The Blueprint

Mike Beggs is senior lecturer in political economy at the University of Sydney. His research focuses on the history of macroeconomic and monetary thinking and policy.

Ben Burgis is a *Jacobin* columnist, an adjunct philosophy professor at Rutgers University, host of the YouTube show and podcast *Give Them an Argument*, and author of several books, most recently *Christopher Hitchens: What He Got Right, How He Went Wrong, and Why He Still Matters*.

Bhaskar Sunkara is the president of the *Nation* magazine, founder and editorial director of *Jacobin*, and the author of *The Socialist Manifesto: The Case for Radical Politics in an Era of Extreme Inequality*.

The Blueprint

How Socialism Can Work in the Real World

Mike Beggs, Ben Burgis,
and Bhaskar Sunkara

VERSO
London • New York

First published by Verso 2026

The manufacturer's authorized representative in the EU for product safety (GPSR) is LOGOS EUROPE, 9 rue Nicolas Poussin, 17000, La Rochelle, France
contact@logoseurope.eu

1 3 5 7 9 10 8 6 4 2

Verso
UK: 6 Meard Street, London W1F 0EG
US: 207 East 32nd Street, New York, NY 10016
versobooks.com

Verso is the imprint of New Left Books

ISBN-13: 978-1-83976-863-7
ISBN-13: 978-1-83976-865-1 (UK EBK)
ISBN-13: 978-1-83976-866-8 (US EBK)

British Library Cataloguing in Publication Data
A catalogue record for this book is available from the British Library

Library of Congress Cataloging-in-Publication Data
A catalog record for this book is available from the Library of Congress
Library of Congress Control Number: 2026944566

Typeset in Sabon LT by Hewer Text UK Ltd, Edinburgh
Printed and bound by CPI Group (UK) Ltd, Croydon CR0 4YY

From the standpoint of a higher economic form of society, private ownership of the globe by single individuals will appear quite as absurd as private ownership of one man by another.

Karl Marx

Contents

1. The Return of Politics 1
2. The Plans That Failed 27
3. Solving the Economic Problem 71
4. What Do Markets Do? 92
5. Workplace Democracy and Finance 137
6. What Does the State Do? 183
7. Income, Equality, and Housing 224
8. Macroeconomic Policy 245
9. Will Socialism Fail Again? 293
10. Is This Even Socialism? 329
11. Civilizational Progress 356

Acknowledgments 379

Notes 381

Index 409

1

The Return of Politics

We live in a time when everything is political—except politics. We routinely treat everyday choices about culture, consumption, and personal identity as expressions of moral allegiance, parsing them for hidden meanings and assigning them to partisan camps. We infer entire worldviews from what people watch, buy, joke about, or post online.

And yet, in this atmosphere of constant ideological conflict, the most foundational political questions are almost never asked. How should an economy be organized? Are disparities in income and wealth intrinsically objectionable, or are they acceptable as long as no one is starving? Can political equality truly exist alongside economic inequality? If democracy is good for governments, why isn't it good for workplaces?

Much of the twentieth century was defined by global rivalry between Western capitalism and Soviet communism. Capitalism's victory was clear by its close. The USSR and its Eastern European satellite states collapsed. Most of the countries still ruled by Communist parties adopted a marketized hybrid of the two systems. In an era of capitalist triumphalism, the basic contours of social and economic life were treated as nonnegotiable.

Decades later, even the most strident critics of capitalism's abuses rarely suggest that we can transcend the system entirely.

The three authors of this book have spent much of their lives advocating for reforms that benefit working people in the here and now. We understand that while history sometimes takes giant strides forward, social progress more often involves daily push-and-pull struggles for short-term gains.

However, those of us who call ourselves socialists must be able to offer not only a thoroughgoing critique of capitalism—one rooted in the lives and struggles of ordinary people—but also a vision of what should replace it. Not, mind you, what such a successor might look like centuries from now, once economic, environmental, and logistical hurdles are overcome by advancing technology, but how an alternative could function in the present. Without that, opposition to capitalism risks amounting to little more than an abstract moral protest.

If the best we can say about a fully socialist society is that it's something that may one day become possible, like radical life extension or colonies in distant galaxies, then being "against" capitalism is a pointless affectation layered on top of our support for reforms within the system.

Nor does it do much good to point out, as Marxists often do, that capitalism hasn't always existed. Consider some other things that didn't exist for most of human history—like modern sanitation, multiparty democracy, or the internet. The question, surely, isn't whether any of these things might cease to exist in the future; it's whether we would *want* them to stop existing. Overcoming capitalism is only desirable if we can replace it with something better.

A key feature that distinguishes capitalism from feudalism or ancient slave systems is that in those earlier modes of production, the class that sat on top of society used direct force to compel what Karl Marx called the "immediate producers" (peasants, slaves, or serfs) to work for them. Under capitalism, wage laborers are made to serve the capitalist class not by whips and chains but by the fear of destitution. No one who works for Amazon is marched into a warehouse under armed guard. In fact, not only can they leave at any time but the threat of job loss is one of the most effective disciplinary weapons in the employer's arsenal.

The results speak for themselves. The tools of extraction might be gentler, but just as feudal peasants were legally obliged to spend part of their time growing crops for the nobility, modern capitalist labor contracts oblige workers to surrender part of the product of their labor to their society's ruling class. The biggest capitalists become so rich in this process that we're rapidly accelerating toward an economy in which the top spots in the distributive hierarchy are occupied not by billionaires but by *trillionaires*.

At the site of extraction, the boss rules like a dictator. Labor unions and the regulatory state sanded off some of the roughest edges of workplace tyranny in the twentieth century, but the forces of capitalist innovation generate creative ways to restore those edges every day. There's a reason why workers at Amazon warehouses race to fulfill their quotas in an atmosphere of electronic surveillance and skip bathroom breaks for fear of falling behind.

As bad as the soft coercion of economic necessity that underlies capitalism can be, though, it's an improvement over the direct coercion that characterized many of the systems that preceded it. But this reduction in human unfreedom doesn't go far enough. Socialists want to radically empower the immediate producers by creating institutional arrangements through which working people get to decide what's produced, how it's produced, and how to collectively divvy up the results. And we want to create a system that does a far better job than capitalism of guaranteeing the social necessities people need to live a good life. This book explores a realistic model of what that might look like and argues that it would be a significant improvement over what we have now.

The Case for Blueprints

That vision begins with a simple question: Who has power, and who doesn't? Short of disrupting the system through collective action, the only shred of control workers have under capitalism is the power of exit. We've already conceded that securing this power is a profound historical accomplishment, but it's also important to recognize its limitations.

For one thing, workers can't exercise this leverage often—your future job prospects suffer if there are too many gaps in your employment history. For another, in most cases, it's far easier for a company to replace one of its workers than for the worker to replace the source of their livelihood. Things are a bit different for those workers whose skills are particularly desired by employers, but supply and demand work much the same way in the labor market as they do in any other market—rare skills confer more bargaining power precisely because they are rare. For most workers, most of the time, wage labor in what we can think of as its "natural state" is a take-it-or-leave-it proposition. Workers whose only freedom is the freedom of exit can decide which *particular* capitalist dominates them, but they still can't fully control their own lives.

A critique of working-class unfreedom isn't the only grievance socialists have with capitalism. We're also concerned with issues like poverty, precarity, overwork, fairness in the distribution of resources, the corrosive effect of all the above on personal fulfillment and interpersonal relationships, ecological destruction, imperialism, and the inevitable link between concentrated wealth and concentrated political power. But at least some of those other problems can reasonably be viewed as lying downstream of the fundamental power imbalances built into capitalist ownership relations. Those imbalances are deeply objectionable on their own terms—or at least they are *if* there's a more desirable society to be found on the other side of capitalism.

After all, the abolition of wage labor only represents a reduction in the overall level of human unfreedom if whatever system replaces capitalism can sustain a sufficient level of material abundance. Attempts to enforce an egalitarian distribution of crumbs can get very ugly, and they don't tend to last for long. The easiest way, after all, to end a system of soft coercion is to bring back hard coercion. Millions of working people are critical of capitalism but hesitant about the prospects for a viable and desirable socialist future. That's exactly why we need a blueprint—a compelling and concrete vision—for how a better system could actually be constructed from the ground up.

Many socialists have thought we don't need to worry about what Marx once called "writing recipes" for "the cook-shops of the future" because, once the working class has vanquished the old order, they'll confront and solve the problems of constructing a new world through mass, democratic problem-solving. It would be foolish and inappropriate, the thinking goes, to attempt to anticipate the results of this process in advance.[1]

We don't deny that there's *something* to this line of thought. It's true enough that no model dreamed up today will fully reflect the complexities of the real world tomorrow. And as a matter of practical politics, new social institutions are often odd and messy hodgepodges—combining bits and pieces that end up surviving from older institutions; new elements shaped by historical accidents; and any number of compromises and improvisations, which would be impossible to predict. Even in our most optimistic moments, we don't expect the citizens of a future socialist society to feel bound by a speculative model devised in the mid-2020s.

Nevertheless, the old-line socialist idea that the details will sort themselves out "after the revolution" is badly misguided. As we'll discuss in this book, the experience of the Soviet Union was a record of systemic economic failure, not just political repression. Authoritarianism doubtless exacerbated the failures of command economies in multiple ways. During the darkest days of Stalin or Mao, even state officials were often afraid to speak out against catastrophically misguided economic decisions. But the apparent assumption of many anti-Stalinist socialists in the twentieth century that democracy by itself would have cured what ailed those societies is hard to defend.

Start with a simple thought experiment. Take the basic structures of Soviet economic planning and graft on the sort of democratic political institutions found in most advanced capitalist societies. There's a free press. There are competitive elections.

Parties debate competing visions for the next Five-Year Plan, and whichever one wins a majority in the Supreme Soviet forms a government and appoints the new head of Gosplan.

This alternate USSR would be superior to the one that existed in our timeline in any number of ways. Certainly, the 1930s Ukrainian famine wouldn't have happened if Stalin had been worried about whether peasants would vote to reelect him. But would the day-to-day frustrations of consumers at grocery stores in 1978 Leningrad really have been much different?

The history of socialism in the twentieth century provides clear evidence against the idea that a viable model will dialectically emerge at the appropriate historical moment. We need to think carefully about these issues in advance. Moreover, you can acknowledge that a particular blueprint might not perfectly match the one shaped by a messy collective process at some future point, and still think it's a good idea to draw one up, for the sake of establishing that there are desirable ways of constructing the *kind* of structure you're asking people to commit their energy to building.

What's more, a blueprint can help galvanize us to fight for a better world. If working people don't think there is an alternative to capitalism, they'll limit their political expectations accordingly. Conversely, it's easy to retreat into comforting vagueness in the face of reasonable worries about how socialism could work. Putting forward a specific model for socialism helps the socialist left steer away from this evasion and grapple seriously with the best objections to our vision of a transformed society.

That's why we've written this volume, even as we fully acknowledge that, for all kinds of reasons, people in the cook-shops of the future might end up using other recipes.

Principles of Construction

Some socialists might object to the thought experiment offered above about a democratic USSR with a riposte like the following:

"Real socialists like me don't think the kind of parliamentary democracy that exists in the most capitalist societies is good enough. I want real bottom-up democracy, with workers' committees, neighborhood assemblies, and so on. I want participatory planning that's radically decentralized as an alternative to Soviet-style economics."

Our imagined objector is giving us a peek at one possible blueprint for a future society. Now we can start to think about whether it's a *good* blueprint.

It overlaps with the model we'll offer here in important ways. Most obviously, we too emphasize the importance of democracy in the workplace. We too want to deepen political democracy in society as a whole. But the extent to which this alternative transfers economic decision-making from a Gosplan to decentralized committees or even to assemblies in which any citizen who cares about the outcome is expected to participate raises at least two major concerns.

First, will the committees and assemblies be in the business of determining the price at which every product will be sold? If so, it's not clear why the empowered citizens of this society would have an advantage over the state planners in either the historical USSR or an imaginary democratic version of it. They'll still have to solve the information problems bound to arise in a complex economy in which a staggering number of items are bought, sold, and produced with a variety of capital goods that themselves must be purchased by enterprises and which are themselves manufactured and so on. Are we imagining public meetings where citizens debate the prices of hundreds of thousands of goods—everything from insulin and diapers to forklift tires, copper-wire gauges, smartphone microchips, and every size of bolt used in a bicycle factory? Is there any reason to predict that the most popular proposals would be conducive to greasing the wheels of economic activity?

At this point in the discussion, we might be offered a second peek at the objector's blueprint and told that money won't exist in this version of the socialist future. If so, that just increases the scope of the problem. Are the committees and assemblies now responsible for deciding what gets produced in the first place *and* what sort of consumption requests will be honored when they come from individual citizens *and* how much of each capital good will go toward each socially owned enterprise to produce the consumer goods?

This is the sort of point that was wielded to great effect by antisocialist economists like Ludwig von Mises and F. A. Hayek. In his famous article on "Economic Calculation in the Socialist Commonwealth," Mises argued that there could be no rational accounting for capital goods in a centrally planned system—that without the prices that emerge from market exchange, there would be no way to know how best to use society's resources to produce what people want. Without markets determining prices for these "higher-order" goods, he thought, planners would be groping in the dark as they tried to coordinate between the needs of various state enterprises and the preferences of consumers. And without money as a common dimension by which to measure tons of coal and iron, hours of labor, and so on, their task would be made that much more difficult.[2]

We don't have to agree with either Mises's overall economic theory or his political proclivities to recognize this as a real problem. It's true that even societies layering social-democratic policies like nationalized health care onto fundamentally capitalist structures have shown that planning can be more effective, in some sectors, than the Austrian school of economics admitted. But these systems operate with monetary budgets in the context of a broader market economy. Experiments in economy-wide marketless planning have been far less encouraging. Those of us who want to try once again to go beyond social democracy to socialism need to reckon with the extent to which our ideological enemies identified genuine problems and calibrate our models accordingly.

This is an *engineering* worry. It's about whether the version of the future we're considering would "work" on its own terms. This is the kind of territory we'll devote the bulk of this book to exploring—laying out our own model of socialism and arguing that it can effectively achieve its goals.

However, this isn't the only objection that can be raised to a particular postcapitalist vision. There's also the question of the goals themselves. Take the sort of ultrademocratic proposal we've been considering, where every detail of economic activity must be democratically planned. Making the dubious assumption that such a model would work in the sense of, for example, preventing shortages in the communal grocery stores, would it be desirable?

Maybe not. Do we really *want* direct participatory control over, say, the municipal water system or the electric grid? Or would we prefer not to think about them at all?

Workplace democracy, we'll argue, matters for many reasons. People shouldn't have to take orders all day from bosses who aren't accountable to them. Earlier socialists were right to stress this point. But they were also right to emphasize that socialism would mean more leisure to pursue one's own projects. Marx's famous image of a person who spends part of the day hunting, part fishing, and part doing literary criticism without ever becoming a hunter, fisher, or critic is an extreme version of that hope: a vision of a society so abundant that consumption is decoupled from work. But even a more grounded, near-term vision of socialism should promise something similar: everyone's needs met, and far more time to do whatever the hell they want with their lives.[3]

Some people may spend more time reading Russian novels or cooking elaborate meals with people they love or hiking and camping in nature. Others might produce work of true genius they never would have had time for otherwise—and still others might just *think* they're doing that. In fact, we confidently expect a better society to lead to a flood of bad poetry and unlistenable albums, as people finally have time to pursue their least self-aware dreams. If that happened, we'd welcome it as a sign of progress.

Twelve million products are directly sold by Amazon. If the prices for all 12 million have to be set as part of some sort of participatory democratic process or, worse yet, if prices are dispensed with altogether in favor of some moneyless formula for determining how much of each product in which combination each worker-citizen is entitled to, a lot of time that people could otherwise spend pursuing their own interests would end up being devoured by meetings.

Of course, there are a variety of social goods that can't be handled through markets and commodity production without degrading important human values. And even when it comes to the most trivial of consumer goods, the economists' metaphor of dollars as "votes" is offensive in a capitalist economy where some people have many thousands of times more "votes" than others. But using regular money at a worker-controlled grocery store to send a quick demand signal by buying a tube or two of a preferred brand of toothpaste sounds a lot better to us than sitting around a committee room, arguing about how many millions of tubes of fluoridated, or tartar-control, or whitening toothpaste will meet the needs of the community in the next year.

This is one reason, alongside concerns about incentives and efficiency, why our model of socialism preserves a role for market coordination, while insisting on a large public noncommodity sector, social control of finance, and workplace democracy across the economy. Our model seeks to combine individual choice with collective democratic decision-making at multiple levels while recognizing the difficulties of coordinating a complex division of labor to meet everyone's needs and wants. For us, efficiency is a socialist virtue alongside equality, security, and freedom, because it is the key to liberating the most important resource of all: our time.

The Veil of Ignorance

This brings us from engineering questions to more basic issues about our normative goals. What values should guide our social design?

Historically, some socialists have preferred to sidestep such questions on the grounds that, once we discover the laws of development of human societies, we'll see that socialism follows capitalism as naturally as capitalism followed feudalism. It was possible, they'd grant, for something to go so catastrophically wrong that society would collapse to an earlier stage of development, but there was only one way *forward*. This quasi-deterministic line of thought is captured in what Marxist philosopher G. A. Cohen calls "the obstetric metaphor": The old society is already pregnant with the new, and all that's necessary is to make sure the baby is safely delivered.[4]

If this had turned out to be correct, both engineering questions about *how* to design a new society and normative questions about the values that should guide the construction would be far less pressing. As we've already discussed, however, history hasn't been kind to this assumption.

In 1918, revolution in Germany created a short-lived socialist republic in Bavaria. Its planning minister was the brilliant philosopher and economic theorist Otto Neurath, who later lamented that "preparation for consciously shaping the economy was lacking" among even the most capable organizers. Briefly imprisoned after the republic's defeat, he reflected on what his socialist training missed: "The technique of a socialist economy had been badly neglected. Instead, only pure criticism of the capitalist economy was offered and the Marxist pure theory of value and history was studied."[5]

As it turns out, design problems are real problems. Conversely, if the only possible postcapitalist future isn't already sitting there waiting for us to arrive, the values question can't be ignored. We need to decide which *goals* we care about, because goals allow us to appraise our design. Like it or not, that takes us into the territory of normative political philosophy. A good starting point is John Rawls's theory of justice.

Rawls believed that just social institutions are ones that we could endorse from what he called "the original position." Agents in this position know everything there is to know about all the facts relevant to deciding between different political and economic arrangements. They would know, for example, how any model would work out in practice—whether they would be faced with shortages of key goods, how easy it would be in practice to switch jobs, and so on. They would also know that they would have to live in the society they were designing. Their vision would be obscured, however, by a "veil of ignorance" on one crucial question: *who* in this society they would be.[6]

Some of the consequences of this are straightforward. Such agents wouldn't endorse the racial laws that existed in apartheid South Africa or the kinds of gender laws that still exist in Saudi Arabia because they wouldn't know the race or gender they would end up with. Similarly, they wouldn't create the type of society where the poor die from easily treatable diseases because they wouldn't know whether they would be born into rich families or poor ones. A less obvious entailment of the thought experiment is that those deliberating in the original position would reject any proposal for a pure meritocracy in which some people got a bigger share of society's resources for no reason other than their greater innate talents. Many liberals and conservatives seem to think such a pure meritocracy would be a utopia, but agents in the original position would reject it for exactly the same reason they would reject racist or sexist laws—they wouldn't know whether they'd be born getting the short end of the stick.

Leftists often end up spending their time arguing that actually existing capitalism isn't particularly meritocratic. Tech CEOs hailed as rare geniuses in the business press often turn out to be the recipients of all kinds of dumb luck. They had seed money from their families, or they were the one entrepreneur of twenty with the same idea who happened to be in the right place at the right time, or they benefited from government favors. That's all correct and worth highlighting, but Rawls's point is that high levels of economic inequality wouldn't be just even if they *did* reflect purely meritocratic principles. Just as you don't get to choose your race, gender, or socioeconomic background, you also don't get to choose whether you'll be even a genuine tech genius.

Granted, nearly all talents need to be developed with hard work before they're of much use to their holder. No one makes it to the NBA Finals or wins a Fields Medal in mathematics without many years of nurturing their skills. But the obvious reality is that the overwhelming majority of human beings wouldn't have the capacity to play basketball or do mathematics at that level even if they devoted their entire lives to the undertaking. No one deliberating behind the veil of ignorance would know their athletic or intellectual potential. And just as they wouldn't know whether they were going to be born into rich families or poor ones, they wouldn't know whether they'd have the combination of cognitive and social skills that—combined with other sorts of luck—help some kids who grow up in poor families do well in school and climb the career ladder.

Once you've internalized that last point, it's easy to see how Rawls's theory cuts against a variety of important sources of inequality. Things get more complicated when we start thinking about which types of inequality *would* be acceptable to people in the original position.

Rawls thinks that, even behind the veil of ignorance, we might grudgingly allow inequalities if they met two conditions. First, the better-off positions must be open to everyone under conditions of "fair equality of opportunity." Second, the existence of any such inequalities would have to work to the benefit of the least well off.

Inequalities, by definition, favor the best off. Rawls's point is that there could still be cases in which the worst off in Society A are better off than their counterparts in a more egalitarian Society B. For instance, suppose that in A—but not in B—computer engineers earn higher salaries than most other occupations. Because of the higher pay, more people are drawn into the field, which accelerates technological progress. That progress then improves the standard of living for everyone, including the poorest citizens of A. If we stipulate that A is, despite this patch of inequality, still more equal than any society today, then an agent in the original position could rationally tolerate the income gap. Even if they lacked the skills to become an engineer, they might see the inequality as a price worth paying for access to the technology available in A but not B.

None of this means that someone born with the skills to be an excellent computer engineer would innately *deserve* a higher salary. To see why not, imagine a Society C and a Society D, where the occupation incentivized with higher salaries in C but not D was defeating giant tigers in hand-to-hand combat. Neither C nor D has the level of technology for *shooting* the giant tigers, never mind computer engineering, and the starting conditions are such that giant tiger attacks are a significant social problem. Just as with the appeal of A over B, it's easy to imagine agents picking C over D. Even if you didn't have the potential to be one of the star tiger hunters, you would be safer from tigers if more of those who did were drawn into tiger-hunting with higher salaries and, on balance, you might well be willing to live with some inequality.

Still, accepting some inequality as a trade-off is very different from endorsing inequality without limits. You might hesitate about allowing such inequalities to grow beyond a certain point. Severely unequal distributions of resources can have devastating consequences for human dignity, social cohesion, and political democracy. You don't want to be eaten by a tiger, but you also don't want to be ruled by a tiger-killing warrior caste.

Rawls was attuned to this point, but one of his most perceptive critics, the aforementioned G. A. Cohen, took the worry a step further. Cohen understood justice in terms of what he called "socialist equality of opportunity": the principle that distributive inequalities are unjust to the extent that they can be traced back to factors outside of the control of the people at the bottom end of the distribution.[7]

This doesn't mean, though, that Cohen necessarily denies that computer engineers in A or tiger hunters in C might have to be compensated at somewhat higher rates for the sake of the greater good. He leaves the door open to such possibilities. He just conceptualizes this as a trade-off between different values—sacrificing a bit of justice for a gain in efficiency—unlike Rawls, who thinks that whatever rational agents would sign off on from behind the veil of ignorance would be just. In Cohen's view, Rawls is making a mistake by obscuring the trade-off.

Cohen's way of dividing up the concepts usefully directs our attention to the fact that something important is lost whenever we permit distributive inequalities that lie outside the control of whoever gets the short end of the stick, even if sometimes the trade-off is worth it. But the gap between their "at the end of the day" positions may be narrower than it looks.

While Rawls leaves open the empirical question of what system would best satisfy his requirements in *A Theory of Justice*, his combination of views—keeping the door open for some degree of inequality for the sake of economic incentives while emphasizing concern for the least well off—sounded to many like an endorsement of welfare state capitalism. But Rawls flatly rejected this interpretation. In *Justice as Fairness: A Restatement*, published a year before his death in 2002, he concluded that his theory was incompatible with capitalism in any form. To see one of the reasons why, think about the difference between worker cooperatives and regular capitalist firms.

Typically, pay scales at co-ops aren't completely flat. Some worker-members may earn more than others. But the range of compensation is barely a bump on a graph compared to the massive levels of distributive inequality produced within standard capitalist firms.

Take the Mondragon Corporation, essentially a federation of worker co-ops in the Basque region of Spain. The virtues of Mondragon are sometimes exaggerated by leftists eager to latch onto positive models. It floats in the sea of Spain's otherwise thoroughly capitalist economy, and often responds to the incentives created by that economy in ways that don't reflect socialist values—for example, by employing nonmember contractors even within Spain and subcontracting to capitalist companies abroad. But the fact that Mondragon's worker-members aren't rigid socialist ideologues but regular people trying to make sensible business decisions makes their relative egalitarianism that much more striking. The pay ratio between the highest-paid executive at Mondragon and the lowest-paid worker-member is 6:1. In leading Spanish companies, the ratio between CEOs and the median worker is 74:1; in the United States, it's 268:1.[8]

The obvious difference between Mondragon and its noncooperative competitors is that in Mondragon the workers themselves get to vote on their pay scales. It's possible to convince most worker-members, who have a rational incentive not to let the company go under, to allow some of their fellow workers to be paid more than themselves for any number of reasons. Workers may agree because those colleagues possess particularly desirable technical skills or because they're willing to take on stressful and demanding responsibilities or because they're willing to take on dirty or dangerous jobs. But good luck convincing your fellow workers that you should be given more of the product of everyone's collective labor so that you can afford to purchase your own spaceship. It's not going to happen.

And even that 6:1 gap must be understood in the context of a Spanish economy where Mondragon must compete for managerial and technical talent with regular capitalist firms. The gap would be even smaller in an economy where workplace democracy and hence far more egalitarian pay scales were the norm.

Rawls's theory allows for distributive inequality when whoever ends up holding the short end of the stick is still holding a longer stick than they would in any otherwise equally desirable arrangement where all the sticks were the same size. What counts as "otherwise equally desirable" is dicey. Agents choosing between possible societies from behind the veil of ignorance may, for example, accept a slightly lower standard of consumption in exchange for the increase in their overall quality of life gained by avoiding the petty social indignities often associated with inequality or by experiencing a more robust sense of community.

Even if you agree with Rawls that *some* distributive inequality can be justified via his "maximin" (maximizing the minimum) principle, it's hard to believe that we need as much of it as is generated by capitalism. The drivers of the limited inequality within worker cooperatives are precisely the kind of factors that are actually relevant to keeping the engine of productivity humming. But you only get some individuals acquiring hundreds of times more of the collective product than others when the direct beneficiaries of that inequality or their benefactors have the power to simply *take* that share without having to justify themselves to the short-stick holders.

Calculation and Incentives

Capitalist thinkers argue that while different ex-post distributional arrangements might be plausible, society benefits from inequality in economic power. They think attempts to bring the means of production under collective economic control will only stifle innovation, discourage investment, and ultimately reduce the wealth available to distribute. Instead of more evenly spreading the benefits of a modern economy around, attempts at socialization will only kill the goose that lays the golden eggs. The citizens of the socialist future would be engaged in egalitarian crumb-rationing. If this is right, even agents in the original position might be willing to give capitalism a second look.

The "socialist calculation debate," which we'll discuss in detail later, centered on exactly this question. On the socialist side, Oskar Lange accepted Mises's argument that managing a complex division of labor required a price system but denied that it required markets. Socialist planners at the center and within workplaces could develop prices and coordinate production by following a set of procedures that would reproduce the optimal outcomes of textbook "perfect competition" models of markets without actually needing the markets. (His system did still involve money, shops, and a labor market, though, to draw out and properly price people's preferences about consumption and work.) He believed this would beat capitalism at its own game, because actual capitalist markets are far from the perfectly competitive ideal and because planners could factor in things like environmental degradation that markets systematically ignore. Socialist pricing would be more efficient, not less. We call Lange's vision and others like it "algorithmic" or "price socialism" to distinguish them from "market socialism."[9]

The Hayekian response was to argue that such a system ran into problems involving information and incentives. It's true that, contrary to the way this debate is often remembered, Lange's algorithms did not require planners at the center to receive and process a vast amount of information from across the economy. It was, in fact, a model of decentralized information processing and decision-making. The problem was Lange's model depended on workplace managers honestly assessing and acting on information about the technical possibilities of production in their own fields. Realistically, though, they would have tremendous incentives to fudge those numbers to maintain their own positions and little reason to go searching for new and better ways of doing things.

On the other side of the debate, Hayek recognized that real-world markets bore little resemblance to the perfectly competitive, static models of general equilibrium theory. But he argued that this objection missed the point about why markets, in their messy, imperfect reality, get the job of economic coordination done in a way for which there's no obvious alternative. The real world is one of uncertainty and continual change; nobody has more than a fraction of the relevant information about technical possibilities and what people want. The pursuit of profit in competition with others gives people the incentives to act on the information they have, and the prices that emerge amalgamate that information, feeding it back to the participants and coordinating their activity. It is chaotic; it is not perfect; but it works.[10]

We grant that there is a point here and that some models of socialism really do flounder on those rocks. We accept an important place for markets and commodity production in our model. But we flatly reject the suggestion that any of this shows that we need *capitalism*.

In what follows, we sketch out a model of a fully socialist economy—one in which, instead of being owned by a class of capitalists separate from the class of workers, the means of production have been socialized. The proposed economic system, like capitalism, is mixed. "Private" and "public" are perhaps the wrong words here, given these spheres are even more entangled under the socialism we envision than they already are in highly developed capitalist economies, but the distinction is clear enough. There's a "private" commodity-producing sector in which costs are covered by market sales and a noncommodified "public" sector operating with publicly allocated funds. The noncommodified sector includes the government bureaucracy and agencies under central control, but it may also include a variety of community agencies with considerable autonomy, which are nevertheless financed by the public purse.

The firms in our commodity-producing sector are democratic in two ways. First, management and administrative structures are chosen by the firm's labor force using a democratic process. Second, each worker receives a share of the firm's residual income. These are *firms*, though, in that they are autonomous commodity-producing entities that must cover costs with revenues and meet their contractual payment obligations.

A variety of enterprise constitutions are possible, but the standard for a midsize to large company would involve representative democracy, with elected directors appointing and monitoring administrators who do day-to-day management. This structure could be supplemented by committees and referenda as needed, but routine administration is often best handled by specialist professional workers with expertise in accounting, logistics, and so on. Democracy does its job by making sure the administrators are ultimately answerable to their colleagues and that working conditions and key questions of strategy have broad approval.

Financial viability constrains the democratic firm, as it does the capitalist firm. The need to cover costs and meet cash flow obligations, while competing with other enterprises, is what ties the firm into the broader division of labor across the economy—a chain of coordination linking everything from the sale of lattes in coffee shops to the federal health service buying cutting-edge medical equipment for use in the nationalized hospitals to car-manufacturing cooperatives replacing failing parts in their drop forges.

This financial discipline enforces the socialist virtue of efficiency, ensuring that the firm is using social resources reasonably well to meet people's needs and wants. Like capitalist firms, democratic firms receive revenue from selling their output and using it to pay for new inputs for the next round of production. Like capitalist firms, they require investment: Some inputs must be paid for long before receipt of the revenue that covers those costs. This investment must be financed somehow or other. (Hold that thought!) As with capitalist firms, their future revenues and costs are uncertain to some degree. Market demand and prices change over time. They must make investment and production decisions in the face of uncertainty and so face financial risks.

So far, so Mondragon. The key differences between the worker-controlled firms in our model and actually existing worker co-ops under capitalism have to do with their legal status and the larger network of institutions within which they are embedded. Empirical research on cooperatives under capitalism suggests that they have similar levels of productivity and survive at about the same rate as any other business once they get going. The main problem is that their birth rate is vastly lower.[11]

Some of this is doubtless attributable to cultural factors. In at least some societies with the legal doctrine of "coverture," under which many of the rights of married women reverted to their husbands, it may have been technically possible for men and women to make more egalitarian marriage-like contracts, but even committed feminists rarely did. Most people in any society will default to normal preexisting institutions as they go through the business of living—getting married, starting families, starting businesses, or looking for work—and even workers who *could* pool together resources with a bunch of friends to start a small co-op won't normally do so.

Other factors, though, loom much larger than that. The most fundamental problems involve finance. To produce, collectives need not only their own labor but also tools, equipment, buildings, and so on. They need to finance these things in some way. The problem is not just that capitalist banks and other financial institutions are leery about lending to collectives because of their unusual legal structure. It's not even that traditional capitalist firms are often a more surefire bet for lending institutions, since they have a competitive advantage over co-ops. Capitalist firms can move around in search of higher profits and don't need to secure the democratic approval of the workers whose lives they upend by doing so.

Even beyond these factors, there are basic things about the economics of worker cooperatives that make them square pegs for the round holes of capitalist financial relations. If worker-members self-finance the organization, they each must bring some personal wealth with them or take on a second mortgage to finance their share. Not only do they depend on their workplace for a wage, they also have a substantial portion of their wealth tied up in it, leaving them especially vulnerable to a firm failure. If the co-op grows by reinvesting some of its profits, its members accumulate collective wealth together, but what happens when someone wants to retire or leave to work elsewhere? What happens when the cooperative wants to expand by bringing in new worker-members? Either new members must come in with their own wealth or incumbent members will find themselves sharing their accumulated wealth with the newcomers.

In the first case, bringing new labor on board becomes a combination of job interviewing and investor courting. In the second case, incumbents may be more reluctant to expand at all, since it means sharing returns with more people. The alternative to member self-financing is borrowing, but this raises its own problems. By borrowing, a co-op promises fixed payments to the creditor on fixed dates, while their own revenues are always uncertain to some degree. By definition lacking the cushion of funding from external investors who can be compensated with equity, co-ops end up highly leveraged, their worker-members' own incomes left exposed to the ups and downs of the business.

Given all this, it is not hard to see why worker cooperatives are rare under capitalism (and why, ironically, they are most common in the form of partnerships of high-income professionals in low-capital-intensity fields like law). And this isn't to speak of the collective action problems involved in co-op formation within a capitalist context. Since our economic lives are governed by capitalist rules that allow for concentrated individual power, anyone whose motive for starting a co-op is simply to have a better life would have every incentive to shoot the moon and try to become an *employer* instead. The firm failure rate for businesses of all kinds is extremely high, and getting a new enterprise off the ground takes an enormous amount of work. Why do all that on the slim hope of marginally improving your position by becoming an equal citizen of a miniature economic republic? Why not spend that effort attempting to win a *much* better life by building a miniature economic kingdom where you get to be the king? If, after all that sweat and blood, the most likely outcome is that you'll end up back in the subordinate working class anyway, why not at least *try* for the throne?

These problems alone mean that workers primarily motivated by their own individual interests are much less likely than committed socialists to be involved in attempts to start co-ops. And those committed socialists are likely to make the rational calculation that their time and effort would have more impact on the society around them if they spent it doing things like organizing unions at large capitalist companies, rather than working fourteen hours a day to get some local cooperative coffee shop up and running.

It gets worse. To see the full scope of the problem, imagine that you could ask a magical genie to instantaneously restructure every existing firm and put it under the democratic, collective ownership of its workforce, without changing anything else about the structure of the economy. The result wouldn't be a stable form of market socialism but an arrangement that market forces would eventually course correct back into something recognizable as capitalism. Firms, whether capitalist or worker controlled, sooner or later go out of business and the people who once worked there need new jobs. Cooperatives looking to expand operations and increase the income of existing members have an incentive to hire new workers as regular employees rather than co-owners, and people who have been out of work for a while have an incentive to accept this reduced status. And whole co-ops would often have an incentive to transition to regular capitalist firms by selling ownership stakes to other enterprises or wealthy individuals.

The lesson here is neither that it's a fool's errand to even try to go beyond capitalism entirely nor that the only way to do so is to learn to live with the calculation and incentive problems caused by totally marketless planning. Rather, it's that just as capitalism required a set of social institutions different from the ancien régime, a stable and thriving socialist economy can only emerge on the basis of new socialist institutions.

Ending Capitalist Realism

Make no mistake, in our model, much of the economy would be under direct state ownership as part of the public sector. A worker-controlled health insurance company, for example, would have the same bad incentives as a regular capitalist health insurance company, and we know from the experience of social democracies that this is exactly the kind of activity for which the social benefits of decommodification vastly outweigh any calculation concerns. Similar arguments apply to sectors like education, energy, transportation, and telecommunications. We also agree with the traditional socialist position that the "commanding heights" of the economy should be taken into the domain of state planning and the noncommodified sector will be larger than is typical under capitalism. We'll talk more about this in chapter six and about the other functions of the state in managing income distribution and macroeconomic planning in chapters seven and eight. Crucially, this form of management includes the banking system, which, in our model, is the whole of the financial system and is entirely under public control.

However, for reasons given above and expanded in chapter four, there will also be a large market sector of commodity production by democratic firms. These will be "private" in the sense that they would be self-governing institutions autonomous from the state. But workers wouldn't own shares of the firms that could be bought or sold any more than citizens can sell their votes in the next city council election to a fellow citizen. Workers can join or leave a firm the way citizens can move in and out of jurisdictions, but pieces of neither are for sale. And the productive assets—the actual physical "means of production"—would essentially be rented out to the firm by the larger community.

Starting new firms and expanding existing ones both involve partnership between public banks and worker-controlled firms. Worker-members do not invest their own wealth in their firms. Investment in capital equipment and other assets comes from the associated banks. The financing arrangements are different from capitalist forms of debt and equity, designed especially to combine workplace-level democracy with national-level democratic control of the use of social resources. The public banking system allocates finance where it is most needed, managing and spreading risk. Individual collective firms become custodians rather than owners of the part of social wealth they are entrusted with. They are free to manage things in their own way, but they are responsible for maintaining the value of social wealth and given incentives to use it efficiently to meet their fellow citizens' wants and needs. The workings of the system are described in chapter five at the level of the firm and chapter eight at the macrolevel.

The possibility of firm failure is a necessary component of a dynamic economy. Short of outright failure, firms and whole industries sometimes need to shrink rather than grow. Our model balances security with mechanisms that give people incentives to move to workplaces where they are needed. A welfare state supports people who are temporarily out of work, with access to education and training for developing new skills. Meanwhile, the public banking system takes an active role in setting up new democratic firms, taking advantage of the detailed information it collects to find the most likely areas for development. Macroeconomic policy is committed to full employment, so that nobody who wants paid work is left looking for long.

This kind of socialism wouldn't be a utopia or some kind of conflict-free endpoint to human history. It wouldn't even fully realize Cohen's "socialist equality of opportunity" principle, since, even with democratically determined pay scales, workers with particularly desirable skills would often be in a position to demand higher-than-average compensation, and some of this would reflect the brute luck of natural talent. (We discuss income distribution and redistribution in chapter seven.) But anyone who sees Cohen's principle as their North Star should acknowledge this model as a massive step in the right direction. Perhaps a path toward an even more deeply egalitarian reorganization of the basic structure of society, without unacceptable losses with respect to other values like economic efficiency, would become visible once we have gotten that far. Just as the degree of social progress that's been achieved in many advanced capitalist democracies would have been unimaginable to a Chartist fighting for universal male suffrage in early nineteenth-century

Britain, it could be that the vision of socialism laid out in this book won't begin to approach the virtues of the kind of socialism everyone will be living under in the twenty-fourth century. We can't know.

However, our purpose in proposing a model isn't to pronounce the last word on all future progress and close off other possibilities. It's to demonstrate that it's possible and desirable to go much further than even most of the people alive right now who have broadly socialist inclinations can imagine going.

We live at a time where unpredictable geopolitical developments and dizzying technological progress can make the future feel uncertain, but where what Mark Fisher called "capitalist realism" prevails on fundamental economic questions. American leftists dream of Medicare for All, British leftists of renationalizing their country's railways, and so on, but it's hard to stretch our minds to picture any alteration to the basic property relations that shape our societies. In providing a blueprint for one possible future, we aim to pry open our imaginations and put the biggest questions of politics back on the table.[12]

2

The Plans That Failed

When Nikita Khrushchev was born in 1894, shoes were a luxury for peasants. In his memoirs, the Soviet leader says he went barefoot from spring until late autumn. "Every villager dreamed of owning a pair of boots." The best they could muster were *lapti*, easily frayed slippers woven from tree bark.[1]

It's fitting that when many people think of Khrushchev today, a shoe comes to mind. By 1960, he'd long outgrown his lapti. The leather shoes he wore to the United Nations General Assembly that year were so new and tight that he found them uncomfortable and took them off after getting seated. Later, angered during the session, he picked one up and started banging the table in disgust. For the Communist leadership it was an embarrassing episode. Yet in the light of Khrushchev's origins, it was a poignant reminder not only of an individual's unlikely elevation from poverty to the helm of a superpower but of the transformation of a Russia characterized by tsarist underdevelopment to one marked by growing abundance.[2]

The pounding of shoes and machinery meant that millions around the world took Khrushchev seriously when, in another well-known outburst, he promised that history was on socialism's side and the system would soon bury capitalism. The Soviet party program aimed to catch up with the United States in terms of infrastructure, labor productivity, and even consumer goods by 1980. "We shall see," Khrushchev told a Moscow crowd of thousands in 1958, "who eats better and who has more clothing." The optimism was matched by worry from Western analysts about Soviet growth rates and technological success, symbolized by the launch of Sputnik, the world's first artificial satellite. Washing machines, televisions, and personal automobiles were still hard to come by, but the Soviet system was delivering on the basics, with promises of more to come.[3]

And yes, at its peak, the administered economy made 800 million pairs of shoes and boots a year, three times as many as the United States made. But these shoes also tell the story of why the system failed. It was expert at churning out vast quantities of footwear, but not the kind people wanted to wear or that necessarily fit. An additional 100 million pairs were brought in from abroad annually. In a country famous for its lines, some of the longest were in front of shoe stores, where people hoped to buy imports. Meanwhile, mounds of unwanted goods piled up in warehouses, while the firms they came from were rewarded for meeting their production quotas.[4]

The lessons of the Soviet experience are many and encompass not just the dangers of political authoritarianism but those of bad economics. Soviet planning made immense progress in its early years, but as time went on, the gap between East and West only grew larger. Unable to keep up technologically, harness the immense resources that it mobilized, or effectively incentivize its managers and workers, the system went from example to cautionary tale. Khrushchev thought he was ushering in the future, but his successors found themselves in the dustbin of history.

This chapter looks at why the economy behind "actually existing socialism" ended up burying itself rather than capitalism. It's a vital story for anyone who wants to dig out from the rubble of the twentieth century and find a socialism worthy of the twenty-first.

Early Drafts

Karl Marx and Friedrich Engels dreamed of transcending capitalism. But most of their lives were spent studying the system—where it came from, how it operated, and how the working class that it spawned could bring about its downfall—rather than speculating on what would come after it. Marx rebelled against the utopian impulse to see socialism as "an ideal to which reality would have to adjust itself." As discussed in chapter one, instead of writing "recipes for the cookshops of the future," he focused on the material developments driving that future and trusted that producers themselves could find a successor system.[5]

Marx, however, did touch on what a postcapitalist civilization would look like, broadly dividing it into a socialist phase and a communist one. Communism would be a thoroughly decommodified world where "the enslaving subordination of the individual to the division of labor," especially the division between mental and manual work, would fade and there would be so much material abundance that society could be organized around the maxim "from each according to his ability, to each according to his needs."[6]

Hints about what a transition toward the socialist phase might look like appear in his writings, as well: "to wrest, by degree, all capital from the bourgeoisie, to centralize all instruments of production in the hands of the state, i.e., of the proletariat organized as the ruling class; and to increase the total productive forces as rapidly as possible." Some sort of democratic planning is implied. As early as 1843, Engels wrote that "if the producers as such knew how much the consumers required, if they were to organize production, if they were to share it out amongst themselves, then the fluctuations of competition and its tendency to crisis would be impossible."[7]

The question of how socialism could work in practice took on greater relevance with the rise of working-class mass parties in the late nineteenth century. But locked out of power, disputes between reformist and revolutionary tendencies within those formations remained abstract until the Great War and the upheavals of the 1910s. In Germany, a debate over the "socialization question" raged after the November Revolution. As chair of a commission on the topic in 1918, veteran theorist Karl Kautsky proposed selective nationalization of large industries combined with democratic administration of other firms. These enterprises would be transferred from capitalist ownership and run by representatives of workers, consumers, and the state. A tripartite organization would enable "the workers and the consumers, as well as science, to exercise the necessary influence upon the adaptation of the processes of production." Kautsky had looked to examples ranging from producer co-ops to "guild socialism," but in the long run, he decidedly aimed at overcoming the role of profit making in socialist enterprise and replacing the anarchy of the market with conscious planning.[8]

These ideas, however, were never seriously considered by the ruling Social Democrats. They wished to establish a functioning parliamentary government by winning over segments of the capitalist class. In the end, their Weimar Republic yielded neither socialism nor a stable liberal democracy. Far from the heartland of industrial capitalism, the assumptions of planning would be tested in, and forever associated with, impoverished Russia.

The Russian Riders

It's said that what distinguished Vladimir Lenin from his Menshevik rivals was a "single-minded, purposeful, and persistent" commitment to socialist revolution. His workers' party, however, faced the daunting challenge of trying to wield power in a country with very few workers.[9]

Lenin's *The State and Revolution*, written just before the October Revolution, had a somewhat libertarian hue. It saw the state not as a neutral vehicle that could be occupied by workers but as a tool of class oppression. The old state would have to be "smashed" and replaced by a new one. Both states were repressive, but unlike the violence it took for a tiny ruling class to control the great mass of working people, the repression needed for the majority to suppress the minority would be minimal. It would bring about "democracy for the vast majority of people" and "exclusion from democracy" for only the "exploiters and oppressors of the people." Over time, it would be possible for "a democracy without any exceptions" to flourish, as in a world without the exploitation of person by person, "people will gradually become accustomed to observing the elementary rules of social intercourse."[10]

For all his genius at making revolution, there was a simplicity to Lenin's views on postcapitalist politics. His thoughts on the economic basis of socialism and communism, however, were more complex. Lenin posits that under socialism "bourgeois law" would only be abolished in proportion to "the economic revolution so far attained." The development of socialism, then, would not happen overnight—much less communism, which required the "economic basis for the complete withering away of the state."

The Bolshevik leader did, however, join most contemporary Marxists in thinking that capitalism was retarding the development of productive forces "to a tremendous extent." While describing socialist construction as a protracted process, he was confident that the expropriation of capitalists would speed things up. The strictest control over that process, not by a state of bureaucrats but by "a state of armed workers," would be necessary until communism arose.

Though it was directed to aims he despised, Lenin drew inspiration from the German war economy and saw its highly organized state capitalism as ripe for capture. After all, capitalism, with its big banks and syndicates, created a ready-made accounting structure. Workers could, he proposed on the eve of winning power, "lay hold of and set in motion this state apparatus." At first, they wouldn't bring an immediate end to capitalism but put strategic sectors under worker control and march toward socialism. In the medium term, they could oversee "the expropriation of capitalists, the conversion of all citizens into workers and other employees of one huge 'syndicate'" managed by a "genuinely democratic state." [11]

Ambition was mixed with caution in these 1917 writings. Lenin's prescriptions assumed a set of preconditions that he knew didn't exist in Russia: universal literacy, highly productive agriculture, advanced industry, and more. But despite these material barriers, in October 1917, Lenin's political talents, his ability to yoke together the seemingly divergent interests of peasants and workers, made a revolution in economically backward Russia politically possible.

What would the Bolsheviks do after October? At the very least, they wanted to hold onto power long enough for workers elsewhere in Europe to start revolutions of their own. In the meantime, they had every intention of maintaining a mixed economy. Their seizure of power, however, created an environment in which an orderly trek to socialism seemed impossible. Long-oppressed workers and peasants seized factories and farms, while the business owners who clung on to control of their workplaces launched capital strikes. A complete breakdown of production resulted, and the Bolsheviks were caught on the back foot. To take one example of the economic chaos of the time, a contradictory November 1917 order gave factory committees a legal mandate to interfere in production and distribution, while still asserting management's right to manage. Neither worker control nor stable production resulted.

What mix of realism and ideology compelled the young Soviet government has been the subject of debate for generations. But amid horrific conditions the revolutionaries pushed on. As Leon Trotsky described their attitude in these difficult days, "Having mounted the saddle, the rider is obliged to guide the horse—at the risk of breaking his neck."[12]

Civil war and foreign intervention in 1918 encouraged policies that would become known as "war communism." These were above all a response to a political emergency—improvised measures to keep the Bolshevik state alive—though they were sometimes romanticized as a genuine experiment in socialist planning. The barely functioning private economy was nationalized, scarce resources were distributed by the center, labor conscription was the norm, and, like the tsarist state before it, the government turned to forced requisition of grain from the countryside to feed its armies and the cities. Peasants had little incentive to direct what they still produced to urban areas—there was a shortage of consumer goods and grain prices continued to decline in relation to those goods. Still, their produce was seized on a stunning scale, backed by hostage taking and collective punishment. The Bolsheviks applied their class analysis to the countryside, which they crudely saw as divided between poor peasants, middle peasants, and wealthy kulaks. They hoped to maintain support by focusing their actions on the latter, but divisions on the ground were far more complicated than this schema accounted for. The presence of armed requisition squads searching for hoarders only served as a further disincentive for cultivation.

The Bolshevik industrial policy also shifted in this period. The government nationalized the entire economy, instituted rationing, and imposed strict labor discipline. Yet shortages of parts and raw materials—exacerbated by the fact that vast swathes of territory were occupied by the counterrevolutionary White Army—meant the wholesale collapse of production. The crises of industry and agriculture went in tandem. As the scholar Steve Smith writes, "Even if the Bolsheviks had not taken a single pud of grain from the peasants, the latter would still have had little incentive to produce more than was necessary for subsistence, since there were no manufactures to buy and money had become almost worthless."[13]

By 1921, Russian industry was less than one-third its prewar size. The state's political base was decimated, too. Many industrial workers died in the Civil War, while others left starving cities and tried their chances in the countryside.

New Economics

War communism persisted until Red victory in the civil war, by which point Russia, according to Lenin, was like a man "beaten to within an inch of his life." The New Economic Policy (NEP) that followed in March 1921 was pushed by resistance from below. Rebellious Soviet sailors in Kronstadt spoke to the demands of peasants by advocating for freer trade, and peasants themselves launched more than fifty major uprisings in the countryside. Even many surviving pro-Bolshevik workers in cities participated in strikes and demonstrations. An alliance of workers and peasants had made revolution possible in 1917, but circumstances and policy decisions had torn the alliance asunder and pushed the revolutionary government to its breaking point.

Lenin still defended the prior policy of requisitioning, which was introduced by tsarist forces in 1916 and, he explained, "forced on us by extreme want, ruin and war," but now he advocated taking a smaller amount of grain in the form of a tax. Whereas, before authorities would seize foodstuffs without clear limitation, now peasants knew how much they would have to surrender. They had clear incentives to produce surpluses and those surpluses, in turn, helped revive the industry-producing manufactured goods.[14]

Market exchange was restored. With a stable currency backed by gold and the return of workers to the cities to produce goods the countryside wanted, the chaos abated. The commanding heights of the economy—large-scale industry, banking, foreign trade—remained under state control. But even state-owned enterprises produced for the market, not for a plan, and strove for profitability. Combined with the reemergence of smaller enterprises, the result was a rapid restoration of production.

Starting from well below prewar levels of output, by 1926 some industrial sectors reached new heights. Most importantly, the country went from suffering mass famine in 1921 to achieving a modest food surplus in 1923, and there were no new revolts.

By the time of Lenin's death in January 1924, the young Soviet state was securely in power, by consent and not terror.

Despite the horrors of the previous years, the revolution finally yielded fruits for a beleaguered people. Peasants won the land rights they had craved for centuries. Workers enjoyed three meals a day, improved living conditions, and democratic outlets through their factory committees and trade unions, and more of them had access to health care and education. Yet problems emerged in the new system—ones with a real material basis, which were made far worse by the power of ideology.[15]

The Bolsheviks conceived of the NEP as not only a way to restore political stability and the worker–peasant alliance but as a route to development. With memories of foreign intervention during the civil war fresh in the mind, they saw industrialization as a necessity for their state's survival. The restored rural sector was meant to produce enough surplus to facilitate exports and allow for the importation of machine parts. But much of that surplus stayed in rural areas to support a growing population and livestock herds. The Communist Party wanted to boost agricultural productivity to encourage collective farms and mechanization, but the pace of change was slow.

In the cities, the NEP had restored prewar construction and light industry but struggled to find the capital to build new heavy industry and expand extractive sectors. Productivity and investment exceeded 1913 levels but only modestly. The NEP was a success relative to its apocalyptic starting point, but the gap between the Soviet Union and its rivals in the West was wider than ever.

Growing levels of inequality; the apparent prospering of many peasants while conditions stagnated for workers; and concerns about corruption and the activity of "nepmen," who amassed wealth through trading and small enterprise, generated fierce debate among leading Bolsheviks. In the direst analyses, the NEP was seen as opening the road for a new ruling class. Trotsky emphasized the conditions of the workers' party's worker base in the cities and advocated more rapid industrialization at the relative expense of peasants. Nikolai Bukharin, the party's foremost theorist, wanted to stay the course, focusing on the need to maintain an alliance with the peasantry, who he said should be allowed to enrich themselves into a consumer base for industry. Progress required stability, and slow development was better than no development at all. Joseph Stalin harbored long-standing criticisms of the NEP but had the political acumen to triangulate between the two positions.[16]

Stalin's chance to move against both the New Economic Policy and the last vestiges of democracy in the Soviet Union came as a response to a crisis of grain procurement in the late 1920s. Economic difficulties were not new to the system. By early 1923, reforms had already helped agriculture rebound, but industry was just starting its slow path to recovery. State industry was still producing few goods, so it demanded high prices from its peasant consumers. At the same time, the state only offered to buy grain from peasants at low prices. After seeing the divergent lines of industrial and agricultural prices mapped out, Trotsky is said to have called the dilemma a "scissor crisis." The problem was far from academic: Without affordable clothing or farm implements to buy from the cities, peasants had little incentive to produce surpluses for urban consumption.[17]

At that point, the situation was resolved by forcing industrial prices down via austerity measures, the expansion of consumer coöperatives, and a steady rebuilding of war-ravaged industry. Terms of trade between town and country remained uneven, but not counterproductively so.

The response to a grain-procurement crisis in the winter of 1927–8, however, led Stalin down the road of revolution from above, not technocratic reform. By fall 1927, the country had a food grain shortage. Only 13 percent of the harvest that season was marketed. The Soviet Union's population had increased by 14 million over the Russian Empire's prewar level, but its grain production was smaller. Many of the roots of the agricultural malaise were the same as those that had plagued the country for centuries: Labor-intensive production on small plots vastly limited potential output. But this was now compounded by the low prices offered by the state for agricultural products and the high prices it wanted to be paid for its still scant industrial products. Peasants faced a "famine of goods" and were offered poor prices for their harvests, but the state could only resolve this problem by procuring the resources needed to jump-start industry.

The peasantry's response followed a commonsense economic logic: Since the prices for livestock and industrial crops were more favorable than grain, peasants consumed grain themselves or fed it to their livestock and sold any remainder to private buyers. As a result, little of the harvest reached the cities and ration cards were reintroduced by the middle of 1928.

Bolsheviks of all stripes supported efforts to improve agriculture through peasant cooperatives and the pooling of resources, but these efforts weren't enough to make a dent in the problem. Yet the scale of the crisis in 1928 and the years that followed could have been mitigated. As historian Moshe Lewin muses, "Given a more logical price policy, a better developed cooperative movement, a more adequately maintained state and collective sector, and a serious effort to provide agronomic assistance for the peasants," some version of the New Economic Policy might have soldiered on. Many of these measures had, in fact, been adopted but only implemented in a halting fashion.[18]

Ultimately, Stalin and his faction of the Soviet leadership felt that their country could not afford to ride, as in Bukharin's formulation, "to socialism on the peasant nag." They wanted to increase investment in heavy industry and feared falling even further behind the West. Though it's hard to separate deliberate bluster from ideological delusion, they claimed to see peasants making rational attempts to survive their policy zigzags, as "kulaks holding the country ransom." After crushing the left and right oppositions within his party, Stalin had free rein to take on enemies in society at large, real and imagined.

What followed is well known: an eventual push toward terror in the countryside, state collectivization, mass famine, crash industrialization, and the command economy. Stalin's turn was a radical departure from the New Economic Policy, but it resonated with the long-standing belief that finding capital for industrial development—"socialist primitive accumulation"—made conflict with the peasantry inevitable. The NEP's unequal exchange became state violence on an unimaginable scale.

Yet at a horrific cost, Russia did industrialize. Taking the long view of twentieth-century economic development, economic historian Robert C. Allen credits the crude 1930s mobilization of resources with substantially raising rates of both investment and consumption and putting the Soviet Union on a fundamentally improved developmental trajectory. The tragedy, Allen concludes, is that much of this need not have required Stalinist terror—the NEP framework could have achieved it.[19]

Now that we know the context of its emergence—revolution in a backward country, war, famine, and the growth of an authoritarian collectivist state—let's look at the mature model most now think of as socialist planning.

An Economy by Decree

What we prefer to call the "command" or "administered economy," rather than, for reasons that will become clear, the "planned economy," was formed in an ad hoc fashion. The bureaucrats around Stalin knew their aim—rapid industrialization and agricultural collectivization—and their pursuit of those aims created an entirely new type of economy. Many of the institutions they wielded to this end dated from an earlier period. Gosplan, for instance, was founded in 1921 as just one of a myriad of planning organs. During the NEP period it developed calculations to help state-owned enterprises set production targets, allocate resources, and coordinate medium-term regional and sectoral plans.[20]

It's hard to overstate the novelty of what Gosplan was now tasked with doing. It created the first national system of accounts, capturing a vast country's entire economic activity years before such a feat would be attempted in the West. In the following decade, it would be asked to do much more. By the 1930s, the mixed economy of the NEP period had been replaced by a system of total state ownership coordinated by administrative resource allocation. Whereas the early Soviet Union pioneered indicative planning, meant to shape public and private investment and smooth out market fluctuations, this new type of planning sought to mobilize immense resources directly through state decree. The market would be dismantled, not influenced.

The system that emerged has been described by one scholar as "the most complex organization ever constructed by mankind," so naturally we only offer a simplified sketch of its operations. Resource allocation began with the Communist Party leadership using information gathered about the country's production potential and consumption needs to lay out high-level priorities for development. These policy directives were made real through the work of an economic bureaucracy. At the top of this hierarchy stood a council of ministers that issued decrees and oversaw planning agencies. Gosplan, which had morphed into the state's vital planning commission, produced plans, translating the party's multiyear goals into specific annual targets. Its bureaucrats relied on functional agencies, such as state banks, the finance ministry, a price committee, and more, to create the "rules of the game" in areas ranging from financial guidelines to compensation agreements. Gosplan itself did not have the ability to prepare operational plans for thousands of enterprises producing millions of goods and services. Instead, it projected aggregate supply and demand for key commodities. It was up to individual ministries, like the ministry for steel production, to liaise with individual firms and eventually generate detailed instructions for them. After complex coordination and vigorous negotiations—between the party and Gosplan, Gosplan and the ministries, and the ministries and firms—these plans were eventually approved and became binding directives for enterprises.[21]

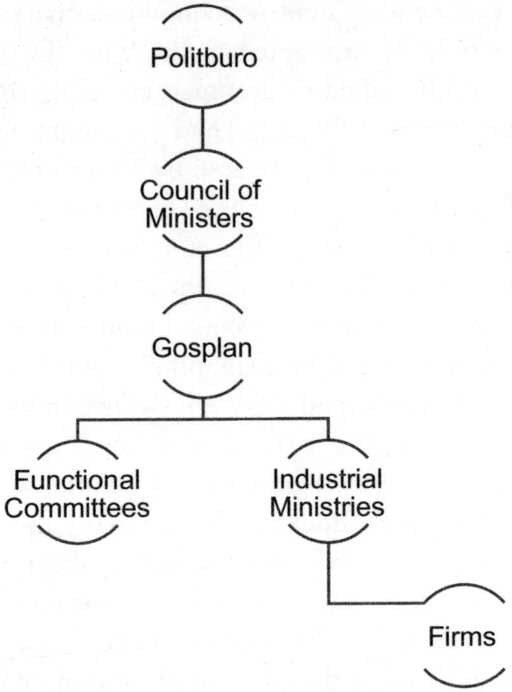

Simple Model of the Soviet Economic Bureaucracy

Since firms received directives for their output and had their inputs strictly allocated, hundreds of indicators had to be managed. Working with firm directors, planners had to decide how many materials would be assigned to each firm, what employment levels they had to maintain, their volume of investment, and how much they had to pay their workers. Every decision created ripple effects throughout the economy.

The basic process was referred to as "material-balance planning." The resources needed for each sector of the economy were calculated in advance. The required production supply (plus foreign imports) was set to match consumption demands (plus foreign exports). Planning was largely carried out in physical terms, and while price was used, it had largely an accounting function.[22]

Above all else, the system was hierarchical. Though locally produced and consumed commodities could be sold by firms without authorization, for most commodities, producers could only sell goods to purchasers with allocation orders. In his pioneering study of the Soviet system, *Factory and Manager in the USSR*, Joseph S. Berliner describes a world in which firm managers were forced to be incredibly resourceful to navigate bureaucracies and meet output expectations, while facing a perpetual shortage of supplies and an environment in which firm autonomy was incredibly circumscribed. In market systems, any given economic activity is presumed to be permitted unless it is expressly banned. In the state socialist economy, a safe assumption was that activity was only allowed if expressly permitted.[23]

From Gosplan to the Factory Floor

To better understand how such a system functioned, let's imagine, following Berliner, the workings of an important 1940s-era factory. The state, naturally, is the lawful owner of the enterprise, and it would entrust its oversight to an intermediary body like the ministry of iron and steel. This ministry selects a firm director responsible for its overall performance. This director has a chief engineer by his side to guide the technical operation of the plant machinery and the design of its products. There is also a chief accountant to keep the books and prepare an all-important annual report. A planning chief is needed to record production results and calculate the degree of plan fulfillment. Finally, the executive management is rounded out by a figure entrusted with preparing the firm's purchasing plan. This department head must not only map out required production inputs but make sure that the plant is getting these materials in the right quantities and in a usable form.[24]

The director relies on his management team to engage with state bureaucracies. As Berliner explains, "It is they who the director usually takes with him to Moscow on critical occasions; the chief accountant to present and defend the annual report; the chief of the planning department to negotiate for next year's plan; or the chief of the purchasing department to press for an additional allocation of some critical material." But, naturally, to ensure the internal functioning of the enterprise, a set of middle managers are employed to play a role similar to the one they play in capitalist firms: to help with product design, quality control, labor discipline, and more. Engaging most closely with rank-and-file workers are, of course, foremen, a figure valorized by Stalin as "the junior commander of production."[25]

However, unlike the head of a capitalist firm, the director nervously awaits orders from Moscow, not sales figures from consumer markets. In late summer those orders come in the form of control figures—tentative targets for the following year, like a call for a 5 percent increase in total output, the production of 150 tractors, or the establishment of a production line for a new product. The firm must respond to these directives with a draft production plan, laying out in detail how it might meet the ministry's wishes (or why it might fall short of them).

The most important part of the overarching enterprise plan is a production plan presenting its target output. Next is its procurement plan, which lists the material and equipment inputs required, and then a labor and payroll plan, which not only encompasses a wage bill but labor productivity goals. Other parts of the plan relate to finances, organization, and capital investment. Creating such a document is a process that involves discussions at every level of the firm as managers try to grapple with the state's desire for "tempo" despite frequent input shortages and low levels of productivity. Once it has draft production plans from all its firms, the ministry creates an overarching plan and sends it to Gosplan for amendment and coordination and the creation of a national economic plan.[26]

Later in the year, once this process is completed, the firm director receives a revised enterprise plan, based on input received from around the country, with far less room for negotiation. He'll continue to plead for more inputs and fewer output requirements, however. The final enterprise plan issued by the state was in theory binding, but in practice it was subject to revision through the year. The ceaseless process of administrative corrections during the year led Polish economist Eugène Zaleski to wonder whether the "trial and error" system could even be considered planning at all.[27]

In communist lore, Soviet managers like our firm director were selflessly committed to plan fulfillment and the state's ideology and developmental project. As we'll discuss later in this chapter, the reality of supply failures encouraged them to hoard labor and material and access a secondary economy to obtain scarce materials or otherwise wastefully devote resources to producing their own inputs. They concealed their true production capacity to obtain better plan targets, overreported output to move up the ranks of the nomenklatura, and had little real interest in ideology.[28]

As for the workers laboring in workers' states, an account by Miklós Haraszti describes Eastern Bloc factory conditions. Though employed at institutions called things like "Red Star Tractor Workers," in many respects their work lives differed little from their peers in capitalist countries. Their managers demanded output above all else and the gains of that output only trickled down indirectly to the workers themselves. Not only did they receive a wage for their labor, but piecework, opposed by generations of labor activists, persisted in avowedly socialist economies. State-controlled unions protected workers against gross abuses, but there was no shopfloor democracy. They were protected by welfare state guarantees, but that was true of citizens in the social democracies of Northern Europe too. Compared to them, socialist workers had an analogous relationship to the means of production but with less robust union representation and far fewer consumer benefits.[29]

For Haraszti, the socialist system was marked not just by a lack of economic democracy but perverse incentives that prized quantitative output over "producing useful goods of high quality." He asks, "What immense force is capable of killing in the worker—who creates everything—the instinct for good work?" Just as factory managers concealed their capacity to produce from the ministries who drafted their control figures, managers couldn't "count on any information coming from us who actually operate the machine."[30]

A generally egalitarian income distribution prevailed under state socialism, though wage differentials were maintained and considered essential to the system. Differential pay was often used to encourage specialization—but also to shift labor from "nonproductive sectors" of the economy like education, health care, and housing to the "productive sector" like industry, construction, and mining. Workers could expect incentive pay, but for those engaged in piecework the extra income often proved short-lived; regular overfulfillment of piecework just pushed target output upward. Such policies were the root of the popular saying, "The government pretends to pay us—we pretend to work." There were moral exhortations to encourage citizens to construct socialism, but workers saw themselves more as wage laborers in a hyperbureaucratic state and less as the collective owners of the means of production.[31]

How citizens ended up at their places of work—or, in the mind of critics like Haraszti, their sites of exploitation—differed greatly from how they ended up there in capitalist economies. In place of a traditional labor market, command economies had what we can call a quasi–labor market, referred to by the state bureaucracy as the "planned distribution of the labor force." Some of the system's oddities seemingly benefited workers: firms hired extensively and avoided job shedding as part of national job guarantees, part-time and fixed-term employment was virtually nonexistent, job security was ironclad, and workers had extensive fringe benefits.[32]

Even though most people—other than certain recent university graduates who were assigned to certain sectors and regions—were not told by the state where they had to work, Communist governments retained control over the internal migration of workers, something that would be unimaginable in the West. After Khrushchev's reforms, the USSR relaxed restrictions, but it still maintained a passport system, which made moving to some cities like Moscow difficult. Generally, socialist planners relied on centrally administered wage rates to cut off or create movements of labor indirectly. As one contemporary text sensibly put it, "In those industrial branches where sufficient labor is not available, we have to make jobs more attractive by raising wages."[33]

In most respects, however, it's hard to overstate what a departure the command economy was from the market system that prevailed across the rest of the world. Production required administrative orders (and the state capacity to back up those orders) rather than horizontal exchange and contracts across the economy and the (in theory) ex ante coordination of this production as opposed to ex post market relations.

Now that we've explored the series of events that created this dizzyingly complex economy and sketched out its basic functioning, let's examine its actual performance.

The Administered Economy Stutters

The Stalinist period, at an inexcusable human cost, saw notable economic gains. Administrative planning generated huge amounts of waste, but it more than made up for it through its ability to mobilize resources. In 1931, Stalin said, "We are fifty or a hundred years behind the advanced countries. We must make good this distance in ten years," and though his regime did not come anywhere near this mark, it made up significant ground, particularly in industrial and defense sectors. While the capitalist world was in the middle of the Great Depression, growth figures coming out of the Soviet Union encouraged millions of workers around the world to see a rational, planned future being built in "the socialist sixth of the world."[34]

In its first few decades, the command economy was able to produce "extensive growth" by tapping into previously idle resources. Large numbers of workers were forced from agriculture into heavy industry; women were brought into the workforce; and new sources of coal, oil, and iron ore were lifted from the earth. The system not only harnessed resources, but it set clear priorities, diverting goods to construct vital infrastructure and develop key sectors. New sources of progress would have to be found once those reserves had been exhausted. By the time Khrushchev came to power dreaming of a more humane and prosperous system, the Soviet Union sought "intensive growth" through technological innovation and productivity and efficiency gains.[35]

Early indications pointed to the new administration being up to the task. "Khrushchev's thaw" famously meant a reckoning with Stalin's terror and a reduction in his police state, but it was also accompanied by economic reforms. The Sovnarkhoz reform shifted planning from all-Soviet industrial ministries in Moscow to regionally based ones, specialists convened to openly discuss production problems, and the planning process involved wider layers of the nomenklatura. The organizational changes were accompanied by lofty rhetoric that recalled a much earlier period of Bolshevism: "We must govern in such a way that nobody governs for society, but society itself does the governing."[36]

One of Khrushchev's overarching goals was to rebalance the Soviet economy from a single-minded focus on capital goods to the production of more consumer goods. Improving agricultural productivity, that age-old aspiration of Russian leaders, was also on his mind. Producers in that sector were offered higher prices and given access to better equipment and fertilizers. The agricultural laborers made redundant by farm mechanization found homes in cities where tens of thousands of new *Khrushchyovkas*, prefabricated apartments that took just days to build, awaited them.[37]

But his well-intended schemes were, on the whole, failures. Consumer goods production skewed toward things that most citizens couldn't afford and created shortages where there was demand. The fleeting attempt at decentralization (the 1957 Sovnarkhoz shift) actually seems to have made coordination of these complex products even more difficult and exacerbated "manager-planner" agency problems we'll soon discuss in more detail. Some agricultural reform was undertaken but it was dragged down by grand failed projects like a campaign to encourage farmers in Ukraine to grow corn instead of wheat.

Yet this period coincided with some of the Soviet Union's greatest triumphs. The world's first satellite, Sputnik, was launched in 1957; Yuri Gagarin traveled into space in 1961, and probes were soon sent to Mars and Venus. It's no surprise that between 1959 and 1961 the *New York Times* produced articles with titles like, "Allen Dulles Sees US Peril in Soviet's Economic Rise," "CIA Forecasts Soviet Output Will Grow 80% in Next Decade," and "Doubling of Output by Soviet Indicated." What Western commentators didn't know was that their rival's agriculture was stagnant—indeed grain production remained almost unchanged from the late 1960s until the country's collapse—and that labor and low-cost natural resources were becoming scarcer, jeopardizing key sources of growth. This truth was apparent to everyday citizens of the USSR and its allies, who dealt with long lines and poor-quality goods.

Patience waned along with growth rates. The command economy was relatively successful in its first few decades when progress could be achieved simply through investment (increasing the capital–labor ratio) without a need for technological or other sources of productivity improvements. It was "all thumbs and no fingers"—good at mass producing steel and tanks during the period of rapid industrialization, while struggling thereafter to cope with the complexity of consumer goods inputs. The system did deliver high-profile innovations, but only where prior technological knowledge was widespread (like aerospace) and almost never in emerging fields (like computing). This technological lag and stagnation more generally were the product of its basic economic model rather than the authoritarian political system it grew from.[38]

Suboptimal Solutions

The 1960s Soviet economy, one contemporary academic calculated, was now 1,600 times more complex than it had been just a few decades earlier. But its techniques of planning were virtually unchanged since the first Five-Year Plan. The need for creative efforts to modernize command economies was apparent to many. We can call one school of reformers—those who wanted to use mathematical optimization and new forms of communication to make planning more efficient—early "cybersocialists."[39]

No one was more important to this effort than Leonid Kantorovich. Kantorovich eventually won a Nobel Prize for his work pioneering linear programming, work that began out of a desire to solve the problems of state socialism. In 1938, the young professor of mathematics at Leningrad University was approached by a plywood trust looking to answer a deceptively simple question: They had eight peeling machines that had to produce five types of plywood in varying quantities; given the raw materials, they needed a work schedule to maximize output. To tackle the dilemma, first Kantorovich formulated an objective function—maximizing the output of finished plywood—and then he identified constraints—the availability of wood and the capacity of machines needed for processing, in this case. He developed a way to measure each machine's output of one plywood in terms of all the other products it could have made. "Shadow prices," a number assigned to inputs in place of market prices, were calculated from opportunity costs, taking into account constraints and thereby helping to show how much more output could be gotten by relaxing one or another constraint.[40]

Kantorovich's method was meant to allow planners to assess optimal pricing; shadow prices would be calculated from opportunity costs without the need for the "total information awareness" that the likes of Ludwig von Mises and Friedrich Hayek had said were necessary for planning to work. As Kantorovich recounts in the plywood example, he was able to obtain "an increase in the output of the product of 5 per cent in comparison with the simplest solution (that is, if we assign work to each of the machines in proportion to the product mix)." Not satisfied, he explained how to use his method to do things like route freight transportation more optimally or improve the cutting of timber and the trimming of metal. All the examples used linear programming to minimize waste and maximize machine and labor power. Kantorovich was plagued by the problems of Soviet planning and he sought a general method for solving them. He and other would-be planning optimizers asked, "Why couldn't the mathematics that worked to fix problems at individual plants be extended to the economy as a whole?"[41]

In the Stalinist era, it was hard to make such a case openly. When Kantorovich's work was discussed at Gosplan in 1943 one speaker noted that "an optimum has already been proposed by the fascist Pareto, a favorite of Mussolini." A follow-up meeting was convened where the arrest of the renegade mathematician was contemplated. Luckily, such a measure was not deemed necessary and after the death of Stalin it became easier to make the case for mathematical methods in economics.[42]

In 1954, an early advocate of Kantorovich's approach, Leningrad University's Sergei Vallander, promised new premier Georgy Malenkov that the new optimization methods would boost GDP by 50 to 70 percent. Yet the ideas were once again rejected on ideological grounds—the prices that emerged from linear programming seemed too incompatible with the labor theory of value and all the talk of investment efficiency based on profitability and cost minimization smacked of the "bourgeois" notion of the profit rate. More practically, Gosplan officials claimed—ironically echoing the supreme bourgeois economist Hayek—that mass application of the method was not practical since it required too much information and impossibly large computational abilities. But this time authorities offered their critiques less harshly and even supported the use of the method at lower levels to shape transport and rationalize cutting. Meanwhile, Kantorovich waited for the chance to prove his ideas nationally, while rebranding his work with invocations of Marx and Lenin and more ideological phrasing—"objectively determined valuations" would be used, for example, instead of "prices."[43]

Under Khrushchev, the Soviet state was finally ready to embrace Kantorovich and his co-thinkers like Moscow mathematician Vasily Nemchinov. Together the two men were allowed to create a research institution that trained a generation of mathematical economists who labored toward an automated system of economic planning and management. Their dreams dovetailed with the aspirations of Victor Glushkov and others who aimed to create a nationwide computer network, a sort of Soviet internet, to share data between firms and planners. As we've discussed, Hayek argued that effective planning was impossible since it required accessing information from across an economy and solving "a system of thousands or more simultaneous equations." Combined, the work pioneered by Kantorovich and Glushkov seemed to offer the solution for a viable, computerized planning: a cybersocialist utopia.

Kantorovich's work was internationally recognized and he was awarded the Nobel Prize in economics. In practice, however, linear programming in the USSR came to be nothing more than a minor planning tool among others. Why that is the case is a matter of debate. Some point to contingent political barriers: The technocratic nature of optimal planning would have disempowered the vast bureaucracy that ran the USSR and limited their discretion to wheel and deal. A less cynical view would be that such seeming distortions of the Soviet system allowed it to function in practice. Excess material, for example, from unneeded inputs ("waste") was often bartered elsewhere in the economy, preventing supply problems. Managers sometimes tapped into secondary markets or lied to planners; they did so not necessarily to enhance their own position but to ensure their firms had what they needed to function in an uncertain economy.

Ultimately, it wasn't optimal planning, but it was this unplanned sector that kept the Soviet system trudging along.

"Allocations from the ministry covered only 40 percent of what we needed," one manager lamented. "You had to find the other 60 percent yourself." As Kantorovich would himself concede, "Sometimes one has to reject models which were the most complete and precise in their design in favor of one which promises practical results."[44]

Soviet decision-makers understood that optimal planning faced not just a mathematical challenge but an incentive one. Managers had little reason to be forthcoming about their capabilities, and workers had little incentive to exceed expectations. These misaligned interests meant that accurate information was systematically withheld at every level of the system. But even if planners could somehow access perfect data, they would still face the staggering problem of computational complexity. As Cosma Shalizi points out, if an administered economy like the USSR had 12 million distinct goods (Alec Nove's estimate) and planners needed to account for just 1,000 locations, they'd be dealing with 12 billion variables. Solving such a system of equations would take even a modern computer a thousand years—not ideal for coming up with an annual plan.[45]

Just as significantly, as Hungarian economist János Kornai argued, what is determined to be optimal mathematically is inherently *relative*. It is "valid only under given simplifying assumptions, regarding definite political targets and expressed in the constraints and in the objective function of the model." Calling the search for optimality the "blue-bird of economic theory," Kornai says that the real use of mathematical planning was more modestly in "the exploration of feasibilities" and the "explanation of interdependences between conflicting goals."[46]

Other critics were blunter, saying that Kantorovich and his collaborators had tried to build economic reform on the basis of microeconomics alone and had confused a social system with a technical system. With a wider lens, they would have concluded that a viable path to economic growth was "not by the reallocation of given resources with given productivity between alternative uses, i.e. the method of linear programming. It is by increasing the productivity of resources by increasing specialization, utilizing economies of scale, raising the qualifications of the labor force and fostering technical progress."[47]

It's not that Kantorovich's economic ideas didn't work at certain scales. Capitalist firms regularly use linear programming tools to make decisions about supply-chain logistics and production scheduling. But it's a massive leap to go from the needs of firms operating in a market economy to those of a state juggling an avalanche of outputs and the complex linkages between them.

Optimal planning and the related dream of cybersocialism, however, still sparks imaginations today, especially via interest in Cybersyn, a promising effort by Salvador Allende's socialist government to enhance coordination between Chilean state-owned industries and provide real-time information to planners. But similarly, if Cybersyn had merits as a planning tool in a mixed economy, it would have run into unresolvable problems if used on a wider scale.

In a critique of cybersocialism, *Jacobin* editor Seth Ackerman discusses the widespread adoption of networked planning in the most industrially advanced state socialist country, East Germany. The German Democratic Republic operated a computerized, networked planning system that collected data and plugged it into linear optimization models. Over 23,000 enterprises submitted 250 monthly reports consisting of thousands of key figures to the Central Administration for Statistics in Berlin. Planners immediately used the information to formulate and adjust plans. Kantorovich himself was impressed by developments in the country.

Ultimately, however, the East German economy suffered the same fate as its less advanced, and less computerized, Communist peers. As Ackerman notes, even more important than the problems inherent in compiling information and making calculations (plan formation) were problems in plan execution. "Beginning with fires, we could draw up a long list of routine mishaps liable to disrupt production: bad weather, broken machines, delivery errors, someone ordering the wrong part by mistake—maybe even a pandemic. All of these are profoundly destabilizing to centrally planned economies. And yet none of them are problems computers can solve."

What if a fresh aggregate plan could be generated every day or even every hour to take into account these changes? Ackerman says that this would only create a worst-of-all-worlds economy, "a system of pure ex-post coordination, just like a market economy; except now every microeconomic adjustment, no matter how small the cause, would force systemwide changes affecting every household and business all at once."[48]

Profit and Plan

In the Soviet Union, other avenues of change received more support from state authorities. In 1962, economist Evsei Liberman wrote an influential *Pravda* article called "Plan, Profit, and Bonus." That such a headline openly touting the importance of "profit" could be published in a mass circulation newspaper reflected both the relaxed environment Khrushchev had created and growing concerns about economic performance. Liberman explained the context of his proposals and the reforms that followed in an interview to the Western press a few years later: "Our planning machinery has remained the same as it was in the 1930s," when it was able to build an industrial base and defeat fascism. But now, with rising living standards, "People are demanding not only more goods but goods of better quality. Now the country must produce high-quality goods in large quantities and at a minimum cost."[49]

Liberman, an elderly and previously obscure academic, became the face of Soviet economics; indeed, his face graced a 1965 cover of *Time* magazine. He was a staunch believer that central planning could be more effective. Liberman saw that in pursuing their output targets, directors paid little heed to costs. In fact, they often tried to boost gross output by decreasing quality or changing their product composition. The story of the Soviet nail factory that, when incentivized according to numerical output, first produced a lot of tiny nails and then, when incentivized according to weight, produced useless giant nails is apocryphal, but it conveys the dynamics at play.

Liberman wanted managers to have more autonomy to make investment decisions and find ways to lower costs, rather than just build up stock. He wanted suppliers to better serve the needs of users and for weak producers to shutter. Workers, he thought, had a right to employment, but not necessarily at their existing firm or even in their current sector. As for profits, a word once taboo in socialist thought, a text on his ideas explains that "Liberman proposed that bonus payments (after fulfillment of the planned output target) should be an increasing function of the profit rate (profit/capital ratio), thus encouraging the expansion of profits but the reduction of capital usage. Profitability norms established for each industry would serve as the basis for evaluating managerial performance."[50]

In the early 1960s, Liberman's proposals were tested in select mines and factories to generally favorable results. Meetings at the USSR Academy of Sciences were held on cost accounting and financial incentives, and a few years later a new Soviet premier, Alexei Kosygin, instituted a set of reforms loosely along the lines of "Plan, Profit, and Bonus." Efforts were made to eliminate slack plans, firms were given more freedom, and a new bonus system encouraged workers and managers alike to value efficiency. Planners and producers were meant to have their interests aligned, without constant monitoring and punitive penalties. By the end of 1968, 72 percent of enterprises were converted to the new scheme.[51]

The Kosygin reform could have signaled a big shift in Soviet economic policy. In theory, reducing the number of centrally assigned targets from forty to just nine was a major change, especially since gross value of output—particularly responsible for encouraging waste—was not one of them. Allowing firms to keep and reinvest more of their profits would not only have rewarded successful enterprises at the expense of less successful ones; it would have shifted resources from flagging heavy industry to more dynamic light industry. These changes would have had to be accompanied by price reform to make revenues and expenditure representative of firm performance (and not just administrative price fixing).[52]

In practice, the shift was less significant. Price reform was limited, as were levels of firm-driven investment. There was only so much that could be done in an economy with administered prices: When more flexibility was offered to managers in the early years of the reform, they took advantage of prices that diverged greatly from marginal costs and avoided much-demanded goods that were not. As one economist recounts, "Some products that Soviet society needed were not produced because they were underpriced relative to social marginal cost and producing them would have reduced enterprise profits and incentive funds." There was no way profits could provide proper signals for investment decisions in an economy without scarcity prices. Allocative efficiency suffered and planners were forced to intervene, essentially replicating the old system. Soon realizing the constraints still in place, firms again hoarded resources and paid less heed to efficiency.[53]

The changes were less dramatic than expected for managers in other respects, as well. The thirty-one targets that were "eliminated" still needed to be tracked and submitted as part of a firm's draft plans. The problems created by the traditional model's emphasis on gross output weren't obviated either. That figure might not have been mandated by planners, but it was still used to centrally determine a firm's wage bill. The larger the wage bill, the more managers could draw from the new bonus fund, encouraging the expansion of employment rather than increased productivity. The wage bill was just one example of the contradictory nature of the reforms, which suffered from problems of both design and implementation. An additional overarching issue plagued any attempt to solve the problems created by the command economy within the framework of command economies: How much autonomy could a firm really have if it couldn't decide what to produce, where it could buy its inputs, or how it could price its outputs?

There was little evidence that the halting reforms were delivering success, making them easy to undermine. After Czech "revisionism" bubbled into 1968's Prague Spring, the Leonid Brezhnev wing of the leadership became even more wary of change, especially any that offered a reduced role for the party's planners and the heavy industry it had so diligently built up. It was better to risk stagnation than political instability.

Those around Brezhnev had their own theory of progress: They looked to the "scientific and technical revolution" sweeping the world through the rise of new computing and information technology. By tailing these advances, perhaps Khrushchev's promised superabundance could come about without fundamental reform. Planning technology, as we saw in the East German example, was already shaping command economies, and in the meantime, soaring oil prices seemingly bought Communist parties time.

The promised growth never came, however. The Soviet system produced shortages and poor-quality goods by its very nature, and technocratic tweaks (seesawing between tighter oversight and more decentralization) proved ineffective. We now have a clearer picture of Russia's economic dysfunction: Perhaps 20 percent of gross national product was spent on the military, and agriculture was at only 55 percent American output. One Soviet economist estimated that out of 90 million tons of potatoes harvested, only 24 million got to consumers because of transportation and storage problems. The real numbers were so jarring that the United States General Accounting Office felt obligated to publish a fifty-six-page assessment of how exactly the CIA had so grossly overestimated the size of the Soviet economy.[54]

Stagnation boiled into demand for reform. After Brezhnev's death in 1982, Yuri Andropov succeeded him as general secretary. During his fifteen months in power, Andropov sought to combat corruption and absenteeism, emphasized quality over sheer volume in production, and promoted young reformers like Mikhail Gorbachev.

Andropov's protégé would soon pursue a more radical course. When Gorbachev became general secretary in 1985, he inherited an economy riddled with supply shortages, declining productivity, and growing dissatisfaction. His twin slogans—*glasnost* ("openness") and *perestroika* ("restructuring")—were meant to address both political sclerosis and economic stagnation. Under perestroika, Gorbachev introduced measures such as the 1987 Law on State Enterprises, which gave firms more autonomy and allowed them to retain profits. He legalized cooperatives, bringing in elements of private enterprise, and launched more campaigns to reduce corruption and absenteeism.

But these changes unfolded within a system in which prices remained centrally administered, inputs were unreliable, and state agencies still attempted to steer outcomes through outdated levers. Managers were formally empowered, yet remained bound by planning norms that no longer functioned. As the state's coordinating capacity eroded, no viable alternative emerged.

At the same time, glasnost eroded the legitimacy of the party. Censorship was relaxed, and criticism of the system—along with rising nationalist sentiment—flooded public discourse. By weakening the repressive and centralizing aspects of the old regime before constructing a durable replacement, Gorbachev cut through the red tape that had been tenuously holding a fragile superpower together. He intended to reform the command economy—instead, he unmade it.

The Soviet Union entered the 1990s with no functioning plan and no functioning market. Food and fuel shortages worsened. Monetary instability spiraled. Nationalist movements gained traction. A failed coup in August 1991 by hardliners weakened the center further. By December, the USSR ceased to exist. In 1977, about a third of humanity lived under socialist command economies of one type or another. By 1992, that figure was 0.6 percent.[55]

Hungarian Market Socialism

After its liberation from fascism by the Red Army, much of Eastern Europe was remolded in the image of the Soviet Union. In the official ideology of these war-ravaged countries, socialism meant a rationally planned economy and capitalism was synonymous with market economies, which were doomed for the dustbin of history. However, these economies quickly caught up to dilemmas plaguing their erstwhile Soviet comrades. The early years of state socialism saw the mobilization of untapped resources and impressive growth rates. Yet before long, the model's problems became clear: low agricultural productivity, firm hoarding, shortages, an imbalance between heavy and light industry, and worker unrest over living conditions and rationed goods.

This discontent boiled over into outright revolt in East Germany in 1953 and in Hungary and Poland in 1956. In Hungary, a revolution, with thousands mobilized in militias and worker councils, threatened to push the country out of the Warsaw Pact and provoked a bloody intervention by Soviet forces. A new Communist leadership, loyal to Moscow, had to restore legitimacy, and fast.

It wasn't clear who the new Hungarian premier, János Kádár, really was. He was arrested and tortured by the Stalinist Mátyás Rákosi administration in 1951 and was only released from prison after the reformist Imre Nagy came to power. A couple years later, he supported Nagy and assumed a leadership role during the early days of the Hungarian Revolution before backtracking and deciding that things had gone too far. After the Soviet invasion, Kádár repaid Nagy by ordering his former benefactor's execution.

Kádár's early economic moves hardly burnished his credentials as a reformer—he appeased hardliners through a massive recollectivization program. During the chaos of the 1956 revolution, collective farms lost 60 percent of their members, most of whom became private farmers. But unlike Hungary's postwar collectivization, Kádár offered peasants more carrots than sticks. Many peasants were pushed back onto state farms, but they were allowed private plots and allowed to hold their own livestock herds. Others were encouraged to form agricultural cooperatives that expanded their activities to construction and small-scale manufacturing. The new regime did away with compulsory deliveries and instead encouraged voluntary sales at good prices. Government investments in mechanization and fertilizer further encouraged growth. Hungary became the only command economy in history to see crop output increase along with collectivization.[56]

With his position consolidated and a better climate for reform emerging in the Eastern Bloc, Kádár had space to chart a new course. His famous refrain, "Those who are not against us are with us," signaled a degree of political and cultural openness. In the new environment, heterodox economic thinking thrived. Hardliners were dismissed and reformers, like new Central Committee Secretary Rezso Nyers, were appointed. They had long identified the command economy's classic problems and knew that isolated changes would be subsumed—as in the Kosygin reforms—by the overarching logic of the old system. A whole package of measures would have to be rolled out at once.[57]

On May 7, 1966, the Communist Party leadership laid out their objectives for the next few years: "The laborious and bureaucratic system of centralized allocations" would give way to "commercial relations." Producers would have autonomy and the ability to decide what and how much to produce and whether to purchase their required inputs. They'd be free to establish horizontal relationships with users within a regulated market, including (within the bounds of national interest) foreign firms. Enterprises would have greater ability to direct investments. Profits would be the measure of their success and the source of incentive payments for managers and workers alike.[58]

While maintaining state ownership of the means of production, this New Economic Mechanism (NEM) represented a shift from imperative planning to indicative planning. Whereas imperative planning relied on binding directives issued from central authorities, indicative planning sought to guide economic activity through indirect means such as prices, taxes, and interest rates—using financial signals to shape firm behavior rather than command it. Hungary's version of Gosplan would still produce five-year and annual plans to guide national development toward light industry and the production of goods for export, but ministries wouldn't break them down into granular firm-level targets. It would instead try to realize them through financial means (like prices, taxes, and interest rates). Crucially, unlike the Kosygin reforms, autonomy and incentives were accompanied by price reform so that differences in profitability actually influenced supply and demand. The prices of some key items remained centrally administered; some were left to market forces, while still others were allowed to bounce between state-set minimums and maximums.[59]

The NEM was an immediate success. Unlike in the Soviet Union, firms became, almost overnight, interested in profit seeking by meeting consumer demand. They stopped hoarding resources and reduced waste. While controlling inflation, the economy grew, productivity soared, and trade increased. Hungary was fulfilling its plan—to become a competitive exporter, with thriving light industry and productive agriculture—with a greatly reduced role for centralized planning. Ordinary workers felt the benefits, as well: The workweek was reduced from forty-eight hours to forty-four hours, shortages abated and there was a more varied assortment of products to buy.[60]

However, the NEM was wrought with contradictions from the beginning. The state, via branch ministries or local governments, was responsible for founding and deciding the scope of firms' activities, but it rarely liquidated them for being inefficient. It appointed but rarely dismissed directors. The national bank was also a crucial source of funding. Directors waited for calls from the national bank, an industrial ministry, or the myriad of other officials they needed to be in the good grace of to get a government loan, subsidy, or tax relief. Economic rules are always set by state authorities, but in Hungary dependence on vertical relationships with the state outweighed horizontal relationships with other firms and consumers.[61]

These tendencies were strengthened by high market concentration in the Hungarian economy. The traditional model favors large, integrated combines. The size of these enterprises made them easier for planners to manage and provided economies of scale. Through the early 1960s, large campaigns of industrial mergers took place. The decade prior to the NEM's inauguration saw the percentage of enterprises employing more than one thousand workers go from 10 percent to 34.6 percent. This composition meant that many firms felt weak competition. What's more, just as directors relied on their state benefactors, party officials were wary of the political consequences of letting even unproductive firms that thousands of workers relied on for employment go under. Instead of designing a properly functioning market socialist system, the Hungarians had seemingly just grafted some elements of a price system haphazardly onto a command economy, piecemeal.[62]

Four years after the New Economic Mechanism's introduction, the Communist Party's centralizing impulses returned to the fore. Certain hardliners had always resented wholesale reform and hoped to just improve on the old system as their peers in Berlin and Moscow seemed to be doing. This was a path of far less resistance than the alternative: breaking up powerful conglomerates to allow productive competition and expressing state development preferences indirectly.[63]

As the world plunged into recession following the 1973 oil shock, these leaders, reluctant to slow down economic growth and risk a fall in living standards, turned their economy inward to insulate themselves from a "crisis of capitalism." Foreign loans fueled a large investment drive in the mid-1970s, wages were increased, and consumer prices often became lower than producer prices. Producers, in turn, bargained for subsidies from the state for which they had no repayment obligations. More products were subject to purchase quotas and more seller–buyer relationships were centrally determined. As production taxes and financial assistance became set on a firm-by-firm basis and the usefulness of price signals weakened, a key part of the NEM was undermined.

Within a few years, however, a new set of reforms were in place that not only returned to the original New Economic Mechanism course but addressed some of its defects. A December 1978 party resolution called for increased emphasis on the profit motive, less government interference, and price reform. The state structure interacting with firms was simplified and made less prone to microlevel meddling, many large enterprises were broken up to promote competition, producer prices were rationalized by aligning them more closely with world market prices, and investment decision-making was decentralized.[64]

But even with the changes, Hungary wasn't generating enough foreign exchange to service the debts it had taken on in the 1970s. As the 1980s went on, worker discontent with stagnant wages, housing shortages, and poverty grew. The measures needed to tackle debt and inflation were politically unpalatable, but efforts to preserve subsidies and consumption levels only fueled a balance-of-payments crisis. As the wider Soviet bloc crumbled, Hungary's new leaders saw the restoration of capitalism as a palliative.

The Hungarian reformers' revision of the Soviet model managed to solve some of its key deficits: its emphasis on quantity over quality (what East Germans called *Tonnenideologie*, the ideology of tons), its low-productivity and incentive issues, and information problems that arose from the hiding of capacities and the hoarding of resources. It was no small feat to overcome the shortage economy. But weak producers were still not punished with bankruptcy and the old bargaining over the annual plan was replaced with new forms of bargaining with state authorities for credits and subsidies.

The New Economic Mechanism has been described as "neither plan nor market," and fittingly many Hungarians took to describing their system as "goulash communism." Goulash, after all, was a stew made up of an amalgam of ingredients: onions, peppers, potatoes, noodles, meats. Despite its flaws, its record holds up better than that of any other socialist state, and if not for contingent economic difficulties and its party-state's fragile legitimacy (big ifs), it might have found a way to move toward democratic socialism. Still, one measure of its relative merits is a public opinion poll two decades after the transition to capitalism in which only 8 percent of respondents said that most people in Hungary were now better off than they had been under communism.[65]

The writers of this book have paid special attention to the case of Hungary and related efforts in countries like Yugoslavia to better understand the contradictions of any system that seeks to meld together plan and market. Any government can make macroeconomic mistakes, but by limiting the purview of state actors, foregrounding the agency of workers as firm stakeholders and founders, recognizing the necessity of enterprise failure, and encouraging competition in our public banking system, we address the key flaws of these examples.[66]

From Soft Budgets to Hard Failures

So how should we summarize the failure of "actually existing" socialist planning? The extensive history of command economies throughout the world tends to reveal the same issues. The first category of outcomes can be described as "agency problems," which involve relations between planners and managers, managers and workers, and even state planners and the public writ large.

To take these agency problems in turn: Command economies rely on accurate and honest information from firms about their production possibilities and their efficient use of allocated resources. But since the resources allocated to firms depend on the information they provide to the center, they have incentives to falsify information and hoard resources. We saw this in

Berliner's study of Soviet managers who almost universally underreported their capacity and overreported their output to obtain easier plans. Once they received those plans—just like the piecework workers in Haraszti's account—they wouldn't even respond to monetary incentives to radically overfulfill targets for fear of ratcheting up future targets.

Directors might scheme to ensure their own career futures, but their firms' survival was almost never in doubt. Kornai labeled a phenomenon we've covered in the Hungarian case the "soft budget constraint." Weak producers were inevitably subsidized by the state and not allowed to fail. This was perfectly logical for policymakers; allowing inefficient firms to collapse would cause destabilizing unemployment and impact other producers reliant on their outputs.

Letting firms shamble on indefinitely when they are producing things in a more costly way than others, or making things nobody wants anymore, comes at a cost. They use resources, including people's time and effort, that could be better applied elsewhere. Mechanisms like limited liability and bankruptcy law have developed within capitalism to manage the impact of firm failures without standing in the way of "creative destruction." Bankruptcy removes managers and restructures the firm to minimize losses to creditors and salvage useful assets. Social insurance programs and sometimes active labor market policies reduce the costs to workers. Central bank lender-of-last-resort action helps stop temporary liquidity problems from snowballing into needless "destructive destruction."

Under capitalism the main concern is protecting creditors and restoring profitability. The socialist impulse to protect the security and conditions of work is a good one. All too often, intensifying work and shifting income risks onto workers in the name of "flexibility" are confused with efficiency, rather than recognized as moving costs off the balance sheet and onto people. A viable socialist system has to find a way to direct competition along the high road of process and product improvement, rather than the low road of wage-cutting, insecurity, and work intensification. Whatever the answer to that—and we provide ours throughout this book—it cannot involve simply letting zombie firms stumble along.[67]

If the soft budget constraint kept firms alive, the Soviet workplace showed how warped incentives shaped how that capacity was used. We've already covered manager–worker agency problems through our look at Eastern Bloc workers who had no real incentive to work efficiently. However, managers also lacked incentives to take risks and innovate using new technology or production techniques. In Hungary's market socialist system—which saw incentives, decentralization, and price reform—this particular issue was mitigated, despite the problems of monopolization and other structural flaws.

Next, there is a category of objection that we can call the "public-planner agency problem." Who plans the planners? In actually existing socialism, there was no democratic control, and feedback from civil society was stifled by political authoritarianism. Planners may have been trying to serve public interests, but poor information flows often forced them to resort to guesswork. They also were unable to take into account the externalities created by their actions—one reason why the Eastern Bloc environmental record, which featured lowlights like the destruction of the Aral Sea through poorly designed irrigation projects, was even more abysmal than that of its capitalist peers.

These are just some of the difficulties we encounter before getting to the most common criticism of the command economy—informational problems. Lenin wrote in *State and Revolution* that "accounting and control" was all that was needed for the proper functioning of the first stage of a communist society. "All that is required," he contended, "is that [workers] should work equally, do their proper share of work, and get equal pay; the accounting and control necessary for this have been simplified by capitalism to the utmost and reduced to the extraordinarily simple operations—which any literate person can perform—of supervising and recording, knowledge of the four rules of arithmetic, and issuing appropriate receipts."[68]

In practice, this proved to be a difficult task even for highly trained technocrats with advanced calculational tools. The 1980s Soviet economic bureaucracy consisted of thirty-eight state committees, thirty-three all-Soviet ministries, twenty-eight republican ministries, and more than 300 regional ministries and authorities. Each of these nearly 400 organizations had sprawling bureaucratic departments within them. Together they oversaw 43,000 factories, 26,000 construction enterprises, 47,000 farming units, 260,000 service establishments, and over 1 million retail trade shops. The factories alone produced around 12 million different products or product variants, each of which required unique inputs and were dependent on each other through complicated supply chains.[69]

It seems impossible that such a system could persist, let alone oversee growth, for over a half century. Yet hidden features of command economies meant that they were more resilient than early critics like Hayek and Mises expected. Despite Soviet boasts about its "scientific" planning process, Gosplan couldn't have planned and priced millions of goods and services. To do such a thing would require accurate knowledge of the needs and abilities of every firm and household in the country.

Planners confronted informational problems by essentially guessing to determine production quotas. For example, they had to set targets for firms in their ministries without knowing what those firms could truly produce. They did know, however, that directors were understating the output that they could achieve. So they used a rule of thumb: They'd ask for what they produced last year, plus a little bit extra, thereby maintaining economic tempo, while broadly accepting the production horizons laid out by directors. Every part of the Soviet economic hierarchy—from supreme party organs down to workers "pretending to work"—all seemed to have an incentive to hide their true capacities. Far from a totalitarian machine, with orders followed and enforced implacably through the hierarchy, we see a system composed of ordinary human beings improvising and navigating difficult trade-offs.

Rather than simply wait for promised inputs that were not forthcoming, firm managers, as we've discussed, exercised an important degree of control and discretion to reach their output targets. They bargained with state authorities and took part in a "second economy," an informal sector in which they joined other enterprises and consumers in bartering or buying goods that they couldn't get through the planners' official channels.

Even with these simplifications, Gosplan's responsibilities were immense. It had to coordinate and amend draft output plans to make them coherent with each other and with material supply possibilities, estimated agricultural production, personal incomes, the budget, and other key items. But its authority flowed indirectly through the highest bodies of government and much of its planning only involved setting aggregate output targets for *planned* commodities. Estimates of required inputs were aggregated by ministries and sent to Gosplan but essentially came from "below," since enterprises were responsible for their own draft plans. "Many orders are written by their recipients," a Hungarian economist remarked.[70]

As the year went on, planners spent much of their time reconciling unfinalized drafts with actual results. It's no wonder Zaleski asked whether the Soviet Union was actually planned at all.

Planning with Markets, Not Against Them

The design flaws of the system yielded real-world problems. Take *Tonnenideologie*, the quantity drive we've covered: Planners weren't ignorant of the pitfalls of that approach but had few alternatives to it within the traditional model. They ended up producing an economy in which paper growth often ruled the day. The Soviet steel industry is a striking example. The USSR almost doubled American steel production, but it did so with far more waste of iron ore, and it yielded a volume of products further up the value-chain that was lower than that of the US economy. Relatedly, the economist Michael Ellman notes that a reform experiment that instructed clothing factories to directly produce according to the needs of shops resulted in less output, since production runs were shorter and a wider array of items were made. By Soviet measures, these facilities had become less effective even though they were more responsive to consumer demands.[71]

This sort of planning developed a general tendency toward shortage. If consumption choices are different from what is anticipated in the plan, there will be shortages of some products and surpluses of others, and bottlenecks (shortages further up the supply chain) may delay adjustments. When people and firms come to expect shortages, they hoard, which makes the shortages themselves worse. These complexities only grew over time as the Soviet Union tried to shift from investment-led growth in heavy industry toward a more balanced path that emphasized consumer goods and efficiency.

What can get lost in an abstract and bloodless recounting of the command economy's pathologies is how everyday people experienced the system. Even if we consider Stalin's bloody terror and totalitarianism to be aberrations, the overall record isn't good. State socialism will never shake its association with lines for groceries and yearslong waits for housing and cars. Long hours spent in queues were rooted in a shortage economy that was supply constrained rather than demand constrained and resentment grew not only about the lack of goods and their shoddy quality but also about the fact that the nomenklatura with power and status could access things ordinary people could not.

Even when workers lived in countries with relatively high standards of living, like East Germany, the political system that accompanied command economies was stifling. Lenin proposed that a much smaller repressive state apparatus would be necessary under socialism than capitalism since the former required the suppression of only a small minority by the great majority. Yet by the late 1980s—a time when according to Khrushchev they should have been living under superabundance—the Stasi had nearly 175,000 informants, 90,000 agents, and kept files on over 5 million citizens. All this was necessary to keep a nation of 16 million people, with a long communist and social-democratic tradition, in check.

Despite everything we've just recounted, readers who share our egalitarian commitments might still believe that a different kind of planning—more democratic, more intelligent, more technologically advanced—could succeed where the Soviets failed. And to some extent, they would be right: Macrolevel planning is indispensable for any serious socialist project. Public investment, regulation, and strategic coordination will always be needed to guide development in socially useful directions. State planning already works in vital sectors of modern economies where outputs and social goals are relatively clear and stable, unlike the vast and constantly shifting realm of consumer production. Take the British National Health Service, a supply-constrained, centrally administered system that in many respects resembles a Soviet institution and that remains one of the most cherished and politically resilient features of the UK welfare state.

The lesson of the twentieth century, however, is that central planning cannot function as the organizing principle of an entire economy. Large organizations in both the private and public sectors are command economies of a sort, but they operate in a broader context of prices, budget allocations, and income-expenditure flows that they do not control. Planning an entity within these given parameters is a completely different order of problem than that of planning the parameters themselves.

The failure of Soviet-style planning wasn't just a matter of missing computers or Cold War pressures. It was a product of an institutional structure that generated perverse incentives, suppressed information, and collapsed worker agency into bureaucratic command. These weren't bugs to be fixed with better optimization algorithms; they were coded into the system itself.

Our book aims to show that the path to more effective planning runs through market socialism, not around it. A functioning market socialist system—with social ownership, worker control, and competitive allocation—creates the material surplus, the embedded information, and the dispersed initiative that make large-scale coordination and democratic decision-making in key sectors possible.

This socialism is not merely a nicer or more flexible variant of socialism—it may be the only viable socialism left. If we are serious about transcending capitalism, we have no choice but to wrestle with how to reconcile democratic control and social ownership with the logic of market coordination. This is how we ensure that socialism offers not only shoes for all but shoes that fit.

3

Solving the Economic Problem

Greet the dawn of a new era. You weren't a morning person before the revolution, and you certainly aren't a morning person now. But you wake up with fewer problems than you used to. After all, debt collectors aren't stalking you like villains in a horror movie, your broken arm didn't come with an itemized bill longer than a Tolstoy novel, and your boss isn't canceling your shift over text.

You stretch, check on your kid who's busy drawing a dinosaur that does not look like a dinosaur, ask your mom about her physical therapy (the clinic has decent coffee now), and you go to work—where you spend just thirty-two hours a week, not because you're employed by a nice billionaire but because law and custom require it. Your workplace environment is like the 2013–14 San Antonio Spurs: Everyone touches the ball, there's a shot clock on meetings, and while some people shine brighter, no one needs to score thirty a night for the team to win.

A cooperative firm isn't organized like a medieval kingdom with fluorescent lighting. Directors are elected (yes, sometimes a person you hate wins), and they're responsive to workplace concerns while keeping production moving along. You and your fellow worker-members can even shape production decisions.

And if the new product you suggest flops—say the fickle masses are not ready for a curry-infused pasta sauce—and if your firm fails, the fall isn't a hard push off a cliff. Instead, you get generous unemployment support, access to routine retraining, and a safety net to land on. Markets still tell you useful things (like "don't retool a factory to produce curry-flavored pasta sauce without consumer testing") and help produce a dynamic and efficient economy, but there are limits to their rule.

Aside from work, the basics are drama-free. Things like health care, childcare, and school are guaranteed as rights. Of course, life isn't perfect. Your upstairs neighbor moves furniture at 2 a.m.; a coworker coasts until a nudge becomes a formal warning; there are meetings that should have been emails. But the fights are bound by rules everyone helped draft.

Call it the ordinary miracle of a just society: Time you can count on; work as the fuel of a good society, not its end; a reasonable say in the decisions that shape our lives; and a politics that can handle people as they are, not as we might wish them to be.

This is, more or less, the world we'd like to travel to in our lifetimes. But first, let's talk about where we are now.

Capitalism is today's dominant mode of production. Its reach is immense, encompassing much of the globe and shaping nearly every sphere of human activity. No earlier social system has ever extended its logic so widely or integrated such vast numbers of people into a single economic framework.

At its core, capitalism is organized around profit. Workers, who are separated from their means of subsistence, must sell their labor power to survive. Capitalists purchase that labor, combine it with machinery and raw materials, and sell the resulting goods on markets. Demand, in capitalism, reflects not just what people need but what they can pay for. The central aim of the system is to generate profit, which is then reinvested to expand production further. Competition between firms makes this dynamic compulsory: To stand still is to be driven out of business. This relentless pressure to reduce costs, raise productivity, and expand markets is what gives capitalism its motor.

The case for capitalism is that it delivers the goods, and without direct coercion. It has a long record of driving technological progress: both making production more efficient and developing new products. Output per person is extremely high by historical standards. Though such high levels of productivity require countless people to play specialized roles in a complex division of labor, capitalism organizes this cooperation on the basis of property rights, freely entered contracts, market exchange, and competition. The most technically efficient cooperative network of production in history is coordinated on an individualized legal basis, in which people participate of their own volition.

Socialists have generally recognized this achievement, but raise three fundamental problems:

- *Inequality:* Resources are very unevenly distributed, and so market-oriented production is geared toward satisfying the wants of those with a lot over those with a little. Freedom to do what you like with what you own leaves those who own less with less practical freedom. Income is also often distributed according to neither need nor effort.
- *Unfreedom/alienation at work:* For most people, the most valuable resource we have to exchange is our capacity to work—the time in our days. Employment is a good bargain for both sides: Thanks to the collective productivity of the division of labor, firms can pay workers much more than the value of what they could possibly produce alone or in their household, and still make a profit for their owners. But this means that our daily lives at work are subject to authoritarian bureaucracies. Capitalism promises freedom of contract and exchange on the market but also imposes hierarchy and discipline in the workplace.
- *Market irrationalities:* For all of their efficiency in organizing the production of private goods, markets have serious flaws and limitations. Though there are few socialists nowadays

who want central planning of toothbrushes and haircuts, climate change has made market irrationalities more obvious and urgent than ever before. Market decisions that satisfy the individuals making them can aggregate into terrible outcomes no one would choose. Modern economics recognizes that market failures large and small are common, and anti-competitive practices and macroeconomic problems are obvious to all. Regulation and public sector activity have developed within capitalism to deal with some of these, but concentrations of wealth and industrial power are often an obstacle to rational collective action.

The socialist project must develop institutions that address all three of these problems, building an economic system that is egalitarian, gives people meaningful control over their lives, and has reliable channels for collective action. We aim to do this without sacrificing either personal autonomy or the well-coordinated division of labor on which modern living standards depend. Socialism, after all, is not simply the negation of capitalism, but its transcendence.

The antisocialist response is that it is impossible to mess with the signals and incentives of capitalism without killing the goose that lays the golden eggs. Socialism cannot deliver the productivity on which modern living standards are based without the capitalist economic system that has delivered it. Trying would interfere with our freedoms and launch us down the road to serfdom. You don't have to be a Pollyanna about capitalism to reluctantly say it is the best system available: Many disillusioned defenders of capitalism accept at least some of the problems socialists have pointed out, but they see them as a price worth paying.

The debate has usually pitted "markets" (capitalism) against "central planning" (socialism). The socialist calculation debate of the twentieth century followed this pattern. We discuss that debate in the next chapter. It raises questions that must be answered by anyone with a vision for socialism. But we do not accept the framing that pits socialism against markets. Our proposal has a role for markets and commodity production, just as modern capitalism has a large role for regulation and the public sector.

We argue on two fronts in the next few chapters. We defend the feasibility of a genuinely socialist economy against the antisocialist critics. We also hope to convince skeptical socialists that markets, money, and commodities should play a role in a socialist economy. Nowadays, this is not a niche position: Many of the most prominent socialist visions in recent decades have been forms of "market socialism." But reservations about markets are still widespread for important and valid reasons. Our system involves markets because we are unconvinced that there are better ways of organizing a complex division of labor that is responsive to people's needs and wants. Market coordination has its flaws, but the alternatives either introduce greater problems or remain too vague to show that they are up to the task.

Hopefully, it goes without saying that we are far from market fundamentalists. As you'll see, our model has a large public and community sector of noncommodity production. Its market sector exists in a context of workplace democracy and an entirely public financial system, with plenty of scope for democratic planning. There is no private ownership of the means of production. This is a vision of, as Diane Elson put it, "socialized markets."[1]

What Is the "Economic Problem"?

To make the case for a socialist model—including the role of markets within it—we need to be clear about what we want from an economic system. As we discuss in the next chapter, the central point of contention in the socialist calculation debate was the argument that "a socialist economy cannot solve the problem of rational allocation of its resources." But what does it mean to "solve" the economic problem? What does it mean to allocate resources *rationally*?[2]

Oskar Lange, writing in the 1930s, tried to answer exactly these questions—choosing to fight on the ground of mainstream welfare economics. Lange was not only a socialist but also a leading neoclassical economist, soon to join the faculty at the University of Chicago. Though Lionel Robbins, the influential British economist, was on the other side of the debate, Lange basically adopted his conception of what economics is all about: "Human behaviour as a relationship between ends and scarce means which have alternative uses." We have limited resources, which can be used in different ways, so we have to make decisions about which ends they should be used for. Time complicates the problem, because the decisions are not just about the present. Today's scarce means can be directed toward today's ends or toward expanding tomorrow's means.[3]

Solving the economic problem involves settling on some way of choosing how to use resources from among all the possible options. Making these decisions requires information, and so part of the problem is finding ways to bring that information to the places where the decisions are made. In Lange's view, rational allocation of resources requires:

1. knowing what resources are available;
2. understanding the alternative ways in which each of the resources can be combined and used—and from this, the terms of the trade-offs that must be made in choosing between them; and
3. developing a preference scale for choosing between those alternatives.

Seen like this, it might seem that a socialist solution involves only a different approach to the third category, with more weight put on egalitarian outcomes and public goods. But it's not that simple. In any complex economic system, decisions will be distributed. A centrally planned economy would especially face problems of coordinating dispersed decisions and activity and collecting dispersed preferences and information. And, since a desirable socialism respects human autonomy, the most important productive resource—our labor—is not, in fact, subject to central command. People must have good reasons to cooperate and play an effective role in the division of labor.

The meta-economic problem involves questions about how decisions are made and coordinated with each other. Who chooses, and how? How do they get the information they need to make decisions? How are people given incentives and coordinated to play a part that not only makes sense to them but is also socially rational?

Capitalist Solutions: Individual Ends, Individual Means

In a capitalist economy, the metaproblem is answered mainly with property rights and contract law. The owner of a resource gets to decide what to do with it, subject to some regulatory constraints. They can use it, exchange it, or hire it out to others. Contract law expands the realm of exchange beyond things to promises, including promises of services. Employment contracts are of a special kind—more open-ended than tightly defined services, they promise disposal of a person's activity for specified periods of time. This framework enables people to hire labor and combine it with an array of other resources—owned or rented—toward a productive end.

We each, then, have our own individual economic problem (though we usually solve it together with others in our household). Our personal scarce resources are our property and our time. Our ends are determined by our own preferences. The terms of the trade-offs we must make are prices: both prices of things we might want to buy and of the resources we have to sell, including our labor power.

With law having secured property and the freedom to dispose of our own time, people have two ways of getting from what they have to what they want: exchange and production. An exchange is voluntary on both sides, and so both parties must feel at least as well off as they would otherwise, and at least one must feel better off if there is any point to the transaction. Agents will also only choose to engage in production if the outputs leave them better off than alternative uses of the inputs. Where there are *markets*, would-be buyers and sellers can seek out the best offers or bids available. Sellers compete with other sellers, buyers with other buyers, and producers with other producers, thus forming market prices.

Both property and contract law allow for corporate entities to own things and enter into contracts. On this basis, production for the market is largely organized by the *firm*: property that owns property, a complex of contracts that enters into contracts. The corporate structure allows for a mobilization of resources well beyond the personal property of any individual. Firms purchase and hire inputs on labor and product markets, coordinate their use in production, and sell the outputs in other product markets.

Firms are internally hierarchical and organize themselves by command—seemingly a suspension of the freedom of the marketplace. But, the argument goes, all are participating voluntarily. If people sign on to work for an enterprise, the wage must be worth at least as much to them as any other use of their time. Firms bring workers together with one another and with other inputs and plan their cooperation in a way that produces more than enough value to compensate them at least as well as any alternatives. Anyone is legally free to start a firm. Find a niche with a profitable gap between the value of inputs and the value of outputs in some production process, and have at it. You don't even need to own resources: You can borrow or raise capital and even hire managers from the get-go. Existing companies are also free to reorient their activities in response to changing market opportunities.

Firms, in this vision, are simply the way in which individuals come together contractually to manage production; they call for labor and other resources beyond the means of a single household.

Some may supply their time and energy, while others supply funds, but all involved are simply making the best use of what they have. In pursuing profits for their owners, firms provide the things consumers want using the cheapest inputs, thus connecting their output and input markets in networks of supply and demand.

Property and contracts and markets and firms therefore resolve the metaproblem about who makes decisions and what the aims are. If all resources are owned privately, there is no "we" to make decisions for. Each person solves the economic problem for themselves—allocating their own scarce resources to their own preferred ends, whether using resources directly for enjoyment or production or exchanging them for other things they want more. This is the basic argument for capitalism: Leaving owners free to exchange and produce as they see fit gives everyone else the chance to find trades, make contracts, and produce together; everyone is better off than they started. "Better" and "worse" off are left to each individual's estimation. From this perspective it seems there is no collective economic problem to solve and no need for planners with the responsibility of solving it.

Of course, this formulation excludes the distribution of resources from the economic problem. At the time of Lange's intervention, the "new welfare economics" did that explicitly, in the name of rigor. The "old" welfare economics of English economist Arthur Cecil Pigou was utilitarian and so could pass judgment on distribution. Downward redistribution would plausibly increase the utility of the poor more than it would take from the rich. Against this, Robbins and others drew on reasonable doubt about the "metaphysical" concept of aggregable utility and argued that if utility could not in fact be quantified, this made comparisons of the relative welfare of different people meaningless, or at least not something that a scientific economics could pass judgment on.

Whether one person was enjoying themselves more than another was not something that could ever be measured—the millionaire might seem better off than the pauper, but who can say what goes on in the minds and hearts of others? The millionaire might be a sensitive soul who would wither without fine wine; the poor man hardy enough to find joy in simply having a tin roof over his head and the companionship of family and friends.

If "interpersonal utility comparisons" were ruled out as unscientific, it was harder to criticize an economic system for inequality, leaving the focus on inefficiency. An economic system could be judged in terms of the concept of Pareto efficiency (after Vilfredo Pareto, who argued along these lines in the 1890s). A Pareto improvement is an adjustment that makes at least one person better off without making anyone else worse off. This required no interpersonal comparison: Every single individual would know whether they preferred one state over another or did not care one way or the other. The optimum of Pareto efficiency is a state in which no further potential Pareto improvements remain: No one can be made better off without making someone else worse off.

This seems like a standard designed to pass a favorable assessment of laissez faire capitalism: If everyone can do what they like with their property, exchanging and producing to get the best outcome as they themselves perceive it, how could the outcome not be a Pareto optimum? But, in fact, this conclusion cannot be taken for granted at all. In the absence of organized markets, for example, people might only be able to exchange on those occasions when they happen to bump into someone who both has what they want and wants what they have, leaving many possible trade gains undiscovered. Even the existence of markets is not enough. There are countless ways of productively combining inputs to generate outputs. To ensure that resources are optimally combined requires that the prices people face for final consumption outputs really reflect the trade-offs between alternative uses of resources in production. But where producers have monopoly power, the prices they ask for something will generally not equal the marginal cost of producing the thing, breaking the link and leaving potential mutual gains untapped.[4]

At the time Lange wrote his essay on socialist calculation, it was acknowledged that the Pareto optimality of market allocation depended on perfect competition—a situation in which nobody had individual pricing power and could only adjust their behavior to prevailing market prices. Public goods and externalities also pose a problem. Production and transactions can impose costs on or provide benefits to people who play no part in the transactions, and so their preferences would not have any impact on the market, leaving public goods underproduced and bads (like pollution) overproduced. In the second half of the twentieth century, economists paid more and more attention to such things, and further expanded the list of conditions that must hold for markets to generate "first best" outcomes, including the structure and completeness of markets, the nature of goods and services and the processes for producing them, transaction costs, the information held by market participants and the cost of obtaining it, the rationality of participant behavior in pursuing preferences, and so on.

Nobody would argue that real-world markets meet these stringent conditions. Of course, people and governments have not been waiting around for economists to provide analytical justifications for public provision and regulation: The economic analysis lagged behind the great expansion of states during the twentieth century. It was long recognized that markets depended on nonmarket institutional underpinnings, even if these only took the form of the minimal "night-watchman" roles of defending property, enforcing contracts, and providing security. Noncommodity production has long been an important part of capitalist societies, and even more so since the great expansion of the public sector after the Second World War.

A substantial amount of paid work is in the public sector—the OECD average is around a fifth of the workforce—in which most products are not sold and production is ultimately directed by governments rather than by profit-maximizing firms.

Government agencies intervene in and regulate private market exchange and production. More noncommodity production also takes place within the household. Americans of working age spend on average more than three and a half hours per day in unpaid work, with the distribution of this work highly gendered.[5]

But commodity production and monetary exchange remain at the core of capitalist economic organization. Household and public sectors are tightly entangled with the commodity sector. Both use its commodities as inputs, and public agencies hire labor just as firms do. Both households and governments must secure funds with which to purchase the inputs. People pay for their groceries, energy, and rent with earnings from paid employment; some also receive income from asset ownership or as transfers from the government. Public production—including general administration—is funded through taxation and by financial means. Households and public agencies alike must manage monetary budgets. Wages, prices, and financial conditions therefore set the key parameters for noncommodity production decisions as much as they do for commodity production. People routinely make decisions about whether to cook a meal at home or eat out, how much child- and elder care to do within the home, how much to pay for and how much to draw on available state services. The extent of public provision, subsidies, and transfers strongly influences these decisions. Public production often overlaps with private in the same field, supplementing or providing an alternative—in education, health, and elsewhere. The system of prices frames and guides economic decisions in general, not only in commodity production. Of course, changes in the public sector and households also shape the market environment, in turn.

This all makes the capitalist economic problem more complicated than one about the purely private, individual exercise of property rights and freedom of contract. In fact, there is no single economic problem but many separate issues appearing as distinct political problems, from health care and education to poverty and unemployment. The ways these are framed and dealt with—whether they are even seen as political problems for governments to resolve—vary enormously across time and place. But the *relatively* self-organizing private sector of commodity production and market exchange tends to be treated as the central sphere, into which the state then "intervenes." Market incomes from property and contractual labor are taken for granted as earned, with taxation and redistribution needing to justify their legitimacy.

Socialist Solutions to a Tougher Problem

What, then, does the economic problem look like for socialists? We said above that our critique of capitalism focuses on inequality, unfreedom at work, and market irrationalities. All these problems are recognized in capitalist politics to some extent, but what sets a socialist project apart is an intention to deal with these issues systematically. Liberal politics may see all three of these areas as problems, but if equality, dignity and empowerment at work, and sustainability are taken as seriously as efficiency, then really existing capitalism must be judged a failure. These failures are not incidental but deeply rooted in the economic system, which is why they have proven perennial. The power of concentrated private property stands in the way of thorough and rational remedies.

However, our socialism does not deny the liberal values of personal freedom and democracy. In fact, it is grounded in a view that capitalism prevents the full flowering of those values. We also value the complex, intricately coordinated division of labor on which modern living standards are based. This is to say that personal freedom and efficiency are socialist values along with equality and economic democracy. If socialism were merely the negation of capitalism or the *replacement* of liberal values, its problems would be easier in some respects because its goals would be more limited. But in fact we have a much more difficult goal: maintaining productive efficiency and personal freedom, while *also* taking egalitarianism, democracy, and sustainability seriously.

This is, in fact, what the calculation debate was all about: whether the specifically socialist aims are compatible with those aims we share with capitalism or whether their pursuit must tragically undermine the foundations of modern life and liberty.

Both "efficiency" and "personal freedom" call for some explanation as socialist aims. Leftists are sometimes skeptical of efficiency or productivity, and for some good reasons. Efficiency is often rhetorically pitted against equality. Productivity sometimes has connotations of churning out consumer stuff, without regard for natural resource constraints or environmental damage, and of subordinating ourselves to the technical requirements of production at the expense of the more enriching aspects of life.[6]

But efficiency and productivity are really about the relationships between costs and benefits. Resource depletion, environmental damage, and alienation at work are all real costs, which ought to be counted on the negative side of the balance sheet. The fact that markets often fail to register these important costs is a major flaw and one reason why markets can only be part of the solution. Conversely, leisure time free of the demands of instrumental work is a great benefit—and one of the reasons to consider labor productivity among our priorities. Efficiency and productivity do not mean maximizing output but minimizing waste in using our resources—including our precious time—to meet our aims, whatever those may be. Efficiency is not only compatible with spare time and sustainability; it is their foundation.

What about personal freedom? The social environment in which the individual uses their freedom is always made up of other people, also entitled to their freedom. Only Robinson Crusoe, when alone on the island, is free of social entanglements, but exiled from the modern division of labor, he is much less free insofar as he lacks access to society's abundance. We are bound to cooperate, and that means people can't just do whatever they want. Freedom must mean something different from that.

Capitalism seems to place overriding importance on freedom because property rights are taken for granted, and these provide a way of resolving who prevails in many situations of conflicting aims. Individuals can at least be free to do what they like with their property, which is to say that others have no freedom with respect to that property. Individuals also have freedom to do what they like with their own person, which entails the freedom to contract, to exchange promises of behavior.

One obvious problem with this standard is the very uneven distribution of property. There are two poles of possible democratic socialist response here. One is to do away with property itself—and with it, exchange and markets. Distribution and the organization of production are about the allocation of collective resources and so should be managed democratically. The other solution is to distribute property in an egalitarian way, find a way to maintain that distribution, and otherwise let people work out the details privately through market exchange and production.

Of course, few if any solutions are all the way to one pole or another. Socialists have generally seen value in *personal* property, but not *private* property in the means of production. A democratic socialism balks at directed labor, at the state assigning people to jobs, however democratically. Oskar Lange presumed both "freedom of choice in occupation" and "freedom of choice in consumption," and so do we.[7]

In fact, those goals we share with liberalism—efficiency and personal freedom—are connected. If economic efficiency is defined in terms of subjective benefits and costs to people, then individual choice plays an important role in signaling people's own perception of those benefits and costs. This choice goes well beyond trivial choices between different brands of consumer goods: It can involve major differences in ways of living, each drawing on roughly equivalent shares of social resources. One person might prefer a lot of travel and flexible, small accommodation in urban centers. Another might prefer a more settled life in a larger house in a suburb. One might choose to work longer hours, producing more for others and accordingly enjoying more of the fruits of others' labor. Someone else might opt for a shorter working week, drawing less from the division of labor. The same person might enjoy each choice at different stages of life.

There is great benefit in an economic system that is flexible enough to provide for such differences. This is what is valuable in the standard definition of Pareto efficiency, whereby one situation is more efficient than another if it makes some better off without making others worse off. In a system where people have reasonably even entitlements to the fruits of our productive resources and cooperation, Pareto's logic comes into its own. Not only is it good in itself; a reasonable degree of such efficiency is necessary for a socialist economic system to keep the support of the population. Without it, either desired things will be more costly in terms of our precious time or not available at all, and many will conclude that living conditions would be better under capitalism.

Lange's argument was that a price system was necessary in guiding production rationally for socialist aims but that markets cannot be relied on to generate rational prices. He was an "algorithmic planner"—a "price socialist" rather than a market socialist. Though markets for labor and consumer products were part of his system, prices were set by a system of administrative rules rather than emerging out of market competition.

The counterargument from Hayek was that market competition is in fact necessary to form the information and incentives that generate reasonably rational prices, and to motivate rational behavior based upon them. This argument has been essentially accepted by market socialists from Nove to Roemer, who nevertheless argue that a reasonably egalitarian economic system can be built around markets. Other socialists have opposed market socialism on the grounds that markets will inevitably regenerate inequalities and entrench alienation at work.

This is a genuine worry, but in our view the best response is to build safeguards into the system, rather than to throw out markets and prices entirely. Our own model is an attempt to navigate between these socialist camps, which are both right to some extent. We follow Lange in recognizing that market prices are not necessarily rational prices. We are not for or against markets in a general way, but take a pragmatic approach to managing them. Market pricing and coordination is a tool to be used, not an ideal in itself.

Overview of the Model

We spend the next few chapters fleshing out and explaining why our proposed system takes the shape it does. In chapter four, we make the case for a commodity-producing market sector as part of the socialist mix. In chapter five, we explain why workplaces should be democratic and what that means, and address the serious criticisms that have been leveled at workplace democracy. Because democratic firms raise distinctive challenges—around finance, labor mobility, and risk—we also outline how a supportive public banking system can help address them. In chapter six, we turn to the socialist public sector—the substantial sphere of noncommodity production—and the ways public agencies will regulate and intervene in commodity production. Chapter seven covers income distribution: how the system guarantees basic needs for all, regardless of whether people are in paid work (since many of us spend long stretches in education, caregiving, or retirement). It discusses how the system counteracts market tendencies toward inequality while retaining incentives to draw people to where their labor is most useful to others. We also cover housing. Finally, chapter eight discusses public management of the economy as a whole: macroeconomic policy, planning through and outside the banking system, and international trade.

Each of these chapters makes the case for specific parts of the model. But before we dive in, it's useful to sketch a basic map of how these parts fit together in the system as a whole.

- There is a market sector in which democratic firms produce commodities for sale and a noncommodity sector operating with budgets allocated by the state. Commodity production is mainly suited to unambiguously private goods, while the noncommodity sector produces public goods. But some things are not well suited to commodity production for other reasons. (We explain why markets are necessary in chapter four and discuss what the noncommodity sector does in chapter six.)
- Workplaces are democratic in that worker-members have equal voting rights. In the market sector, worker-members typically elect the top management of their firms or the directors who appoint and set goals for managers. In small firms without specialized managers, decision-making may be more directly democratic. In the noncommodity "public" sector, workers are organized in unions with collective bargaining rights and a degree of workplace codetermination to help shape the ways in which social objectives are reached. (We make the case for workplace democracy and discuss democratic firms in chapter five and discuss democracy in the noncommodity sector in chapter six.)
- In the market sector, firms are autonomous and must at least cover their costs with revenues. Worker-members receive a regular wage at a predetermined rate and are also entitled to a share in any profit the firm makes after covering costs and financial obligations to partner banks. The profit share is paid out periodically in dividends. (See chapter five.)
- Firms and their worker-members are custodians and users, not private owners, of the means of production. Investment in productive assets involves a partnership between democratic firms and public banks. Profit for worker-members is what is left over after making financial payments to the banks. Firms do not retain or reinvest profits. The financial arrangements are designed to share risk and returns appropriately between firms and public. (Also in chapter five.)

- The public purse receives some of its capital income from commodity production, through firms' financial payments to the public banks. Beyond what is reinvested to maintain and expand the capital stock, state funds will be available for the noncommodity sector and for income transfers. However, the purse will need to be supplemented with taxation of labor incomes. (Chapter eight discusses the banking system, social wealth, and public and private income flows.)
- The tax-and-transfer system will be used to (1) provide income to meet the private consumption needs of those not formally employed and to supplement labor income where needed; (2) smooth the distribution of labor income with progressive taxation; and (3) fund (or provide macroeconomic space for) the noncommodity sector. (Income redistribution is discussed in chapter seven, and the macroeconomic relationship between commodity and noncommodity sectors in chapter eight.)
- A national labor board sets and periodically reviews central benchmarks for wages and conditions in each job category. Individual workplaces are free to exceed these benchmarks but cannot undercut them. There are several purposes for central benchmarks, and so they are discussed at several places in the coming chapters. Benchmarks ensure that competition is channeled along the "high road" of productivity and product improvements and not the "low road" of wage-cutting and work intensification (chapter five); they reduce labor income inequality (chapter seven); and they aid in macroeconomic management (chapter eight). Because there are multiple goals, tensions need to be managed.
- Housing makes up a large part of society's capital stock. People will have secure tenure in their homes and the ability to direct renovations but pay rent to a public housing authority. Rents are set by the public authority and adjusted to match demand in order to supply housing in particular locations and of specific types. The authority organizes construction to develop supply in response to projected demand. Residents

are entitled to periodic maintenance and renovation work and can initiate additional renovation beyond the regular allocation by meeting costs in a financial arrangement with the authority. (See chapter seven.)

- The banking system is made up of a central bank and a number of public banks. Only the central bank provides deposit facilities used by households, firms, public agencies, and banks. The public banks therefore have quite different balance sheets than capitalist banks do—instead of "borrowing short and lending long," they borrow funds for investment from the central bank, rather than directly from depositors. This gives the central bank considerable control over the overall pace of investment, whether through the cost of credit or direct quantitative controls. When this is coordinated with public transfers and spending in the noncommodity sector, experts, under direction from elected government, enjoy considerable control over macroeconomic income–expenditure flows. (See chapter eight.)
- The banking system is also a vehicle for planning across the economy. Most banks will be tasked with pursuing high returns consistent with a given level of risk. There are, however, ways to provide finance for investments in the commodity sector that do not meet that commercial bar but are desirable for other reasons—for example, to support employment in a depressed region or to get a new industry off the ground. This can be done by specialized investment banks or with subsidies to regular banks for particular investments. Public banks also assist in the organization of new democratic firms. Their information and expertise put them in a good position to play an entrepreneurial role in identifying niches, bringing in worker-members, and assisting them in getting a new enterprise off the ground. This role helps to keep labor mobile, making dynamism compatible with worker security. (Chapter five discusses the relationship between banks and firms, and chapter eight discusses planning through the banking system.)
- International trade and participation in the global division of labor are important for maintaining living standards. They

raise macroeconomic and planning challenges, but the latter are manageable with the coordinated use of the labor board, the banking system, and fiscal policy. While trade is generally free, private capital flows are not—and since there is no private capital in the system there is no place for international private capital. Cross-border investment takes place only through public banks and state-to-state arrangements, rather than through private financial markets. Exchange rates should generally be flexible to help absorb international shocks. (We go into more detail on this point in chapter eight.)

We started this chapter with a sketch of life under socialism: It's not utopia; but it is mornings without debt collectors or bosses texting away your shift. What follows is the scaffolding that makes that world possible: markets that help us coordinate, democracy where we work, banks owned by the public, and a state strong enough to guarantee stability while expanding freedom in our daily lives.

None of this abolishes conflict or hard choices. But it means those conflicts unfold on fair ground, with everyone guaranteed dignity and security. That's the promise of socialism: a society decent enough to make everyday life more hopeful.

Next, we make our vision more concrete by asking how things get made and distributed in practice. That means starting with markets and what they do.

4

What Do Markets Do?

You stop by your favorite coffee shop on the way to work. The barista behind the counter is a worker-member, just like you are at your firm. You chat for a minute about how the place has been packed lately and how they're training a few new people for the morning rush. You tap your People's Bank of New Jersey debit card, pick up your latte, and step back into the flow of the city.

When you buy a cup of coffee, you're reaching into a chain that links farmers in Colombia, container ship crews from Copenhagen, roasters in Massachusetts, the labor of baristas, and countless other people. No one person designed this system of market interactions. But it holds together and manages to deliver you a latte.

As we saw in the last chapter, the prosperity of modern life rests on a sprawling division of labor. The challenge for any society—capitalist or socialist—is how to coordinate that complexity and answer some hard questions. How do we know what people want to consume? How do we choose between countless ways of producing goods? How do we motivate people to contribute and to be honest about the information they hold?

Markets offer real solutions. They transmit information through prices and motivate people through incentives. At the same time, they generate inequality, fail to account for social and environmental costs, and subject people's lives to impersonal pressures they can neither anticipate nor control. Markets, in other words, are Janus-faced institutions. They give us the morning coffee that links strangers across continents, but they also reproduce inequalities and neglect needs that don't register through purchasing power. They solve coordination problems with astonishing elegance but also, when left to their own devices, generate outcomes that clash with democratic values. A viable socialism must figure out how to both harness the strengths of markets and limit their pathologies.

Karl Marx's section on "commodity fetishism" in the opening chapter of *Capital* is a classic reference point for socialist skepticism about markets. For Marx, the price system obscures the fact that production is really a form of social cooperation. Products and their prices can feel as if they're generated in a self-contained system, and we can all too easily forget that this system rests on an elaborate series of social decisions about how to organize our collective lives—I do this much labor making coffee for you; you do this much fixing my car. The market makes social cooperation appear as relations between things: goods exchanged for money—a cup of coffee for a few dollars, a day's labor for a wage. The people whose labor connects it all recede behind the play of commodities and their prices.[1]

As Marx put it, the price structure "conceals the social character of private labour and the social relations between the individual workers, by making those relations appear as relations between material objects, instead of revealing them plainly." To many readers this insight has been revelatory, and it explains why any socialism that accommodates commodity production and markets is often seen as a betrayal of Marx's vision.[2]

The reply from political economists is that the price structure in fact helps to choreograph individuals' pursuit of self-interest into outcomes better than a conscious plan could manage. How? The shape of the answer has been the same since Adam Smith: Free enterprise is tempered by competition.

Where resources and products can be bought and sold and funds can be borrowed and lent, in theory anyone who comes up with a profitable way to turn inputs into higher-value outputs can do so. Yet whenever someone finds such a method, competitors can quickly imitate or undercut it. When producers battle with one another for resources, customers, and funds, the price structure that emerges from the interplay of their strategies ensures that resources are allocated efficiently to satisfy people's wants and needs.

Abnormal returns in one production line or another are a sign that resources are not being used in their most valued ways. There is an incentive to respond by shifting resources away from less profitable and toward more profitable uses. In doing so, entrepreneurs erode the excess profits and restore the general beneficence of the price structure. Persistently high rates of return in an activity or in the ownership of some resource signal a block on competition, and removing such obstacles are the progressive project of the enlightened liberal. If the market system works properly, nobody needs to understand how the division of labor holds together. They need only take account of the prices that matter to them.

Marx himself was steeped in these arguments and was well aware that the market price structure was not simply a veil that could be stripped away to leave the underlying social relations transparent and intact. Prices are not measurements of something that is already there waiting to be measured.

People set prices strategically, within contexts involving factors such as costs, demand, and the competitive landscape. The price structure forms part of the context for producers' decisions, and their decisions in turn form and reform that price structure. Marx's complaint about commodity fetishism is not that the price system is epiphenomenal or false in some way. It is that the price system can make the division of labor look like a self-running mechanism—an impersonal play of prices—rather than a pattern of human cooperation that we reproduce through institutions, rules, and power. And it is also all too easy to take for granted wages and profits and interest and rent as naturally occurring features of the economy, missing the ways in which class positions depend on the arbitrary, deeply unequal distribution of property. This is not only a matter of unequal income but of unequal freedom, unequal control over work, and unequal power over the course of one's life.

Marx contrasts all this with a picture of

> an association of free men, working with the means of production held in common, and expending their many different forms of labour-power in full self-awareness as one single social labour force . . . The social relations of the individual producers, both towards their labor and the products of their labor, are here transparent in their simplicity, in production as well as in distribution.[3]

But he does not explain *how* labor power would be applied "in full self-awareness," here or elsewhere such as in the *Critique of the Gotha Program*. The answer is far from obvious. Who decides how to allocate productive resources, how much to produce of each thing, and how to organize production? What motivates people to play their part in the division of labor, to provide and transmit accurate information, to make choices that cohere into that "conscious organization"?

In other words, plausible answers must solve both information and incentive problems. Decisions about how to apply labor and other resources require technical information about the possible alternatives and information from people about which alternatives they prefer. Reconciling personal freedom with the technical needs of an efficient division of labor requires incentives, ideally presenting choices to people in ways that accurately reflect trade-offs. The information problem has its own incentive problems. Knowledge about what is technically possible in an intricate division of labor is widely distributed, and individual consumption preferences obviously so. This knowledge does not collect and transmit itself, and people may even choose to deliberately falsify it, unless given good reasons to accurately share it.

Some of these problems might be lessened if we could drop the objectives of personal choice or efficiency or both. Planners would find allocation problems easier if they could simply direct labor and decide on standardized consumption baskets for all. But this, of course, is at least as much of a departure from the Marxist conception of socialism as markets would be. Nonmarket organization might also be easier if the productive forces were so fruitful that we did not have to worry so much about the tight coordination of the division of labor. But modern abundance depends upon that very coordination, and inefficiency is a waste of the time we could otherwise spend in leisure, free of instrumental labor.

These were the issues at the heart of the socialist calculation debate, and the issues we explore in this chapter. Rather than present another blow-by-blow narrative of that historical debate, we go through the problems of nonmarket allocation systematically. First, we focus on the problem of drawing consumption preferences from individuals. This is a good place to start, because there is broad consensus among socialists that production decisions should be responsive to individual consumption preferences (though not exclusively, of course, given the importance of public goods and bads). There is narrower, but still wide, consensus that such preferences are best collected through people making consumption decisions much as they do under capitalism, allocating a budget among priced goods and services. By exploring the reasons for this consensus in the next section, "Consumer Choice," we establish the usefulness of a consumer-facing price structure.

There is less consensus around a market for producer goods and competition among firms. In the section "Production," we review Ludwig von Mises's claim that, without markets, central planning would be unable to allocate resources between producers effectively, as well as Oskar Lange's famous response. Lange argued on two fronts: first, to convince fellow socialists that Mises had posed an important problem that should be taken seriously, and second, to refute Mises's argument. Lange's proposal was that planning could replace markets by following a set of rules designed to mimic the idealized workings of markets set out in neoclassical general equilibrium models of perfectly competitive markets. They could even outperform actual markets, which are far from perfectly competitive.

Lange's model is one example of a broader type of "algorithmic planning," which takes information and coordination problems seriously and tries to solve them by specifying a set of rules planners and local production managers can follow. His argument was not that planners at the center would allocate everything by solving an enormous linear algebra problem. Lange's proposed system was itself decentralized, did not require extravagant computing power, and relied on feedback between production managers following rules but using local information and judgment, a planning board setting prices to balance supply and demand, and consumer markets.

Though Lange-type models respond effectively to some anti-socialist objections about the informational problems of planning, other problems remain, as we discuss in the final section of this chapter. Algorithmic planning particularly struggles to resolve incentive problems. At the same time, to the extent that it coordinates the division of labor by following rules, it is subject to some of the standard criticisms leveled at market coordination. Are its rules not "blind," coordinating cooperation through "impersonal economic laws"? If the response is that the algorithms provide leverage points for conscious planning choices, the same is true of markets. If the algorithm is meant to mimic markets yet still faces these incentive problems, why not simply use actual markets?

Our view, elaborated below, is that markets and democratic planning are compatible. In fact, Marx's goal of a community of people "working with the means of production held in common, and expending their many different forms of labor-power in full self-awareness" would find markets extremely useful in bringing that association to life. Rather than standing over people as an alien and unknowable force, markets would be knowable and provide many points of leverage for conscious intervention. Properly set up in combination with the other elements of our model—democratic workplaces, a public banking system, and an expansive noncommodity sector—the grid of prices and incentives generated by the market sector would facilitate planning, not act as an obstacle to it.[4]

Of course, one immediate objection is that "incentives" are simply a euphemism for discipline. The worry is that even if markets work, they work through pressures that seem at odds with socialist ideals. But any system involving a division of labor requires some way to get people to play their respective part; this is just as true of a nonmarket system. We take seriously the objections that markets and competition come with alienation, insecurity, externalities, and inequality. In subsequent chapters, we explain how our model responds to these very real problems.

Consumer Choice

An important part of the economic problem that any socialist system must solve is how to decide what to produce from among the countless things our limited time and resources could go toward. Most recent socialist proposals hold that individuals—by themselves and as part of households—should play a major role in choosing the goods and services produced for their private consumption. That stands in contrast to a system where people receive standardized consumption baskets determined by planners, democratic or otherwise.

Despite this consensus, it is worth making explicit the rationale for personal consumer choice, because it has implications both for how we organize that choice and for how production is coordinated. It is not hard to imagine a socialist argument along the following lines: Since production is a cooperative, social activity, outputs should be decided democratically rather than privately. The issue, then, is not whether those democratic claims have force but what follows in practice when private choice is curtailed.

In such a system, people would make individual consumer choices even if they were allocated standardized baskets without any individual say in the baskets' contents. We would trade among ourselves to get what we preferred. Mises suggests an example in which the state distributes to each person an arbitrary number of cigars and cigarettes and a market exchange rate forms between them as people swap for their preferred mix. Unless the state is draconian enough to stamp out voluntary trades altogether, prices and consumer choice will emerge anyway.[5]

These will not be socially rational prices, however, if there is no signal back from people's choices to production. The quantity of cigars and the quantity of cigarettes in circulation are predetermined by the planners' production decisions, democratic or otherwise, and exchange can only reallocate those quantities. Yet tobacco and other inputs can be reallocated between the production of cigars and the production of cigarettes.

There is some definite rate at which cigars can be swapped for cigarettes, not through exchange, but through different choices about how much of each to produce in the first place. More generally, if tastes shift away from tobacco products entirely, as they have since Mises chose the example a century ago, tobacco fields could be devoted to something else. But absent feedback from consumer choice reaching production decision-makers, the rates at which things can be exchanged may be far out of line with the marginal rate of transformation between the things—that is, the rate at which one thing can be produced in place of something else by transferring resources between them.

This is the fundamental reason to have consumption decisions directed by individuals, so that production can be rearranged to give people what they prefer without leaving anyone else with less. Since production is flexible enough to adapt to individual wants, there is no reason for decisions about consumer outputs to be made by a larger collective. It makes perfect socialist sense to let each person choose how to direct the share of collective resources devoted to their personal or household consumption. In addition to the more efficient allocation of resources, there is the benefit of participating in choosing—of deciding for ourselves without the approval, or even knowledge, of others. Much more than minor choices about toothpaste flavor or coffee blend is at stake here. This mechanism opens space for entirely different lifestyles.

There are, of course, also many products that are not well suited to selection by private consumption decisions, such as public goods whose benefits are widely distributed—basic scientific research, health infrastructure, or flood control. More broadly, there are many things whose production or use affects people beyond those who make the decision to consume them, from greenhouse gas emissions and air pollution to vaccination and antibiotic use. These must be managed through collective decisions, and we discuss the issues and the options in chapter six. These decisions include how much labor and other resources to devote to noncommodity public production, a decision that cannot be made through an aggregation of private consumption choices.[6]

Why Prices?

It is not really in dispute among socialists that a lot of production will be for private consumption and that production should be guided by people's own preferences. The point of making the case explicit is that the rationale for allowing consumer preferences to direct production has implications for the institutional arrangements required to coordinate supply and demand. And on that question, there is far more debate.

Most socialist proposals, even those that aim to generally replace markets, involve collecting consumer preferences by having people buy things in shops, much as they do in capitalism. This is the case in Lange's model; he even calls it a "market of consumers' goods." It is also true in Paul Cockshott and Allin

Cottrell's model, which sees prices adjusting to clear consumer product markets. But there are exceptions.[7]

According to the Belgian Marxist Ernest Mandel:

> The assumption that consumers can only determine their needs indirectly, by the allocation of their money incomes to different goods and services, is absurd. Why should individuals have to take the detour of the monetary form to ascertain what they require? . . . The simplest—as well as the most democratic—way of adapting material resources to social wants is not to interpose the medium of money between the two, but to find out people's needs just by asking them what they are.[8]

Having people allocate their personal budget to choose between priced products, however, *is* a way of asking people what their wants and needs are. That particular structure of choice—with a limited budget denominated in the units in which things are priced—happens to be well suited to the problem of allocating scarce but flexible resources to meet those needs and wants. If we are to make meaningful choices about what to consume, the trade-offs inherent in using resources for one thing rather than another must be presented to us in some way. But because of the interconnection between our needs for different products and because resources can be transferred between making different things, it would take an extremely complicated set of questions to "just ask" people. Planners could not simply ask people questions like, "How much coffee are you going to want next year?" Unless there are infinite mountains of coffee, there must be a limit. If there is nothing to encourage people to economize, some might reason that coffee grounds make good garden fertilizer and add an amount well beyond what they might drink to their request.

As soon as trade-offs are introduced into the questions consumers are asked, the questions begin to snowball. Which things would you consume less of to make room for more coffee? How much less for how much extra coffee? Different people would have completely different answers, and each person's answers would be bound up with other trade-offs. The desire for a single product is tied to the desire for others. Coffee is a substitute for some things, like tea and energy drinks. It is a complement for others, like croissants and oat milk. It is not possible to take products in isolation and ask about needs for each one by one. Meanwhile, on the production side, resources can be transferred between different things. Some resources are versatile and can be redeployed very widely: Labor, at the very least, is involved in all production. This means the trade-offs relevant to consumers are not only between related things but between everything and everything else.[9]

We can see how difficult this informational challenge is by looking at textbook models of consumer choice that do turn it into a solvable problem. Each person in these models is presumed to have a complete set of preferences and to be able to rank every possible combination of consumer products from most to least preferred. With direct access to such data, planners could in principle find out the trade-offs each person would be willing to make—not only between coffee and energy drinks but between, say, gasoline and jeans. But it is one thing to say that each person has a ranking in the sense that they could in practice make a choice when presented with some specific options. It is another thing entirely to think of such a ranking as something the person could make explicit and communicate to a planner ahead of time for any possible structure of trade-offs.

It is not even that this kind of private knowledge is hard to communicate. It is that we do not ourselves know in advance the answer to a question like, "How much coffee would you drink each week if its cost in terms of milk were twice what it is now." And without prices and budgets, the questions are much trickier than that, because we would have to be able to consider trade-offs not only with milk but with everything else. Even if we drastically cut the possibilities by relating them to combinations of consumer products within some limited range of typical past choices, we are still talking about a stupendous number of possibilities. And this is not the kind of problem that can be solved by throwing computer power at it, because it is about finding out the structure of our subjective preferences.

When the trade-offs are put to people in the form of prices and a budget to spend, choice becomes manageable. In the hypothetical case in which planners somehow did have access to each person's preference rankings, solving the allocation problem would still generate a set of "shadow prices" and each individual would have a "shadow budget" in terms of those prices. Since they would emerge anyway, what is the harm in bringing the prices and budgets into the light? And because planners cannot, in fact, have access to people's raw preferences, the case seems closed.

Why Shops?

Because of the issues above, there is a broad consensus among socialists that alternatives should be presented to people in the form of prices, or something very much like prices, with each person having a budget to allocate. There is almost as much consensus that this can be done through people spending money in shops much as they do under capitalism. One prominent exception is Robin Hahnel's "participatory planning" model—a serious attempt to flesh out how a democratic allocation of consumer products might work.[10]

Hahnel's system does give people personal budgets to work with and presents them with consumer product prices. But instead of people directly spending from their budgets in stores, there are layers of collective decision-making:

> In a participatory economy every household in a neighborhood is a member of the neighborhood consumer council, where every household (1) submits its personal, household consumption request for approval; (2) all members of households participate directly in discussions about what neighbourhood public goods to ask for; and (3) all members vote for recallable delegates to

higher level federations of consumer councils at the ward, city, county, regional, and national levels.[11]

The consumer councils aggregate and make consumption proposals, to which worker councils respond with production proposals specifying the outputs they propose to make and the inputs they need to make them. An Iteration Facilitation Board then looks at all the consumption and production proposals together and sums the total demands for and supplies of each product, resource, and kind of labor, and then moves each "indicative price" up or down according to the balance between demand and supply. The new price list is issued to the councils, and the process is "repeated in subsequent rounds, or 'iterations,' until there is no longer any excess demand for any final or intermediate good, capital stock, natural resource, or category of labour."[12]

Whatever we might say about the resource-allocation mechanisms of the Iteration Facilitation Board, this is an enormously cumbersome way for people to make consumption decisions. Households would need to work out their consumption plans for a year at a time, at least several months before the start of the year in question. They would also need to share those plans with their neighborhood committees.[13]

Any system of production that is responsive to consumer wants is going to face uncertainty about unexpected changes in needs and tastes, partly due to the development of new products. Most production uses long-lived equipment that cannot be quickly and costlessly repurposed and skills that cannot easily be transferred to make different things. Investment and production decisions, therefore, are speculative. In capitalism, this manifests in various kinds of slack: stocks held by retailers and wholesalers, extra room in appointment calendars, inventories held by producers, spare capacity in the use of equipment. It may seem that a system of preordering like what Hahnel envisions could mean great gains in efficiency over market allocation. But it would impose the costs of mistaken expectations on people as consumers.

Forget the tyranny of the state: what about the tyranny of your past self? Unless suppressed, markets would inevitably develop as people trade the kale they intended to eat for the whiskey they end up wanting to drink. Recognizing the issue, Hahnel says that "nobody is going to hold households to their consumption requests when it turns out they want to consume more of some things and less of others than they pre-ordered." The system simply records on people's accounts the over- and underconsumption of the various products and encourages them to adjust their requests accordingly the following year.[14]

Does this not mean kale piles up while whiskey runs out, with some who correctly anticipated their whiskey needs going without to meet the whims of others? These real-time shifts in demand would need to be met with some combination of a pricing system and rationing. In the first case, whiskey would be reallocated by offering those who give it up more claim on other things. Having been shooed out the door, consumer markets return through the window, as the terms of exchange would need to be calibrated to match demand with availability. In the second case, simply allowing some of a good to go to those who hadn't ordered it at the expense of those who had, on a first-come first-served basis, seems unfair. The system might mitigate these problems by maintaining surplus stocks of goods, and spare room in the appointment calendars of services. Inventory adjustment would absorb some of the shifts in demand, with price adjustment called for more rarely. The consumer councils would need to look at what people actually consumed and not only at what people believed or hoped they would want over the next year. They could take into account the needs that people do not anticipate a year in advance, which are more predictable in the aggregate, from the arrival of new children to car repairs.

But now we have reinvented the shop, posting prices and holding stocks to meet the ups and downs of demand in real time. There seems nothing to be gained through a cumbersome and intrusive back-and-forth with consumer councils about private wants. The slack in market distribution and retail may look like inefficiency, but flexibility in responding to unpredictable needs is an important, often overlooked positive feature of the division of labor. Alec Nove argues that overtaut plans were an important reason for the tendency toward shortages experienced by consumers in the Soviet Union.[15] Shortages are not only annoying in themselves; they come with other undesirable features of a "sellers' market," with producers buffered from having to pay attention to the quality expectations of customers who "can't be choosers." This is a problem we return to below.

Personal and Collective Consumption

Hahnel's system mixes private consumption needs with democratic decision-making about community needs at various scales. Households submit their personal consumption requests to their neighborhood consumer council, where they also participate in community decisions about collective consumption requests, and elect representatives to negotiate on their behalf in councils for several layers of wider geographical areas.

There is much to be said for wide participation in decision-making about public goods, but it is a mistake to have all private consumption decisions go into the same process. Not only is the loss of privacy and convenience a high price to pay, but majoritarian decision-making over personal consumption is misplaced. After all, individual differences in consumption preferences can be accommodated by a flexible division of labor without affecting what is available to anyone else.

There is a gray area of collective consumption between individual private goods and public goods. Even some collective consumption decisions are best handled privately—that is, by groups voluntarily pooling some of their personal purchasing power to purchase commodities together—rather than through democratic processes involving everyone in some geographic area. Relevant groups are often bigger than the household but smaller than the neighborhood and can cut across geographical administrative boundaries.

Some mundane examples are familiar from capitalism, such as the apartment building with a shared laundry, a gym, and swimming pool, or the sports club. Some socialists have envisioned an expansion of both shared consumption and cooperation in reproductive labor, from community gardens and childcare arrangements to experiments in communal living. Some have speculated that flexible fabrication technology could make some small-scale craft production more efficient again relative to factory-scale workplaces. If so, this has potentially profound implications for the boundaries between household, community, and commodity production.[16]

We do not prescribe any of these things as core elements of our model. By their nature, they depend on voluntary participation and grow organically to the extent that they appeal to people. But our system does facilitate such self-organizing cooperation. These possibilities can only be discussed once we have detailed other aspects of the system involving work, finance, and the noncommodified public sector.

But we make the point here that personal incomes and commodity production open one important channel for such cooperation. They enable people to pool some of their purchasing power to acquire and maintain shared durable infrastructure (premises and equipment) and to access shared services for any such collective project. Often, of course, such facilities are better provided by the public sector. But the option of self-organized "club good" purchasing is valuable, especially where the shared consumption in question is a special interest, such as a hobby. It also allows for motivated private groups to get experiments off the ground as "proof of concept," in the hopes of persuading fellow citizens of their value as public goods deserving of broader social resources.

This channel is missing in a system that channels everything through democratic decision-making at various scales. There is an important role for consumption decisions that are collective but still private, made by people associating voluntarily and sharing some of their personal purchasing power. This kind of cooperation should need no majoritarian permission from a consumer council beyond the group, because it comes from people's personal share of the fruits of social resources and the division of labor, which is theirs to direct.

Price and Quantity Signals

We are left with the conclusion that allocating private consumer products to people is best organized in a way already familiar to us: People have monetary incomes, from which they spend as they choose on goods and services at prices quoted to them. This is not a necessary evil, but a genuinely good way of collecting consumption preferences in order to allocate flexible resources to meet them.

Sets of prices present options to people and leave us to work out how best to allocate our budgets. In practice, most of us buy with some combination of habit, planning, and impulse. We don't always fully consider the trade-offs we make, but because the cycle of income and expenditure is repetitive, we have plenty of chances to adjust our choices. Whether our typical choices are more deliberate, habitual, or impulsive, they are still choices, and one way or another take into account the trade-offs established by prices and our budgets. In making these decisions, we receive price signals and send *quantity* signals with what we choose at the going prices, given our budgets. These quantity signals can then be used to guide production decisions.

This conclusion in favor of money, prices, and shops as a means of socialist allocation presupposes that

1. budgets are egalitarian, so that each person's purchasing decisions represent a claim on their share of those collective resources devoted to private consumption;
2. prices facing consumers accurately signal trade-offs in the use of labor and resources—for example, the costs of production, including environmental and social costs; and
3. the quantity signals people send in their purchasing choices feed appropriately back into production decisions.

All of these things are ideals, which no realistic system will meet perfectly, but they are a set of features that the system should prioritize. To begin dealing with these conditions, we must discuss how production is structured.[17]

Production

We now come to the point where there is more disagreement: The role of markets in organizing production. This was the central issue in the socialist calculation debate of the twentieth century, and it is worth reviewing the core arguments—not only between socialists and antisocialists, but also between market socialists and comprehensive planners. We begin with Mises's antisocialist challenge to planning. This challenge was the spur to Lange's landmark contribution on the socialist side. He countered Mises by proposing an algorithmic planning system: a set of rules for allocating resources efficiently, using information about available resources, the technical possibilities for combining them, and consumer preferences.

Lange's argument is ingenious and clearly defines the problem, but his solution raises serious objections. It depends on people being motivated to discover and accurately transmit the information the algorithm requires—and to follow its rules. Even in a centrally planned system, coordinating many dispersed decision-makers across the division of labor poses challenges. Hayek offered the most famous critique, but socialists, too, have since developed these concerns.

Mises's Challenge

Mises's challenge to central planning was that without prices there would be no way to rationally choose between the countless recipes through which resources could be transformed into consumption goods and services. People are able to make rational consumption decisions based on their own subjective preferences, but we are not equipped to work out what this implies for "higher-order goods," like the inputs used to make consumer products. Resources can be used in many different ways to make many different things, and it is a very complicated problem to work out how each should be deployed.

Imagine the options that would present to planners making decisions about cement, a staple intermediate good. Any cement making will require the use of some inputs that could otherwise be used for something else, but there are many different techniques using different combinations of inputs. There are choices about materials: whether to use hard limestone or chalk, clay or shale, and whether to obtain these from quarries or as the byproducts of other industrial processes. There are choices related to energy source: the type and size of the furnace; whether the factory can be more or less automated, which calls, in turn, for different types and quantities of labor.

Transportation is an important part of the cost of something as bulky as cement: should it be shipped, trucked, or piped and where should the production plants be located in relation to the quarries, the power sources, the sites where the concrete will be poured? Then there is the big question of how much should be produced. It is used as an input in the production of many things, from building materials to roads to pipes, but in each case there are substitutes—plastic for pipes, asphalt for roads—and all the substitutes have their own webs of techniques connecting them to possible inputs and outputs. To use bitumen in place of cement frees up the quarried material for other uses, or frees up the resources that would have gone into the quarrying, but uses more energy directly and draws on petroleum products that could have been used for something else. We must also take into account that bitumen requires more frequent repair and replacement.

For the planner, deciding how much cement to make and how to make it cannot be separated from deciding on the alternative uses of its inputs: their substitutes, the substitutes for cement itself, the substitutes for everything that uses cement as an input, the alternative uses of all the inputs to those processes, the inputs to those inputs, and the substitutes for their outputs and the outputs of their outputs. It seems impossible today—and it certainly seemed impossible to Mises in 1920.

But where there are markets for all these things, producers have a clear way to decide what to make and how: profit. Many technologically possible processes are ruled out because the outputs are worth less than the inputs. Among economically viable possibilities, firms choose those that generate the highest rate of return. Capitalism's legal framework of property rights and contract law allows anyone, in theory, to take advantage of gaps between the cost of inputs and revenue from outputs. Anyone can look at the price structure as it is and consider whether they could make more profit by combining inputs in different ways.

So markets make it possible for firms to use resources rationally for their own gain, but how does it follow that this leads to a *socially* rational use of resources? The answer is competition. Opportunities for outsize returns will not last long once others notice them and try to get a piece, so long as there are no barriers to entry. Competitors must bid against one another for inputs and compete for customers. The field will attract new entrants or induce existing players to expand until, one way or another, profits are eroded. At this point, resources have been bid away from lower-value uses and toward higher-value uses, ultimately directed by consumer preferences (effective in proportion to each consumer's budget).

The questions of how to produce cement, and how much to make, are then answered. The decisions are ultimately made by the managers of cement firms in pursuit of profit, but the parameters of those decisions are shaped by the decisions of many others through the markets for things connected to cement—as inputs, substitutes, and complements and as inputs of inputs, substitutes for substitutes, and so on. Producers are effectively bidding against one another for inputs—and not only against their direct competitors but against those in other industries who could potentially use the same things. The intuition is that resources are bid to the use in which they are most highly valued. Of course, most inputs are not absolutely scarce, but themselves capable, at least after some time, of being produced in greater quantities, so long as *their* producers can bid more of their own inputs away from other uses, or induce more production of those inputs. The ripples of cause and effect eventually reach resources that are not themselves produced commodities, like labor and natural resources.

It is difficult to trace or even imagine all the complex pathways of cause and effect between people's preferences at one end and the allocation of basic resources at the other, through the labyrinth of potential techniques for using the latter to satisfy the former. This is the Austrian point: It is because we cannot comprehend it—certainly not in enough detail to manage it—that we must rely on markets to coordinate.

Lange's Response

By the time Oskar Lange responded to Mises in the 1930s, this kind of argument had been formalized in a particular way, with the combination of general equilibrium theory and Paretian welfare economics. Lange himself was an important contributor to this literature. Given a number of stringent assumptions, it could be shown mathematically that a competitive general equilibrium would be a Pareto optimum, a situation in which no reallocation of resources or products could make anyone better off without making someone worse off.

A "competitive general equilibrium" is a market situation in which no individual has pricing power, so each must take going prices as given, and those going prices are such that supply matches demand in every market. Nobody has pricing power because competition checks any attempt to sell for higher, or buy for lower, than others are offering. There are plenty of others ready to buy or sell at that going price, so no one will accept your higher offer or lower bid price. Market decisions just involve choosing how much to buy and sell at going prices.

In other words, firms and households alike receive price

signals and send quantity signals. Though nobody in particular sets market prices—and no player is big enough for their quantity decisions alone to have a noticeable effect on price—prices move in response to aggregate imbalances between supply and demand, and equilibrium prices are those that clear the market: The amount of each thing agents want to sell at that price equals the amount other agents want to buy.

In equilibrium, the structure of prices reflects both subjective preferences and technological possibilities. On the one hand, the relative prices of any pair of goods must be in line with each person's subjective trade-off between the two. If anyone can do better by consuming less of one thing and spending an equivalent value on something else, they would do so, and we are not in equilibrium until they have. Meanwhile, if any producer could make more profit by switching techniques, using less of some inputs and more of others of equivalent value, they would do so. Likewise, if they could make more profit by producing more or less of anything, they would do that too. Equilibrium prices are those that balance supply and demand when every person and every firm has made these adjustments and optimized from their own point of view.

The claim was never that actual markets worked like this. The artificiality of the assumptions was clear from the beginning. For the socialist Lange, the point of the model was not to describe how markets really worked, but to give a rigorous answer to the question of how resources *should* be allocated, given people's preferences and the many ways resources could be combined to meet them. It provided a vision of interconnectedness across the web of production and consumption. It was a framework for thinking about how different consumer preferences or a new technology could have consequences for something else, which seemingly lay at a distance on the web of inputs and outputs. The equilibrium itself was the point, not any story about how markets would get there. Real-world capitalist markets did not meet the assumptions made in the theory, and so would not get there—and so much the worse for markets. For Lange, the point was that the framework established what information was necessary and how that information should be used in order to allocate resources efficiently. A planned system could collect that information and issue directives to get closer to the model's ideal than markets could.

Lange's argument was not, however, that planners would plan by collecting the data centrally and plugging it in to solve the model's system of simultaneous equations. There are serious doubts about whether this would be feasible for an economy with tens of thousands of products and complex, nonlinear production techniques, and in the 1930s the doubts were even more serious. By the time of Lange's essay, Hayek and Lionel Robbins had already acknowledged that the planning problem could be solved *in theory* by planners with complete information and, in Lange's words, "retreated to a second line of defence"—namely, that capitalist competition and markets provide ways of *practically* approaching the optimal points, methods which were not available to planners. As Robbins put it:

> It would necessitate the drawing up of millions of equations on the basis of millions of statistical data based on many more millions of individual computations. By the time the equations were solved, the information on which they were based would have become obsolete and they would need to be calculated anew.[18]

Lange's response was not to anticipate advances in computing to solve the problem faster, like the cybersocialists we discussed in chapter two. Instead, he suggested it could be solved in practice by iterative processes of trial and error. This was how, it was presumed, markets did it, after all. Planning would need its own set of processes for approaching equilibrium, and it could improve on capitalist markets in not being held back by monopolistic practices and by taking into account social and environmental costs and benefits that were not factored into private exchange decisions.

What Lange proposed is an algorithmic socialism, in which planning decisions are made and implemented based on a set of rules designed to coordinate efficiently across the division of labor. There would be a central planning board, but it would not be an omniscient eye in the middle of it all. It would be one node in the network of decision-making, and it would be assigned specific tasks. In his view, coordinating production required three sets of information about

1. people's preferences about consumption and work;
2. the quantity of available basic resources of each type; and
3. the alternative ways they could be combined and used in production processes.

Together, these would be sufficient to guide production choices to make the best use of resources to meet people's wants and needs. This information did not need to be centralized, any more than it did in capitalism. It only needed to be transmitted to the points where it was needed to make particular decisions. Workplace managers would pick how much to produce and how to produce a given good in a decentralized way. Consumption decisions and decisions about how many hours to work would be made by individuals. In each case, the decision-makers would only need local knowledge and knowledge of prices that mattered to them.

For individuals, the local knowledge would be their own preferences, just as we described above: They would be quoted prices in shops and choose what to buy from their budgets. They would see the wages available in different jobs and choose where to work accordingly. In Lange's view, wages would adjust to match supply and demand for different kinds of labor, and so in equilibrium, relative wages would fairly reflect the relative perceived difficulty and unpleasantness of each job. Each person's income would come partly from paid work and partly from the social dividend representing their share of returns to publicly owned resources. Lange's system involved markets for consumer products, and even a labor market. He was not opposed to markets in a doctrinaire way but saw them rather as a decision-making device within an overall administered system.[19]

For workplace managers, the local knowledge would be the alternative methods available for producing their output. Each would need only to know their own branch of the division of labor. Unlike consumption and work decisions, managers are required to follow rules in making their decisions, not their own preferences. They would be instructed to look at the prices quoted for both their outputs and inputs. Each would then choose their production technique and level of output so as to minimize the average cost per unit produced. The lowest-cost technique for a given output depends on the relative prices of possible inputs. For some price configurations, for example, a cement plant manager will choose a relatively labor-intensive process, for others a more automated one. (Where the technique involves fixed capital equipment, from machinery and tools to buildings, the cost includes not only a depreciation factor based on replacement cost, but also an interest rate.) Such data can be used to construct an average cost curve, based on the minimum cost per unit for any quantity of output. The manager then chooses the scale of output according to which the marginal cost equals the price of a unit of output.[20]

The central planning board sets and periodically adjusts the prices for all products and for nonproduced inputs. They do this by monitoring how much is being produced and ordered of each thing at current prices and adjusting to bring supply and demand in line. Since the number of prices is vast, presumably this is done mainly by automatically following algorithms, with the potential for more deliberate intervention to meet special circumstances as the board determines. The central planners do not themselves need information about preferences or production techniques: They only need information about what is ordered and produced, and this information is easily collected.

Following these procedures leads to the same set of prices and production decisions as profit-motivated firms reach in a standard model of long-run general equilibrium in perfectly competitive markets. The difference is that Lange's socialist managers are ordered to aim directly at minimizing average cost, while capitalist firms are driven there by chasing profits in competition with others. There are no profits in a long-run equilibrium in hypothetical, perfectly competitive capitalism, because profits draw new competitors or drive existing firms to expand until price meets average unit cost, eroding profits away. There are no profits in Lange's equilibrium because managers do not aim for them in the first place. (Profits generated by workplaces out of equilibrium end up in the public purse anyway.)[21]

Thus, Lange argues, his system meets the efficiency standards claimed by competitive general equilibrium's utopian capitalism, while actually existing capitalism does not because it is not in reality all that competitive. Workplace managers are instructed to minimize average cost because this minimizes the "alternatives sacrificed" in producing each thing. People's decisions as consumers filter into workplace decisions about resource use that end up allocating each input, and the inputs required to produce those inputs, to where they are most valued. Excess demand for a given input—say, steel—will lead the planning board to raise its price. This may induce steel producers to make more steel. It could also induce some users to switch to alternative techniques that are now lower cost, where other inputs substitute for steel, leaving the available steel to those uses in which it cannot be replaced so cheaply. It all depends on the reactions of demand and supply in the web of industries connected in some way to steel: its inputs, its users, its substitutes and complements, and so on. The planning board need not track these ripples or even be aware of them: It must only adjust prices in response to supply-and-demand imbalances as they arise.[22]

This does not mean planners are just passive rule followers who must act blindly. Having this standard algorithm to fall back on frees up their information-gathering powers and decision-making attention for targeted interventions. For Lange, one great advantage of planning over even idealized, textbook markets is the possibility of internalizing externalities. The market system only takes into account costs and benefits as perceived and borne by those involved in transactions. It ignores environmental and social costs imposed on others and takes no account of benefits to third parties either. The central planning board could assess these public bads and goods and adjust prices to take them into account. Even in the case of regular products (without clear externalities) planners would have "much wider knowledge of what is going on in the whole economic system than any private entrepreneur can ever have." They may be able to use this knowledge to find equilibrium prices faster than a blind algorithm (or markets) would and avoid destabilizing disequilibrium dynamics. But where they make mistakes or are faced with too much uncertainty, they have standard procedures to fall back on to correct them. The algorithms provide a baseline that can be left alone across much of the economy, freeing planners from a need to monitor and decide everything, in order to focus attention on strategic or problematic sectors.[23]

Lange's model as presented in his answer to Mises is extremely simplified and was intended as proof of concept rather than a detailed guide. For example, like the model of markets it is based on, it focuses on equilibrium points where producers have followed price signals to fully adjust their techniques to prevailing tastes and technology and does not track the paths from one equilibrium to another. Production techniques optimized for a particular set of prices call for a particular set of capital equipment and a built environment. But such things can take a long time, much work and many other resources to produce and install, and then have a long productive life—over which the basic parameters of consumer preferences and technology will surely change.

It would be far from an optimal use of resources to scrap equipment and install new machinery in response to every change in price that would theoretically call for it. Investment inevitably circumscribes choices of technique in a workplace for some time to come. At the workplace level, this separates planning decisions into (1) shorter-run choices about how best to operate the capital equipment inherited from past investment decisions and (2) longer-run, forward-looking decisions about how to replace, modify, and expand or contract the capital stock for the future. Investment should not be mechanically decided as if the current prices at the time of decision will prevail for the life of the equipment. More judgment than that is called for.

It is also doubtful that short-run decisions about how much to produce from week to week are best directed by price signals alone. Capitalist firms in most manufacturing and service industries are guided in their short-run output decisions mainly by shifts in sales and orders rather than by prices, which they tend to adjust infrequently. They typically operate with spare capacity to flexibly meet fluctuations in demand, so that marginal cost is relatively constant over a wide range of "normal" outputs. It would make sense for socialist workplaces to maintain similar flexibility—and so price signals will not be enough to guide their short-run output decisions.

But Lange's point is not bound to the specific, simple set of rules he gave as an example at a high level of abstraction. Real-world capitalist-firm decision-making is also much more complex than it is portrayed in the utopian capitalism of general equilibrium theory. His central point is that there could be decentralized socialist analogues to the same rules of thumb capitalist firms follow in deciding how to invest and what to produce. A real instance of a Lange-style algorithmic socialism would need a more intricate set of rules and also leave more room for judgment at the workplace level—but it would not need a supercomputer or omniscient planners at the center to track everything and solve a vast, ever-shifting system of simultaneous equations.

Against this, some of Hayek's antisocialist arguments about the use of knowledge in society fall flat. Hayek argued, rightly, that the kind of knowledge producers need to have about techniques is not only the type that can be codified in blueprints and engineering manuals. A complex division of labor is dynamic, often being disrupted by unforeseen accidents and opportunities. Dealing with these calls for improvisation and adjusting skillfully depend on local knowledge and experience that can only really be expected from people involved in the day-to-day production.

> The continuous flow of goods and services is maintained by constant deliberate adjustments, by new dispositions made every day in the light of circumstances not known the day before, by *B* stepping in when *A* fails to deliver. Even the large and highly mechanised plant keeps going largely because of an environment upon which it can draw for all sorts of unexpected needs; tiles for its roof, stationery for its forms, and all the thousand and one kinds of equipment in which it cannot be self-contained and which the plans for the operation of the plant require to be readily available . . . The statistics which such a central authority would have to use would have to be arrived at precisely by abstracting from minor differences between the things, by lumping together, as resources of one kind, items which may be very significant for the specific decision. It follows from this that central planning based on statistical information by its nature cannot take direct account of these circumstances of time and place, and that the central planner will have to find some way or other in which the decisions depending on them can be left to the "man on the spot."[24]

However, there is already room for this kind of local judgment in Lange's proposal. The plant manager under algorithmic socialism is in a similar position to the manager under capitalism. They face a set of input prices they do not control, and those prices are the parameters they must take into account in pursuing a given goal. Again, the difference is that while the capitalist manager is supposed to pursue profit, the socialist manager is supposed to minimize average cost. In both cases, pursuing the goal involves decision-making in the face of uncertainty. An investment choice locks in particular variables and constrains future decisions, and it may turn out in retrospect to have been wrong. Sometimes, there may be dilemmas between what seems to optimize in the short run and what better optimizes over longer periods. For example, laying off workers in a temporary slump might be more costly over the long run if it is expensive to recruit and train new employees in the recovery or if layoffs hit morale enough to undermine productivity. Cutting corners on quality might reduce costs now but erode customer loyalty. Capitalist managers routinely make such judgments in the pursuit of profit; socialist managers would make similar calls in the pursuit of lower average cost.[25]

Lange's fundamental point is not that a set of socialist pricing and decision-making rules would make the economy operate mechanically, as if it were finding a solution to a system of simultaneous equations. Nobody believes that real capitalist markets work like a textbook general equilibrium model either. His argument is that there are plausible, practical procedures through which socialists might generate a rational set of prices, which would work as parameters for local decision-making, just as market prices do for capitalist firms.

Whether such a system could in fact be fully fleshed out is an open question. Fundamental problems may not be apparent until the general approach is operationalized, fleshed out to take into account the many specific issues encountered in applying it in the real world. In a fictionalized account of a debate about such things in the Soviet Union in 1960, Francis Spufford has Leonid Kantorovich remark:

> I'm afraid that the computer cannot digest some of our economists' scholarly products. Long talks and articles which people think they understand prove impossible to put into logical, into algorithmic, form. It turns out that, once you remove everything that's said "in general," once you pour away all the water, there's nothing left. Well, either nothing . . . or one big question mark.[26]

Spufford's novel is in part a dramatization of both the promise this kind of thinking had in the Soviet Union and the problems it ran into in practice, as we saw in chapter two. Lange himself went on to work in the highest levels of government in communist Poland. The ideas of the neoclassical socialist economists—including homegrown geniuses like Kantorovich—certainly had a good deal of influence. But it cannot be said that algorithmic socialism, in a form that would have satisfied its theorists, was ever truly tested. Political and sociological constraints intervened at every stage.

However, politics and sociology will always get in the way. Our view is that an economy with a substantial market, commodity-producing sector is likely to be more robust than algorithmic planning in the face of some of these issues, and therefore a better vehicle for the socialist project. Unlike Mises and Hayek, we do not argue that marketless planning is impossible. The Soviet experience, after all, shows that a complex division of labor could be managed, even if planners were often muddling along with methods far from the economists' ideal and rates of progress in efficiency that were underwhelming over the long run. Nevertheless, we believe marketless planning is systematically vulnerable to some predictable, fundamental problems, which algorithmic planning fails to properly address.

The Limits of Algorithmic Planning

As we've already discussed extensively, a viable socialist system needs to have plausible answers to information and incentive problems. Information problems involve failures to discover or transmit accurate information to where it is needed to inform decisions, so that those local decisions can be made consistent with systemic efficiency. Incentive problems involve failures to motivate people to make decisions and act in accord with systemic efficiency. Some of the thorniest problems combine both—when people lack the incentives to collect, honestly transmit, or use accurate information.

Democratic marketless central planning, algorithmic or otherwise, depends not only on the accumulation of information but also on the following of directions in order for the plan to be carried out. Three channels of direction are especially important:

1. Managers of production units must follow instructions from the plan.
2. Workers in the production units must follow instructions from their local administrators.
3. The plan must gather and follow instructions from the public, whom the plan is supposed to serve (including individual consumption preferences and collective decisions on public goods).

This is fundamentally different from commodity production for markets, which involves a direct channel from customers to production units, and where the managers of those units are not directed by an external plan.

John Roemer argues that marketless planning faces principal-agent problems in each of the three channels, which tend to create fundamental problems in coordinating the division of labor efficiently. A principal-agent problem involves conflicts of interest between those making decisions and those they rely upon to carry them out. Market commodity production of course has its own such problems. They will arise in any complex division of labor—the questions are whether and how they can be managed. In this section we explain why even a sophisticated algorithmic system of central planning will be plagued by these problems and why we therefore conclude that a commodity-producing sector is a better vehicle for socialist aims—in spite of its own problems, which will be tackled in the following chapters.[27]

Lange-style algorithmic planning mainly deals with the transmission of consumer desires and the coordination of production. Its advance on traditional central planning is that it recognizes that much of the information planning needed is developed and held locally—with consumers and producers—and that it takes account of the difficulties of collecting and transmitting that information to the center and processing it once there. In Lange's system, the center sets prices but leaves much decision-making to local levels, which take those prices as parameters. People choose their consumption goods from shops; managers decide how much to produce and how based on their knowledge of possible techniques. And the center sets and revises prices mainly by responding to differences between supply and demand. In this way, algorithmic planning deals with one of the main Hayekian objections to central planning—namely, that planners have no access to the critically important information that is available only to the "person on the spot."

But it runs into some other fundamental problems:

- Local managers are likely to face pressure to act in ways that conflict with instructions from the center to follow the rules. Since the managers have local information that the center does not have, it is difficult for the center to monitor compliance. The strongest of these pressures will come from the interests of workers in job security and good working conditions. These are legitimate interests and priorities for the socialist project. The system has no way of openly managing the trade-offs between people's preferences as workers and as consumers. It will therefore tend either to fudge the tensions with inefficient results or depend on capitalist-style labor discipline.
- Work units do not need to directly respond to customer wants. Though customers express preferences between available products, there is no incentive built into the system to experiment with ways of better meeting people's wants. The extra distance between customers and producers makes it harder for the former to effectively signal preferences about trade-offs between cost minimization and quality. It also exacerbates informational asymmetries between customers and producers about quality.

The Inputs Include People

Though local production managers have responsibility for critical decisions, the coherence and efficiency of the system requires them to faithfully follow the rules of the system. The directives from the center are not detailed instructions telling them how much to produce and how to produce it but guidelines for how to decide these things. The coherence of the system does not require managers to transmit their local information up the chain but does require them to honestly make their best effort to collect and apply accurate information themselves while following the rules—for example, by choosing the technique that minimizes average cost per unit.

But managers will likely often face pressures that compete with the demand to follow the rules faithfully. The resources allocated to their production unit depend on their choices, and they may have incentives to fudge information. As was the case in the Soviet Union, it will often be easier to settle for less efficient arrangements, to overstate input requirements and underestimate output possibilities. The more that the rules leave local managers to use their judgment, rather than fully specifying their responses to data in a mechanical way, the harder it will be for planners to monitor management decisions. As we argued above, since production decisions must be made in conditions of considerable uncertainty and constantly deal with many unforeseen issues, efficiency calls for a certain level of autonomous judgment for local managers. But then not only will it be easy for managers to fudge numbers, it will often feel like the right thing to do, even by managers most committed to making the socialist system work.[28]

The basic reason is that the choices about production are also choices about people—the workers in the production unit—and what they do all day. Managing production is managing a workplace full of human beings who must ultimately have reasons to work and apply themselves to a part in the division of labor. It does not matter to electricity or coffee beans if the algorithm calls for production to use more or less of them, but it matters very much to people. Machines and buildings do not care how intensely they are used or how pleasant the process is, but human beings are conscious throughout, and work takes up much of our waking life.

This is perhaps the most important blind spot in Lange-style algorithmic planning. Most standard economic models of production—including the ones on which algorithmic planning systems are based—treat labor as an input like any other, with a predictable, mechanical relationship between input (hours worked) and output. In reality, there is a lot of room for movement between hours on the job and results. The relationship depends on all kinds of things: effort, morale, talents, skills, and the ways in which people cooperate. These things can be difficult to monitor and manage—and attempts to intensify monitoring and discipline can backfire, harming morale and commitment. Even from a purely instrumental perspective, motivating workers to play their part effectively in the division of labor requires that workers' own subjective feelings and views be taken into account.

Struggles over labor processes and the terms of employment have always played a large part in shaping capitalist production. Capitalist managers also face demands for security, respect, reasonable workloads, and so on, but they are expected and allowed to give priority to the bottom line and profitability. The possibility of job loss exercises a powerful discipline on workers, and macroeconomic policy deliberately keeps the labor market from becoming a sellers' market. But under socialism worker well-being, preferences, and security are core priorities for the system. This creates new dilemmas.[29]

It is not that there is a tension between efficiency and worker preferences. Properly defined, even in the sense of traditional welfare economics, the yardsticks of efficiency should take into account worker preferences. (There is nothing more efficient at the system level about achieving greater output by forcing more strain on the workforce—gains to customers come at the expense of the workers.) The issue is that more satisfaction of worker preferences can often come at the expense of consumer preferences and vice versa. A lighter workload with more breaks, other things being equal, makes the product more expensive. Tighter security of job tenure can make it slower and more difficult for production to adjust to changing conditions.[30]

Since workers are also consumers, this is not a conflict between different groups of people. We produce for others and consume what others produce for us. From a purely selfish perspective, each person might prefer that everyone else work as hard as possible, for long hours and on flexible terms, but no one wants this for themselves. Conversely, an utterly leisurely day at work—rolling into the office mid-morning as we feel like it, a long lunch, and then a pleasant afternoon of light duties interspersed with a few beers—comes at too high a price if everyone else is doing it too. (If we lived in so much abundance that people would be perfectly happy with that level of output, most would probably still prefer to work more productively over fewer hours, and more fully enjoy leisure time completely outside the workplace.)

True efficiency therefore demands some way for people to weigh up their preferences about their producer preferences alongside their consumer preferences and to have the full set of preferences systematically taken into account. We argue more fully in the next chapter that a labor market is not sufficient and that workplace democracy within cooperative commodity-producing firms best allows for the trade-offs to be better managed. Worker-members collectively decide on how to manage their production. Because each shares in whatever profit the firm makes, they have an incentive to seek more efficient ways of working and strike a chosen balance between workload and income.

Marketless planning—central or algorithmic—has much more difficulty resolving these problems. Lange himself simply did not address them. Employment relations in his system were the same as under capitalism. He treats the labor market as an arena of empowerment for workers, who can express their preferences through their choice of job. But he does not consider whether motivation at work depends on fear of job loss, whether a degree of unemployment is necessary to maintain such fear, or the implications of a nonclearing labor market for his claims about the efficiency of pricing labor.

The idea of solving the incentive problems through tight labor discipline and flexibility of employment is not appealing. But the temptation to looseness is also the root of a number of systemic problems, which played out in the experience of state socialism. If the system depends on local production units following rules to pursue local efficiency, there must be some monitoring of local managers and consequences for not following the rules. Situations inevitably arise when following the rules implies reducing the workforce within a unit. Other situations may arise when the rules imply units should be shut down entirely. If loss of a position in the unit means workers face a large fall in income and uncertainty finding work elsewhere, it is easy to understand why employment becomes a good in the system in itself, competing with the rules. If this is not openly acknowledged, and no way found of integrating such a goal within the rules, it will be pursued informally in ways that corrode the system's efficiency.

This brings us back to Kornai's concept of the "soft budget constraint," a general expectation that local units will not face consequences from inefficiency, at least within wide bounds. Once that expectation takes hold, it has wider consequences beyond the protection of jobs within the unit: It is harder to enforce all kinds of efficiencies on local managers when budget limits are easily fudged. The system breaks down or sags as the rules it depends upon no longer effectively connect local decisions with one another. Kornai found that "protection of jobs" was the most frequent reason for the loosening of the budget constraint in socialist economies.[31]

Again, security of worker livelihood is a legitimate priority for the system. But the system must be built to openly recognize and manage the tensions it brings—tensions with flexibility of adaptation and with incentives to exert effort at work. Roemer sees this as an important part of the manager–worker agency problem any viable socialist model must solve: How can workers have a reason to work hard if they do not fear unemployment? Our answer involves workplace democracy and workers as residual claimants on income to their unit, along with the exit opportunities afforded by a robust public welfare system. This aims to motivate workers in positive ways, allowing them to balance their interests in income and working conditions. But the balancing act depends on being able to meet the needs of customers, who are free to choose the products of other workplaces if they wish.[32]

The Outputs Are for People

This brings us to problems transmitting consumer preferences to production. We established early in the chapter why most socialist models still involve people expressing their consumer preferences much as they do under capitalism—by spending a monetary budget as they choose across priced goods and services. These frameworks have consumer markets in this sense, even if they replace markets for producers, allocating resources between production units and organizing the division of labor in some other way. This means that, under these systems, the choices consumers make affect producers only indirectly. In this mediation some obstacles are likely to arise between people's wants and production.[33]

If each type of product were standardized—were essentially identical—with characteristics and quality easy to assess, this would not be such a hard problem. Consumer choice would then just be about allocating a budget between broad categories: how much soda, how much breakfast cereal, how many restaurant meals, how many haircuts. Some products are indeed standardized: wheat, oil, aluminum, coffee beans, and so on. Each of these have grades, but are considered identical within a grade, and there are clear, widely accepted, and easily applied criteria for grading. But most products—manufactures and especially most services—are not like that at all. One restaurant meal, or haircut, or breakfast cereal, cellphone, or denim skirt is not like another.

Under capitalism, each firm is responsible for deciding the specific qualities of its own products and directly bears the consequences of customer choice. Its products are substitutes for the products of other firms. If your pasta sauce is more expensive than the next one on the shelf, buyers might be more inclined to get the other one. But they are *imperfect* substitutes: if a buyer likes your sauce better, or is simply more familiar with your brand, they may be prepared to pay extra. Firms do not compete only on price; they also compete with respect to quality—and of course through pure brand differentiation and marketing.

It is tempting for socialists to focus on this last part and point to the waste of large marketing budgets and to the seeming inefficiency of so many different brands of functionally identical toothpaste. It is certainly true that product differentiation based on pure branding rather than true quality differences is inefficient, as are marketing arms races. But wherever people have genuine preferences about the quality and qualities of things, product differentiation is important. This is not to say that people always want the highest-quality version of something. Quality is costly. Some tastes are more expensive to cater to than others. One person might be perfectly happy with a single pair of canvas sneakers but enjoy single-malt whiskey. Another might prefer to maintain an extensive shoe collection while drinking mass-produced lager. The important things for efficiency are that prices accurately reflect the costs of the qualities and that people are able to accurately identify the qualities they care about.[34]

Can this be dealt with in a nonmarket socialist system? There is a tension involved in allowing for product differentiation in any system of marketless planning, whether centralized or decentralized in the Lange style. Allowing for product differences effectively means multiplying the number of distinct products that the system must manage. It is not hard to come up with at least half a dozen meaningful distinctions in almost any product we can think of, and for some there are many more. These subcategories are usually more or less close substitutes for one another both on the demand side and the production side. In other words, on the demand side, people will be willing to swap between them on the basis of reasonably small variations in relative cost, and on the supply side, switching between them usually calls for relatively minor adjustments in production processes. This means a fiendish set of interdependencies for any central planning system to estimate—never mind the calculability of the equation system with so many millions of variables; just estimating the parameters to plug in seems to call for a godlike omniscience.

Sensing the difficulties that quality distinctions pose for a marketless system, Mandel envisions whittling down product subcategories by referendum:

> A consumer, having the right to receive six pairs of footwear a year, would cross six samples in a sheet containing a hundred or two hundred options. The model mix would then be determined by the outcome of such a referendum, with post-production corrective mechanisms reflecting subsequent consumer criticisms.[35]

Considering that we would need to scroll through countless catalogues for referenda on every product category, we are back to the problems discussed above about cumbersome, time-delayed systems for expressing consumer preferences.

Meanwhile, a Lange-style decentralized trial-and-error algorithmic planning system runs into its own problems. In that model, all products of a particular type are pooled to form the supply of that product. Potentially, many different production units (workplaces) contribute their output to the pool of each product category. If, over some time period, the amount people want to buy at the going price is appreciably below that supply, the central planning board reduces its price. If demand exceeds supply, it raises the price. This then feeds back into the decisions of the production units, who adjust supply in response.

If this worked smoothly, it would seem to have no trouble registering choice between related but distinct products and feeding these into production decisions. If consumers begin to favor more "pasta sauce–curry" and less "pasta sauce–basil," firms contributing production to both of these categories take account of the price shifts and adjust their production accordingly. Most workplaces will be producing things in multiple categories and be capable of producing more.[36]

But there is a fundamental problem. Wherever there are multiple workplaces making a particular product—and presumably this generally would be the case—they collectively bear the consequences of demand for that product category, not demand for their own contributions specifically. There are many possible recipes for "pasta sauce–curry." Some will use fresher, costlier ingredients than others. There is no material incentive for a workplace to make a product customers would prefer over other products in the same category. There is no mechanism encouraging workplaces to experiment to find out what customers want. Since the standard rules instruct managers to minimize average cost per unit, there is no direction to consider quality beyond what is necessary to qualify the product as fitting the category.

Since higher quality often comes at higher cost, there is no easy way to add rules to managers' directives requiring them to take quality into account. The system cannot find out, for example, how many customers would be prepared to pay the extra cost for a fresher sauce or how many would prefer reduced salt or lower calories—not, at least, without multiplying the product categories still more, to take into account all the possible permutations: "pasta sauce–curry–reduced salt–low calorie," and so on. But the more the categories multiply, the more difficult the system becomes to manage. Since there is no way to register whether customers prefer one workplace's product over another's within a category, an independent system of quality assurance would bear the burden of making sure that each product met the standards for its category.

Alternatively, the system's subcategories could be defined by the individual workplaces themselves. Instead of "pasta sauce–curry–reduced salt" including all products meeting that definition, we would have "Bongiovi Sauce Factory's reduced salt pasta sauce with curry," "Springsteen Sauce Factory's reduced salt pasta sauce with curry," and so on. These unit-based product categories could then see prices (or orders) move independently in response to consumer choice, which is now able to express preferences over quality within product types. Each unit's production decisions, following the system rules, would then respond to those choices in a way that takes those quality preferences into account. There would even be incentive to experiment with new products that might find a customer base.

But this is for all intents and purposes a market.

Against all this, the dedicated nonmarket planner might reply that the benefits of planning are worth the sacrifice of frivolous product distinctions. Isn't it a sign of deep contamination with capitalist values to insist on the many fine distinctions between commodities? Couldn't we make do with, say, three pasta sauce varieties, a standard dishwashing liquid, ice cream limited to vanilla, chocolate, and strawberry? Would that be so bad, if the reward is an egalitarian society?

Our response is that we do not need to choose between socialist aims and consumer choice, so long as the system has ways of dealing with the problems that come with commodity production. Showing that our system does have such ways is the aim of the subsequent chapters. But we also maintain that effective customer choice is a genuine necessity for a viable system. Even if *consumer* choice were trivial and frivolous, which is not our view, quality signaling is vitally important in the production of inputs too. Quality and fine distinctions of type are key in all kinds of production equipment, materials, and buildings. A system unable to transmit producer preferences regarding these products will run into serious problems, however much we simplify consumer product categories.

Alec Nove has discussed how this problem played out in the Soviet system, in a passage worth quoting at length:

> Plan-instructions have to be expressed in units of measurement: tonnes, square metres, millions of roubles, thousands of pairs, and so on. In any instance where there is a product mix, or different types or dimensions, plan indicators must of necessity be *aggregated* . . . But an order aggregated (e.g. in tonne-kilometres) incites the recipient to act in a particular way. If the measure is gross value in roubles there is benefit to be derived from making expensive goods, using expensive materials. Tonne-kilometres incite transport undertakings to carry heavy goods over long distances. Examples of wasteful or otherwise irrational practices designed to fulfil plans . . . could fill several bound volumes, all the examples being taken from Soviet publications. That so well-known and well-studied a problem still resists solution is proof enough that it is genuinely difficult to solve. The basic contradiction arises from the simple fact that the centre *cannot* know in full detail what is in fact needed by the customer, and yet the entire logic of the Soviet system rests upon the proposition that it is the duty of all subordinate management to obey the plan-instructions of the centre because these supposedly embody the need of society. In practice, the detailed specifications can generally only be determined in negotiation between producer and user, with or without the intermediacy of trading organs.[37]

In other words, to make production genuinely responsive to needs, user preferences about product specification and quality must be transmittable to producers, who must have incentives to make products that meet them. It is very difficult to organize this through a marketless plan.

False Choices

As discussed, Oskar Lange aimed to contest both antisocialists who did not believe planning could solve the allocation problem and socialists who did not see the nature and seriousness of that problem in the first place. He called Mises the "great advocatus diaboli" of the socialist cause, deserving of a statue occupying "an honourable place in the great hall of the Ministry of Socialisation or of the Central Planning Board of the socialist state," because "it was his powerful challenge that forced the socialists to recognize the importance of an adequate system of economic accounting to guide the allocation of resources in a socialist economy."[38]

Though we do not ultimately endorse Lange's algorithmic planning solution, we have highlighted his most famous contribution to the "socialist calculation debate" because it explains important aspects of the problem so clearly. Lange gets a statue right next to Mises. His model did not involve firms producing for markets; it involved firms producing according to decision rules based on neoclassical general equilibrium theory.

In this chapter we have set out why markets and commodity production play an important role in our own model. Not only do consumers express preferences by spending from their budgets in shops, but firms produce directly for markets, rather than following a comprehensive central plan. This does not mean we are blind to problems of markets raised by socialists and many liberals. But our view is that it is much easier to meet socialist aims by addressing these problems than it would be to fix the problems of central planning.

In David McNally's view, the notion of a *limited* role for markets is incoherent. To give any ground to the idea of market rationality is to open the door completely to Mises and Hayek. He claims that "if the market is the only mechanism of rational economy, then it should govern all aspects of economic life." This is Hayek's *Road to Serfdom* with the direction of the slippery slope reversed.[39]

Thankfully, it is not true. It is easy to combine markets and commodity production with regulation, noncommodity production, and all kinds of other public intervention. Markets and planning are not mutually exclusive. A grid of prices and a network of monetary flows are a great aid to democratic planning, both at the macro scale and within collective workplaces. In fact, they help to knit these spheres together to make local and national democratic decision-making inform one another, while also taking account of individual needs and wants about both consumption and work. In our system, the commodity-producing sector overlaps with workplace democracy, socialized financial institutions, a large noncommodified sector, and an active democratic state.

The coming chapters are devoted to explaining how this set of institutions not only are compatible but support one another in meeting socialist goals for equality, personal freedom, empowerment at work, efficiency, and welfare.

5

Workplace Democracy and Finance

You've worked at the pasta sauce firm for years. Lately, arguments have been heating up over whether to introduce a new kind of bottling machinery. The "Alfredo of administration," as your elected director half-jokingly calls himself, insists the upgrade will boost efficiency. Others worry it will speed up the line, make the work feel more mechanical, and disrupt the cooperative rhythm they've built.

Mr. Alfredo's team is reelected narrowly, and it plows ahead with the capital plan. You join a few fellow dissenters and decide to leave and form a cooperative of your own. You'll need to convince a public bank to finance you, of course, and you and your fellow worker-members start under the same rules as everyone else: democratic governance and no private accumulation of capital. If your ideas work, they'll find customers and maybe even set an example for others to follow. If not, the lesson will still be shared.

We believe that, in a socialist society, workers should have democratic control over their own workplaces. Most anticapitalists think that's obvious. But among economists who have developed proposals for how a successor system might work, the question is much more controversial. Some of the most well-known models do not involve democratic workplaces.

We have already seen that Oskar Lange's system features a labor market and conventional employment relations. In a more contemporary proposal, *A Future for Socialism*, John Roemer also rejects labor management, at least as part of socialism's "first step," and possibly even as part of an ideal vision. He argues that "an organism with one mutation is more likely to survive than one in which two mutations occur simultaneously." For Roemer, it is "more important to change the private nature of the financing of firms than the management structure."[1]

From a completely different angle, other socialists are skeptical of combining workplace democracy with market commodity production. How can workers truly be said to be in control when they are subject to the discipline of the market? But the question could just as easily be asked of a nonmarket socialist model: How can workers be in control when they must play their designated role in a central plan? The problem is general. As we've seen, individual workplaces are small nodes in a vast and complex division of labor. These nodes must be coordinated to meet people's needs efficiently, but if each workplace must play a part, what is the scope left for local democratic decision-making? Any viable system must constrain the choices made within the firm and structure those choices with incentives to bring local interests in line with broader social needs. That is easier said than done.

We argued in the last chapter that nonmarket socialism has difficulty managing the tensions between consumer preferences and worker preferences. It tends to elide the conflict in ways that breed major inefficiencies. Our model makes workplace democracy meaningful not by pretending that each workplace is an island but by clearly representing other social interests in the parameters of the decisions made by workers.

Interests of customers are represented in the need to attract them to buy the unit's products, when they could otherwise choose products made by other firms. The interests of the community are represented in the need to obtain finance from public banks. Workplaces make use of social resources that might have been used elsewhere. The financial system ideally allocates those resources to where they are best used and shares returns from using those assets with the community.

There are two major safeguards that protect the space for local workplace decision-making in the context of these broader interests. A system of robust minimum benchmark wages and conditions prevents workplaces from taking the low road of self-exploitation, channeling competition instead toward productivity and quality. It also helps to spread gains from productivity improvements across the economy. What's more, the public financial system allows for risk to be shared, shielding workplaces from temporary bad luck and helping them adjust to changing conditions.

Workplace democracy is not a module that can be plugged into a socialist model without affecting the system as a whole. It is tangled up with questions of finance and labor mobility. It brings challenges around risk, income distribution, and efficiency. Critics have pointed out serious flaws in some models, and this has convinced many that worker management is simply unviable. The problems are real and must be faced squarely.[2]

The aim of this chapter is to do just that. In the next section we defend workplace democracy as an aim. We argue against those who hold that a labor market is enough to express worker preferences and make the case that there are meaningful decisions for workers to make locally, even in complex economies.

After explaining the basic structure of a democratic firm in our model—what makes it democratic and what makes it a firm—we review the problems of workplace democracy discussed in the economics literature. We then explain how our model gives a plausible solution to those problems, namely, with a financial system that treats investment as a partnership between democratic firm and public bank.

What Makes a Democratic Firm?

Our proposed economic system, like capitalism, is mixed. "Private" and "public" are the wrong words here, given that both sectors are socially owned in our model, but they are convenient descriptors. The division is between a "private" commodity-producing sector whose costs are covered by market sales and a "public" noncommodified sector whose costs are covered by publicly allocated funds. The noncommodified sector includes the government bureaucracy and public agencies under central government control, but it may also include a variety of community agencies with considerable autonomy, which are nevertheless still financed through the public purse. We discuss the noncommodified sector in the next chapter, focusing here on democratic firms in the commodity-producing sector.

In the system we propose, a firm is *democratic* insofar as the "management and administrative structure are chosen by the firm's labor force using a democratic political process." Those who work in the firm are also members, each receiving a share of the firm's residual income. Democratic firms are *firms* in that they are autonomous commodity-producing entities that must cover costs with revenues and meet their contractual payment obligations.[3]

A variety of firm constitutions are possible, but the standard for a midsize to large firm would involve representative democracy, with elected directors appointing and monitoring administrators who would be responsible for day-to-day management. This could be supplemented by committees and referenda as needed, but routine administration is best handled by specialist professional workers with expertise in accounting, logistics, and so on. Democracy does its job by making sure the administrators are ultimately answerable to their colleagues and that working conditions and broad questions of strategy have general approval.

Financial viability constrains the democratic firm, as it does the capitalist firm. The need to cover costs and meet cash flow obligations, while competing with other enterprises, is what ties the firm to the broader division of labor across the economy. It ensures that it is using social resources reasonably efficiently to meet people's needs and wants. Like capitalist firms, democratic firms receive revenue from selling their output and pay for the inputs used in producing that output. They require investment: Some inputs must be paid for long before receipt of the revenue that covers those costs. This investment must be financed in some way. As with capitalist firms, their future revenues and costs are uncertain to some degree. Market demand and prices change over time. They must make investment and production decisions in the face of uncertainty and so face financial risks.

However, a socialist economy with democratic firms calls for financial arrangements very different from those suited to capitalism. In our system, labor-managed firms undertake investment in partnership with one or more public banks, who finance firms' productive assets and can help in other ways. We explain the workings of the system in the course of this chapter.

In a fundamental way, democratic firms are very different from capitalist ones. Capitalist firms are ultimately controlled by their owners, who are also the claimants to the residual income left after suppliers, workers, and creditors have been paid. Labor-managed firms, on the other hand, are ultimately controlled by their workers.

Wages in the Democratic Firm

Worker-members receive two forms of income from their firms. They earn a regular wage, fixed in advance, and a periodic dividend, their share of the firm's profit. Since worker-members are the firm's residual claimants, it may seem redundant to divide their entitlement between wage and dividend. But fixed wages have a number of advantages.

First, they give workers income stability. It is important for household budgeting to know in advance what regular income to expect. When recruiting new worker-members, they indicate what baseline income the new member can expect. Second, they provide a vital reference point for price setting and accounting, pricing labor as an input. This is important for the coherence, stability, and rationality of the price structure. Direct labor costs are a substantial, often majority, portion of most firms' costs. Fixing these costs in advance is important for planning and pricing decisions. Finally, they allow for differences in pay among worker-members according to duration and type of work. Some worker-members may prefer to work fewer hours than others; some may want overtime while others may not. Different levels of compensation may be necessary to attract workers to different positions.[4]

As we've argued in our discussion of John Rawls, some wage differences are justifiable even on egalitarian grounds: They compensate people for doing jobs that are more difficult, strenuous, or otherwise unpleasant; for putting in extra effort; and for developing skills that are in demand. The wage is specific to a particular type of work and potentially to an individual. Each wage rate must at least meet a benchmark for that work type, as described below. But the firm has the discretion to pay margins above the benchmark. The collective might decide to pay extra for all members doing a particular kind of work or to use individual promotion or bonus schemes to motivate effort. Such payments subtract from the dividends that are paid evenly to all members, so people are likely to agree to them only if they expect them to pay off—for example, by motivating productivity gains.

There is undeniably a tension between the egalitarian and efficiency aims of socialism here. Firms will try to attract members with skills and talents that are in short supply, and the wages for these attributes will be bid up across the economy. If this leads to wage premiums that encourage the development of undersupplied skills, this is positive and self-limiting, as the supply of people with those skills adjusts to meet needs over time. But talents—personal attributes less responsive to training—are a different story, and the talented will enjoy compensation persistently above what would be necessary to induce them to bear the difficulties of the work itself. The system must face the reality of persistent differences in talent and use extramarket tools to limit income differentials, such as progressive income tax and transfers. Labor income inequality must be addressed across the economy, not only within individual firms, though it also seems likely that democratic firms will settle on radically more egalitarian pay structures than today's nondemocratic firms. We discuss these ideas at length in chapter seven.

In this system, the democratic firm treats precommitted wages as a cost, even though they form part of member income. A firm that is unable to meet its wage commitments is considered to be in debt to its own members and potentially insolvent.

Wage-Setting and the Labor Board

Alongside local workplace democracy, our system also has a national-level venue for coordinating wage-setting. In setting wages and conditions for particular jobs, firms must at least meet benchmarks set by a national labor board. Benchmarks would be specified for particular job categories, with margins for skill or experience, and potentially allowing for regional differences. The benchmarks function as a floor, but the board would adjust the benchmarks periodically to keep them not too far off from the wages actually paid across the economy. They are intended as genuine benchmarks, not safety-net minimum wages as they exist in many capitalist countries.

There are a few main reasons for this framework. First, it prevents democratic firms from getting stuck in a self-exploitational low-cost spiral. Competition over costs can take a high road involving the pursuit of more efficient techniques and technologies or a low road of wage restraint and work intensification. Even in a democratic firm, members might be tempted to accept lower incomes as an alternative to restructuring around new technologies. This can hold back labor productivity growth that could free up people's time for leisure. Wage benchmarks block the low road, encouraging lagging firms to catch up with new techniques and technologies or even, with the financial support of a partner bank, transition to new products.

Centrally determined benchmarks also help to spread gains from productivity growth to workers across the economy. Some sectors, especially in manufacturing, are more prone to labor-augmenting technological change than others, such as personal services. Central benchmarks help to make sure that the incomes of day care workers, teachers, and hairdressers are not left lagging because gains from technological improvements are captured in industry. Spreading the gains to labor productivity growth also helps to counteract a perverse incentive around labor mobility. If wages rise faster in the sectors where productivity gains are generated through technical change, worker-members will be more likely to cling to positions precisely where technology has made labor-saving possible. When instead these productivity gains are spread around—through some combination of lower prices in industries with improved technology, and rising wages across the board—it encourages workers to move where their talents are best used. After all, we know from long experience under capitalism that consumers often prefer to take some of the gains from technological improvements and spend more on other things, rather than simply increase consumption of the things that have become relatively cheaper.[5]

Wage benchmarks can be used as a policy and planning tool. While market trends should factor into labor board decisions, they need not be decisive. Egalitarian and development goals can be taken into account. The benchmarks can be used, for example, to maintain gender pay equity, which is undermined in labor markets if women are more likely to have time out of work for childcare and under the long shadow of historic pay penalties for traditionally feminine jobs. For development purposes, benchmarks could vary between geographical areas, allowing for lower pay in lower-cost regional areas or rising at different paces to narrow regional disparities over time. They could be used to draw people into growing industries and away from declining ones.

Finally, wage benchmarks can be a powerful macroeconomic tool. In the early years of macroeconomic policy, economists like Jan Tinbergen argued that influence over wages would be critical to making full employment compatible with price and exchange rate stability. However, in most capitalist countries policy had little leverage in the wage-setting process and so relied on labor market slack (unemployment) to keep wages under control. There are precedents for centralized wage determination in capitalist countries—for example, in postwar Australia and Sweden—with good track records over long periods of high productivity growth and macroeconomic stability.[6]

The categories in the system need not be too fine-grained. They do not need to be continually tweaked—a schedule reviewing each every few years should be sufficient. With an established system of relativities between job categories, the whole structure can be shifted more often, without needing to individually assess each one. The national system of minimum wages in Australia currently has about a hundred industry-based "awards," each setting out minimum wages for a number of related jobs. Only a dozen of these awards cover most of the workforce who rely on them. The system we envision would be no more complex than this.

There are some tensions among the different aims that wage benchmarks try to serve. Benchmarks can be set to promote fairness between sectors, to encourage efficiency and labor mobility, or to protect employment in struggling regions—and these goals can pull against one another. Centralized bargaining in capitalist countries revealed these same difficulties. But such conflicts are a normal feature of democracy. Our system channels them through two levels of democratic decision-making: the labor board sets economy-wide benchmarks that balance equality and efficiency, while each firm decides locally whether, and how much, to exceed them in light of its own circumstances. We return to this in chapter eight, where we discuss how the labor board fits with other aspects of macroeconomic policy and planning.

The Case for Workplace Democracy

In the previous chapter we argued that even for socialists there is a good case to leave many economic decisions to individual choice rather than democratic decision-making. Fundamentally, this is because of the flexibility of production. Resources can be combined in many different ways, and it is often possible to shift how they are used to better satisfy individuals without making anyone worse off. It therefore makes perfect socialist sense to consider everyone to have a fair share of a claim on productive resources to allocate as they see fit for their private consumption—and this is expressed through purchasing decisions from a budget. Democratic allocation of every resource would be much inferior.

Why, then, do we see a role for democracy at the workplace level? Some argue that the same logic we applied for consumer choice applies also to choice of work in the labor market.

In this section we lay out the case for workplace democracy. First we explain why labor markets generally fail to transmit producer preferences in the way markets transmit consumption preferences. Then we lay out the moral and efficiency cases. In themselves, these do not decide the question. They give prima facie reasons for favoring workplace democracy, but these might be outweighed by disadvantages. In the rest of the chapter we respond to important criticisms of workplace democracy and suggest ways of overcoming its problems.

Contested Exchange

How is a labor market different from a grocery store? This is a controversial question. There is a long tradition in economic thinking that treats labor market decisions as equivalent to consumption decisions. Since people are free to choose whether to accept any given contract for their time and seek the most agreeable terms on the market, wages should already price in preferences about working conditions.

Armen Alchian and Harold Demsetz pushed this argument to its limit in a defense of the traditional firm. They claimed that employers exercise no special authority distinct from ordinary market contracting: A boss can only "punish" a worker by ending the relationship, just as a consumer can stop buying from a grocer. For them, even the act of directing labor—telling an employee to type this letter rather than file that document—is simply a moment in an ongoing process of renegotiation between equals.[7]

They did, however, acknowledge that production requires coordination. In their terms, the employer serves as the "centralised contractual agent in a team productive process"—the node that holds together a web of contracts among different inputs—not a commanding authority.

From this perspective, there is no rationale for worker democracy. On the one hand, there are other parties beyond the workplace with legitimate claims to direct firms: customers and suppliers of other (nonlabor) inputs. On the other hand, workers already possess all the power they need and deserve, in that they can choose whether or not to contract with the firm. The potential for exit means there is no need for voice to ensure that the terms of employment take workers' interests into account. The market wage for a job with a particular set of working conditions moves toward an equilibrium that balances the willingness of firms to employ with the willingness of workers to accept those conditions at that wage.

In this view, the employer's role is purely functional: to coordinate a team process and design production so that it is as efficient as possible for a given level of acceptability of working conditions. Competing employers must keep those conditions at least as attractive as those their rivals offer for comparable pay. Workers will not necessarily get the precise combination of comfort and income they want, any more than a grocer can charge whatever price they please. They offer their labor alongside many others, and if others are willing to work on worse terms, their offers will be outmatched. Equilibrium wages and conditions simply reflect the marginal trade-offs both sides are prepared to make.

This argument is unconvincing because it takes no account of the unequal distribution of assets. Someone without wealth has worse alternatives to labor than someone who can draw income from other sources. Simply, workers have to work to meet their needs, and dressing it up as a "choice" is a stretch.

But once there is a reasonably equitable distribution of property, does the Alchian and Demsetz argument become more compelling? Could we then leave the labor market to manage wage and working conditions? This seems to have been Oskar Lange's view, a key reason for maintaining regular employment relations in his model. He thought wage rates would adjust to reflect the relative marginal disutility of work in each occupation. The worker's ability to exit one workplace and choose alternative contracts elsewhere checks the power of any firm's management: To keep workers, they would need to match conditions elsewhere or compensate for less desirable conditions with a higher wage. Worker preferences over conditions would be factored into their labor supply decisions, alongside their other preferences. If wages adjust to match supply and demand in the labor market, the resulting wages and employment will appropriately reflect each individual's trade-offs (at the margin) between pay, conditions, and leisure.[8]

Pay corresponding inversely to the agreeableness of the job is a nice ideal. Capitalist labor markets, though, don't work like that. Tougher, dirtier, riskier, more emotionally draining jobs are very often less well paid than cushy jobs, interesting jobs, and jobs that offer workers more autonomy. People in the former job category would often prefer the conditions of the latter and would be willing to do them even if paid at the lower rates of their current jobs.

The obvious reason why labor markets function the way they do is that they are divided by qualification, skill, and talent. An employer's demand for labor is rarely a demand for just *any* warm body. It is for people who can do particular jobs competently—and, for a given pay rate, the more competently the better. Those who lack the relevant qualifications do not form part of the supply for that particular kind of labor. So even if wages rose or fell until supply met demand for labor with each skill—"clearing" the market, as economists put it—it is easy to see how different wages and employment conditions could come to prevail in different professions.[9]

If there were a calculable, predictable relationship between training and competence and if qualifications reliably measured that competence, things might be simpler. The cost and agreeableness of training would be easily factored into people's preferences about their jobs, and qualifications would make it easy for employers to identify who met their criteria. To the employer, the potential worker would be as knowable a unit as a tool in a supplier's catalogue. The worker would know exactly what education they needed to get a particular job and could weigh up whether the time and effort was worth it. The Lange ideal might then come back into its own: Relative wages would reflect not only the relative agreeableness of the jobs but also the relative opportunity cost of developing the skills.

Even in this predictable world, there would be challenges to egalitarianism. People have different capacities for developing particular skills, and an accessible education system can only make so much difference. Not everyone is cut out to be a heart surgeon or a long-haul truck driver. We discuss the consequences for income equality in the next chapter, but here we are concerned with the implications for people's ability to express their preferences about working conditions through market choices.

Here the unpredictability of the real world matters in important ways. Potential workers are *not* as knowable to employers as tools, machines, and raw materials. People with the same training develop competence to different degrees. Certification measures this only in highly imperfect ways. Beyond capacity, workers also differ in their motivation to work as the employer would like them to. The employer is interested in the results of work, but for most jobs, results cannot be explicitly contracted for.

Labor contracts cannot provide a fully enforceable promise of what employers want to pay for. The contract is for time spent under the direction of the employer. The wage pays for time, but the employer is ultimately interested in the *results* of an employee's work, which depends also on the employee's ability and effort over the time for which they are employed. But usually neither effort nor ability are fully observable, it is costly to monitor them, and the firm cannot rely on external legal enforcement.

This makes employment a *contested exchange*, as Sam Bowles and Herb Gintis put it. For various reasons, the results of employment cannot be contracted for explicitly, especially because much production is done by teams, often involving heterogeneous tasks, and it is difficult to identify the contribution of individuals. (Piecework and independent contracting are exceptions, but are impossible in many fields.) Level of effort cannot be contracted for in an enforceable way either—it is even more difficult to observe. What can be contracted for is time at work, under direction of the employer, within the parameters of a job description.[10]

This matters to the question of whether workers can effectively express their preferences about working conditions on the labor market. It means that much about work is not determined, and so not fully priced, at the point of transaction. It is bargained for among parties already in a contractual relationship—sometimes formally, but more often informally and from day to day. It plays out in employer decisions about how to monitor, discipline, and motivate employees, as well as employee decisions about how to work in response.

Terminating the contract is a move both can play in this game, and the possibility hangs over the bargain. This brings the state of the labor market back into the picture: General conditions of supply and demand for labor affect people's willingness to take the exit option. But, crucially, *the labor market generally does not clear, and labor is usually on the long side of the market*—that is, supply of labor typically exceeds demand at going rates of pay. Unemployment is a perennial feature of capitalism. If a worker can expect to quickly find an equivalent job at their current salary and conditions, the risk of job loss does not have much sting. But workers usually face much more uncertainty than that. Many may be reasonably confident about being able to find *some* work, while being very nervous about finding a job that matches their current pay and conditions. This makes the exit option costly and gives management an upper hand in negotiations about how work is to be done.

How employers use this advantage varies across jobs. They have to deal with the fact that they have paid for people's time and that those people are not robots or tools. Employees still have to be motivated to work. In some jobs, a monitor-and-discipline approach works. The employer keeps tight surveillance over the production process or its results and threatens dismissal if the worker does not meet the benchmarks. Amazon warehouse and delivery tracking systems are a pure example, but this strategy has a long history in factories everywhere.

Many jobs, however, are not as easy to monitor. Here employers depend on some amount of internal worker motivation, which tends to be undermined by aggressive surveillance and discipline. High employee turnover is costly to employers too—it takes time to train new workers and replace lost experience. Employers are especially loath to lose their most productive employees, even if it is not always easy to identify which those are. Since it is exactly these employees that are most likely to feel confident about finding work elsewhere, employers try to make sure they have something to lose. Most employers therefore use some combination of carrot and stick, the arts of the human resources department: performance reviews with the possibility of both promotion ladders and disciplinary measures.

All this means that wages are not much like the market-clearing prices Lange had in mind, representing an equilibrium in which people weigh up pay and conditions and choose from a menu of options the mix that suits them best. The labor market generally does not clear—there are unemployment and multiple qualified applicants for jobs at most levels. Pay rates and conditions for different jobs evolve over time out of the interplay of strategies in bargaining. Norms develop across professions. While the evolution of these norms can be affected by market conditions, it is far from determined by them. Nominal wage rates are famously inflexible and especially resist falling.

The position of the typical worker is not much like that of Alchian and Demsetz's grocer. Unlike the grocer, they are dependent on a single customer who buys what they have to sell. This customer has much of the initiative in setting terms, and the worker cannot be too confident of quickly finding a replacement. Some may sell more valuable wares than others and enjoy high wages and more autonomy, but even those are often dependent on a single buyer and risk losing considerably in trying to find another. Only a lucky few professionals are really in a commanding position in the labor market.

We Need Workplace Democracy

The case for workplace democracy follows from the nature of labor contracts as a "contested exchange" and the consequences of the fact that workers are generally on the long side of a nonclearing market—that is, it is generally easier for employers to replace them, than for them to replace an employer.

The argument for labor markets has been made from the Left. For Amartya Sen, "free seeking of employment" is a key part of his ethical case for markets, and he invokes Marx in making the argument. For Lange, "freedom of choice of occupation" implies a labor market, just as "freedom of choice in consumption" implies a consumer market.[11]

Both of these are arguments for the right of the worker to be free from assigned or forced labor. A labor market is compared favorably to feudal or slave bondage and to state assignment of occupation respectively. Neither argues that a labor market guarantees everyone their occupation of choice. Whether workers find their occupation of choice depends also on the choice of employers on the other side of the market. The right in question is the right of exit.

There is no way of efficiently maintaining a complex division of labor that would guarantee everyone their dream job. In our system, membership in a workplace, and appointment to specific roles, both involve agreement of the worker and the democratic organization itself. Worker-members are free to leave but not to be automatically accepted in a role elsewhere.

Workplace democracy is not in itself an alternative to the labor market, but to the right of exit it adds the right to a voice within the firm. Exit is not enough, not only because of the limited practical freedom people often have to leave a job or to be picky about job offers but also because the cooperative nature of production makes colleagues' preferences about work highly interdependent with one another. They cannot be accommodated in the same way as individual consumer preferences. Cooperative work needs to be coordinated: For example, in many jobs people have to be on shift at the same time.[12]

For Alchian and Demsetz, this is part of the rationale for regular employment relations: Someone must coordinate a team process. But without an effective way for workers to voice their preferences and have those preferences be taken into account, the coordination will happen on the employer's terms. Workers can only express objections in negative ways: by leaving, by quietly not cooperating, by working less diligently and energetically than they might. At best, collective bargaining through a union gives workers a seat at the table, but they are still usually restricted to responding defensively to employer initiative. In contrast, in a democratic workplace, administrators are accountable to their colleagues. Not only must worker preferences be taken into account, but they must be actively sought. Those preferences can now be expressed positively, with those working together also working out together how best to do the job.

Bowles and Gintis, who developed the concept of employment as a "contested exchange," argue for workplace democracy on two grounds: There is a moral-political case for accountability and an economic case on efficiency grounds.[13]

Liberal philosophy typically excludes the workplace from its arguments for democracy on grounds that it is part of a zone of voluntary exchange in which individuals are best able to freely pursue their own interests. But, as discussed above, because of unemployment, the boss finds any individual worker replaceable, whereas the individual worker cannot be sure of finding an alternative buyer for their labor power at the going wage at will. Because there is a relation of power rather than a relation of free and equal exchange, there is a liberal political justice argument that the power should be accountable to those over whom it is exercised. Not only are workers not inert "inputs" but agents with their own will, conscious subjects whose experience and wishes should be taken into account. Liberal arguments for democracy in the political sphere apply also to the firm.

Bowles and Gintis draw on Robert Dahl's observation that "exit" from a firm is often so costly that membership is, for all practical purposes, compulsory. When leaving one's job entails serious loss of income and stability, the government of a firm begins to resemble the government of a state: Because exit is costly, membership is not significantly more voluntary than citizenship in a country. In that sense, the same democratic principles that justify accountability in political life can be extended to economic life as well.[14]

If worker management were to fail to effectively organize the team processes of production, the accountability argument could fall flat: People might consider workplace despotism a trade-off worth making for higher living standards. This is why an efficiency argument is also needed.

Efficiency in the economic sense is broader than technical efficiency in turning inputs into outputs. It is not necessary for our argument that cooperative firms outperform nondemocratic firms in productivity. Other advantages may make up for some deficiencies in productivity. Workers may prefer less pressure on the job to higher income but be unable to effectively express such preferences in capitalist conditions. However, it is important that labor-managed firms are at least reasonably productive. If workplace democracy came at too high a price in terms of real income, the claim for economic efficiency in the broader sense would be shakier.

Empirical evidence offers little support for the idea that democratic workplaces are inherently inefficient. Cooperative firms perform at least as well as conventional ones in productivity and survival, and often better. As Gregory Dow notes, real labor-managed firms do not conform to the familiar caricature of chaos: Their members generally do not shirk work, fight over wages, or rebel against supervisors, nor do such firms quickly collapse or drift back into capitalist control. They manage to coordinate production and maintain discipline without replicating the coercion of capitalist management. Of course, we should be cautious about generalizing too far from these findings, since they come from cooperatives operating within capitalist markets, in which only those suited to particular industries or competitive pressures survive. Even so, the evidence sharply undermines the intuition that only authoritarian management can make production work.[15]

The intuition that democratic firms must be less disciplined than their traditional peers rests on the idea that participation will weaken managerial authority and lower effort. Bowles and Gintis point instead to several mechanisms that can raise productivity. Democracy obliges management to consider the social costs of supervision and the pace of work. While democratic firms still rely on monitoring and incentives, these must win broad consent and so tend to be less arbitrary and more legitimate. Legitimacy makes work less alienating and morale higher—conditions usually associated with better performance.[16]

Workers are also better placed than managers to gauge one another's effort. Peer pressure and pride in shared achievement can do more to sustain discipline than orders from above, since slacking off harms colleagues rather than distant owners. Profit sharing adds another spur: when returns go to the workforce, each member has a tangible stake in the firm's results. The effect weakens as enterprises grow larger, but even then measures to improve efficiency are easier to support when their benefits flow to workers themselves rather than to external shareholders.

A further source of strength lies in workers' practical knowledge of the labor process. Democratic firms give them both the means and the incentive to use that expertise to refine techniques and reorganize work. Innovations adopted through open deliberation gain legitimacy, and the direction of technological change is more likely to reflect workers' interests than the capitalist bias toward control.

How democratic firms respond to labor-saving change, however, depends on how the broader system manages labor mobility. The risks cut both ways: If workers fear redundancy or shorter hours, they will resist innovation; but on the other hand if the workers within an enterprise get all the gains from greater efficiency—less or easier work at the same pay—the benefits are not socialized.

Beyond the question of productivity—efficiency in turning inputs into outputs—there is efficiency in the broader economic sense. Capitalist labor markets systematically hinder the expression of worker preferences, especially given their tendency to chronic unemployment.[17]

We argued in the previous chapter that there is not a tension between worker preferences and efficiency as such. Economic efficiency, properly defined, treats people's preferences about the production process, working conditions, workload, job security, and more, on the same level as their consumption preferences. It is not necessarily an efficiency gain if a diner is able to provide coffee and lunch more cheaply in making its workers' lives more precarious by quickly adjusting shifts according to demand. The gain to the customers comes at the expense of the security and income of the workers.

There is, however, a tension between worker preferences and consumer preferences. In many cases, better satisfying worker preferences increases the cost of production or makes it harder for firms to adjust when demand changes. And though almost everyone is both a producer and consumer, the things we produce at work are only a tiny proportion of our own consumer basket. As a consumer, other people's working conditions affect what we can afford. Other things (like quality) being equal, we normally choose a lower-priced product over a higher one, and even if we care about the conditions of production, we usually do not have much information about them. The increased flexibility of employment at the cafe benefits us directly, even if we would be much worse off if the same conditions prevailed in our own workplace. Conversely, if it came at no loss of income, we might prefer to work in a place where we can come and go as we please, but if that was how things also worked at the workplaces that produce what we consume, we would be poor and frustrated.

John Roemer has suggested that socialism calls for people to engage in Kantian (or golden rule) optimization, rather than the wholly self-interested utility maximization of standard economic models. That is, it calls for people to act with solidarity and consideration of the well-being of others. It is of course wishful thinking to premise the system on a deep change of heart on the part of people everywhere. But the way in which decisions are structured can make a big difference with respect to the choices made.[18]

Our model structures people's choices in ways that make it easier to reach a balance between our producer and consumer interests. It does this by democratizing decisions about work and pay. Unlike many consumption decisions, these are choices that are properly collective. In production, there are so many interdependencies between people's preferences, and formidable collective action problems to reaching generally preferred positions on the basis of individual bargaining. Because workers are also the residual claimants on firm profits, they can directly make decisions over any trade-offs between income and working conditions. To the extent that superior positions can be reached, with higher income *and* better conditions, democratic workplaces are better equipped to find them, given their advantages in morale, mutual monitoring, and likelihood of revealing information about labor processes in an environment of trust.

Democratic firm management would not mean producer preferences override everything else, because in a market socialist system firms must still take into account the preferences of their customers and make enough revenue to cover their costs. Competing firms may make different choices about the pace of work, but they sell into the same markets and no firm can charge higher prices simply to cover higher costs. The trade-off between higher income and a more leisurely pace of work is put directly to the workers in each workplace. The labor board's benchmark conditions set economy-wide lower limits, preventing competitive downward spirals, but there are still meaningful decisions to be made above those limits.

Problems of the Democratic Firm

We just established the prima facie case for workplace democracy as part of a socialist system. But those reasons are not sufficient if democratic firms are nonviable for other reasons. Some economists have raised some concerns with workplace democracy that must be taken seriously. In our view these problems can be overcome, but they have important implications for the financial structure of democratic firms and call for a supportive banking system to be built around them.

At the root of these problems lies what Gregory Dow calls a "fundamental asymmetry" between capital and labor: Ownership of nonhuman productive assets can be transferred from one person or group to another, but the same is not true for endowments of time, skill, and experience. Both capitalist and labor-managed firms organize people to work with productive assets, but they differ in two decisive respects.

In a capitalist firm, labor is hired in exchange for a wage or salary tied to contracted time. Employment can expand or contract at the discretion of owners, though longer-term contracts often constrain this flexibility. Wages appear as a cost on the firm's books, subtracted from revenue and other expenses to yield residual profits. In a democratic firm, by contrast, the worker-members supply their own labor. The collective cannot hire or dismiss workers without altering its membership, and each member's compensation includes a share of whatever surplus the firm produces. Any change in the firm's size affects how many people that residual is divided among.

The second difference concerns ownership and control. In a capitalist enterprise, ownership can be divided into tradable shares held by people with no involvement in the firm's daily operations. In a labor-managed firm, by definition, both control and income rights are inseparable from active participation. They cannot be transferred or sold to outsiders.

These structural asymmetries have far-reaching implications for economic behavior. Economists studying cooperatives have long treated them as sources of instability or inefficiency, raising a set of objections that any credible vision of an economy based on democratic firms must address.

Perverse Responses to Market Signals?

The most familiar of these objections concerns how cooperatives respond to changes in market conditions. In traditional theory, a capitalist firm chooses its level of production so as to maximize total profit. Hiring another worker simply adds a wage-cost, without changing how profits are shared. The democratic firm, on the other hand, is committed to sharing the residual among its workers. It is therefore presumed to aim at maximizing income (revenue less nonlabor costs) per worker. Bringing more workers on board adds to both the numerator and the denominator of that equation: The new workers add more output but also take their share of total income. A capitalist firm expands until the value of the extra output from another worker just covers their wage, whereas the existing members of a cooperative firm have an incentive to expand only so long as the extra workers bring in enough revenue to cover their share of profits too.

Neoclassical models of such behavior concluded that if such firms were dropped into a textbook-perfect competition setting, cooperatives would react the "wrong" way to changes in demand and fixed costs in the short run. They would respond to a lower price of their product by producing more and to a higher price by producing less.[19]

This conclusion has had outsize influence in the economic literature on labor-managed firms to this day, in spite of its dependence on unrealistic assumptions. It assumes that democratic firms can easily adjust employment by taking on or expelling members but not at all by adjusting the hours that members work. It assumes a diminishing marginal product of labor (i.e., that each additional worker produces slightly less output). And the model applies only in the hypothetical short run, in which firms can adjust the number of workers but not the equipment those workers are using. In long-run equilibrium, with firms able to adjust all inputs, the standard model predicts the identical behavior for capitalist and labor-managed firms.[20]

These are not realistic conditions. In his landmark analysis, Jaroslav Vanek argued that democratic firms would be unlikely to adjust their membership quickly, and especially not by laying off their own members. They would be more likely to react to modest shifts in demand by adjusting the hours worked by those already in the firm, which would shift output and income but not the number of workers among whom the residual would be split. This made the "perverse" short-term results of the standard model fade away. Empirical research on cooperatives has found that they do not tend to behave in the real world as the early neoclassical models suggested they would.[21]

However, it is not unreasonable to believe that democratic firms would be less responsive to market conditions than capitalist firms in adjusting their workforce in either direction. Turkeys are not expected to vote for Thanksgiving, so it would be harder to lay off members involuntarily. Because of that, firms would be more reluctant to bring in new members if the persistence of favorable conditions were uncertain.

Capitalist firms also face severance costs in laying off workers on longer-term contracts—and there is nothing stopping democratic firms from offering severance payments to sweeten separations—so the difference is not absolute. But capitalist firms often have a buffer of workers on insecure contracts that can be adjusted at will, an option not open to the democratic firm. In our model, greater security of employment is "a feature not a bug," but we should acknowledge that, for democratic firms, labor input is likely to be less flexible, except to the extent that hours can be varied for existing members. Labor is more of a fixed factor, especially in the short run. Over longer periods, attrition from retirement and voluntary resignations makes downward adjustment easier. But labor mobility will be lower than under capitalism because people will have more say in their own separations. This has consequences not only within firms, but also for the transmission of price signals and the flexibility of labor allocation across the economy. We discuss measures for dealing with this below and in chapter eight.

More problems come with the financial structure of democratic firms and their members' stake in them. When the partial owner of a capitalist firm wants to exit, they can sell their equity and so recover the market value of their share in the firm's future income. For most large companies in a modern capitalist economy, there is an active stock market with enough liquidity that shareholders can quickly sell when they wish. The market valuation of a firm's equity reflects market participants' expectations about future earnings prospects, becoming an important reference point in investment decisions.

But a member's stake in a democratic firm—their share of control and earnings—is tied to their continued participation as a worker. In the standard model, they have no marketable stake to sell when they leave. (Some proposals involve a membership market, which we discuss below.) This means that individual workers have a horizon of personal interest within the firm: their expected date of departure. Exit may be due to retirement, a move, a career change, or a layoff. The end date may, of course, be very uncertain: it may come next year, in five years, or in twenty.

This changes the logic of investment decisions. A firm investing from retained earnings is using funds that might otherwise have been distributed as personal income to its owners or members. If it makes economic sense, the investment must be expected to increase the firm's future earnings. Shareholders of a capitalist firm can expect to reap rewards from the investment either by enjoying higher dividends later or by selling their shares in the meantime at a higher price reflecting the higher expected dividends. They favor an investment project as long as the expected payoffs are at least as good as they could otherwise get by personally putting their funds somewhere else with an equivalent risk profile.

Members of a democratic firm, on the other hand, do not get their share of wealth out of the firm when they leave. They will be entitled to extra income generated by the investment only so long as the investment pays off and only if they are still at the firm when it does. But the funds for the investment come directly out of the profit dividend they would otherwise get as personal income now. Decisions about the use of the firm's profits thus become a trade-off between certain income now and possible income later, with the possibility of higher future earnings offset by the chance that the individual member will not be around to get them.[22]

This may lead to divisions among members: between the young and those nearing retirement or between those whose skills or preferences tie them to the firm and those who have opportunities elsewhere. Those who expect to be with the firm long term will be more willing to invest, while the others will be sacrificing income now for a very uncertain reward. In general, shorter-term payoffs are less risky, and long-term investment will be more difficult to support. An economy made up of such firms will tend to forgo a lot of investment that otherwise makes economic sense. This has come to be known as the *horizon problem*.[23]

The other side of this is the *common property problem*, which relates to joining rather than departing a democratic firm. The net worth of a democratic firm is essentially a form of collective wealth held by its members. When members decide to invest with retained funds, they are collectively saving, since otherwise the earnings would have been distributed to them as personal income, which they could individually decide to save or spend. But when the firm expands, new members immediately acquire their share of this collective wealth, with an equal entitlement to residual earnings and therefore to returns on the wealth collectively accumulated from the sacrificed personal income of incumbents. This may make those incumbents more reluctant to take on new members than they otherwise would, or it could reinforce a reluctance to invest with retained earnings in the first place, leading to suboptimal employment and investment.[24]

Finally, the absence of a share market deprives the economy of an institution for allocating resources and managing risk. Capitalist financial markets, at least in theory, provide information and incentives to allocate investment efficiently across the economy—that is, to where it can bring the highest returns for a given level of risk. The same is true for a Roemer-style market socialism with an equitable distribution of financial claims. The parceling of equity into tradable shares allows wealth holders to diversify their portfolios and choose their own preferred point on the risk–return trade-off curve. Just by holding a range of financial instruments, the individual can lower the risk they are exposed to for a given return.

The worker in a cooperative firm, on the other hand, has a substantial amount of wealth tied up in a single firm, and it is the same firm on which they rely for their employment. They have many eggs in that single basket and cannot diversify away their exposure to their firm. The more democratic firms must rely on internal finance—their own workers' collective savings—the more the system lacks mechanisms for rationally allocating finance across the economy to where it is most useful.

The Membership Market Solution?

One possible solution to the horizon and common property problems is to make a worker-member's stake in the firm's control and residual earnings transferable and explicitly valued. In effect, membership would function more like a capitalist share—though ownership of these rights would remain tied to working in the firm, so that control stays in the hands of its workers. If a worker left an enterprise, for whatever reason, they would sell their membership right either to an incoming worker or back to the firm itself. If these membership rights were valued in line with the present value of the worker-member's claim on the firm's future residual earnings, departing members would not forfeit their share of the collective assets built up during their tenure.

Existing members' stakes are no longer diluted when the firm expands. The newcomers bring their own share of equity into the firm when they purchase a newly created membership. (If the firm chooses to expand its workforce faster than its capital stock, some of the funds brought in by new members might even be distributed as personal income to incumbent members.) When the firm reinvests with retained earnings, this increases the value of members' stakes so they can keep their personal share of collective savings by selling when they leave.

The membership market features prominently in Gregory Dow's *The Labor-Managed Firm*, the most thorough recent work on the economics of the democratic firm. For Dow, the idea is strongest as a response on the abstract terrain of the economic models from which the traditional problems emerged. Critics had presumed cooperative firms were stuck with particular "realistic" constraints while traditional capitalist firms were free to enjoy all the benefits of competitive capital and labor markets. However, in idealized textbook conditions with a complete set of perfectly competitive markets, there is nothing to stop collective firms from working on the basis of scalable memberships.

The problem, as Dow himself makes clear, is that the real world is not one with a complete set of competitive markets.

And a membership market is likely to be especially imperfect, because of the inherent asymmetries between asset ownership, which is alienable, and labor, which is inalienable, because it is available only as a flow of activity from a human being. The democratic firm must seek labor and funds from the same person, who must wish to both work at and invest in the same enterprise—and must have the wealth to invest in the first place or be willing to take out some kind of job mortgage. The capitalist shareholder is an absentee owner: They simply own a claim and need do nothing else but let the dividends roll in. The worker-member must actually work. The decision to buy a membership is also a decision to accept a job. And while managers of a capitalist firm, hostile takeovers aside, can generally be indifferent about who owns its shares, when a democratic firm takes on a new member, existing members get a new colleague. They care about the person as a worker as well as a source of funds.

Individual members thus could not be allowed to sell to any taker at their own discretion. The outgoing member has no material interest in the appropriateness of the person replacing them, only in how much they are willing to pay for the job. Instead, the outgoing member would need to sell their stake back to the firm, which would sell new stakes to incoming workers. Taking on new members would then combine the hiring search with the selling of equity. Job interviews would combine questions about experience and education with questions about how much the candidate is willing to pay for the position. Perhaps this is not so different from negotiating over pay, but it means that the value of a membership would not simply reflect the present value of a share of the firm's expected future earnings; it would also reflect bargaining over the value of the future work to be performed by the incoming member, with the firm interested in the worker's productivity and the incoming worker interested in the opportunity cost of their time.

On the other side, the prospective member would lack information that incumbents have about the prospects of the firm, which may leave them cautious and unwilling to pay the full value of membership in a successful enterprise. The membership market would therefore be nothing like the deep, liquid share market of a capitalist economy. Memberships would be rarely traded, and the prices at which trades took place would be specific to individual workers, given the combined labor and capital transaction.[25]

Salable membership rights thus create as many problems as they solve for the democratic firm. The proposal in this book takes an alternative approach, avoiding as much as possible any collective wealth accumulation by worker-members in their own firm. Finance for investment comes entirely from a public bank. This mitigates the horizon problem, because members no longer make a choice between spending their firm's earnings on investment and receiving them as personal income. It mitigates the common property problem, because members do not actually sacrifice income to collectively build wealth, which they might resent sharing with newcomers.

It is true that members can still benefit from firm-specific returns to intangibles like market position and customer goodwill. These are not assets that can be straightforwardly invested in, like capital equipment, so the firm does not owe a bank for them. They come from some combination of good luck and good decisions, and members might feel they have earned those returns to some extent, leaving some trace of the common property problem. They do not pose as clear a dilemma between certain income today and uncertain extra income later. But there may still be some elements of the horizon problem: Members who do not expect a long-term future with the firm might be more inclined to burn customer goodwill—with higher prices or lower quality—for short-term gain.

So although the external finance solution described below will much reduce these problems, there will still be a need for mechanisms that could compensate incumbent members for losses from expanding membership upon leaving the firm. But there are alternatives to the membership market that avoid its drawbacks. For example, there could be a time lag between joining the firm and receiving a full share of residual income and then a period after departure during which the former member continues to receive a dividend. More simply, the horizon problem can be dealt with via a severance payment capitalizing a departing member's share of expected future profits.[26]

As for the problems of managing risk within the firm and across the economy, external finance raises a new set of issues. How it is handled links the fortunes of individual enterprises to the stability of the whole economy.

Finance and the Democratic Firm

The horizon and common property problems arise from firm worker-members accumulating collective wealth in their firm, which individuals lose their claim to when they leave and which incumbents must share with newcomers when they arrive. If the membership market solution is not viable, these problems must be solved in some other way.

The other option is to minimize workers' collective equity in their firm. This was Jaroslav Vanek's solution. He thought that democratic firms should be externally financed. The firm's investment decision is then not muddled by individual member preferences about savings and consumption or by the risk members take on when they concentrate their wealth in their own workplace. All profit is distributed to members as personal income, leaving individuals to decide how much to save and how much to consume. Instead of keeping all their eggs in one basket, individuals save financially through the public banking system.[27]

However, requiring firms to rely on external finance raises its own problems, since democratic firms cannot issue shares to those who do not work there. Borrowing involves promises to pay definite amounts by definite dates, but earnings are always uncertain. Equity comes with no absolute payment commitments; its owners are entitled only to residual earnings, and so in capitalist firms equity works as a risk cushion. A debt-to-equity ratio of around 50 to 60 percent is typical, though firms vary widely in their leverage—not only because of different decisions about risk but also because different business models face different levels of earnings volatility.[28]

Workers in a democratic firm depending largely on debt finance would find their incomes—and the very survival of their firm—highly exposed to downturns in earnings. One argument for the traditional employment relationship is that the wage gives workers more security of income than they would have as residual claimants. The wage gives the worker in a capitalist firm a predictable income as long as they remain employed, though tenure of employment may itself be uncertain. A share in the residual of a cooperative firm means the worker's income can swing up and down unpredictably. It is not hard to imagine that many workers may prefer the certainty of a fixed-wage income, even if the riskier residual income were usually higher.

So it seems that an economic model based on democratic firms is caught in a dilemma. Either firms mainly finance investment from their retained earnings, hitting the horizon and common property problems, or they rely on borrowing, leaving them fragile and their members exposed to high income volatility.

Fortunately, we are not stuck with the financial instruments and institutions that have evolved to meet the needs of corporations and financiers under a capitalist set of property rights. A socialist economy may have a large commodity-producing sector and yet involve noncapitalist financial forms better suited to egalitarian distribution and democratic decision-making. That means finding a way to allocate social resources rationally, pool risk, and share returns, while taking advantage of the local knowledge and initiative of workers, giving them meaningful decisions to make while aligning their interests with social needs. The task is to design financial institutions capable of holding these goals together—and that begins with the public banking system.

The Investment Partnership

In our model, investment in productive capital assets involves a partnership between the democratic firm that uses them and a public bank that finances them. This is consistent with the socialist principle of social ownership of wealth, and it allows for an efficient use of resources to meet people's wants and needs.

Democratic firms are custodians of social wealth—not owners. The equipment and buildings they use in production need to be themselves produced with labor and resources that might instead have been used for other purposes. It would not be fair for these assets to be treated as part of the wealth of the members of the firm that uses them. Some kinds of production are more capital intensive than others, so power plant workers, for example, would be much wealthier than day care workers. And workers in the "private sector" would have collective wealth not enjoyed by those in the public sector or by those not engaged in formal work at all. It is fair for firms to pay for the use of these assets, sharing proceeds from their use one way or another—and since this will form part of the cost of production, it will be reflected in output prices charged to customers.

Furthermore, rational resource allocation requires that the services of productive assets be priced appropriately. Not only should their own cost of production be recovered over their productive lives (the depreciation component), but there should be charges to cover *interest* and *risk*. Individual firms are well placed to understand the technical possibilities of production and the present and possible futures of the market situation, but they do not have the wider perspective needed to say whether resources would be best used to expand their own capacity or for something else. A socially rational financial system selects investment projects to make best use of limited resources, and this means appropriately pricing capital and risk.

What is the rationale for interest in a socialist setting? Investment in the economic sense means adding to the stock of productive real assets. Resources devoted to producing some particular capital asset might instead have been used for another kind of capital asset or for producing goods and services for current consumption, or they might have been put to some noncommodity use, such as leisure. Investment means using resources now to increase income in the future. The interest rate sets a minimum standard for how much extra future income an investment project must be expected to generate to be worth the use of resources today. Projects promising less will be shelved. The "room" for investment is ultimately a question of how much productive capacity is available and unused for public or private consumption. This is a macroeconomic question, and the authorities will set the basic interest rate as part of overall macroeconomic policy, as we describe in chapter eight. Around the baseline interest rate, particular kinds of investment might face higher or lower rates depending on developmental, environmental, and other forms of industrial policy.

Investment is inherently risky because future economic conditions are unknown. But what exactly is at risk? At a social level, the risk is simply waste; it will turn out that the resources devoted to producing one thing would have been better used for something else. Either they might have produced capital assets better suited to the unexpected pattern of demand that developed, or they might have been used to satisfy more consumer or public wants directly instead of augmenting future production, or people might have enjoyed more leisure time instead of producing at all. In a market system of commodity production, this waste shows up as disappointing rates of return compared to what had been expected when the investment was made.

The financial system should be designed to minimize this kind of waste, but because the future is inherently unknowable, it is impossible to eliminate it. Holding back on investment because we can't be sure of outcomes would itself be wasteful. Ideally, the system puts a price on risk so that it is taken into account when decisions are made, but it should also allow for and even encourage risks to be taken.

By pooling risks and diversifying exposures, a financial system lowers the amount of risk to which anyone is exposed. A socialist financial system can take full advantage of this principle of insurance and of modern portfolio theory. But to make up for the equity financing that is not available to an economy based on democratic firms, we also need novel financial arrangements. The banking system must socialize the downside risks of commodity production, but it must also charge firms appropriately.

Under capitalism, equity finance makes it possible for shareholders to manage risk by building a diversified portfolio. In considering investment in new capital assets, a firm's managers can assume its owners hold the firm's stock along with that of many other firms. If it invests in a new plant making solar panels, for example, and it turns out that an unexpected new technology is about to make that plant's processes comparatively inefficient, that is bad news for the firm's profits. But for its stockholders, the bad luck is likely balanced out by good luck elsewhere in their portfolio: Perhaps they also own stock in the firm pioneering the new technology or in a firm that's having a good run in a completely unrelated field. Equity holders with a diversified portfolio are not worried by a firm's idiosyncratic risks—that is, by those risks that are uncorrelated with the ups and downs of the market as a whole. They tend to cancel one another out across a portfolio.

Investors are, however, concerned with the extent to which a firm's returns move with the business cycle as a whole. This cannot be diversified away; but some firms, and some investment projects, are more exposed than others. For example, restaurants might be highly exposed to changes in consumer demand, while grocery staples are "recession proof." An asset's sensitivity to market fluctuations is measured as its beta. Individual stockholders are free to choose their own level of exposure by choosing the mix of stocks in their portfolios and combining them with safe government securities. They will only be willing to hold high-beta assets if they expect these to bring higher returns on average.

This gives a capitalist firm a metric by which to assess its potential investment projects. Standard principles of corporate finance hold that a firm should invest in a project if its expected rate of return is high enough to compensate for its sensitivity to market risks. The assessment depends on estimates of both the expected payoffs on the investment over time and the risk profile. Neither of these are straightforward things to estimate. Average past experience on similar projects can be used to estimate the profile of future possibilities, but, of course, situations never quite repeat, the economy evolves, and there is no guarantee that the past is a good guide to the future. It is not always easy to choose appropriate comparisons against which the project should be judged: the whole firm, a set of similar firms, or a set of firms that specialize in the project type being considered. The metric cannot be used mechanically, then, but it provides a structure for bringing together data and judgment to decide whether an investment is a good use of resources—if this is judged in terms of maximizing return for a chosen level of risk.[29]

Can this metric be adapted to socialist investment planning? Ideally, financial arrangements are set up to take advantage of the ability of banks to reduce risk through diversification. They will enable democratic firms to invest in projects with a socially desirable level of risk, while avoiding moral hazard and leaving incentives for the firms to pursue efficiency. In the system proposed here, firms will generally have a long-standing partnership with a public bank, which provides them with not only finance but also advice. The banks may even have played an active role in establishing the firm. But it is possible for firms to switch banks, getting a better deal or a second opinion on a project not favored by the current partner.

A potential investment project—whether a new firm start-up or the expansion of an existing firm—can be analyzed in a familiar way. It begins with a cash flow forecast: the cost of initial investments, later maintenance, and net income (after other costs) from employing the assets over their useful life. The forecast includes a central estimate of expected net cash flows in each period as well as scenario analyses considering upside and downside risks. The specific financing arrangements make a big difference in whether the firm's members will approve investment. If fixed-rate loans are the only available financing, member income is fully exposed to the risks. Even if expected income is more than enough to cover interest payments, the downside risks—from subpar demand or cost spikes, for example—can be substantial. With no equity cushion, worker-members might, in bad times, find their personal incomes radically cut to ensure the collective was able to meet its obligations and remain solvent. Since the individual firm cannot diversify its way out of its idiosyncratic risks, members face the full range of things that could go wrong, from a shift in consumer tastes to an energy price shock.[30]

If banks can offer variable-rate finance, however, the situation is transformed. Different arrangements would suit different kinds of businesses. In some cases, a firm's payments to the bank could rise and fall with its income, cushioning members from short-term shocks. In others, the bank might guarantee a minimum level of income, insuring workers against particularly bad years. Alternatively, the bank itself could own the firm's productive assets, charging a rent that moves with industry conditions—taking on the risks of ownership while allowing the firm to turn a fixed cost into a variable one.[31]

In each case, the bank takes on some of the risk but receives a higher average payment in return. This transforms the risk profile of an investment from the perspective of a firm's members: Cash outflows to the financier are made to correlate with uncertain revenue inflows and other cost outflows. The protection from risk comes at the cost of lower expected income, but there is a lot of room for a beneficial trade. Firm worker-members will be more risk averse with their labor income—their bread and butter—than people and the public purse will be with their income from wealth. Further, because banks have a diversified portfolio, idiosyncratic risk has no cost to them. They need only charge according to the strength of the relationship between returns on the instrument negotiated with the firm and the ups and downs of the whole market.[32]

The price of risk in the system ultimately depends on policy settings and potentially the preferences of bank depositors. There are regulatory capital and liquidity requirements on bank balance sheets. The public treasury, as the ultimate owner and residual claimant on the banks, can set acceptable boundaries around the volatility of bank returns and discipline management that fails to meet them. But if private depositors are themselves willing to take on more risk with part of their wealth, the banks might be allowed to off-load some volatility onto them. They do this by offering alternatives to deposits—products offering higher, variable returns without the guaranteed principal of deposits. Essentially, these would be mutual funds, with customer funds pooled and attached to diversified groups of investments in particular firms. The holders of these funds would enjoy higher average returns but would also take on the risk of lower returns.

Forecasting an investment project's expected returns and assessing its risk profile relies on access to a wide range of data about market and production trends. It also calls for specialist judgment to draw informed conclusions about the future from historical experience. The banks will be in a good position to collect a range of information from their partner firms, and there could be more extensive requirements for public reporting of accounting and production data. As public utilities, the banks will be empowered to assist democratic firms with their planning and decision-making. Small firms, in particular, will not have their own finance specialists and will depend on a bank for advice. These financial partnerships allow for risk to be pooled at a social level, while still leaving incentives for democratic firms to value efficiency and seek better ways of doing things. Bank assessments of risks and expected returns are based on industry- and economy-wide benchmarks. Because members remain the residual claimants on profit, they have something to gain when their firm outperforms those benchmarks.

The fact that a firm's members may be insured against the immediate income consequences of losses does not let them off the hook indefinitely. When time for refinancing arrives, such experiences will be reviewed and factored into future arrangements: They may be assessed as temporary runs of bad luck, as a sign that the original forecasts were misjudged, or as showing that economic changes have made continuing the project unviable.

It is important that loss-making firms not be supported indefinitely and that refinancing terms reflect sober, informed, and honest assessments of future prospects. As discussed in chapter two, soft budget constraints deeply undermined the efficiency of historical socialist systems. When workplaces are kept alive despite chronic inefficiencies or despite demand for their products having faded, they continue to use resources that would be better used elsewhere. Expecting to be bailed out indefinitely reduces the incentive for workplaces to meet customer needs and adopt improved processes. At a macroeconomic level, regular bailouts can feed inflation.

The answer, however, is not a system without any emergency support for workplaces at all. Budget constraints that are too strict can also be very inefficient, turning even temporary liquidity problems into permanent insolvencies, wrecking workplaces that might have recovered or adapted, and wasting much that had been invested in them. Hard budget constraints can worsen recessions as dominoes fall and demand declines. János Kornai, the Hungarian economist who coined the term "soft budget constraints" while analyzing chronic shortages under communism, himself clarified that he did not suggest "that the hard budget constraint is 'good' and the soft is 'bad' . . . There is no general solution; one has to search for acceptable compromises in each case."[33]

Our system aims to make the critical financial decisions open and clear. It is up to policymakers to ensure that the banks are not prone to lean too far in either direction. The appropriate stance at a given time will depend not only on the circumstances of individual firms but also on general economic conditions.

Options for Democratic Firms

Though in our system democratic firms are mainly externally financed by one or more public banks, it makes sense to allow them to retain some profit rather than always fully distributing it to their members. Besides their physical capital stock, firms need to maintain a fund of working capital, because their receipts and payments are not perfectly synchronized and are uncertain to some degree. They need to be confident of being able to make promised or otherwise necessary payments to workers, suppliers, and their partner banks but cannot always be confident that the pattern of expected revenue will be timed to match due dates. Typically capitalist firms operate with a buffer of cash and other easily liquidated assets and can deal with fluctuations within reasonable bounds.

It is perfectly possible to operate without much of an asset buffer, if the firm has prearranged lines of credit or an overdraft with a bank. It would be quite possible for democratic firms in our system also to have a public bank finance its working and fixed capital along with similar arrangements to those described above. We discussed above how partner banks can protect democratic firms from revenue volatility but that firm worker-members might still have good reasons for preferring to maintain a cash buffer, which would give them some room to move without having to negotiate everything with the bank. One of the reasons we have argued that democratic firms should generally finance investment externally rather than from collective savings in the form of retained profits is that it avoids the all-eggs-in-the-same-basket problem. If worker-members have substantial savings tied up in the same enterprise in which they work, they have a lot to lose if the firm fails. But even if the firm's capital equipment is largely financed by a bank, worker-members still have quite a lot of their eggs in that basket because it pays their labor income.

For this reason, firms should have the option of retaining funds to maintain a financial buffer rather than disbursing everything to members. And once this is accepted, it is hard to entirely rule out internal financing of investment in fixed capital. It is not easy to draw a neat line between investment in capital equipment and in working capital. Expenditure on maintenance shades into equipment replacement, which shades into investment. The system does not depend on prohibiting firms from all self-financing of investment. It depends only on public bank financing being the norm for large investment projects.

There is also a good case for allowing former worker-members to retain a share in the firm's residual (though not a vote) for some time after their departure or to receive as part of a severance payment an amount reflecting expected future dividends they will no longer be entitled to. This helps with the horizon problem and also encourages people to depart the firm when it makes economic sense to reduce some jobs—whether because of labor-saving technical change or because of changing demand.

Even with most of a firm's investment externally financed, worker-members in successful firms will build implicit stakes. When a capitalist firm is persistently abnormally profitable relative to what would be expected for its tangible assets like capital equipment, this may be imputed to intangible assets like goodwill or intellectual property. Goodwill and other intangibles might reflect customer loyalty or something else that keeps the firm's extra profitability from being eroded by competitors, like a reputation for quality that competitors cannot easily replicate. Such things were never paid for in the way capital equipment is paid for, so there is no original value of investment. There might have been costs associated with acquiring them, like research and development or design efforts, but there is no predictable relationship between these outlays and their valuation. There is a lot of luck involved. The value of intangibles is estimated according to the profitability left unexplained by tangible assets. It needs to be valued by those considering buying the firm. Tangible assets alone would be a poor guide to the value of a capitalist firm with considerable market power, whatever the basis of that power. Intangible valuations are always imputations, estimates—until a firm or intellectual property actually changes hands at some definite market value, and even then there is no guarantee the intangible will work for the new owner like it did for the old.

Because neither democratic firms nor their equity can be bought and sold, there is no market basis for valuing their intangible assets. And yet a democratic firm might find itself persistently achieving higher rates of return than would be expected given what has been invested in its tangible assets. Some causes might be undesirable. If the firm enjoys monopoly power from some feature of the market in its industry, then there are good reasons for government to intervene or tax a monopoly rent, as discussed in the next chapter. But if the high returns are due to making a popular product or capturing lightning-in-a-bottle having to do with the effective way the collective works together, this should be welcome as a prize motivating firms to meet people's needs, either by innovating or just being dependable.[34]

But this is another reason that worker-members in successful firms will have collective wealth in the institution. This wealth may not appear as an asset on the firm's balance sheet like the financial buffer discussed above. It manifests as an expectation of continued relatively high dividends to worker-members, but it can be thought of as an intangible wealth just as invisibles are accounted for in the case of capitalist firms.

The common property and horizon problems then are back in play, though much reduced if investment in tangible assets is mostly externally financed by partner banks. Worker-members must share the expected high profits with new members and know they will lose their own share of them when they leave. This may make them more reluctant to take on new worker-members, to support costly measures to build or retain customer loyalty, and to willingly leave the firm when it needs less labor.

These may therefore be reasons to modify the standard assumption that only current worker-members get dividends from the profit residual and that all members share equally. Allowing former members to keep receiving a share of profit for some time after they depart makes the firm's structure more adaptable and eases the reallocation of labor across the economy. It also keeps current members interested in the future of the firm beyond their own expected horizon as a member. The duration of this postmembership entitlement need not be long—perhaps three to five years—and the size of the share might also decrease over time. Alternatively, firms might simply pay out a severance package proportional to a departing member's tenure as a member.

Conversely, new members might not receive a full profit share at the beginning of their tenure. (They would of course start receiving a wage immediately.) If their stake is not diluted in the short run, incumbent worker-members might be more inclined to expand the workforce. It should take no longer than a year or two for new members to enjoy a full share, however, and it should follow them (along the lines just described) even if they depart early to stop firms from taking advantage of temporary labor.

This is not to say that worker-membership should never be intended as temporary. In some industries where work is seasonal or otherwise periodic, there may be a good case for fluctuating membership. In such cases, however, the worker would need to be compensated for the unsteadiness through higher wages. The rhythms of these kinds of work could be synchronized with breaks in the education calendar, allowing for synergies between the technical conditions of an industry and the needs of a special part of the workforce. In such cases, the meaning of worker-membership would need to be adapted. The general approach laid out in this chapter is intended as a baseline from which such adaptations can be made to fit the special circumstances of different kinds of production.

Ours to Master, and to Own

The question running through this chapter has been whether a society can combine democratic control at work with the efficiency and dynamism of a market economy. We have argued that it can, especially if the financial and institutional architecture supports that purpose. The democratic firm does not need to be an isolated cooperative struggling to survive in a hostile environment. It can be a basic cell of a larger, coherent system—one where social ownership, public banking, and market coordination work together to organize production efficiently and on democratic terms.

One of the biggest influences on our model is the work of Jaroslav Vanek, who proposed an egalitarian market economy with production by democratic firms. His monumental 1970 book *The General Theory of Labor-Managed Market Economies* crystallized the conception of democratic firms within the economic literature of the 1970s. His approach was to model worker-controlled firms using the familiar tools of neoclassical economics.

Vanek's strategy was similar to Oskar Lange's in the socialist calculation debate decades earlier: he used impeccable standard neoclassical theory to make the case for a socialist system. And just as Hayek had responded to Lange by arguing that neoclassical assumptions ignored important features of capitalist reality, so did Vanek's critics. For these writers of the 1970s, the fatal weakness of the democratic firm was the incentive structure it set up, leading to the horizon and the common property problems discussed above. The implication was that even if democratic firms were theoretically viable, real-world complexity would restore the case for hierarchy, private ownership, and profit-driven finance. Capitalism's property rights, financial instruments, and managerial hierarchies were ideally suited to coordinating the complex modern division of labor—or so the new economics of property rights, transaction costs, agency problems, incentives, information, and finance claimed. That body of theory, born partly in an encounter with the democratic firm, became a defense of capitalism's existing institutions against the very possibility of systemic reform.[35]

A second wave of thinking about democratic workplaces came in the 1990s, as part of a burst of thinking about alternatives after the collapse of the Eastern Bloc—also the milieu in which Roemer's original model of market socialism emerged. Sam Bowles and Herbert Gintis (among others) turned the "post-Walrasian economics" that have been deployed against Vanek back in favor of workplace democracy. They argued, as discussed above, that the capitalist employment relation was one of "contested exchange," because what employers want from their workers cannot be fully specified in enforceable contracts. What they want is effort, but they pay for time. Drawing effort from workers depends on some combination of monitoring and loyalty, sticks and carrots—all of which are costly. They coupled the efficiency argument with a normative argument for democratic accountability at work, building a case for labor self-management.[36]

Yet by the 1990s, the stakes of the debate had changed. Market socialism and workplace democracy came untangled. On the one side, John Roemer was agnostic at best about whether worker management fit with his model, the best-known vision of market socialism. On the other, the literature on democratic management increasingly focused on cooperative firms under capitalism, rather than as part of a broader socialist system. This trend is exemplified by Dow's *The Labor-Managed Firm*, which brilliantly reviews decades of theoretical and empirical literature on democratic workplaces. Dow's career-long interest in the subject was sparked by reading Vanek in the 1970s. But the political context was now very different. The driving question of Dow's book is why cooperatives are so rare under capitalism, in spite of the evidence suggesting they are at least as productive as traditional firms. Because part of the answer involves the difficulty cooperatives face in getting external finance, he suggests they are better off mainly self-financing out of retained profits—the opposite conclusion to

Vanek's. Because the prospects for a broader systemic transition currently seem remote, Dow's modest proposals understandably focus on policies that would foster collectives within a capitalist environment.[37]

Here we have the advantage of imagining a broader institutional framework, one designed not to accommodate cooperatives within capitalism but to make them the foundation of a new system. We've just sketched the financial institutions and instruments suited to that purpose. The next step is to show how the state sustains that framework by shaping the wider economy.

6

What Does the State Do?

You stand in line at the post office on a Saturday morning. The man behind the counter scans a package and stamps it with a small emblem of public authority. The woman next to you is renewing her passport; another customer is sending letters for a neighborhood ballot initiative. Everyone's doing something different, but they're all interacting with the state—not as a power standing over society but as a means of its own self-organization.

The state arose in tandem with the first class divisions: to collect surpluses, raise arms, enforce order, and guarantee that those who ruled could keep ruling. Over centuries, it evolved in tandem with changes in the mode of production and under democratic pressure from below, but this basic form remained.

Under capitalism, the state has been marked by a supposed separation between "the political" and "the economic." Property and contract were made to look like private affairs, while the public authority stood at arm's length, umpiring the game whose rules it had written. Yet the state was never a neutral brain hovering above society. It has always been an ensemble of institutions staffed by people with social backgrounds and interests, embedded in dense ties to business, and operating within structures that privilege capital's needs. That ensemble can exercise relative autonomy from capital but mainly to manage capitalism more effectively—resolving crises, disciplining labor when necessary, socializing costs when profitable.[1]

So socialists have always had a double task: to contest the state and to transform it. Every durable egalitarian breakthrough—universal schooling, the eight-hour day, social insurance, national health services—arrived through public power, wrested free by class struggle. The question is not whether we use the state under socialism, but what kind of state we create: who controls it, what it is asked to do, and whose interests it is structurally organized to serve.

In a democratic socialist society, the state becomes the organizer of social cooperation. Our goal is a state capable of mediating disputes, conducting the politics that will persist even after the end of class society, guaranteeing universal goods, shaping investment, and stabilizing the economy, while creating the space for pluralism, experimentation, and everyday freedom.

As we've discussed, our system does not involve the comprehensive central direction of economic activity. Instead, it features a market sector of commodity production and exchange. There, people are free to spend their personal incomes as they choose. Worker-controlled firms choose what to produce and how, subject to their ability to at least break even and to finance their operations. Regulations will of course limit some activities and mandate others. For example, they will require firms to maintain democratic structures and meet wage benchmarks. Beyond these basics, which establish the architecture of the system, there will be specific rules around many things from carbon emissions to safety standards. A market sector does not mean laissez faire. But the point of a commodity sector is that planners are not generally prescribing what is produced and how—that is left to the self-organization of the firms.

Public agencies do not have to organize everything but *can* organize just about anything the democratic process decides it should. The market is not an obstacle to state activity but facilitates it. Without having to worry about the right balance between pasta sauce and frozen peas, planners can focus on specific gaps and problems. The gaps are large: A lot of things people value—clean air, safe drinking water, public parks—are not well suited to commodity production. Problems like market failures, macroeconomic dysfunctions, and the regeneration of inequality all call for coordinated public action. Planners have the capacity to take a longer and broader view of production than individual firms, coordinating investment in particular industries and regions wherever useful.

So our model involves a mix of state and market sectors like modern capitalism itself. On the one hand, this should be grounds for confidence. The basic structure of what we propose has decades of at least some kind of precedent, which offer many lessons. On the other hand, it might be asked, "Is that all there is? A mixed economy?"

But this reaction downplays fundamental differences between the capitalism of today and the socialism of the future. To call the new commodity-producing market sector a *private* sector does not seem right. This sector is quite literally socialized: Commodity-producing firms are not privately owned, but collectively run by their workers and financed by public banks. It is not an arena for private wealth holders to expand their wealth by exploiting labor. There is a commodity sector because this is a generally good way of allocating resources to meet individuals' preferences about private goods. So long as personal income is distributed fairly and workplaces are democratically managed and take into account people's preferences as producers, it organizes things the same way a benevolent social planner would *if* they had the relevant information and ways of motivating people in accordance with the plan.

There is also an expansive public sector because some production is not well suited to commodity production. While the market sector is shaped by the public, the public sector is shaped by the market environment. State agencies have monetary costs. They pay their workers, who need incomes for their own commodity consumption. They buy other commodities as inputs into noncommodity production. This means that public agencies face monetary prices and work with monetary budgets. To the extent that wages and prices represent real trade-offs in resource use, they transmit useful information for coordinating public decisions and plans. They help to prioritize public action, which draws from the pool of labor and other resources just as commodity production does.

This is not to say that prices and market conditions are formed by the commodity sector and then given to the public. Collectively, across its myriad agencies, the public is a massive customer and employer and, through the public banks, the main source of finance for commodity production. On top of that, it has powers to tax and transfer and to regulate. Public decisions have huge effects on market conditions, both because state agents are participants in those markets with vast resources and because they have regulatory power over other participants.

The state, given its control of the banking system, does not have the same budget constraints as a household or firm—though each individual public agency (except for the central bank itself) does have a budget constraint. With this power comes responsibility: Its constraints are ultimately macroeconomic. The state is a giant that must understand and moderate its strength so as not to crush what it grasps. Its actions must be coordinated: The many public agencies engaged in many different plans must be managed into overall economic coherence.

Though commodity and noncommodity sectors are intermeshed, the institutions themselves can be classified more straightforwardly. Firms in the market sector fund their budgets through the sale of goods and services. Public agencies, by contrast, receive budgets allocated from higher levels of government, ultimately coordinated by a treasury accountable to elected officials. These agencies may be overseen by democratic bodies at local or community levels, but their funding still originates from the center. We will use "market sector" and "public sector" to refer to organizations grouped in this way.

The public has a number of tools for action, some through interventions in the commodity sector and some directly organized within state agencies:

- *Regulation*: limiting some actions and mandating others;
- *Public production*: directly organizing activities;
- *Public consumption and subsidies*: spending public funds on commodities—either directly purchasing goods and services or subsidizing the purchases of others;
- *Finance*: influencing the terms and availability of funding for investment in particular branches of commodity production; and
- *Taxes and transfers*: adjusting the distribution of private disposable income.

With these tools, the socialist state has three main responsibilities:

- *Allocation*: shaping production to meet people's wants and needs, both by direct noncommodity production and by influencing commodity production;
- *Distribution*: pursuing a relatively egalitarian distribution of personal income; and
- *Stabilization*: macroeconomic management to avoid involuntary unemployment and excessive inflation.[2]

These tools and objectives are familiar to us from modern capitalism. What is new is the thoroughgoing use of the tools to meet the objectives. Capitalist states have failed to live up to the ideals of even orthodox public sector economics, largely because many state actions that would improve efficiency or equality threaten wealth and market power, and the wealthy and powerful have successfully defended their class interests. We do not presume that socialist society will be free of conflicting interests. But there are reasons to be optimistic that a democratic socialist government overseeing a set of public agencies will be in a better position to fulfill the promises of rational, egalitarian administration than even the most social-democratic governments today.

With investment finance under the control of public banks, there is no need to fear bond market vigilantes or capital strikes—a central source of capitalist economic power. Without concentrated personal wealth, there is no outsize political influence of the wealthy.

Most returns to wealth used in the market sector flow first to the public purse: Firms pay for the use of land and natural resources and make contractual payments on the financing of investments in the means of production. This capital income gives the democratic public a substantial flow of income to use and distribute. It will not replace taxation, but shifts the starting point enough to reframe political debate. There will still be differences of interest along a number of axes. But the institutional structure of our system at least makes distributional consequences more transparent and has more points of leverage for conscious public intervention than in a capitalist society, widening the scope for democratic resolution.

The Socialist Public Sector

It is widely acknowledged even by nonsocialists that markets are not good and are sometimes outright bad at dealing with certain important aspects of production. Markets transmit signals about wants and costs only through decisions about transactions. The ideal private commodity is a discrete package of benefits enjoyed solely by the buyer, whose costs are fully priced in. Then, a voluntary purchase signals that someone finds the benefits worthwhile enough, relative to those of other things they could use the money for instead, to compensate the producer for those costs, and profit-seeking producers bid for resources accordingly. The resulting market prices for resources factor into the price of the good, thus structuring the terms of buyers' choices. The shadow prices generated by a socialist system like Oskar Lange's mimic this process by presenting individuals with prices that reflect the real cost of using resources one way rather than another. In both cases, the ultimate decisions are left in the hands of individuals, who use the price to decide whether the benefits are worth it.

But in reality many products are not like this, with benefits flowing to a single consumer and costs neatly attributed to the production process. There are positive and negative externalities, so-called because they fall on parties who have no influence on the decisions about producing or consuming. Market prices will thus not fully reflect real costs and benefits, and markets will misprice products.

In some cases, products escape the commodity package entirely, because it is hard to exclude people who have not paid for it. Public safety and broadcast media before the advent of signal scrambling are classic examples of nonexcludable goods. There are costs involved in producing them, but it is difficult to prevent anyone from enjoying them. In other cases, there are benefits that nonbuyers can be excluded from, but there are also spillover effects that benefit or cost others. Education and journalism are examples of products with positive spillovers: It may be possible to keep individuals from classes and put news behind paywalls, but everyone benefits from a generally educated and informed population. Carbon emissions and other pollution are examples of negative spillovers: They impose costs on people whether or not they are the ones consuming the dirty products. Left to themselves, commodity producers will tend to underproduce public goods and overproduce public bads relative to what people want, because prices and transactions do not carry the right signals and incentives to profit-seeking firms.

A More Complete Accounting

Oskar Lange saw the ability of planners to take externalities into account in setting prices as a key advantage of socialist over capitalist organization. This was another of his jiu-jitsu moves using neoclassical theory against capitalism. The Pareto efficiency of a market in general equilibrium depends not only on the assumption of perfect competition but also on an absence of public goods and externalities of all kinds. Market resource allocation is inefficient—perhaps vastly so—wherever these matter, because it ignores preferences that cannot be expressed in transactions. Lange's answer was not to abolish the price system but for planners to adjust the price structure to factor in estimates of public costs alongside the directly observable production costs and to supplement individuals' demand signals from personal income with "a sector of socialised consumption the cost of which is met by taxation." He acknowledged that capitalist states had always provided for some public goods and that "much of this waste [negative externalities] [could] be removed by proper legislation, taxation, and bounties . . . within the framework of the present economic system." But, he argued, "a socialist economy can do it with much greater thoroughness."[3]

Capitalist public sectors are now much larger and more regulative than they had been when Lange wrote. Public spending is substantial and tends to be higher relative to gross domestic product in higher-income countries: typically between a third and a half, including transfers such as pensions and unemployment benefits. The public sector's share of employment is typically between a tenth and a quarter. Decades of "promarket" reaction never reversed the mid-twentieth century's great expansion of the capitalist state, though it limited its further advance.

This raises the question of whether the socialist noncommodity sector and state spending more broadly would be bigger still. It seems likely that both would be at least in line with the higher reaches of social-democratic states. But it is worth not taking this for granted and exploring why.

At about the high-water mark of social-democratic optimism, amid talk of the "convergence" between capitalist and socialist models, Richard Musgrave considered the question of whether a socialist society would be likely to devote more resources to public goods than a capitalist one. Musgrave was an economist who had played a major part in crystallizing the modern neoclassical paradigm of public economics. He believed that *in theory* the optimal division between public and private goods would be the same in a socialist and a capitalist economy. A capitalist economy would inevitably develop a noncommodity public sector, because public goods are essential but by definition not adequately provided by production for market. Conversely, an efficient socialist economy would need to organize the production of private goods in a way that would at least emulate markets in drawing out individual consumer preferences.[4]

The benefits of public goods and the costs of public bads to individuals could in principle be weighed according to each person's preferences. There is some rate at which a person would be willing to give up income for spending on private consumption in favor of more enjoyment of public services or of less pollution. They simply have no way of expressing those preferences through private purchases. Both capitalist and socialist systems would face the same challenge of collecting information about those preferences that can't be revealed through market exchange. These would instead be conveyed, however imperfectly, through a political process, and, as social choice theory reminds us, there is no flawless way to aggregate individual preferences into a single collective will. Yet finding some method of choosing is unavoidable, and again, *in principle,* any political mechanism for directing public production could be replicated in either system, just as a Lange-style system emulated a perfect market to direct the production of private goods.[5]

But *in practice* there were good reasons to expect the political process in a socialist country to settle on devoting a larger proportion of resources to producing public goods than it would in a capitalist country, even if the citizens in both countries shared identical personal preferences. First, Musgrave suggested that socialist polities would be likely to have more public provision because of what he called "ideological externalities." Public goods are available to all and so are inherently egalitarian. That they are organized by the state rather than the market is congenial to the socialist. This is the weaker side of his argument. The fairer distribution of personal income under socialism might in fact reduce the importance of the egalitarian motive for public provision. With firms run democratically by their workers using publicly financed capital, public bureaucracy loses some of its ideological advantage for the socialist.[6]

The other part of Musgrave's argument is more decisive. Socialist economies are likely to more completely meet preferences for public goods, because they do not have to worry about undermining the profit motive for investment. In both capitalism and socialism, there is a trade-off between the resources devoted to public production and those devoted to commodity production. Provision for social goods reduces disposable private income for spending on commodities, while usually providing the social goods for free. In a capitalist system, expanding the public sector at the expense of income from wealth may threaten incentives to invest, because investment decisions are left in the hands of the wealthy. In a socialist economy, however, the state has direct control over investment.[7]

In our system, the pace of investment is under the control of the public banking system. Any effect of marginally smaller expected revenue on firms' decisions to invest is easy to counteract. Furthermore, Musgrave's argument still presumes idealized political conditions. The limit private capital places on public sector expansion in a capitalist economy often expresses itself politically long before it would be expressed in a quiet, unorganized way through a lower propensity to invest. The threat of a capital strike, or of offshoring, is a potent deterrent to any policy that would eat into capital incomes—and it is a threat that does not arise in a socialist economy.

Ultimately, we cannot predict how much of the economy a socialist polity would devote to public noncommodity production. It is a matter for the democratic process. The trade-off between public goods and personal income is genuine, and where the system lands depends on the balance of preferences across the citizenry.[8] Assuming full employment, for a community with a given amount of resources, using more for noncommodity production means less commodity production and vice versa. For citizens of a democratic socialist country, a vote for higher public spending is also a vote for lower disposable income, one way or another. At the margin, higher public spending will come with higher income tax. Some of the noncommodity sector can be funded out of public capital income from commodity production (payments from firms to the public banks for their financing of investment). But the surplus from commodity production must cover a range of things: investment and income transfers, as well as the costs of noncommodity production. The alternative to taxation is to increase capital charges on investment, raising what firms pay to the public banks. But this would still come at the expense of personal disposable income—it widens the gap between wages and prices—and in an uneven way that increases the relative costs of capital-intensive commodities. Taxation is the most transparent way of allocating between commodity and noncommodity production and allows a progressive tax structure to temper inequalities in market-derived personal income.[9]

We expect the socialist electorate to maintain a larger noncommodity sector than is typical in capitalism and certainly one that is substantially bigger than exists in the United States, where the "atmosphere of private opulence and public squalor," as John Kenneth Galbraith put it decades ago, persists to this day. We do not think it is necessary here to justify every form of noncommodity production, especially where there is already broad agreement under capitalism in favor of public provision—the justice system, roads and other forms of basic infrastructure, and so on.[10]

Much of the room for growth is in Musgrave's middle zone "where both the private and social alternatives are present." Here capitalism often has a bias toward commodity provision not because it is more efficient but because wealth owners defend the rents they derive from private production against the public alternative. In what follows we explore this middle zone, explaining the reasons why a socialist state might be more likely to expand noncommodity production in certain areas.[11]

- Many intellectual and cultural products are nonrival goods that, once produced, can be reproduced at essentially no cost. Under capitalism, their reproduction is often artificially restricted by intellectual property law, so that the initial cost of production can be covered by commodity sales. Combining direct public funding with free reproduction is much more efficient, taking advantage of the negligible marginal cost. It is possible to organize this public funding along "crowdfunding" lines, so that each person individually directs a share, rather than leaving cultural funding to state commissars.
- Under capitalism, education and health care are often provided through a mix of public and private channels, with the mix varying a great deal from country to country. Rival and excludable, they are in fact not classic public goods, despite often accounting for a large proportion of public spending. Problems of information and uncertainty, as well as social cohesion, make these unsuited to commodity production even in a socialist environment with an egalitarian distribution of personal income. Both should have comprehensive public provision.
- Care work—for children, the elderly, and those with disabilities—overlaps with health and education, and faces some of the same issues. But here, alongside public and commodity provision, a third domain becomes essential: the household. As socialist feminists have long argued, public support for care work should combine public provision with support for informal care in the household. This calls for income support and the structuring of employment schedules to accommodate people's household care responsibilities, with gender equality as a guiding principle throughout.
- The efficiency case for commodity production breaks down wherever concentrations of market power develop. In capitalism, competition policy is mainly restricted to

prohibitions on collusion and erratically applied trustbusting. A socialist state should directly organize natural monopolies (like energy and communications networks) rather than trying to engineer artificial markets. There is also a case for the public organization of at least some wholesale or retail, because public intermediaries can counteract concentrations of market power wherever they emerge across the economy. This kind of market-making, what Diane Elson has called "socialised markets," plays an especially important role in our system, because of the problems market power poses for workplace democracy.

Intellectual and Cultural Products

Pure public goods are both *nonexcludable* (no one can be prevented from enjoying their benefits once they are produced) and *nonrival* (one person's use does not get in the way of another's). Nonexcludable goods and services are difficult to provide as commodities at all: They are costly to produce, but no one needs to pay to enjoy them. Nonrival goods, on the other hand, can be produced as commodities so long as they are excludable.[12]

Many intellectual and other creative products are nonrival, from pharmaceutical research to music, film, and games. They can be enjoyed by any number of people without leaving any less for others. The problem with treating them as free goods is that they require substantial costs to produce in the first place, even though the marginal cost of providing them to additional people is negligible. The traditional capitalist solution has been to commodify such products as intellectual property, making them artificially excludable, so that the initial costs can be covered with sales. This suppresses potentially vast Pareto gains.

A socialist society could reap these gains by publicly funding research, journalism, and artistic creation, and then making the products freely available. This can be done in ways that allocate funding to self-organized groups of creators on the basis of audience preferences, rather than having it organized directly by state agencies. The funds might be partly allocated according to actual audience (by tracking streams, downloads, etc.) and partly by giving each person an amount to direct to creator studios of their choice—public crowdfunding. This distributes resources on the basis of both track record and new ideas that capture the imagination. This sort of system would strike a balance between sustaining successful studios and individual creators and allowing for newcomers to pitch new ideas.

But while it works for art of many kinds, it is inappropriate for science. This is because most of the people who ultimately benefit from research do not have knowledge of the fields required to make judgments about the most promising avenues for research. Here, though, we have existing models of public research funding to build upon. The funding system can combine public allocation between fields with peer review–based allocations within fields. Universities should remain centers of research, given the synergies with teaching.

Applied research and development directly related to commodity production calls for special measures. In capitalism this is motivated primarily by attempts to capture competitive advantage, which is reinforced by intellectual property law that delays the diffusion of advances to competitors. There are very good reasons for encouraging R&D within workplaces. Much of the knowledge and incentive for innovation in products and processes will lie with the immediate producers. When firms are dissuaded from innovating because they know that competitors will quickly copy them, there is a net social loss. But there are models for encouraging innovation other than long-lived patents. A system of substantial public bounties and prizes paid only on public disclosure of the innovation could provide the incentives without leaving the innovating firm with a monopoly.

Finally, there is some justification for public funding of news media. Much of this can follow the same lines as other cultural products, with people using their personal allocations of public funding to vote for media. This allows for a pluralistic media that is state-funded but not state-controlled. But journalism has some of the characteristics of research—it is social research in real time and absolutely necessary to an informed citizenry. The audience does not necessarily have the information or inclination to fully assess newsgathering and analysis, since we do not know what we do not know. On the one hand, there is a risk of underfunding expensive reporting about dull but essential topics—local government, say, or trade news. On the other hand, there is a large risk of privileging analysis and other choices that flatter the sensibilities of an audience rather than providing truthful but challenging information. Public support of some media independently of the regular audience-directed system therefore has a role to play. It might be directed along the same lines as research funding, based on some kind of peer-review system—though here choosing the appropriate "peers" is more fraught. Ideally, this part of the media prioritizes honest reportage and analysis regardless of the political direction in which it leans. But care must be taken not to let performative nonpartisanship substitute for genuine orientation to the truth. Pressure to cater to "both sides" of issues can be almost as corrosive of journalistic ethics as pressure to favor the government of the day.

Education, Health Care, and Hidden Problems of Commodity Production

Education, health, and care services more generally cross the public–private borderline in capitalist societies. Public provision of both takes up a large proportion of state spending in many countries, but there is wide variation. Even in countries with expansive public health and education systems, there is often mixed production: Private health care and schools exist alongside public services. And yet there is usually strong support for public health and education where they exist. The classic theory of public goods does not really explain why. They are excludable, and so they can be produced as commodities. As personal services that depend on workers' individual attention, they are also rival.

One reason for their popularity surely stems from an egalitarian sentiment. Inequality has a degree of political legitimacy under capitalism, but that legitimacy rests shakily on the idea of equal opportunity. Education is seen as a pathway to meritocratic success in a capitalist society, and it is hard to justify denying children access to it because of their parents' lack of resources. As for health care, the life-or-death nature of needs, combined with the arbitrariness of their distribution, makes inequality of treatment harder to stomach.

If inequality of access to these services were the main problem, public provision would not necessarily be the answer. Needs could be met with cash transfers or vouchers usable with private providers. After all, food, clothing, and housing are also basic needs, but these are generally left to the market, with welfare systems (often inadequately) providing people with income to pay for them. In a socialist system with more equal income distribution, this specifically egalitarian rationale for public health and education would fade. But there are other, more fundamental, reasons why education and health care are not well suited to commodity production. These reasons have to do with uncertainty and imperfect information—issues that have loomed larger in analysis of market failures since the 1970s. These problems disrupt the chain between preferences and resource allocation as much as externalities do.

Uncertainty appears in two major guises: (1) about the future consequences of current decisions and (2) about how well a product will actually meet preferences. It appears all over the economy in small and large ways but in especially important ways in education and health care. With everyday purchases, we make mistakes all the time. We splurge on an impulse buy that we later regret. We buy a shoddy appliance or pay too much for one with features we don't end up needing. These are usually relatively inconsequential, and we have the opportunity to fix them the next time around. The benefits of the commodity form outweigh the imperfections. With education and health, though, we make irreversible, consequential life decisions about services that are very expensive.

Part of the problem is uncertainty about what we will need down the line. In both health and education, we make decisions with ramifications that come years and decades in the future. Education builds skills that last, but people cannot be sure about the future demand for those skills. Lifetime health care (and aged care) needs are extremely uncertain for any individual and tend to be concentrated later in life. Left to individuals as market decisions, these are financial choices involving the spreading of costs over a lifetime as much as they are choices between particular educational and medical products. When this kind of uncertainty is resolved because the future has arrived, we may discover we have spent too little or too much relative to our needs and our preferences.

Then there is uncertainty about the quality of the products themselves. For both education and health care, most of us do not have the knowledge we would need to assess the product in advance. We must make decisions about education before we have the knowledge and skills in the field with which we could assess it. Unless we are ourselves medical professionals specialized in the right field, we are not able to make skilled judgments on what procedures or medicines we need. In both cases it is also hard for us to assess the quality of a given service, especially in advance.

The problem is not only that we lack the knowledge with which to make a decision but that providers know more about quality and needs than we do. Where information is asymmetric, profit-motivation comes with temptations to cut corners in ways that lower costs or to overprovide services. The fact that users come to expect such behavior from for-profit providers can actually entrench the problem. If they cannot reliably distinguish high-quality from low-quality services, they are less likely to be willing to pay the higher prices that cover the higher costs of quality, making it harder for high-quality for-profit provision to survive in the market.[13]

Institutions for dealing with these problems have evolved under capitalism. Private insurance has long rivaled public provision as a solution for the problem of uncertainty about health care needs over the lifetime. But it runs headlong into the problems that come from combining asymmetric information with the profit motive, now with an extra profit-motivated party, the insurer. Insurers have strong incentives to avoid high-risk patients, design opaque contracts with exclusions and copayments that are hard to understand, and contest or delay claims, while healthier people have incentives to opt out if premiums are high. The result is underinsurance and gaps in coverage alongside large marketing and administrative costs that do nothing to improve care. The American system based on private insurance is a model of inefficiency as well as inequality: It is more expensive per person while yielding worse health outcomes over the population as a whole. But the same basic tensions appear, in milder form, in all systems that rely heavily on private insurance.

Comprehensive public noncommodity provision of both education and health care can be fair, efficient, and relatively simple, pooling risks across the whole population and separating access to services from ability to pay. Within that outline, the hard questions concern the appropriate overall level of resources to devote to each sector and the institutional rules through which these resources are managed, rather than how to cajole a structurally perverse insurance market into serving public purposes.

Care Work: Between Household and Public Sectors

Public services like health care and education necessarily involve work by professionals like doctors, nurses, and teachers. The question about their provision is therefore about the nature of the formal workplaces through which they are provided. Care work (childcare, elder care, disability care) is different in that much of it can also be provided informally within the household. Under capitalism we see care work done in all three sectors—

private, public, and household—with different mixes in different countries. In our model, care work is provided formally in the noncommodity sector and informally within households.

The reason much care work happens within the household is obvious: It is provided out of love and responsibility for our family members. But while it can be rewarding and meaningful, it is also often physically and emotionally draining. It takes time that could otherwise be spent on other activities, including paid work. And so it is also obvious why much care work is provided by people who are paid to do it.[14]

The standard model of consumer choice is not well suited to understanding care decisions. The notion of "the household" as a unitary decision-maker with collective interests breaks down here and socialization and ongoing societal expectations cause preferences to diverge along gendered lines. Nancy Folbre describes this as "prisoner-of-love dynamics":

> Most women would prefer to share care responsibilities more equally. But they are seldom willing to threaten withdrawal (or non-commitment) in order to achieve this. The pattern is evident in family structure. Most mothers would prefer the active and loving cooperation of a father, but if they cannot obtain that, they do not relinquish their children, but rather assume financial as well as direct care responsibilities for them.[15]

It is all too easy to exploit this structure of "preferences" and leave women to bear more than their share of the costs of care. For example, women will also "prefer" jobs whose hours accommodate the informal care they "choose" to do—and so will accept such jobs even at lower pay rates because they are "compensated" with flexibility. And so, across the capitalist labor market, women end up not only doing more unpaid work but also getting lower rates for their paid work. The fact that women feel obliged to step in as carers of last resort takes the pressure off the rest of the community. It also restricts mothers' options: The choice between a bad relationship and poverty is common in a capitalist society. Women are more likely to find themselves caring for elderly parents and providing care for husbands whose poorer health and shorter life expectancy mean they often need intensive support in old age.

A socialist system of care provision should be based on the principle that support for care is also support for those who provide the care. Change in the gender relations of care will require cultural change, but the institutional environment can help promote the cultural change. It can do this especially by (1) providing certainty of *quality* care so that women no longer feel the pressure of being the carer of last resort and (2) addressing penalties carers face in paid work. Though the system should recognize the gendered reality so long as it continues, carers should be supported regardless of gender. A system that aimed only to redistribute more of the costs of care toward men within each household would still be highly inegalitarian, doing nothing to share costs across households. It may also backfire: It is harder to encourage men to take more responsibility for care work so long as it still comes with additional costs beyond the work itself.[16]

The underlying problems are complex, but the system for dealing with them is straightforward. There have been debates about the priority of public formal care provision or the adaptation of workplaces to accommodate informal care responsibilities. Like scholars Janet C. Gornick and Marcia K. Meyers, we think that the right answer is both.[17]

There are three basic principles in our model.

1. *The costs of care should be socialized.* Care is expensive however it is provided. Socializing these costs is as much about redistribution across each person's lifespan as it is about redistribution between different people. We all need care as children, and most of us need it toward the end of our lives. Many of us will face disabilities in the course of life, with the severity and duration largely up to chance. Our need for care falls exactly when we are least equipped to earn income through work. When this is left as a private problem, we manage this

mismatch partly through intergenerational care and financial support within the household and partly through financial vehicles of saving, borrowing, and insurance.

Socializing these costs means shifting them so that we each pay them when we are most able to. Guaranteeing care as needed removes the anxiety, arbitrariness, and waste of needing to provide individually for uncertain future needs. This is the principle Nicholas Barr describes as "welfare state as piggy bank": It may be costly, but for the typical person this approach will shift their costs around their lifespan, rather than shift "their" income to someone else; it works like insurance.[18]

Of course, not everyone is the typical person. Some will have more children and some have none. Some will live decades in a retirement home; others will never get there. So the system does also redistribute between people and between households. The redistribution is egalitarian, coming from people according to their capacity to pay and going to people in line with their needs, and so needs no further justification in a socialist system.

Some might object that while old age and disability are not a choice, having children is, and so the responsibility of care for children properly rests with the parents. But the web of reciprocity between generations stretches out well beyond the family unit. To be crude about it, raising children has many positive externalities. As Gornick and Meyers put it, other people's well-cared-for children are "this generation's healthy playmates, creative peers, and well-behaved students, and who become the next generation's productive workers, social insurance contributors, and civic participants." Whether they have their own children or not, everyone was a child once and relies on the work of other people's children—and so, also, on the labor that went into raising them.[19]

The same argument also justifies income grants to parents and other carers to help cover the cost of commodities (like groceries) that come with caring for someone. Such family payments are discussed along with other transfers in the following chapter on income redistribution.

2. *Quality public care facilities should be available to all who choose them.* Everyone should have access to a good standard of institutional childcare, aged care, and disability care.

For childcare, this means an entitlement to professional early childhood care and before- and after-school care on an as-needed basis. Some socialist models propose including collective, nonprofessional care as at least part of the mix. Diane Elson, for example, proposes a universal "duty, on the part of able-bodied adults, of undertaking some unpaid household work of caring and providing for those who are unable to take care of themselves." Johanna Brenner proposes collective provision of care as part of cohousing arrangements or community-organized semi-formal facilities. Here, instead of a service organized by the state for households, a group of households cooperate to collectively organize their care provision. She argues that such commons arrangements, "managed, cared for, and primarily enjoyed by a group of people cooperating with one another, committed to ensuring its availability to future generations, and capable of engaging in democratic decision making about how it will be used," may be superior to "public goods delivered through bureaucratic, hierarchical, and inaccessible organisations."[20]

In our view, such semi-formal interhousehold arrangements have a place for those who choose them and can be supported with public subsidies. But a system of public, formal care is vital to make sure that everyone is covered. Some will prefer or need a professionalized system.

However provided, the cost of this care should be met publicly. There may be a case for limited user charges to encourage families to take into account the relative cost of various kinds of care. But if there are such fees, they should be payable out of the income grants received by households with children or with other care obligations.

3. *Jobs should accommodate informal care responsibilities.* Formal care is rarely a complete substitute for the care of family, especially when it comes to childcare. Parents and carers will still have major responsibilities. They must either be able to fit

these responsibilities in with paid work or be unable to fully participate in paid work.[21]

The availability of formal care goes a long way to solving this problem. Vacation care and before- and after-school care can bridge the gap between school time and work time. But many parents will want to spend more time directly with their children or may be involved in helping to run such care in a community-based program. Babies and younger children typically need more direct parental care. Children of all ages get sick and require home care, and disability and aged care may involve periods of high need for family care.

There should be paid family leave, mostly for the weeks and months after a child's birth, but also for other periods when there are exceptional care needs. These entitlements can be flexible: It may be more helpful to take some on a part-time basis and to split the leave over different periods rather than taking it all in one block.

Beyond these intensive periods, the working day should be adjusted to accommodate ongoing care responsibilities. Gornick and Meyers suggest:

- a full-time baseline work schedule that is reasonable for everyone, not only carers, with thirty-five- to thirty-nine-hour weeks and at least four weeks of vacation (a socialist society may well favor substantially more free time than this);
- per-hour pay parity for part-time work; and
- flexible working arrangements wherever possible.

These proposals are generally a good fit with the democratic workplace of our model, but they also raise challenges. A labor-managed firm is already inclined to make its work practices suit its members' wants and needs. But the model will still require central support and regulation. Care responsibilities are widely distributed across the working population, so it is unlikely that carers will find themselves in a minority. But it is still possible for carers to be more concentrated in particular jobs and for such jobs to face a penalty through the unconscious workings of the labor market if the system is left unchecked. This is a matter for the labor board that sets benchmark pay for positions across the economy. The board should also enshrine work flexibility as a standard employment condition, so that individual workplaces do not trade it away.

Pay for those on leave should come from the public purse, rather than the individual workplace—otherwise workplaces would have an incentive to avoid bringing on members likely to be entitled to it. But the replacement of workers on leave raises a bigger problem for our system. Under capitalism, there is a floating pool of unemployed and underemployed workers who can be brought in temporarily to fill in for those on parental leave. The system we have envisioned does not have this pool of insecure, unattached labor.

Large workplaces can be expected to have the spare capacity among their members to deal with parental leave from their own membership, reassigning people into particular positions as necessary. They would have an expected small proportion of their workforce on such leave at any given time and would build their membership accordingly. This is not the case for smaller workplaces, where each spare worker would be a substantial cost. The system may accordingly need to allow for some temporary employment, at least for such cases. It would draw from pools of people who are otherwise not in the labor force or who are generally happy to work sporadically or on a part-time basis. This could include, for example, the recently retired, students, and artists. Short-term positions could pay a premium to compensate for the sporadic nature and to draw in people who are otherwise not looking for work. To some extent such temporary roles could be built into training programs, though there may be problems matching training needs with care responsibilities.

Socialized Markets

One of Oskar Lange's key arguments for his algorithmic planning model was that real-world markets were nothing like the perfectly competitive markets of the textbook ideal. Socialist planners could simply direct workplaces to act as firms would in that idealized environment and so actually fulfill the efficiency promises of competitive general equilibrium. Our own model does not follow Lange here, and instead has a commodity sector with actual markets, for reasons discussed in chapter four. That means we must take seriously the problems of real-world market power.

The economist Joan Robinson warned that giving socialist firms full autonomy—including control over their own prices—risked reproducing the problems of capitalist market power. Too little competition, she argued, would allow firms to enrich themselves by leveraging dominant positions against suppliers and customers. Too much competition, however, meant no planning horizon and threatened instability: the "hog cycle" of oscillating prices and output all too familiar from the capitalist business cycle.[22]

Diane Elson later extended this critique, arguing that many defenses of market socialism relied on an idealized vision of competition. Real competitive markets, she observed, tend toward mergers, predatory strategies, and collusion, generating the concentration and centralization of capital identified by Marx, Schumpeter, and Kalecki. Competition, she pointed out, is not simply the opposite of monopoly; it is often the mechanism through which monopoly power emerges. But neither Robinson nor Elson ultimately argued for a command economy, an alternative with its own major problems. For Robinson, the challenge was to avoid both monopolistic abuses and chaotic fluctuations without reverting to rigid central control, which she also deemed unworkable as living standards and consumer expectations rise. She writes that "by and large, the freedom of the consumer to spend his money as he chooses may be accepted as the basis of the concept for a rational price system." Elson likewise concludes that for all the problems markets bring to socialism, they are ultimately indispensable.[23]

For both economists, the important thing is to understand markets as they are, warts and all, rather than to idealize them—and to design institutions to address the problems. Elson describes her vision as one of "socialised markets," in which certain critical parts of market infrastructure are run as public utilities. These utilities create leverage points for public agency to tackle the problems that emerge from markets without undermining the latter's ability to allocate resources to meet individual preferences.

Capitalist competition policy is mostly regulatory: banning cartels and price-fixing collusion, blocking mergers that would create dominant companies, and breaking up firms that have already come to rule a market. Only cases of natural monopoly—where economies of scale; network effects; or very high, fixed capital requirements make competition inefficient or hard to sustain—are traditionally seen to call for suspension of the commodity form and direct public organization. Even there, socialization competes with the artificial regulatory construction of markets (or pseudo-markets).[24]

Regulation and socialization remain options in the socialist system and can be more consistently applied. The line between unacceptable natural monopoly and acceptable natural oligopoly is a blurry one, and a socialist policy might well draw more industries into direct state management. In this "public commodity sector" most would still charge for those products that are private goods, but they would be directed to cover costs and not to exploit their market position.

But Elson's conception of socialized markets provides other ways to deal with problems of competition beyond bringing them entirely into the public sector. To socialize markets is to create points where public authorities can address problems that emerge from markets without undermining their benefits. The point is *not* to attempt to force real markets to work like an idealized textbook vision of perfect competition, which is neither a realistic nor desirable benchmark. The aim is not competition for competition's sake—but to keep producer choices responsive to customer preferences and to ensure that the fruits of social resources are not unduly captured by particular producer groups. At the same time, people's wishes as workers—their producer preferences—are as important as their consumer preferences, and it is important that market pressures are not so tight as to make firm democracy meaningless.

Here we consider three different domains in which our system can use public agency to sustain the benefits of markets while minimizing their problems.

Public Banks, Public Entrepreneurs

In a capitalist system, persistently high rates of return on investment that are unmitigated by volatility generally indicate some barrier to entry. Otherwise the high returns would attract competitors, who would erode profits by drawing away customers and potentially by bidding up the cost of inputs. Whatever stands in the way of entry, from intellectual property rights to economies of scale, the firm enjoys a rent from its market position, a return over and above the rate of return new investment is expected to receive elsewhere.[25]

A version of this principle applies in our system but needs to be adapted for the way democratic firms work, with investments being a partnership between the worker-members and a public bank. Firms are not allowed to reinvest profits beyond a modest safety margin of working capital. Most finance for new investment, whether by an existing firm or a new one, comes from public banks. The baseline interest rate is uniform, moving with monetary policy and adjusted to guide the pace of investment across the economy according to macroeconomic conditions. But around this baseline, the rates and terms for individual investment projects can vary substantially. A bank, informed by higher-level public policy, may offer lower rates for special purposes; for example, to encourage investment in a particular location or technology. More generally, banks and firms will agree to risk-sharing arrangements that lead to higher average interest payments in return for adjusting those payments according to variations in firm sales or costs.

Each firm must also at least meet benchmark wage rates set by the labor board for each job category. A firm's gross surplus for a given period is its revenue over this period minus (a) benchmark wage-costs, (b) interest and other financing costs, and (c) other input costs. Gross surplus per worker-member share provides an indicator of the firm's commercial success, from the perspective of its individual members. Some of that surplus will be used to pay above-benchmark wages. The rest will be distributed periodically across all members as their share of profit. Both forms of surplus must be considered together when comparing the surplus-per-member amounts between firms. If only postwage profit were considered, a monopolistic firm could simply convert its advantages into permanently higher wages for members. Taken together, these measures give a clear picture of how well a firm is doing—and, crucially, whether its success reflects genuine efficiency or the exercise of market power.

One of the key roles of the public banks is to actively organize the formation of new entrants into persistently profitable industries. In other words, some of the entrepreneurial function is performed by the banks themselves. They do not have to wait around for existing firms and workers with start-up ideas to approach them for funding. They can actively arrange the formation of new firms, with which they will partner. They can advertise for worker-members and advise them on setting up together as a cooperative.

This is one of the reasons to have a plurality of banks, even though all of them are ultimately owned by the public. While a single bank might face a conflict of interest in setting up new firms to compete with those it already finances, other banks would not. The system would also depend on critical financial information about businesses being public, not on trade secrets known only by the firms and their partner banks. This goes well beyond the mandatory annual reports of public companies under capitalism: It should involve a more comprehensive array of data, be much more frequent, and apply to all firms. The raw data would have already been collected by the banks and standardized publication could be more or less automated. Analysts within the banks could then use the data to track industry trends and look for areas where new firms are warranted. The surpluses of existing firms would be an important indicator, though not the only one.

This arrangement also helps to identify entrenched market power needing other remedies. If a firm persistently earns an abnormally high surplus-per-worker, this may indicate some kind of barrier to competition. The reason for that barrier could be identified, and if appropriate, regulatory remedies applied. If there are natural barriers to competition, the firm will be considered to be drawing rents from its occupation of a market position. If there is no way to remove these barriers or if other considerations make this a bad idea, there are other ways to transfer these rents to the public—effectively by charging the firm for the "asset" of its privileged market position.

For example, consider a firm that comes to occupy a dominant position in its market because of network effects—that is, when the benefit to the user of a product increases the more other users there are. This is common, for example, with social media or when a proprietary file format (like Microsoft Word or Excel) becomes a standard. It is difficult for competitors to build alternatives, because they must reach a certain critical mass before they can develop network effects of their own and it is hard to tempt users to convert before the effects arrive. Forcing a breakup of the monopolist here would undermine the network effects, which are genuinely useful to the users. But the position lets the company capture outsize returns and encourages behavior that takes advantage of the captive user base.[26]

Instead, the answer could be compulsory public acquisition of whatever the network effect is based on. In one case, this might be as simple as making a file format open; in another, it could involve transferring the network's administration to a public agency. In the latter case, some or all of the people doing the engineering and running the network could choose to remain in place while the organization transforms from a firm to a public agency. In still other situations, administration might remain with a cooperative, while the firm is charged a rent on the asset. In all these cases, the worker-members of the enterprise that developed the successful network would be compensated for the public acquisition, giving them a substantial one-time windfall while preventing the entrenchment of a source of private rent forevermore. This does not necessarily mean paying the full present value of its future expected revenue streams, as it would under capitalism; it means paying enough to reward the labor that went into it and to motivate attempts to build such useful things in future.

The arrangement reflects the fact that the value to users of what was built came partly from the software and partly from the interaction of the users themselves—an emergent public good. Just as tech start-ups begin today with the ambition of selling out to venture capital, this system encourages teams of developers to build something in the hopes of selling it to the public. But it also reshapes the incentives about what to build: Where venture capitalists are interested in the outsize profits that can be squeezed from a captive user base, the socialist public will pay more for networks designed in users' interests.

The Commanding Heights of Wholesale

Elson's own proposals for socializing markets, which build on Robinson's, tackle competition from a different angle: that of consumers. Both are skeptical of the notion that market competition is sufficient for people's preferences to adequately shape production and resource use.

> In the great majority of cases, choice can only be exercised within a pre-specified set of goods at pre-specified prices, which households are free only to take or leave, in conditions in which

> large resources are expended by enterprises to mould household preferences and to control household knowledge of product characteristics.[27]

As Robinson writes, "No-one who has lived in the capitalist world is deceived by the pretence that the market system ensures consumer sovereignty. It is up to socialist economies to find some way of giving it a reality."[28]

Consumer information about products is limited, acquiring such information is costly, and the information environment is dominated by advertising that aims to massage wants and maintain product differentiation. Cosmetic differences can be difficult to distinguish from substantial differences in quality. Competition is often channeled into marketing and advertising, which add to producers' costs without adding to value to customers. In any case, our ability to switch between products is a limited way of expressing preferences over what should be produced. It is "exit" without "voice."

Robinson's proposal is to have public wholesalers as intermediaries between producers and their ultimate customers. It is not that the role cannot be performed by profit-motivated businesses—capitalism has never faced a shortage of merchants—but that there is great potential for using the position of wholesalers for public ends. As monopsonistic buyers, they can be a counterweight to any monopolistic power that develops among producers. Instead of facing many disorganized, isolated buyers, firms negotiate with and sell to a wholesaler. A public wholesaler can be tasked with using its market power on behalf of households: "Market research, which in the capitalist world is directed to finding out how to bamboozle the housewife, could be directed to discovering what she really needs; design and quality could be imposed upon manufacturing enterprises and the product mix settled by placing orders in such a way as to hold a balance between economies of scale and variety of tastes." Public merchants can solicit and organize consumer preferences effectively into "voice."[29]

Such arrangements would in fact have their benefits for producers too, especially if democratic firms tend to stay smaller than capitalist ones. The system would not need to *require* producers to sell to the public intermediary. In general it is better to allow firms to sell their products directly to willing buyers if they can do so in competition with the public option. But that public option is likely to be attractive to the seller as well as the buyer. By negotiating longer-term supply contracts and using their own stocks to absorb fluctuations in demand, the wholesaler brings stability. By consulting customers about their wishes, it can provide producers with requested product specifications, taking some guesswork out of the picture. Some products could even be standardized and supplied by multiple producer collectives—store brands rather than producer brands.

Elson expands on Robinson's idea. She proposes public commissions and "network coordinators," which take on some of the functions of Robinson's public wholesalers without actually being directly involved in buying and selling. They collect and distribute information but leave buyers and sellers to take action on that information. They are in some ways a softer option than Robinson's public wholesalers, since they do not directly wield the power of mass purchasing. But they can be more broadly applied, working as well with services as they do with goods.[30]

One of the key roles of these bodies is to collect and analyze commercial data that under capitalism would be considered the proprietary information of private firms. In our system, this collection role is performed by the public banking system, and we have already described how the banks use the information to guide their allocation of investment funds. But this data would also be useful in many other decisions across the economy. It would be helpful to firms themselves in planning their investment and production to have data about the rest of their own industry and about their suppliers' and customers' industries as well. It would also inform consumer purchasing decisions.

But this data does not analyze itself. Elson's proposed agencies also do the work of interpreting the data and packaging it for particular uses. A price commission could analyze cost structures in industries and recommend benchmark product prices. Enterprises remain free to price as they choose, but the data helps firms to compare their own operations to others in the industry; makes any outsize gaps between costs and prices transparent and aids customers in shopping around; and can take other non-price factors into account, like environmental impacts. A consumer union acts to collect information on product quality on behalf of customers and feed information about consumer preferences to firms to inform product design. Network coordinators would play a similar role in facilitating communication and planning among groups of related firms. They could also incorporate the banks and other government agencies as a vehicle for participatory planning.[31]

Robinson's vision of public intermediaries that actually engage in commerce and use market power for public ends and Elson's vision of public information gatherers and networkers are not mutually exclusive. Both could have a role to play, each with its own approach suited to particular industries and situations. The specific mix is a matter for democratic governments to decide. Both extend possibilities for public agency and planning not against but through the market.

Elson's point is that markets have a real virtue: They allow initiative to be widely dispersed rather than concentrated in a central authority. Their weakness, however, is that they also erect barriers to sharing information and coordinating decisions. A socialized market retains this decentralized initiative—essential for any society that aims to liberate people—while creating new channels for "individual incentives to serve the common good."[32]

Shifting the Boundaries of the Firm

One of the most challenging problems in our model is the tension between workplace democracy and market power. In a system that mandates democracy but allows for contractual arrangements between firms, it is easy to imagine situations where collectives shape the boundaries of their firms so as to rely on contract labor rather than extending membership to those in less privileged market positions. And what is to stop the exploitation of one democratic firm by another?

When there are many potential customers for what a firm makes and many potential suppliers of the inputs it needs, it does not depend on any of them in particular. But if a firm is dependent on a single customer or supplier, that institution has power over it. For example, a small manufacturer that specializes in making parts for a particular car firm is beholden to that car firm. The car manufacturer might squeeze it by threatening to end the relationship and find a new supplier, and the parts firm may acquiesce because of the cost of finding an alternative buyer and retooling to make different kinds of specialized parts. The firms are cooperating in a supply chain making a joint product, but the workers in the supplier company have no democratic say over the process.

Alternatively, firms might engage people as independent contractors—sole traders or small firms—to do specific tasks, either on an ongoing basis or sporadically. Even if they can potentially find contracts with other buyers, they work essentially as employees rather than as full members with democratic rights. We can imagine, for example, firms engaging small cleaning teams as contractors rather than bringing in cleaners as members of the collective. What is to prevent Uber-style gig working arrangements from emerging in this system, with notionally independent contractors finding themselves essentially in capitalist employment relations in which they have little say over their working conditions because they are outside the boundaries of the collective that contracts for their services?

The system has remedies for these problems. First, the legal system should define workplaces in functional terms. Routinely buying the services of individual contractors, for more than a few hours per week, should entitle them to full worker-membership in the firm. When the work is a generic service that could be performed for a number of other firms—for example, cleaning or accounting—the workers might be organized as members of their own specialist collective firms. In this case they would not be dependent on any particular firm to buy their services, and contractual market provision may work fine. The labor board's wage benchmarks protect these contractor firms from becoming second-class members of the labor market. These wages, along with an ordinary profit margin, will be priced into service contracts, preventing a competitive race to the bottom among contractors and preventing the engaging firms from using contractual arrangements to cut costs. The legitimate use of contractual arrangements is limited to work that is needed only occasionally or for fractions of a full-time job.[33]

Finally, it is possible that many industry structures will look quite different when composed of democratic firms. When a capitalist firm expands its workforce, it need only pay the going wage, but when a democratic firm expands, it also shares profits with the newcomers. Also, since it is likely to be harder for a democratic firm to downsize, it may be more cautious in expanding in the first place. So long as economies of scale remain to be exploited, the gains to expansion may outweigh these considerations. But it seems less likely that democratic firms would grow into very large corporations over many sites. Once economies of scale have been exhausted at particular sites, an industry's expansion is more likely to happen through the banks financing new democratic workplaces at new locations.

For his model of market socialism, with a large commodity sector of democratic firms, Alec Nove argues that large enterprises may warrant public ownership not only when competition is lacking, but also because of their sheer size. "Even when there is no monopoly, it is hard to envisage giants of the size of a socialist Du Pont, or Shell, being meaningfully 'self-managed' by the workforce," he writes. But Nove also notes that the structure and size of firms are not determined only by the technical aspects of their production process. It is not the case that under capitalism a Du Pont or a Shell reaches its enormous scale because production technology requires it. If a firm owns scores of factories producing a wide variety of goods, its size clearly derives from corporate strategy and consolidation, not from any need to house its activities "under one roof."[34]

This is not to say that a hundred separate factories would be just as efficient if they were all separate enterprises. Some of what makes a large, multisite enterprise successful involves information and the management of uncertainty. But tangled up in that, of course, is that very large firms tend to occupy positions of considerable market power.

A socialist system has other potential ways of replicating the informational and risk management advantages of large corporations while maintaining democracy at the workplace level.[35] It can use tools like those proposed by Joan Robinson and Diane Elson. One option would be for a public organization to act as a hub enterprise, buying the products of a number of separate democratic firms and reselling them, deliberately balancing the problems of competition and cooperation. Just as Robinson imagines public wholesalers doing, the organization could standardize the product and put in orders to the multiple suppliers—potentially selling them under its own brand. Alternatively, along the lines of the Elson "network coordinator" model, the hub could be a federation collectively run by the democratic firms themselves. In either case, the hub would also be connected to associated public banks to coordinate investment across the industry.

All of these possibilities would need to be fleshed out and adapted to circumstances by the government, banks, and cooperative enterprises of the day. But clearly there are many ways in which the boundaries of firms might form quite differently in our system than they do under capitalism—and those boundaries will often blur the public–private divide.

Workplace Democracy in the Public Sector

Our discussion of workplace democracy in the previous chapter focused on the commodity-producing firm. In that setting, the producer preferences of worker-members meet the preferences of their customers through the markets for their products. Those customers have the choice of alternative products made in other workplaces, so their wants must factor into the decision-making of the worker-members, along with their own preferences as producers. Collective firms must also secure agreements with public banks to finance their investments—which is to say they must justify using social resources. Both these things limit workplace-level democratic decision-making, but constraints are inevitable in any complex division of labor.

The point of workplace democracy is to give effective voice to people's preferences about how they work, which is at least as important to their daily life as their consumption outside of work. Under capitalism, these preferences can usually only be expressed imperfectly through the possibility of leaving a job. This is a limited form of expression, especially when the labor market is macroeconomically managed to prevent it from becoming too tight, so that most workers bargain from a position of weakness.

The context is very different in the noncommodity public sector where there is no market for the products provided. The state might be seen as a single "buyer" for services "sold" by the workers of an agency, but neither side has alternative transaction partners. It is possible to imagine cases in which a government department might have competing provider collectives bid for contracts—say, for garbage collection—but in such cases the government would have monopsonistic power as the single buyer, placing provider collectives at their mercy, without real negotiating power.

Contract models for public service provision under capitalism often leave workers in the sector especially disempowered: Job security is limited by the length of the contract cycle, workers have little capacity to bargain over funding, and nonrenewal is a constant threat. On the other hand, if worker collectives have security as *the* designated providers of a public service *and* autonomy over how to provide it, there are no checks to their producer interests. They are monopolists, without effective mechanisms to ensure they are responsive to the needs they are supposed to meet or to ensure they use social resources efficiently.

In an ideal world, perhaps, selfless public servants would always put the quality of the services they provide above their producer interests. But it would be unfair to hold them to that standard. It would be just as much a mistake to picture them as lazy pigs at the trough as right-wing critics of state workers often do. Many in today's public sector go above and beyond what is expected of them because they are dedicated to the services they provide, and public sector unions have often defended the integrity of those services—not only their members' direct material interests.

Still, conflicts of interest can arise between those who provide services and those who rely on them. Most of those who would welcome teacher-run schools would blanch at police-run policing. But many of the differences of interest that need to be managed will be mundane matters and not great issues of principle: Alec Nove gives the example of train workers who would prefer to limit night shifts, versus theatergoers in need of a way home.[36]

One possibility is to simply default back to familiar capitalist-style employment relations in the noncommodity public sector. There would still be two extra safeguards for worker interests here. First, they would be covered by the wage and condition benchmarks—which would be more robust than minimum entitlements under capitalism—determined by the labor board just as commodity sector workers are. Second, they would be protected by the possibility of exit. If work in the democratic collectives of the commodity sector were substantially more attractive than work in the public sector, workers could vote with their feet, forcing the public as employer to match pay and conditions elsewhere. (Since worker-members in the commodity sector also get a dividend share from any profit their firm makes, wages in the public sector would need to be higher—though a guaranteed wage boost is worth more to most than an uncertain dividend fluctuating around the same amount.)

But the possibility of exit is limited by the fact that workers' professional skills will be tailored to the sector in which they work. A teacher, doctor, or nurse, for example, cannot migrate to equivalent positions in the commodity sector if education and medicine is organized within the noncommodity sector. Individuals are trapped by their own specialization.

The answer is to support public sector unions with certain codetermination rights. Since workers in these sectors don't control production directly, their unions must persist as independent organizations. Unions representing the relevant workforces would have guaranteed bargaining rights, ensuring that high-level decisions reflect the experience of those delivering services while ultimate authority remains with elected officials.

The principle is that worker influence should be real without displacing democratic accountability. For example, the public health system and the education system would each be governed at the top by departments answerable to the elected national government. There is a role for union representation here, but workers should not have the determining say over policy or funding. At the level of the individual workplace—the individual hospital, clinic, or school—unions and community committees would share structured roles in consultation and oversight within the budgets and policy frameworks determined democratically at higher levels.

The appropriate mix of representation at each level may be different for different kinds of service and even for different kinds of decision with a service. For example, it may be appropriate for community representatives on a hospital board to leave decisions about shift rosters to workers.

The allocation of funding across the noncommodity sector must come from the top, with ultimate oversight from the elected government. Broad decisions about the services to be provided must also be made from the top. The top-level policymakers may well devolve some decisions about both budget allocation and services to lower levels, but it is the prerogative of higher levels to determine the level at which those decisions are made. For example, government may decide that a standard curriculum should apply across the education system, or it may allow for variations at the regional or even school level. The Department of Health may determine protocols for prioritizing funding across medical procedures at a central level or devolve some of this decision-making to lower levels.

The important question for our purposes here is where worker representation should play a role. For broad policy decisions like school curriculum or medical procedure prioritization, professionals play an essential role as expert advisers—but this is quite different from representing their producer interests as workers. Police should not have final say over what constitutes appropriate use of force, and teachers should not have the final say over the curriculum—though in both cases their expertise is helpful. Similarly, the workforce of a particular branch of the public sector cannot determine how much funding it should be allocated—there will always be more that could be done with more funding. There are limits to the resources available, and the allocation of resources can only be done at higher levels weighing up trade-offs between different branches—with the ultimate constraint being democratic decisions about how much should be allocated to noncommodity production as a whole.

But these bigger-picture decisions on funding envelopes and the form of services do have an impact on working conditions. A change to the curriculum, for example, comes with workload implications, as teachers must plan lessons and build class materials. Decisions on medical procedure priorities have implications for the rosters of nurses and doctors and for which specialists are employed. Workplace democracy is meaningless if it must take both service parameters and funding envelopes as given, without any collective bargaining.

Ultimately, the state in our model is neither a distant nightwatchman nor an all-controlling central planner. Its role is to shape the overall framework: to set priorities; coordinate across sectors; and align decisions made by individual firms, public agencies, and national institutions. The state's agency is exercised not against markets but through them, ensuring that decentralized decisions add up to social priorities.

With this architecture in place, the next part of the book turns to the two remaining pillars of a democratic socialist economy. Chapter seven examines the question that markets cannot settle and planning cannot avoid: what to equalize. Because labor cannot be socialized in the way land and capital can, inequalities of capacity, ability, and circumstance remain—and so must the institutions that determine how income, risk, and opportunity are shared across the life-course. Chapter eight then turns to macroeconomic issues and the constraints of an open economy. These areas call for forms of democratic control different from the governance of firms and provide the foundations for long-term planning and collective security.

Taken together, these chapters complete the institutional picture begun here: a system in which democratic firms, public services, and macroeconomic institutions operate within a coherent framework that protects both equality and stability. The task now is to understand how that framework distributes life chances and how it enables a society to steer its economy deliberately.

7

Income, Equality, and Housing

Your child was born at a public hospital on the same day as another baby down the hall. From the start, both lives were shaped by the same public institutions.

Because they were born in a socialist society, the children grew up with the same excellent public schools, the same quality childcare, and the same access to health care, safe neighborhoods, and reliable housing. They were free from the disparities of your youth, the kind that emerge early on and often never close.

But even in this society, which has evened out the playing field almost entirely, some differences remain. Your child struggles with a chronic condition and finds certain kinds of work harder, no matter how much support is available. The other child takes to reading quickly, seems naturally coordinated, and picks up new tasks without much coaching.

None of this is anyone's fault. It's just the part of the lottery of birth that no amount of equal public provision can fully erase. And it matters. When both children grow into adults and enter the world of work, they won't bring identical capacities with them. One will be able to do certain jobs more easily or to work longer hours without strain; the other will have to make different choices.

Labor is one resource a socialist society can't socialize. People arrive in the world with different abilities and different strokes of luck. And unless we consciously decide how to handle those differences, they will turn into differences in income—even in a world that has eliminated capitalist wealth, privilege, and social advantage.

So we're still left with a basic question: If everyone starts from the same social foundation, but not everyone can do the same work, what does a fair distribution of income look like?

Philosopher Ronald Dworkin once remarked on an irony about the relationship between markets and distributive equality. It is because of market valuation that we have concepts of income and wealth as quantifiable aggregates that can be divided fairly in the first place. But markets tend to generate and reproduce the very inequalities they make easy to quantify.[1]

Without prices reflecting real trade-offs in resource use, it would be hard to define equality of income. A bundle of products would be just a collection of diverse things. If everybody got the same standard bundle, then sure, the bundles would be equal. But as we argued in chapter three, everyone is much better off when their individual preferences direct the use of resources to make consumption bundles tailored especially for them. If John goes through three pots of coffee on a slow day and Jane gags at the smell of the stuff, no egalitarian would say the goal should be to make their coffee consumption more equal. But we can compare what they have to spend on coffee, shampoo, garden gnomes, rare books, power tools, and everything else.

With markets, though, come inequalities. One big reason for unequal outcomes is that people come to the market with differences in what they have to sell—different *endowments*. In our model, most wealth is socialized. Land and natural resources are publicly owned and leased to the firms that use them. Investment in the capital stock is financed by public banks, which receive the interest income. For this reason, the system will be much more egalitarian than capitalism, even before extra policy measures aimed at deliberate redistribution are taken into account. Modest differences in personal wealth may emerge out of differences in savings from income, but it will be hard for wealth to concentrate, especially if it largely can't be transmitted between generations.

However, the most important resource of all—labor—cannot be socialized. Time in the day is already evenly distributed: We each have the same twenty-four hours. But the value of our time, attention, and effort is not. We each have different capacities to work. Not only will those two babies born just down the hall from each other have different abilities but all of us have different abilities at different stages of our lives. Childhood, education, and retirement occupy significant portions of our lifespan, as do responsibilities like childbearing and childrearing.

So most of the questions around inequality and redistribution in our system revolve around labor income: first, the relationship between work and income and what that means for those with less capacity to work and, second, the distribution of income among those who are working.

Equality of What?

We said no egalitarian would want to equalize John and Jane's coffee consumption. What, though, does the egalitarian want to equalize?

Modern ideals of equality have always had to deal with the fact that the goods to be distributed are cooperatively produced. They do not simply fall out of the sky ready to be divided up. So, distribution is a more difficult problem than serving evenly cut pieces of a birthday cake. One reason that absolute equality of personal income is not the answer is that work costs the laborer; they pay in effort, stress, or time away from things they would rather be doing, and this cost needs to be taken into account when determining what counts as an "equal" package of goods.

This might suggest equal "utility" as the goal, with the disutility of work or of disabilities compensated with utility from more personal income. Utilitarian arguments for egalitarianism could rest on the idea that income itself is subject to diminishing marginal utility, so that redistributing from a millionaire to a pauper hurts the former less than it helps the latter.

However, the idea of quantifying utility, and especially of making quantitative comparisons of the utility enjoyed by different people, comes with some tricky conceptual headaches. Even if some reliable way of measuring the happiness of different people could be found, trying to equalize it could have perverse implications. A person's subjective welfare depends on much more than the products they receive and the work they do. Some people are temperamentally more easily satisfied than others. Do we give more to the person with expensive tastes, who requires the finest wine, food, and surroundings to feel at home in the world and to whom labor feels like an unbearable imposition? Do we give less to the jolly pauper who has learned to work hard, lower their expectations, and be content with little?[2]

But if neither income nor utility are the right things to equalize, what is? One influential answer was put forward by socialist economist Duncan Foley: Distribution is equitable if each person is at least as happy with what they get as they would be with what anyone else gets. "What a person gets" here is understood not only as the products the person consumes but their whole economic situation including how much they had to work to get those products.[3]

If Anjali works a lot and ends up with enough income to take plenty of vacations and build a deck in her yard and Arun has a more laid-back and frugal lifestyle, there is no problem of inequality if these simply reflect different choices, and either one of them *could* have the other's life if they decided differently. Foley's test doesn't require any objective measure of utility or satisfaction.[4]

Even so, this form of egalitarianism is open to the objection that people have different needs. Some students require more resources than others to reach their educational potential. And some differences in capacity run much deeper than that. Disability and sickness call for extra care and accommodations, and people in such conditions are often less able to work. If you're easily exhausted and you need an expensive wheelchair to get around, it's cold comfort to say that if you *could* work long hours, you'd be able to afford as much as anyone else. Equalizing resources alone would leave many people less well off in arbitrary and unfair ways.

Amartya Sen's "capabilities approach" is one of the great rivals to resource equality in modern egalitarian philosophy. This is the view that the equality that matters is the equal right to the means for a flourishing life. Sen argues that flourishing itself can neither be guaranteed nor forced by policy. Society guarantees resources; it is up to individuals to use them. But it will often take an *unequal* application of resources to bring everybody closer to this equal standard. This is, more or less, Marx's "to each according to their needs."[5]

All of this might seem like a frustrating, confusing mess. Given all the complexity of debates about what we should be equalizing, how can we pick one of these options and use it as a yardstick to see how well our economic model measures up to egalitarian ideals?

The good news is that these views are not as far apart as they might appear at first glance. There are tricky cases in which we might get different results depending on whether we prioritize utility, resources, or capacities to flourish, but across a very wide range of situations, all of these oars row in the same direction. If our form of socialism distributes both income and leisure far more equally than what's possible under capitalism without introducing new sources of unfairness for those with greater needs or less capacity for work, then it counts as an improvement on *any* of these standards.

And indeed our model distributes things much more equally than capitalism. When productive resources are collectively owned and worker-members of the firms that lease those resources can vote on wage scales, gaps narrow in both individual resources and the utility people derive from those resources, bringing people closer to each other in their capacities to flourish. And redistributive state policy can do a lot to attack the inequalities that are left.

Distribution is not just about the division of the fruits of our labor between different people. Recall that we all have very different needs at different times in our lives. The aged, the sick, children, people with disabilities—these are not separate categories of person; they describe most of us at different periods in our lifespan. And we each face the possibility of bad luck. In the absence of adequate socially organized redistribution, people make private arrangements to smooth consumption across their lifetimes, saving or paying off debt in prime earning years and borrowing or running down savings at other times. Parents provide for children. When they have the means, people may protect themselves from some forms of bad luck with insurance. Social democracy already socializes quite a bit of this risk, and a socialist society would go even further. As Nicholas Barr puts it, not only does the welfare state provide the "Robin Hood" functions of redistributing from rich to poor, but it also has "piggy bank" functions that smooth consumption over a lifetime and provide social insurance.[6]

Will Equality Kill Incentives?

As we move from thinking through these more general principles to applying them to our model of socialism, we should start by addressing one of the most common concerns about *any* vision of a more equal economy. Egalitarianism, it's often alleged, kills incentives. If a socialist society guarantees its members the products they need to live a flourishing life, what will motivate them to produce those things in the first place?

This concern is misplaced, because no serious egalitarian ideal rejects rewards for work. Certainly, for the resource or endowment egalitarian, labor deserves to be compensated. The worker bears costs from work, and were they not compensated for it, they would have reason to prefer the bundles provided to those who could work but did not. More intense effort, duller work, more stress—all these things deserve further compensation.[7]

On the face of it, the to-each-according-to-their-basic-needs ideal of the capabilities approach might seem to promise everyone what they need to flourish without asking anything in return. But any realistic conception of flourishing must take into account the conditions required to produce those goods.

Participation in the division of labor must be part of the generally expected lifestyle in any society with the per capita output necessary to provide these things. That does not mean everybody works—there are children, the retired, those in full-time education, and those who cannot work due to disability. But work must be at least compatible with that society's conception of the good life, and it can even be understood as a valued part of it.

Again, labor is the resource that cannot be socialized: People must be incentivized to provide it voluntarily. Firm democracy can reduce the unpleasantness of work, but we don't expect people to stop valuing leisure just because they control the means of production. The public, in redistributing resources, will inevitably stand in an exchange relationship with the individuals who supply labor. Even if many people might be willing to do some work because "it needs doing" or because they take pride in it, pay helps to draw out the additional effort that won't arise on its own and, crucially, directs it to the specific places where it is most needed.

It is quite compatible with egalitarianism to make a distinction between those who cannot (or are not expected to) work and those who can. Even if we assume that the equality that matters most is equalizing the *means* to live a flourishing life, this doesn't mean we have to give "flourishing"-level incomes to those who can work and choose not to. If their personal conception of flourishing includes a lot of things their fellow citizens must labor to make, it's reasonable to ask them to join in helping to produce them.

For similar reasons, John Rawls denied that "those who surf all day off Malibu" were "entitled to public funds." But this may take things too far. The Malibu surfer of Rawls's potshot later became the poster child of the idea of a guaranteed basic income, beginning with Philippe Van Parijs's "Why surfers should be fed." The full-time surfer's income may rightly be lower than those of workers, but Van Parijs thought that as citizens who deserved a fair share of other social resources they were still entitled to something—and if they were able to live their version of the good life with more leisure and less material consumption, he insisted, there is nothing wrong with that.[8]

There is also a pragmatic case for a guaranteed minimum income. Ultimately, a socialist system is not going to allow people to go homeless or starve under any circumstances, so it is best to honestly provide an unconditional baseline. Lentils and rice, a room in a shared apartment—such basics are not terribly expensive, and for some are quite compatible with a flourishing life spent on chosen pursuits, while still leaving plenty of incentive to work for those whose versions of the good life require more.[9]

The idea of a guaranteed minimum income has some support even among conservatives who have no egalitarian instincts. One reason is the expense of maintaining a conditional welfare system, which requires monitoring to distinguish between those who meet certain criteria and those who don't. A universal minimum income, perhaps in the form of negative income tax below a threshold, is simple and much less costly to implement. But this requires that the lentils-and-rice-and-shared-apartment-level income replace all other forms of public income transfer. Pensioners, the disabled, and the unemployed all subsist at this level—along with the surfers who do so by choice. This is not fair according to the logics of either capabilities or resources equality.

A fair system will maintain higher levels of transfer income for those who cannot work than for those who can but choose not to. There is no moral problem at all in choosing leisure over much or all of that potential consumption. But those who make the choice show that they value their leisure at least as much as what they forgo. We can't make the same assumption about the person who *cannot* work or can work only at lower capacity.

This means adding a system of *conditional* income transfers for citizens in these categories—a straightforward-enough project in the case of retirement incomes, since entitlement is based on age. For the others, practical problems will inevitably arise in distinguishing between a choice not to work and the inability to work. Our system aims at full employment in the sense that everybody who wants paid work can find it within a reasonable time frame, as we discuss below. But even if that aim is generally achieved, there will always be at least frictional unemployment while people are between jobs, and it may take some longer to find new workplaces than others. There will be a need for an unemployment benefit for those temporarily out of work. If it is higher than the basic income, as it should be, there is an incentive for those choosing not to work to feign a job search. It is costly to maintain an administrative system to separate out those earnestly seeking workplaces from those who are not—costly not only in terms of administrative work but in terms of the effects on those who are subjected to the surveillance and hoop-jumping. More generally, there are gray areas (for example, involving people with certain emotional disorders) in which it is genuinely hard to distinguish between reduced capacity for work and decisions not to work. Disability deserves full compensation, but any distinction between deserving and undeserving creates an incentive to present as the former. Policing the boundary imposes serious costs on those policed, inevitably excluding some deserving people and creating anxiety for those on both sides of whatever line is drawn—including some of the people least equipped to deal with the anxiety.

There is no simple answer to this problem. To not police a boundary at all would erode the distinction between basic and compensatory incomes, probably at the expense of the latter. But this problem can't be solved at the level of a model. It will be up to democratic politics to work out where and how to draw the line.

That task will be easier the more a culture of solidarity prevails. Our hope is that changing the economic structure of society will be conducive to producing such a culture in two ways. First, while we're under no illusions that worker control of production will be sufficient to make everyone love work, we do think firm democracy can substantially reduce any incentive to game the system. Second, we're optimistic that a more equal and less materially precarious society will incubate more generous attitudes toward people who need help than those that often prevail in capitalist democracies.

It's also worth remembering that the choice between work and leisure is not an all-or-nothing one. Many kinds of work are well suited to part-time or seasonal patterns. Ideally, these jobs can be matched to people's preferences for working hours. Many surfers will be perfectly happy earning extra income as baristas or bartenders a few hours a week or wintering as instructors at a ski resort. Many other jobs beyond the traditional hospitality sector could potentially be redesigned to meet a preference for casual, part-time, or seasonal patterns—and workplace democracy enables such redesigns by giving their beneficiaries a direct say in the matter.

All the tax-and-transfer system needs to do to accommodate this is to make sure that the basic income tapers off gradually as more labor income is earned. For example, the basic income could be structured as a negative income tax (a payment from the government that decreases as earnings rise) so that a person's post-tax income continually rises with additional income, without discontinuities that could discourage taking on occasional or part-time work.

Labor Income Inequality

So far we have discussed distribution between those currently working and those not. What about pay inequalities among those who do work?

Differences in pay are not inegalitarian if they compensate for differences in the disutility of jobs. In Oskar Lange's model of socialism, workers find jobs and earn market wages, and he presents the labor market as working in textbook fashion, matching demand and supply. He implies that market wages are both fair and efficient. He even suggests that rather than compensating for inequalities of labor income, the social dividend from public capital income should be distributed to people in proportion to their wages, so as not to disturb the allocation of labor or its rewards. Being free to choose where to offer their time, workers will accept more difficult or unpleasant work only if compensated by higher pay, and so market wages appropriately price these aspects of work. "Each industry or occupation may be regarded as producing a joint product: the commodity or service in question *and* leisure, safety, agreeableness of work, etc." Not only do such wage premiums reward workers fairly for doing more difficult jobs, but they also ensure that people's preferences about working conditions factor into production decisions. People thus express their producer preferences in the labor market just as they express consumer preferences in the product market.[10]

This is a nice idea, but glosses over something very important: the differences in people's skills and talents. We take stress, difficulty, and other unpleasantness into account when deciding where we would like to work, but we can only actually choose from among jobs on offer to us. The options available to a person depend on organizations also choosing them for a job, in circumstances where employers are choosing between candidates. Where a role requires particular abilities, those without them are simply not part of the pool considered—unless they can be trained on the job, in which case training costs will be part of the consideration.

In actual labor markets, highly paid jobs are often also more pleasant than lower-paid jobs, and some of the reasons this is true would still hold under socialism. The people filling these positions are not competing with everyone who would like a job but with the smaller group of people who would both like it and be able to do it competently. In other cases, a job can be done competently by a wide range of people, but some do it better than others—they work faster or produce work of a higher quality. If these things are valuable to an employer, they might pay these individuals more to avoid losing them to a rival.

The differences in pay that emerge would be no great challenge to egalitarianism if it were open to anyone to develop the abilities desired for a job through education, training, experience, or effort. Pay differentials reflecting not skill but effort need not come with differences in status—someone could personally choose a more relaxed work pace with fewer responsibilities and find it perfectly fair that someone taking on more stress receive compensatory pay. Lange's optimistic vision of the labor market could be adapted: The equilibrium wage structure would reflect differences in training costs along with the disutilities of the work itself. There might be temporary premiums given to particular skills beyond the cost of developing them, because the economy evolves in unanticipated ways. Tastes and technologies change and the division of labor adapts. People with skills suddenly in increased demand might enjoy unexpectedly high wages for a while, but this premium would be eroded as others respond and develop those skills themselves. This would be nothing more than market signals doing their thing, creating the incentive for others to meet the social needs that have created the premium. All a socialist state need do is make sure people have access to whatever training is required.

So far, this is close to the typical liberal response to inequality under capitalism: education. Unfortunately, it is wishful thinking to believe education alone will bridge gaps in pay. There are differences in people's abilities within particular jobs and differences in their ability to train for those jobs, and not all of these can be erased by education, experience, or effort. We call whatever remains otherwise unexplained "talent." Whatever combination of nature, nurture, and blind luck produces it, the important point for an egalitarian project is that this residual difference is not something we can reliably cultivate through personal effort or public policy. (To the extent that a trait can be predictably cultivated, it is not "talent" in the sense used here.)

There is an understandable impulse among some egalitarians to deny the existence of any such ineradicable differences in potential. But the effect of this denial is to lay the responsibility for inequality on the lap of the individual. If someone is not able to make it as a neurosurgeon or rocket scientist, the implication is that they or their teachers should simply have tried harder.

From a resources equality perspective, talents are arbitrarily distributed among people's endowments, and since they cannot be redistributed, they call—at least in theory—for compensation to the ungifted. But it is not easy to do this in practice. Part of the challenge for egalitarianism is that while talent may be a matter of luck, the actual use of talent also depends on effort. The *potential* neurosurgeon is no use at the operating table—we need someone who has actually gone through extensive training and is willing to carry out challenging and stressful work on a routine basis. The relationship between talent and effort is not something that matters only for the likes of doctors and top athletes but right across the division of labor. Some people can repair a car or balance a set of accounts faster than others with a similar level of training and experience. Some people will be more beloved teachers or more efficient administrators than others who put in the same effort. But the expression of talent requires some effort.

This is the root of a familiar economic argument that there is a trade-off between income redistribution and efficiency. If people's decisions about how much and how hard to work and what work to do are at least partly influenced by pay, then redistribution is not about redividing a fixed amount of output. Taxing and transferring income alters incentives and so potentially changes the quantity and quality of what there is to distribute. Completely leveling income from labor would remove any income incentive to do one kind of work rather than another or to work harder. Though there are other incentives besides income, it seems very likely that a flat pay distribution would lead people to produce less and to produce less-valued products than they would with incentives from pay differentials. But with such differentials, the more talented will find it easier to get the more desirable positions, to do the higher-quality work, to produce at the faster rate that gets them the higher pay. They have to sacrifice less for the reward than the less talented: thus the trade-off between fairness and efficiency.[11]

For some, this is a reason to give up on the egalitarian goal entirely. But this all-or-nothing conclusion does not follow at all from recognizing the possibility of a trade-off. There is a large zone between complete leveling and complete laissez faire. It is one thing to acknowledge that some inequality may be justified by making everyone better off, and quite another to suggest that whatever inequality emerges on the labor market is justified.

There is a large economic literature on "optimal taxation," which explores the trade-offs between public revenue, redistribution, and output, given that people's behavior will respond to taxes and transfers in deciding how much to work and how to manage their finances. From the beginning, this work has sometimes been associated with counterintuitive claims, such as that marginal rates should be flat or even decline as income increases, and such arguments have been used as cover for cutting taxes on high earners and flattening the tax structure. But the conclusions are very sensitive to the assumptions on which they are based, and evidence has accumulated that labor supply responses to higher tax are typically much more modest than some thought experiments tend to assume. The consensus now seems to have turned back in favor of progressive taxation and high marginal rates on high earners.[12]

One reason may be that traditional models tended to presume idealized labor markets in which individual workers are willing to work up to the point where the (rising) marginal disutility of labor is just compensated by what they are paid, while employers are willing to employ up to the point where the (declining) marginal productivity of labor meets what they must pay. Because tax appears as a wedge between what employers pay and what workers get to spend, a higher tax rate will lead to a lower labor supply—the only question is how much lower. But in a more realistic situation, there are a number of reasons why workers would be "off their supply curve" and paid more than the bare minimum needed to induce them to work as much as they do. Such workers would be willing to work the same amount even at a lower pay rate, or, conversely, they would not be willing to work more even for higher pay. There are a range of possible pay rates between the lowest the worker would accept and the highest an employer would be willing to pay, and within that range bargaining decides. Those with rarer skills and talents are particularly likely to have the bargaining power to secure pay substantially above what they would be willing to do the work for. Taxation can thus appropriate some of that "rent" without costing the social benefits of their skills and talents.[13]

Ultimately, how the behavior of individuals and the organizations that employ them respond to different tax regimes is an empirical question, and since the setting of our system is substantially different from the capitalist societies we have evidence about, we should be cautious in drawing conclusions. But there are good reasons to believe that high marginal tax rates on high incomes will be both desirable and viable.

The behavioral response to tax rates includes not only decisions about work but also about how to arrange one's finances to take advantage of loopholes in the tax structure. The higher propensity of those with higher incomes to find ways to minimize their tax burdens is one factor that limits the effectiveness of progressive taxation. The answer is a simple tax structure designed to reduce the scope for such behavior.

Our system has some built-in advantages here. The nexus between democratic firms, worker-members, and public banks makes wage and dividend payments transparent. (Labor income should be taxed regardless of its composition between "wage" and "dividend.") There are no official vehicles for financial savings outside the banking system. Cash withdrawals and deposits are easily traceable across the public banks. There will always be the possibility for leaks into international or off-system stores of value, but again, the banking system can catch systematic patterns into and out of accounts.

Economists Peter Diamond and Emmanuel Saez draw on estimates of the response of high earners to tax changes in the United States to conclude that optimal top rates on labor earnings are much higher than the status quo: 80 percent if the structure were reformed to remove deductions and broaden the tax base. This particular figure should not be taken as a guideline for a socialist society. Other features of our model make it quite unlikely that the high inequality of pretax labor income that exists in the contemporary United States would develop in the first place. With a more compressed pretax income structure, the optimal top marginal rate could well be lower in a socialist society than a capitalist one. But the example should give some confidence that progressive taxation can lop off the top of the income distribution.[14]

So far, we have discussed incomes at the top, but our system also tackles labor income inequality at the bottom. In the previous section we covered guaranteed and conditional minimum income transfers for those out of work by choice or otherwise. If such transfers cut out entirely once someone took on any amount of work, people would be actively discouraged from working part time, so they should phase out gradually as someone's pay from work increases. In essence, the guaranteed minimum is a negative income tax, for which there is broad support across perspectives in the optimal taxation literature.

Beyond redistribution of disposable income with taxes and transfers, the wage benchmarks in our system maintain a floor on pretax pay rates. Some high-income capitalist countries—mainly

Sweden and Australia—have had long experience with wage-setting systems in which minimums are determined centrally while local workplaces are free to pay in excess of those benchmarks. These systems have been used to pursue wage compression, among other goals.[15]

Wage compression does, of course, have an impact on the price structure. Those in jobs that might otherwise pay much less, such as hospitality and retail, have incomes much closer to the median in these countries, and the services they provide are consequently relatively more expensive than they are in societies where such jobs are done for pay well below the average. But this is what egalitarianism means. Going out for dinner is more expensive, but those who make and serve the dinner can themselves afford to dine out, and afford much else besides.

Countries that have pursued wage compression through centralized bargaining systems do not generally tend to have worse unemployment outcomes or lower average real incomes. But the workings of the wage-benchmark system are best understood alongside macroeconomic policy, and so we save a fuller discussion for the next chapter.

The Housing Question

In a capitalist society, housing inequality is more than a symptom of broader income and wealth inequality. Homes are both places to live in and vehicles of wealth. In fact, residential real estate typically makes up more than half of the total value of wealth in a capitalist country. Individuals hold only indirect financial claims on most means of production, but they tend to own dwellings directly, whether they live in them or rent them to others as a landlord. While housing wealth is itself very unevenly distributed, the reality is that owning a home is a widespread experience and ambition; and the fact that it is such a *personal* form of wealth for the owner-occupier complicates the politics of inequality in contemporary capitalism. Most middle-class wealth is in housing, and its accumulation is often a lifetime project involving paying off a mortgage over many years.[16]

Many of the features of housing that make it unusual as a consumer need will still be there in a socialist society, and so it calls for special consideration. Housing stock is expensive to produce and very long-lasting if maintained, and occupies space in particular locations. People care about *where* they live—in terms both of their home's position relative to other places that matter to them and of the character of the natural and built environment around it. There is an ineradicable element of scarcity to desirable locations. A given patch of land can be used more or less densely, modifying the supply of dwellings in an area, but density and type of housing are themselves aspects of a location that people care about.

A home of your own, which you can customize to your tastes and needs and in which you have secure tenure, is a genuine good worth preserving. But capitalist homeownership binds together choices about your home with choices about finance and wealth that inevitably come with risks, and the dynamics of the housing market are prone to generate arbitrary inequalities.

The households deciding whether to meet their housing needs by renting or by taking out a mortgage can compare expected interest and maintenance costs with the rent on an equivalent property. Some households may be willing to pay a premium for the security of ownership and the freedom of renovating; on the other hand, the illiquidity and risks of ownership may lead others to prefer to rent. For some, there is no choice: Since mortgage borrowing requires the prior accumulation of a deposit and the lender's confidence in the borrower's ability to repay, those on low or insecure incomes are not able to finance a purchase.

Even sustainable capital gains—driven by rising incomes and population rather than anything the homeowner has done—are arbitrary. Such gains can widen a wealth gap between homeowners (and their descendants) who got in early and those stuck renting or only "getting on the property ladder" later in life.

There are a number of ways a socialist society might structure the provision of housing. We suggest a simple approach. In our model, the land and housing stock is publicly owned, but households have secure tenure in the dwelling they live in, and the capacity to renovate to their taste. People make regular rental payments for housing, rather than being involved in a financial relationship paying off a large asset purchase over decades. Households take neither the risks nor the capital gains that come with ownership—these are socialized—but have all the other benefits of a place to call their own.

Rents are set by a housing authority, generally aiming to match demand to supply. A household's rent may shift over time according to changes in supply and demand for dwellings that are similar in location and type. In other words, rents adjust in response to market conditions and are not simply set forever at the beginning of tenure, though movements can be smoothed to avoid sudden shifts. The housing authority will be tasked with developing supply in response to projected demand, so that significant general increases in rent would be considered a policy failure to be remedied. Urban planning and development are in public hands and engage democratic construction firms to do the building.

This system allows each household to make its own housing choices, each bearing the appropriate cost. Some may prefer a modest apartment so as to have more to spend on other things, while others put more of their budget into spacious villas. Many people will make different choices at different stages of life. The system can accommodate experiments in self-managed collective living for those who want it—as well as handling the traditional family home.

Residents are in a similar position with respect to their dwellings as firms are in with their means of production. They are custodians rather than full owners of that part of social wealth, but they can use and adapt it as they choose. They can initiate renovations in partnership with the housing authority or its associated bank. Instead of paying up front, the costs of renovations are factored into rents and paid over time. Because maintenance costs and depreciation are already baked into the rent of all dwellings, each will come with a budget and schedule for renovations. Households only need to pay extra for modifications that are idiosyncratic or costlier than the standard.

The housing board can adjust the pace of renovation in order to smooth activity for the construction sector, which is notoriously cyclical in capitalism. If a lot of new construction is going on, renovation can be made temporarily more expensive or limited with a waiting list. When new construction slows, this can be reversed. The pace of renovation can also potentially be varied to help with macroeconomic stabilization beyond the sector, as we discuss below.

Capitalist housing markets are riddled with externalities. As such, this is an excellent place to reduce the role of markets and open up a considerable role for public planning. Our model of socialist housing accommodates the diversity of household preferences and needs and provides all the features of "a home of one's own"—except the arbitrary financial risks and windfalls that come with the capitalist model of ownership. This simple but versatile system locates planning and initiative for housing supply within a public agency. This can, in turn, be integrated with macroeconomic policy.

In the end, a fair distribution of income in a socialist society is not a puzzle solved once and for all by philosophical principle or a perfect schedule of taxes and transfers. It is something sustained through institutions that make those principles workable in practice: democratic firms that narrow pretax gaps before the state intervenes, public programs that meet needs across lifespans, and a tax-and-transfer system designed to reconcile equality with the real demands of work. These arrangements do the heavy lifting, and they do it in ways that make the remaining disagreements about "equality of what" matter far less than they do under capitalism. When wealth is socialized, when workplace democracy compresses incomes at the source, and when needs are met as a matter of citizenship rather than luck, our distance from egalitarian ideals shrinks.

But distribution never sits in a vacuum. Even the most coherent system of wages, transfers, and guarantees is only as stable as the wider economic environment allows it to be. A society committed to full employment and generous minimum incomes has to ensure that downturns do not take the form of exclusion from work and that inflation does not quietly undo the gains of redistribution. A society that aims to compress wages needs a way of coordinating those wages with the rhythms of investment, productivity, and changing conditions. In short, egalitarian distribution depends on macroeconomic stability, and stability is not something markets reliably deliver on their own.

That is the subject of the next chapter. There we turn from questions about *who gets what* to the institutions that keep the whole model standing.

8

Macroeconomic Policy

You can sense a downturn before anyone names it. It's the quiet on the shop floor between orders and how long the foreman stares at the scheduling board before walking away.

In your region, precision tools for industrial robots play a crucial role in the economy. Whole towns depend on them, directly or indirectly. So when sales start to dry up, no one needs a press release to explain what's happening. The problem doesn't feel local for long. You hear from friends in other industries—warehouse shifts cut back, fewer deliveries, a slowdown in construction bids. Something bigger is at play.

At your cooperative's monthly meeting, the spreadsheets make the story plain enough: With less revenue coming in, there are fewer hours of work to go around, and you can expect dividends that won't look like last year's. Under capitalism, this is the point where people would start guessing who will be laid off first. Now, layoffs are still possible, but the first question is how to share the adjustment.

People suggest trimming a shift each week for a while. New-member recruitment can pause until the cooperative knows where demand will land. The extended summer break everyone had built into the schedule can wait until you have a clearer sense of where things are headed. None of it is costless. People feel it in their routines and their wallets.

No bailout is on offer, so if the downturn lasts, the firm may have to make tougher choices next year. But that doesn't mean that the state is idle. You catch a short video about the central bank making borrowing a little cheaper after signs of slower activity across several sectors. It's nothing dramatic, but it might make it easier for firms like yours to retool or keep viable investment plans alive.

Around town, public notices go up for infrastructure crews starting work earlier than planned, and a couple of your coworkers sign up for the extra hours. You see more people from nearby cooperatives showing up at the free skills-training center—another sign that the slowdown isn't confined to your line of work.

Over the next few months, the pattern becomes familiar. A few older members retire earlier than planned. One younger machinist moves to a newly forming cooperative assembled out of a pool of underemployed technicians. They plan to make components for electric farm equipment, a sector suddenly picking up steam. Hours fluctuate and dividends come in lighter. You feel the slump, but it doesn't define your life.

The downturn doesn't vanish right away. People worry as spending dips and some firms will eventually shrink or shutter. But the shock is absorbed by institutions rather than borne by individuals as sudden firings and personal crises. The first line of adjustment involves reduced hours and lighter dividends. Public agencies bring forward maintenance and renovation work where they can; retraining programs expand. Slack appears, but it does not take the form of a queue outside an unemployment office.

The business cycle hasn't been abolished—there's still real adjustment at a real cost—but it's no longer allowed to take the form of mass joblessness, and the fear that one bad month will upend your life no longer grips you. And for that you're grateful.

Along with money, markets, and commodity production come the possibility of macroeconomic problems like unemployment and inflation. At the root of these issues is the potential for a disconnect between the resources available and the monetary claims on those resources.

Spending money is how each unit—household, firm, and public agency alike—exerts its claim on the available resources. Each unit is constrained in its expenditures by the funds it has access to, whether it gets those funds through employment, sales revenue, borrowing, or budget allocation from the public treasury. But while each individual unit is constrained by funding, production across the formal (monetary) economy is constrained by the labor and other resources available to it.

The formation of claims is, of course, connected to production. It needs to be for prices and incomes to coordinate activity coherently at all. Commodity production involves a circular flow of income and expenditure. A broader economic system with a noncommodity sector that purchases commodity inputs and pays its workers so that they can purchase consumer commodities expands and fits into this circular flow. The standard national accounting system can be used to map these patterns and stocks of value in our system, just as in a capitalist country. Income from production over a given period equals the value of final output produced. And the value of final output is equal to total expenditure on that output. The formation of prices, the formation of incomes, and decisions about production happen together as part of the same process, and so incomes are not arbitrary with respect to output or the resources expended on it.

There is no guarantee, however, that all those spending decisions will come together to motivate production decisions that just absorb the capacity of the available resources. Effective demand can be too low, leaving people unemployed who want to work at going pay rates. Or it can be too high, driving up prices as producers bid against one another for limited inputs. The essence of the Keynesian revolution, which gave birth to macroeconomics, was that there are no automatic market processes that bring these things back into line. A monetary economy can get stuck in an unemployment equilibrium or an inflationary spiral because the actions of the countless individual units, each with their own aims and their own constraints, can interact together to sustain one or the other.

But along with macroeconomics came macroeconomic policy and the notion that deliberate action by public agencies could intervene in the circular flow to nudge the system out of these traps. This requires, first, that the agencies coordinate their actions around the goal of system stability, rather than chasing the individual goals all the private units are chasing. It requires, second, that their actions are informed by a model of the flows in which they are intervening: macroeconomics itself. And it requires, finally, that public agencies actually have enough leverage and freedom to adequately shift the target variables.

There has not been much analysis of the macroeconomics or macroeconomic policy specific to a market socialist economy. But on the third condition—the points of leverage within the system for public action—there is room for socialist institutions to improve over capitalism.

We are used to taking for granted fiscal and monetary policy as the two branches of macroeconomic policy. Each of them depends on the existence of public institutions that operate within the networks of monetary flows and financial claims, occupying strategic positions that policymakers can effectively exploit. Fiscal policy—the management of demand by adjusting taxation and public spending—could not come into its own before government budgets were large enough to matter. Monetary policy was possible because central banks in some form already existed at the heart of national financial systems. Turning public budgets and central banks to macroeconomic policy involved, and still involves, political projects that are often resisted and compromised by other powerful actors in the capitalist economic system.[1]

We do not assume that macroeconomic policy will be conflict-free and smoothly technocratic in a socialist society. But there are fundamental features of the architecture of our model that make coherent, rapidly deployable policy easier.

One major difference is that investment in the commodity sector is much more tightly under policy control, and returns from this investment flow to the public banks and public purse before any distributions to individuals are made. In the next section we discuss how this is managed by the central bank and public banking system and how it enables both tightly coordinated monetary and fiscal policy and strategic public direction of investment between sectors.

In the following section we discuss another important difference, the centralized wage-benchmark system managed by a labor board. It was once common for economists to argue that policymakers needed some degree of control over wages in order to make full employment compatible with price stability. However, most capitalist countries did not have such an instrument, and instead it has become normal to accept a degree of slack in the labor market to check inflation. In our system, wage benchmarks give the state a nonrepressive, economy-wide tool for maintaining stability without relying on unemployment as the adjustment mechanism.

Finally, we consider the challenges for economic management that come from international flows and prices on world markets. We argue that the system has nothing to fear and much to gain from trade. Policy will need to manage fluctuations in foreign demand and world prices, but this is manageable, especially given that the system will be relatively isolated from international capital flows.

The Banking System and Investment

In our system, the public banking system is the whole financial system. We have so far discussed the banks as the partners and sources of investment finance for democratic firms, but we have not yet discussed how the financing of the banks themselves works or how they connect to the central bank.

In modern capitalism, private bank deposits make up most of what we use as money. The payments system is mostly administered by commercial banks, who settle net flows between themselves with central bank deposits. They borrow from one another on the interbank market to make up shortfalls as necessary. As the issuer of the higher-level currency and as lender of last resort, the central bank usually has tight control over short-term rates in the interbank money market, and this has become the staple instrument of monetary policy. Variations in the short-term interbank rate affect other rates, and ultimately expenditure, indirectly, through a number of channels, each of which involves lags and uncertainty.

The banking system works very differently in our model. First, the payments system is a unified public utility run directly by the central bank. Households, firms, public agencies, and the banks themselves hold deposits directly with the central bank. The banks, in turn, borrow from the central bank and do not offer deposits or borrow in any other way directly from households or firms. The central bank is the only institution in the system with substantial short-term liabilities. The regular public banks cannot expand their balance sheets without borrowing from the central bank, which therefore controls the pace of credit expansion more directly and surely than under capitalism. The central bank is the wholesaler of credit, the other banks the retailers.

This is very different from the capitalist framework in which private finance takes the initiative in stretching the liquidity of the system, relying on the central bank to step in as lender of last resort when it snaps. This familiar banking form developed historically under capitalism because the "borrow short, lend long" model of intermediation is profitable, and central banks came to support the strategy by heading off crises with liquidity. It is not necessary in our system because banks are run as public utilities and not businesses. There is no reason why the institutions that lend for investment should also be the institutions that provide deposit facilities and run the payments system. (Indeed, under capitalism most corporate financing does not come from commercial banks.)

Separating investment lending from deposit-taking avoids one of the major sources of instability in the capitalist financial system—liquidity crises—and also allows for more direct policy influence over finance and therefore investment. The financial system is vital infrastructure for the rest of the economy, but macroeconomic stability is an externality from the perspective of profit-seeking financial institutions. Capitalist policy deals with this in an endless cat-and-mouse game between regulation and financial innovation. In our system, the institutions are built from the ground up as public utilities.

Competition Between Banks

Why then have multiple public banks at all, instead of having firms partner directly with one big central bank? If the banks are all themselves funded from the same source, why not cut out the intermediaries?

Investment decisions call for complex analysis and often involve a great deal of uncertainty. Remember that the banks in this system are generally not lending to their partner firms at fixed rates, but with risk-sharing arrangements in which the bank absorbs some of the firm's risk in return for higher average payments. Here, banking is fund management, with the financial arrangements having some of the characteristics of bonds, equities, or insurance policies, as well as loans. There are benefits to allowing for a plurality of financial analyses and strategies and cultivating limited competition between them.

Those who make the decisions for banks get bonuses based on the extent to which the returns the institution makes across its portfolio exceed what they pay the central bank for funds. The bonuses should be big enough to encourage analysts and fund managers to take decisions seriously, and yet they will be much lower than the profits and bonuses extracted by their counterparts and by the executives and shareholders of financial institutions under capitalism. Partly, this is because the margins will be lower in the first place, with the banks generally borrowing at higher wholesale rates from the central bank than capitalist banks pay on the money market and for deposits. But also, it is because the bonuses need not distribute the full profit made by the bank. It only needs to be enough to motivate skilled people to want to do the work well, equivalent to the dividends in democratic firms.

Because it is an allocated bonus rather than a straight share of earnings, the formula can be shaped to avoid certain incentive problems that plague the capitalist financial system. For example, payments of the bonus accrued in a given year can be deferred and disbursed only over a number of years, with the sum reduced by any losses in the meantime. This discourages a short-termist bias toward investments with front-loaded payoffs. It also discourages fund managers from taking on too much risk with the intention of leaving the bank if the gamble fails. The bonus formula could also directly take the volatility of returns into account and penalize exceeding a target level.

Though the public banks will *generally* be expected to seek the highest returns compatible with a given risk profile, the system also opens channels for public funding of projects that are not expected to make a competitive rate of return in cases in which they are valued for other reasons. Funds can be directed through specialized development banks with different targets from the regular banks, or the central bank could make funds available for such purposes at lower rates to regular banks. This is not the only way of organizing investment in public goods. Often it will be better to do this directly within the noncommodity public sector, especially when the projects supported are not connected to commodity production at all or ever expected to generate a competitive rate of return. But it can work well for longer-term planning for things otherwise well suited to the market sector—for example, developing a depressed region or helping an infant industry find its feet.

This banking system gives the socialist central bank considerably more direct control over aggregate investment than its capitalist counterparts. It can exert this control by setting the wholesale interest rate at which it lends to the banks.[2] To cover ordinary default risks, the banks will apply a margin over this wholesale rate to the baseline rate at which they finance firms. Risk-sharing adjustments agreed with each firm according to their circumstances will mean the average rates paid will generally float somewhere above this baseline. But this whole structure of rates for new investments will move up and down with the wholesale rate. There is no complex channel of transmission between the rate controlled by the central bank and the rates relevant to investment decisions.

There is still some potential for slippage between policy instrument and ultimate target (investment) because bank and firm perceptions of risk are liable to change. Bank margins may expand or compress with these perceptions, and swings in firm optimism and pessimism may swamp the effect of interest rate movements on investment, as they do under capitalism. But the policy transmission channel is still simpler than under capitalism, and the more successful the policy is in maintaining macroeconomic stability, the less volatile such economy-wide swings in risk perception are likely to be.[3]

In any case, the central bank will always be able to set an upper limit to investment, as it is the only ultimate source of funds for the banks. It cannot force banks or firms to borrow and invest, however, so in the event that investment in the commodity sector undershoots policy targets, macroeconomic policy must rely on other measures. Fortunately, it has them.

Integrating Monetary and Fiscal Policy

Demand stabilization is made easier by the fact that the central bank also finances investment in the public noncommodity sector, as well as in construction, maintenance, and renovation across the housing and commercial building stock. Fiscal and monetary policy can be more tightly coordinated. Most of the capital income from investment in commodity production flows through the banking system to the public purse, where it joins taxation receipts. How much of this total revenue is reinvested in the commodity sector, how much used for public noncommodity production, and how much redistributed as personal income in transfers to households is a decision for elected government. But for purposes of macroeconomic management, it makes sense to leave certain aspects of this to specialist policymakers, who work under the ultimate authority of a democratic government. Such a body needs only the discretion to adjust public outlays at the margin, not to make decisions about the whole shape of public activity.

One of the reasons fiscal policy has tended to be subordinated to monetary policy under capitalism is the lag in fiscal decision-making: While the central bank can adjust interest rates immediately, it takes time for fiscal policy packages to be negotiated politically and delivered in a budget. It is often neither easy nor desirable to increase or decrease public noncommodity production and income transfers to make room for the vicissitudes of the commodity sector. (Should education or health spending or pensions bear the burden of macroeconomic adjustment?) Public infrastructure projects seem like something whose timing could be adjusted for stabilization purposes, but they tend to be very long in the planning and execution and so not easy in practice to roll out and pull back fast enough for macroeconomic management.

But in our system, public management of the housing and commercial building stock opens a wide field for relatively rapid adjustment to meet shifts in investment or other components of demand. All buildings need maintenance over time, but the schedule is flexible. Renovations and upgrades are rarely urgent, but nice to have. Unlike full-scale construction, renovations and maintenance are usually smaller-scale projects: easier to get started quickly and faster to finish. The pace of renovation can be adjusted in response to changes in investment activity. There are limits, of course, because such work requires skilled labor, which cannot be expected to wait around on call. But if the pace is set normally to keep the industry with some spare capacity, there is room to adjust. Overtime pay can be used to encourage more work in the short run, and there may be a "reserve army" of labor living on the guaranteed minimum income willing to take on short-term work. If commodity sector investment is expected to be lower for a longer period of time, the construction sector can absorb workers on a more permanent basis with training. Since much commodity sector investment also involves building work, there is likely to already be skill overlap.

The system can also quickly and easily boost consumption demand with direct injections of purchasing power if necessary. These can be framed as tax rebates or as social dividends. It is best for these to be paid out more-or-less universally, assuming that the tax-and-transfer system is already designed for equality and to meet needs. They should be windfalls and not become regular enough for people to permanently adjust their consumption expectations to them. Directly dampening consumer demand with temporary tax increases is likely to be politically more difficult but also possible. An alternative is deferring income: collecting a fraction of income into a special account to be released (or credited toward tax obligations) later. Income transfers to meet specific needs—such as pensions, disability, and family payments—should be stable and not hostage to macroeconomic fluctuations.[4]

Beyond the management of short-run demand fluctuations, a coherent approach to fiscal and monetary policy allows for the public, through the democratic political system, to broadly guide the mix of production between sectors over the longer run. So long as full employment is sustained, the ultimate macroeconomic limits are set by the labor and other resources available to formal production (i.e., production other than that informally done within households). These must be allocated between (1) production for current commodity consumption, (2) public services and other noncommodity production, (3) investment to expand future production (and replace depreciating capital stock), and (4) exports. Spending on exports is not under domestic control, nor is the proportion of consumer expenditure devoted to imports—important facts we discuss below. But the overall division of national income between households, public noncommodity production, and investment (in both commodity and public sectors) is broadly under public control.

Capital income generated by financing investment in the commodity sector flows to the banking system. Central bank financing decisions determine how much of this income is reinvested in production and how much is transferred to the public purse, where it joins tax revenue. The point is not that the public sector needs this income in order to spend: The central bank can always expand public purchasing power by crediting government accounts. Rather, siphoning income from the commodity sector is necessary to create macroeconomic room for state spending and transfers, since these ultimately claim a share of the commodity output. Public spending generates demand for commodities indirectly, because state employees and transfer recipients use their incomes to buy consumer goods. The public sector also purchases commodities directly as inputs. For this reason, there must be a gap between the value of commodities produced and the demand generated within the market sector itself. If the state does not create this gap deliberately, the results will be inflationary.

The combined public control over investment, public spending, taxation, and transfers allows this division to be made deliberately. Neither private nor public spending needs to adjust passively to make room for uncontrollable fluctuations in the other. The overall pace of investment is not determined by private savings decisions. All these things are determined together, ultimately subject to democratic government.[5]

Deposits and Consumer Spending

In the banking system we describe, the central bank has deposit liabilities to households and firms, to other public agencies, and to banks. The central bank's lending decisions are also decisions about the size of its balance sheet and therefore about the aggregate volume of deposits in the hands of those other units. It must take this into account when engaging in macroeconomic policy. Financing decisions do not only affect demand by directly adding to investment (or public spending) and indirectly inducing others to spend out of the income they receive from the investment spending. They also leave a monetary residue in the form of deposit balances, and for each unit, these are a reservoir from which future spending might come, independent of current income.

Assuming that central public authorities have control over the spending of public agencies, deposits in their accounts are of no great concern. Agencies cannot freely spend these balances, and any undesired excess can easily be mopped up by transferring them to the central treasury or just canceling them by administrative decision. The central bank deposits of the public banks are likewise under more-or-less direct policy control. Firms in our model do not retain funds for further investment. Beyond enough working capital to manage the uncertain gaps between revenue inflows and payment outflows, they are supposed to periodically distribute spare funds as dividends to their worker-members. Since how much working capital is necessary might be interpreted generously, there is certainly room for firms to accumulate spare liquidity, giving them more maneuverability and more confidence in expansion. This does need to be monitored by macroeconomic policymakers. But the main pool of liquid assets (deposits) will accumulate with households.[6]

Even in as simple and flat a financial system as this one, the relationship between net flows of new finance and the accumulation of deposits in the hands of households is complicated. Investment spending becomes income and induces further consumption spending, generating more income. Each time around, some deposits will find their way back to the public purse through taxation, where they can be canceled at policy discretion. When people spend on imports, deposits are canceled as foreign currency is purchased from the central bank, but, conversely, deposits are created when income is earned from exports. (Trade and foreign exchange is discussed below.) This is still simpler than in a capitalist financial system, with its multiple layers of financial intermediation, where the liquidity of the banks, other financial institutions, and markets themselves matter. In our system, there is no formal financial store of value except for bank deposits.

This means that household decisions to hold deposits are bound up with decisions about savings—there is not one decision to save and then another decision about how to allocate savings. There are no equities, no bonds, no mutual funds outside the banking system. There is no real estate investment. There are thus no competing assets with rates of return that compete with central bank deposits, leaving monetary policymakers mostly free to choose the interest rates on deposits.

There is no necessary connection between the interest rates paid on deposits and the rates of return on finance for the democratic firms. Even if a substantial portion of central bank deposits are held by private individuals, they are not on that basis the ultimate beneficiaries of capital income from production, even if in an accounting sense their claims on the central bank have counterparts in the assets of the banking system. The public captures the spread between the interest paid on deposits and returns from investment. If individuals receive part of this as private income, they receive it in the form of transfer payments distributed to them as entitlements (e.g., as a pension) rather than as a return proportional to personal wealth.

More broadly, there is no particular moral reason to pay interest as a reward for saving. It is a fiction that a market rate of interest acts as a meaningful way for individual preferences to decide how to apportion resources between consumption today and investment to increase consumption later—there are simply too many other factors at play. This is a macroeconomic decision and better made via the democratic political system, which determines the longer-run allocation of funds through the central bank and fiscal system.

Households have fewer reasons for personal saving under the system we describe. Many of the reasons for personal saving under capitalism—including transferring income over the lifecycle—are taken care of by public transfers and through the public housing system. There is no need to save for a comfortable retirement or to take on a mortgage and pay it off over decades. With basic income security, there is less need to privately prepare for a rainy day. A 100 percent inheritance tax means that substantial intergenerational wealth transfers are not possible. People are still welcome to save from their incomes to spend later, but for most this likely means relatively small-scale saving for vacation travel or consumer goods. There are fewer reasons for long-term saving and no channels for the private accumulation of wealth by reaping returns from production or capital gains, so the propensity to consume out of disposable income is likely to be higher than under capitalism.[7]

The central bank can adjust household-facing interest rates and consumer credit as part of the toolkit for influencing consumer spending. Potentially this could even include paying higher rates on term deposits to sequester purchasing power. But how responsive consumption will be to interest rate changes is an open question. In a sense, the interest rate facing individuals sets a rate of exchange between current and future consumption, and other things being equal, higher current prices would reduce it. But other things are rarely equal and this effect may not be particularly strong within feasible bounds of interest changes. It may be easier for policymakers to adjust other things in the face of shifts in consumer demand than to moderate those swings. The central bank must watch for build-ups in household deposits and consider what they imply. It can also make limited consumer credit or overdraft facilities available as an alternative way of smoothing consumption expenditures over the medium term and then ration consumer credit to throttle consumption demand in a pinch.

Financial Controls: A Small Price to Pay

The workings of the system as described here depend on the public banking system remaining the whole of the financial system. The central bank is the only custodian of deposits and the only source of finance. But if there is one sure lesson from the history of the capitalist financial system, it is that *finance finds a way*. However complicated they get, at base financial instruments are an agreement made between two parties promising future payments, whether on particular dates, on demand, or given particular contingencies. There are ever so many ways to structure them. Every regulatory regime in capitalist history has prompted the emergence of new instruments, institutions, and practices designed to route around it. Completely eliminating financial agreements outside the formal system is not a realistic expectation. But the system can be built to be robust enough to keep such arrangements marginal.

It is not hard to think of points where pressures for financial arrangements outside the system might build up. For example, if the central bank rations consumer credit as just discussed, a frustrated would-be borrower could go looking for a would-be private lender who has savings in the bank earning little interest, and a deal could be made. A market for household-to-household loans develops, and now there is a channel for private wealth accumulation. Alternatively, individuals with savings look to a capitalist country abroad, see returns beyond what they get in the domestic banking system, and find ways to convert their deposits into foreign assets.

Such pressures limit the extent to which official rates within the system can depart from accessible alternatives outside it without provoking unintended consequences. However, while it would be foolish to ignore the potential for private financial relations, we should not assume that nothing can be done about them.

First, the state can simply refuse to give legal weight to private financial contracts and so refuse to enforce them. This makes private finance of any kind much riskier and so greatly widens the scope for setting rates within the system, while not outright prohibiting the kind of casual lending that might take place among friends and family.

An effective prohibition on financial relations between "consenting adults" seems to stand in the way of mutual gains. After all, if one person prefers to spend now and another prefers to spend later, why shouldn't they be able to trade claims across time? Does this not "misprice" the cost of future consumption in terms of present consumption by preventing the market from finding an interest rate that reflects those preferences? It does—but only under the assumption that a market-clearing interest rate reliably guides real resource allocation between consumption and investment so that the economy as a whole moves toward the full use of available resources. But modern macroeconomics is based on the insight that there is no necessary connection between the rates that clear financial markets and those that fully employ available resources. A financial market can "clear" at an interest rate that is compatible with persistent unemployment or, conversely, at one that is compatible with excess demand and inflation.

In our system, the allocation of resources between investment, commodity consumption, and noncommodity production is recognized as a social decision, to be determined through macroeconomic decisions under the ultimate direction of an elected government.

Second, the central bank should maintain a monopoly on currency conversion and use it to prevent individuals from investing or transferring personal savings abroad. Firms should also be prevented from directly borrowing or investing abroad, except through a bank partnership with permission from the central bank. People and firms are free to buy and sell foreign currency in the process of importing and exporting and for personal travel but not to buy and sell assets, financial or otherwise. Capital controls are essential to monetary autonomy. Without them it is difficult for policy to keep interest rates and flows of funds in line with socialist aims of egalitarianism and workplace democracy while also maintaining macroeconomic stability.[8]

It is not possible to completely prevent capital movements, as they can be disguised within trade transactions, but it is very possible to make them hard to do at any scale. The democratic firm structure has capital controls built into it, because there is no place for private capital of any kind to make returns. There is no role for outside investors, domestic or foreign, as the only claimants on a firm are its members and the public banks it has partnered with for investment. Firm cash flow and accounts are transparent and continually tracked within the banking system, so that it is difficult to engage in illicit transactions outside the system and later bring any proceeds back in.

There is a place for cash transactions in which the purpose and identities of the parties involved remain unrecorded and unobservable by others. If the system does not include a legitimate vehicle for this, people will undoubtedly develop illegitimate ones. The key is for the system to monitor the points of conversion between deposits and cash and flag flows that are significant relative to personal income or firm revenue. Large flows of cash do not necessarily indicate illegal activity, but flagging them ensures that they become declared income for tax purposes and makes it harder to hide commodity production outside the democratic workplace system. Most everyday retail products and utilities should require transactions within the formal payments system to make it difficult for a cash economy to develop. It will never be possible to completely eliminate black markets and the evasion of regulations, but their potential to erode the formal economic system can be diminished.

The controls described here are a small price to pay for macroeconomic stability and egalitarian distribution. They are justified on the grounds that within the system, one's financial resources are not only personal property, but represent claims on fellow citizens. Personal income and spending is a device for allocating to each person a fair share of the resources available for consumption and allowing them to direct that share as they see fit. Money is a device for managing the complex division of labor so as to meet people's needs, not a vehicle for accumulating power over others by capturing a disproportionate share of available resources.

Unemployment: Capitalist and Socialist

The previous sections established that the socialist state is well equipped for macroeconomic demand management. But will unemployment and inflation respond to demand in the same way as in a capitalist economy? Since democratic firms are unlikely to fire and hire in the same way as capitalist firms, this is unlikely. For example, slack from deficient demand will manifest partly as underemployment within firms, rather than in people put out of work entirely. The banking system may need to play an active role in forming new collective firms to absorb unattached labor, since democratic firms have less reason to expand once economies of scale are exhausted. But despite these differences in the labor market, there is no reason to expect demand management to be problematic.

It has been argued otherwise. One of the few discussions of the macroeconomics of a market economy with democratic firms suggested that the dynamics would be very different from capitalism. In an otherwise favorable engagement with Jaroslav Vanek's scheme for a worker-managed economy, James Meade argued that "the problems of macroeconomic control of inflations and deflations of price and employment would be strikingly different." A cooperative economy would be prone to "much greater fluctuation in price" in response to fluctuations in demand than a capitalist economy would be.[9]

But this conclusion was drawn from a model with very questionable assumptions. First, it assumes a perfect competition setting in which firms are price-takers, and shifts in market demand appear first as shifts in price, to which firms then respond by changing their output. Second, it assumes that firms can only change their output by changing the number of workers. For a democratic firm, changing the number of workers also means changing the number of members among whom income is divided. With such assumptions, a democratic firm choosing its output to maximize income per worker-member responds the "wrong" way to shift in demand: An increase in demand leads to a rise in price, which induces the firm to reduce its output and its membership.[10]

This means the market supply contracts as demand rises, thus raising prices further, but the vicious cycle does not go on forever because new firms—likely in part made up of the downsized former worker-members of the incumbents—will form to chase the profits. Meade concludes that the long-run equilibrium of democratic firms is much the same as that of capitalist firms; the democratic economy just rides a roller coaster to get there.

Neither of these assumptions are likely to apply in practice. First, firms do not need to change their membership to change their output. Even capitalist firms do not hire and fire in line with every shift in demand. They also let output per worker adjust, partly through changes in hours and partly through changes in output per hour worked. For example, a slow season at a cafe might mean baristas work fewer shifts or that they serve fewer customers per shift. This is why labor productivity (whether defined in terms of output per worker or per hour) usually moves up and down with the business cycle.[11]

As we discussed in chapter five, democratic firms are likely to be more reluctant to lay members off and also more reluctant to take new members on until they're confident of a lasting opportunity for expansion, in part because of the difficulty of downsizing later. This means they will do more of the adjusting in-house, in their "internal labor market." To the extent they do this by varying hours of work, the revenue changes will be borne specifically by those worker-members whose hours change. To the extent they involve changing output per hour worked, the income effects will be spread across members through their dividends from profits.

Second, most firms will not be "price-takers" as they are in the hypothetical situation of perfect competition. Under really existing capitalism, shifts in demand do not first drive market prices up or down and then induce firms to adjust output in response. That may be the case in some markets—specifically, in primary commodities (agricultural and mineral) markets with standardized products—but not across most of the economy. Things are usually the other way around: A shift in demand first leads firms to respond by adjusting their output. They adjust prices only over time and mainly in response to changes in costs. Firms typically operate with spare capacity, allowing them to adjust output in response to demand shifts in either direction without steep changes in marginal cost.

There is no reason to expect democratic firms to be fundamentally different, with one big exception: They will eject their worker-members less readily than capitalist firms fire theirs and, partly because of that, they will not take on new members as readily as capitalist firms hire. This means that labor costs have a more fixed character in democratic firms than in capitalist firms. As explained, we should not exaggerate the rigidity of labor costs for democratic firms. There is some room for adjusting hours worked without adjusting membership, and there will still be a flow of people leaving a firm voluntarily—to retire, to temporarily take time off, or to move to another workplace. Democratic firms *can* still choose to downsize if necessary.

We should not exaggerate the flexibility of labor costs under capitalism either. Many workers in capitalist firms are on longer-term contracts and can only be made redundant at some cost. The flexibility varies greatly from country to country, depending on the industrial and regulatory environment. But in general, capitalist firms are likely to have at least a periphery of marginal workers who can be let go and rehired more easily.

Again, the other side of less flexibility for the firm under socialism is greater security for the worker-member, in itself a very positive thing. The flexibility of the capitalist firm in hiring and firing places more of the burden of adjustment to shifts in demand on the personal incomes of the workers with the least secure employment. This is efficient from the employer's point of view because the costs of adjustment are external to the firm, borne by insecure workers and their families and by the public purse—to the extent that the latter provides income support to the unemployed.

In a socialist system with democratic firms, the income effects of fluctuations in demand are more spread out rather than concentrated on marginal workers. Such firms are more likely to change working hours before changing headcount, thus spreading changes in work over more workers. To the extent that paid hours do not fully adjust, changes in revenue will mean changes in profit, spreading to all members through their dividend share.

Risk-sharing arrangements with partner banks will spread the impact still further. If the firm has negotiated an arrangement whereby payments to a financing bank adjust to fluctuations in revenue, then it has turned some of what would otherwise be fixed cost into variable cost. A capitalist firm typically owns most of its capital equipment, and when it does not, contracts for long-term leases. Equipment and structures are mostly fixed costs. In the case of a democratic firm, on the other hand, it is as if the partner bank owns the equipment, which the firm rents, and the rental price adjusts with the state of the market. Equipment and structures become variable costs, because the bank takes on the risk of low capacity-utilization. This compensates for some of the inflexibility in labor costs.

Such risk-sharing arrangements will not insulate democratic firms from shifts in demand forever, especially those which are specific to the firm or its industry and not general movements in aggregate demand. This is because the banks will have payments information available in more-or-less real time and be able to distinguish between fluctuations that are common across a whole sector or a particular industry and those that are not. The contracts between bank and firm will be able to use these distinctions and provide more or cheaper insurance for the more general fluctuations—with the central bank in turn insuring the banks for macroeconomic fluctuations. The system does not insulate a firm from persistent losses, because over time trends will be distinguished from random fluctuations. A firm persistently underperforming its peers will find it harder to refinance. The secular decline of a whole industry—say, because of shifting tastes or technology—will be managed over time with lower investment.

However, macroeconomic fluctuations in aggregate demand will be partially absorbed via changes in flows to the banking system. This works as an automatic stabilizer in both directions, because flows to the banking system do not show up in anybody's personal income. When demand surges, profits are unexpectedly high, but some of that will be absorbed in higher payments to the partner banks, skimmed off, and added to the public purse. When demand slumps, the opposite is true. This contrasts starkly with capitalism, where fluctuations in profits flow more fully into the personal pockets of shareholders or into reinvestable retained funds for firms.

Besides the personal cost to those who lose income from work, the real social cost of underemployment is the loss of products that the idle workers would otherwise have been happy to make. Both capitalism and socialism have slack of this nature. Some slack is functional, if not inevitable, in any economic system with a complex division of labor that responds to individual choice. The idea that planning could entirely do away with spare capacity of equipment and labor is an illusion. "Overtaut plans" were one factor behind the shortages and unresponsiveness to consumer tastes in the Soviet economy we discussed in chapter two. Alec Nove saw this as the result of the impossibility of anticipating fine-grained demand in a dynamic economy. Even if aggregate supply exactly matched aggregate demand, mismatches would still emerge at the microeconomic level as tastes, techniques, and preferences shifted. In a system producing thousands of distinct goods—say, spare parts for vehicles or dishes for restaurants—perfect balance in the aggregate would still leave "not enough of a given type of carburettor or radiator-cap, not enough seats in certain restaurants, not enough duck or apple tart," while other items sat in excess supply. Some slack, Nove argued, is therefore the price of adaptability rather than evidence of irrationality or waste.[12]

Slack involves spare capacity with respect to capital equipment as well as labor. Under capitalism more of the cost of slack in labor falls to a smaller number of unemployed and marginally employed workers. Under our socialist system, to the extent that labor slack manifests as reduced hours or work intensity within firms, the costs are more widely distributed (across the firm's members) or socialized (as some of the income risk is absorbed by the banking system). Two questions remain: whether the system will tend to foster more slack than necessary within firms, in the form of underemployed worker-members who could be better employed elsewhere, and whether it will also leave pools of the involuntarily unemployed who cannot find work in a democratic firm or public agency within a reasonable time. Both kinds of "excess slack" are genuinely costly.

To the extent that a slump in demand in some industry is cyclical or otherwise temporary, it is not only fairer but also more efficient to keep workers attached to the workplaces where they have developed skills, experience, and personal connections, even if they are temporarily producing less, than to lay them off, only to rehire or replace them later. But when demand has shifted elsewhere indefinitely or when technical change means that some labor is permanently redundant in an industry, it is better for workers to find their way to other fields. There is a risk that a system that protects workers from cyclical unemployment worsens structural unemployment, even if this structural unemployment is partially hidden in pools of underutilized worker-members. There is also a risk of developing a divide between insider workers connected to workplaces and a pool of outsiders unable to find work at all.

The answer—reached by both Jaroslav Vanek and his critic James Meade—is an active public role in fostering new cooperative firms and providing incentives for worker-members to shift from declining firms and industries to rising ones. Democratic firms have reasons to grow to scales that are technically efficient but not to grow to be empires. This means that longer-run supply responses to growing demand for something depends more on new enterprises and less on the expansion of existing ones.[13]

In our model, the public banks do not simply wait for existing firms and entrepreneurial groups to approach them to request financing. With their bird's-eye view of economic conditions, they can identify likely niches for new firms and advertise to bring people together into new collectives, which they finance and partner with from the beginning. In this role, the banks are not just financiers but also advisers and even providers of accounting services to cooperatives, especially small ones. The banks can take the emergence of pools of unattached would-be workers as a reason to pick up the pace in firm creation, unless the government decides instead to increase employment in the noncommodity sector.[14] The prospect of more hours of work alone may attract underemployed members of existing firms, but mobility can also be encouraged with further measures if necessary. If worker-members continue to receive partial dividends from a firm for some time after they leave it, the prospect of being able to stack dividends by joining a new firm increases the incentive to move. The sponsoring bank or the public purse might provide sign-on bonuses at new firms to further encourage mobility.

Inflation and Unemployment: More Than Demand Management

Macroeconomic policy would be a lot simpler if there were a clear point of "just right" demand, with unemployment on one side and inflation on another. Unfortunately, it is quite possible for price increases to begin to accelerate in response to higher demand before the economy reaches full employment in the sense that everyone who wants a job at going wages can find one reasonably quickly. This has been somewhat obscured in modern capitalist macroeconomic policy since the 1980s by the replacement of full employment as a target with the "nonaccelerating inflation rate of unemployment," or NAIRU. This gets rid of the gray area between full employment and rising inflation by defining the minimum unemployment rate as that consistent with price stability. The standard view is that aiming at better than this with demand-management policy alone is futile. An unemployment rate below the NAIRU will set prices and wages spiraling, as workers and firms alike get used to higher-than-expected inflation and start using that as the baseline in their bargaining and price setting, driving prices still higher. Some labor market slack is necessary for price stability.

In this way, the burden of stability is carried especially by the unemployed and those most at risk of losing their jobs. Continual insecurity is the sacrifice imposed on some for the stability of the system as a whole. And the sacrifice cannot be fully ameliorated with generous unemployment benefits, because keeping down wage pressures requires that people keep competing with one another for the limited pool of vacant positions. Taking the pressure off the need to find a job would, other things being equal, raise the level of unemployment necessary to keep inflation under control. Though many higher up the professional ladder are less at risk of being thrown completely out of work, they are still at risk of falling down to lower rungs should they lose their job. Labor market slack imposes insecurity well beyond the marginally employed.

Our system tries to do away with such pervasive insecurity and the anxiety that comes with it. Security is supposed to be one of the key advantages of socialism. But does this doom the system to price instability? Is true full employment—beyond the inevitable pool of people temporarily between jobs in a dynamic economy—impossible in a market system?

The NAIRU story is often seen as conservative, an ideological justification for abandoning full employment and using the power of central banks to prevent the bargaining position of labor from ever getting too strong. And this criticism is valid enough. But socialists argued that capitalism could not sustain full employment long before the NAIRU analysis developed. Karl Marx said that capitalism depended on and would reproduce a reserve army of labor, because wage rises from a tight labor market would eat into profits and choke off investment, reducing the demand for labor. The Polish economist Michał Kalecki argued that though macroeconomic demand management made full employment economically possible, capitalists would reject it politically because worker security would undermine employer authority. Well before Milton Friedman theorized a "natural rate of unemployment," Joan Robinson recognized that wage rises would not eat into profit margins if firms could raise prices in response and posited an "inflation barrier," a point of low unemployment at which wages and prices would begin to spiral, chasing one another.[15]

Later Marxist and post-Keynesian economists developed models in which inflation arises from this kind of conflict over income distribution—conflicts in which unemployment is an important factor determining labor's bargaining power over the nominal wage. Such models imply a rate of unemployment at which inflation remains stable—but only given other factors such as firm market power, worker militancy, and the norms and institutions of wage-bargaining. These models imply a NAIRU that shifts when these other factors shift.

In fact, this converges with the standard conception of the "time-varying NAIRU." Although economists understand the NAIRU to be mostly independent of macroeconomic policy in the short run, they also understand it as movable over the long term. Estimates of the NAIRU find it to be different at different times and different places. It is widely seen as subject to hysteresis—sustained higher unemployment raises the NAIRU, and lower unemployment reduces it. A deep and prolonged slump not only knocks people out of work, but also leads to many business failures. It takes time for new industries to emerge, and it often calls for different skills from those developed for the previous jobs. Long-term unemployment leaves people discouraged, their skills rusty, and employers less ready to hire them. Low unemployment, on the other hand, leads firms to hire people they normally would not, training them on the job and adapting their skills to the needs of expanding industries.

This would seem to favor a macroeconomic strategy of pushing demand to its limits, but policymakers have generally been cautious. The NAIRU is not something that can be precisely and confidently estimated in advance for real-time policy purposes; it can only be calculated looking backward at historical data, and even then the calculation is imprecise. Meanwhile, monetary policy takes full effect only with a lag of many months, so policymakers are always making policy for an unknown future. Since they believe it is difficult to lower inflationary expectations once they become entrenched, they are cautious about testing the perceived limits: If they let the labor market get too tight, they will have to put the brakes on harder for longer. In practice, policy depends upon leading indicators (and rumors) of wage pressure to help with deciding when to choke demand. The role of a NAIRU model is not so much about generating precise estimates for technocratic thermostat twiddling as it is about lowering expectations for what demand-management policy can do.[16]

Instead, the story goes, the main hope for a sustainably lower structural unemployment rate is "labor market reform"—that is, creating flexibility for employers. Regulation and bargaining frameworks that protect wages and job security are abandoned, and conditions on unemployment benefits are tightened to better incentivize those out of work to keep looking for jobs.[17]

This simple story has a problem, however. Unemployment was generally lower in high-income countries in the decades after World War II; there was no runaway inflation, and these countries had highly regulated labor markets at the time. As economists Olivier Blanchard and Justin Wolfers argue, explanations of cross-country differences in unemployment based entirely on differences in labor market "rigidities" face a basic empirical difficulty: "Many of these institutions were already present when unemployment was low (and similar across countries), and, while many became less employment-friendly in the 1970s, the movement since then has been mostly in the opposite direction."[18]

Blanchard and Wolfers's view, however, is that the key change lies not in labor market institutions as such but in the rougher shocks experienced in the last decades of the twentieth century. In that context, they argue, what they call "employment-friendly" policies can make unemployment less persistent than it otherwise would be. On their account, minimum wages, job-security regulations, and collective bargaining protect "insiders" but slow the market's ability to reabsorb the unemployed. Generous welfare programs and a reduced stigma around unemployment may also weaken the pressure to compete for jobs. As they put it, to the extent that labor market institutions blunt the effect of unemployment on wages, they tend to make unemployment more persistent after economic shocks.

The deeper issue is not that price stability requires unemployment as such but that it depends on wage restraint and unemployment only insofar as unemployment helps enforce that restraint. Lower unemployment rates can be compatible with wage and price stability if the link between low unemployment and wage pressure is weakened or broken altogether. This is not so different from the Marxist or post-Keynesian account of inflation as distributional conflict: Labor market "flexibility" is a euphemism for disarming labor in that conflict.

The orthodox response is to deny that *real* wages are at stake here. Given firms' pricing power, any gains workers secure through higher nominal wages, the argument goes, are simply passed on as higher prices. But critics of this view do not claim that the solution to this problem is simple. Their models also imply wage–price spirals if workers and firms both have the economic power to defend incompatible income claims.

For some the point is merely critical: Capitalism's macroeconomic stability depends on labor's ongoing insecurity or quiescence. For others, the point is to propose an institutional framework for coordinating wage claims so that low unemployment rates do not lead to inflationary spirals. In that sense, the question is not whether unemployment restrains inflation but whether there are other, more democratic ways to do so.

This was once, in fact, a perfectly mainstream position. During the postwar long boom, economists widely recognized a tension between full employment and price stability. Counter to the later myth, policymakers did not generally choose to exploit a perceived stable trade-off, accepting more inflation as the price of lower unemployment. First, they did not believe the trade-off was stable: Wage-price spirals were understood. Second, even if they had believed in a trade-off, the fixed exchange rates of the Bretton Woods system meant that no country could sustain higher inflation than its trading partners for long before running into balance-of-payments crises, with foreign exchange reserves dwindling.[19]

One possible response to the tension was to abandon the goal of full employment and lower standards on that front. If this was not politically palatable, the other option was to try to manage wage-setting more centrally. According to Jan Tinbergen, a pioneer in building econometrically estimated macromodels for policy purposes and winner of the first Nobel Prize in economics, "wage rates have to be a deliberate instrument of economic policy if employment targets and monetary equilibrium are to be pursued at the same time."[20]

Most capitalist governments had no such instrument, no way of intervening in a wage-setting process that was dispersed over many firm-level wage negotiations across the economy. In some countries, though, such as Australia and Sweden, institutions for centralized bargaining had evolved within the industrial relations system. Union and employer representatives, mediated by state agencies, would settle agreements covering whole industries. Though these systems had not originally developed with macroeconomic considerations in mind, they were adapted to that purpose with varying degrees of success. As venues for mediated bargaining, they were certainly not policy levers under the control of the state. But they opened possibilities for coordinating wages across the economy.

Other considerations inevitably competed with macroeconomic objectives. Even so, coordinated bargaining tended to insulate wage determination somewhat from short-term labor market pressures, loosening the automatic link between low unemployment and accelerating wages.[21]

Cross-country studies often find that high union membership and extensive collective bargaining agreement coverage are generally associated with higher unemployment—with a vitally important exception: "highly unionised economies where bargaining is centralised are able to sustain low unemployment rates over long periods of time." This result is surprising for those who see labor market "flexibility" as the key to combining low unemployment with price stability, but not for those who view inflation as the outcome of distributional conflict.[22]

Under capitalism, however, there are problems for the labor movement and Left with a strategy of centralized wage determination. It works by voluntarily restraining wage claims below what workers might get were they to fully exercise their bargaining strength in full employment conditions. The system has no corresponding control over the prices set by firms. Wage control alone amounts to unilateral disarmament in distributional struggle. Attempts to combine it with broader price and income controls have been contentious and politically fragile. The wage structure is complex enough but at least still capable of central administration. The price structure is much more difficult to centrally administer while still remaining a market economy. Central wage determination itself tends to be unstable because groups of workers in particularly strong market positions who have a material incentive to negotiate extra payments break away from centrally determined rates. Not doing so seems to let their employers get away with fatter profit margins. In the Swedish Rehn–Meidner framework, it's worth noting that outcome was part of the design: Solidaristic, centralized wage-bargaining deliberately compressed wages in a way that raised costs for low-productivity firms while leaving the most productive firms with wider margins. The point was to force weaker firms to restructure or exit—and to let stronger firms invest and expand.

The more that firms or sectors succeed in breaking away from a centrally negotiated wage structure, the more the system is strained. Labor strategy in centralized bargains can be torn between further restraining wage rates to avoid inflation and letting them catch up for egalitarian reasons. A strong ethic of solidarity is needed to hold the strategy together. This stuck for longer in Northern Europe than Australia, but even in most of the Nordic countries central negotiations have given way to more decentralized pattern bargaining.

However, in the socialist system we propose, the wage-setting environment is different in ways that make the maintenance of centralized benchmarks easier. In the commodity sector, worker-members receive both a wage and also a dividend share of their firm's profits. The wage is the component of income that is set in advance and paid regularly. The dividend is a fluctuating residual paid out in the form of bonuses. Unlike in capitalism, a higher wage is not the worker's only way to secure a higher income from the firm. Other things being equal, higher wages come out of dividends. Beyond the benchmark wages set nationally by the labor board, wage-setting is about how to divide among members what is left over from revenue after meeting other costs. A firm-level decision to increase wages above the benchmarks—whether for everyone or for particular job categories—does not come out of anyone else's fixed-wage income. First, it is a decision about how much revenue to precommit as fixed payments to members and how much to leave as dividends. Second, since pay rates can differ between jobs and between levels of jobs, it is a decision about income distribution among members.

Since wages, once rates are set, become contractual obligations of the firm to its members, a firm must be confident of enough of a gap between revenue and other costs to meet those obligations for the foreseeable future. Shifting member income from dividends to wages lowers the cushion a firm otherwise has, since dividends are variable and not a commitment. Wage increases indicate, then, confidence that the firm has a sustainable efficiency advantage that can be converted into above-benchmark pay. Since the labor board already adjusts the benchmarks to transmit economy-wide worker productivity gains across the economy, firm-specific wage premiums reflect firm-specific advantages.

Wage increases specific to particular job categories come immediately at the expense of other worker-members' dividend incomes. A democratic firm is likely to be generally biased against unequal increases, except in circumstances in which paying some individuals more demonstrably pays for itself, raising the dividend income of other worker-members also. That might be the case, for example, when a firm wants to attract or retain members with particular specialized skills or when higher pay motivates more effort.

These pay hikes are not likely to represent cost increases that will be passed on in prices. That is because they are associated with firm-specific labor productivity increases, and unit-labor costs depend not only on the wage but also on output per hour. So long as the labor board manages the benchmarks themselves in line with macroeconomic stability, full employment is less prone than in modern capitalism to spark inflationary wage-cost growth. So long as competition policy and the public banks are doing their job in responding to anticompetitive market power, firms should not be able to permanently increase their own wages simply by raising prices.[23]

All this makes wage-driven cost-push inflation less likely under socialism but does not entirely sever the link between demand, wage-costs, and prices. It is still possible that competition for worker-members with particular skills drives up labor costs before general full employment is reached. But the combination of centrally determined benchmarks and the logics of democratic firm wage-setting are likely to make things manageable. The more that particular skill mismatches can be anticipated and planned for with active training and labor market policies, the less structural unemployment the system will be left with.

The benchmark wage-setting strategy of the labor board itself remains to be discussed—but this requires, first, an understanding of the international context.

Trade

Residents and firms will buy and sell across international borders. International prices and the state of markets abroad therefore matter across the domestic socialist economy. This is not just a matter of actual imports and exports. In many cases, international prices matter even when the products are both produced and used locally. *Tradable* is a broader category referring to commodities that could potentially be imported or exported. Many domestic firms will produce things for domestic customers who could otherwise choose imported versions. The local prices of these tradables are therefore limited by what suppliers abroad charge. Exports must likewise be priced competitively for their foreign markets. If a tradable commodity cannot be produced profitably given those international prices and domestic costs, it will not be produced domestically—at least not as a commodity.

Some tradable prices matter as costs. Many of the commodities people consume are tradable, and their prices are directly part of what we measure the real value of our incomes against. Other tradable commodities are inputs into nontradable products, and so their prices form part of the cost of production. Some tradable prices matter because they represent revenue: Domestic firms make those products, and the worker-members and the public (through bank earnings and taxation) draw income from them. Many tradable prices factor into both domestic incomes and domestic costs, because they are both produced and purchased locally.

In other words, the grid of prices within the commodity sector has nodes that are beyond the reach of domestic policy and often not much affected by domestic conditions at all. National macroeconomic flows will also be exposed to the ups and downs of demand among trading partners.

Does this undermine the model we have developed over the last few chapters? Is workplace democracy bound to be subordinated to a drive for international competitiveness? Can policymakers tend the flows of income and expenditure through the public banking system when so many of those flows pass to and from the wider world? We argue that it is possible for the state to manage and socialize the constraints and risks of integration into a world economy, protecting the socialist model even while leaving cross-border trade mostly open.

Getting this right matters because the alternative to international trade is not sovereignty but self-imposed inefficiency. Autarky would turn what is feared as a risk of entanglement with the world economy into a certainty: lower incomes for more work. In any case, autarky is not an option for any country that lacks essential primary resources. Economies of scale, specific resource endowments, and advantages that come from specialization mean that a country will be better off concentrating on what it has relative productivity advantages in and trading for other things.

Trade works something like an alternative technology for converting resources into products. Often the indirect route of using resources to make other products and trading those for what is actually wanted will bring more of what is desired than using the resources directly to make them. A socialist government does not control the terms of trade—that is, the rates at which domestic resources can be converted into desired outputs via exports and imports. But neither does it control the rates at which resources can be converted into desired outputs at home through production techniques.

No directive can order a power plant to generate an extra hundred megawatts if the technology does not allow it. Technical possibilities also set limits, and the socialist approach is to share the costs and gains of production within those limits. If we do not consider technical limits fatal to socialism, we should not consider trade fatal either.

There is no reason to expect a market socialist country with democratic firms to be less *technically* efficient than a capitalist country with equivalent resources and technology. The citizens of a socialist country may however *choose* more leisure time, more noncommodity production, or a more relaxed pace of work than is typical in a capitalist society. If deliberate, these are not inefficiencies but different choices about how to use the available resources, people's time and energy especially. These choices do mean lower real personal income per capita in terms of commodities than would otherwise be possible. Openness to trade will not in itself force different choices on the whole country in the name of international competitiveness. The choices will instead make themselves felt partly in the affordability of products made abroad—but whatever the choices, the terms of the trade-offs will be better with trade than without it.

Having said that, *changes* in the international situation can have different impacts on different groups, creating domestic winners and losers in the short or long run. For example, demand for a major export might boom, driving up wages or the exchange rate and increasing real incomes overall but squeezing the margins of collective firms producing other tradable goods. Sometimes developments may make just about everyone worse off. For example, there could be a sharp rise in the world price of a critical import used as an input across the economy but not produced domestically. And sometimes international shifts can be macroeconomically destabilizing. For example, a slump in a key trading partner could hit demand for exports, first lowering income in that sector and then elsewhere as exporting firms and their members lower their own spending in response.

The worker-members of firms in tradable industries will be more directly exposed to changes and especially to things that permanently affect the margins between the domestic costs they must pay and the international prices they receive. Even if it would be better in the long run for labor to shift into other industries, workers have skills, experience, and relationships where they are and value staying put. And so, they may find that even if "international competitiveness" of a whole economy in the abstract is not a worry, the specific competitiveness of their particular firm is. Since they have no way as an individual firm to share the burden of adjustment, they find themselves under pressure to work harder or restructure their operations.

When such things happen, it can be cold comfort to know that gains to the winners exceed losses to the losers or that outcomes would be even worse in the absence of trade or that conditions will improve over time. As Keynes said, in the long run we are all dead. We live in the world of dynamics and never reach the static destination of welfare models before more disturbances arise.

It is a commonplace of trade discourse that gains to the winners are generally enough to more than compensate the losers, but under capitalism that compensation rarely actually happens. The socialist system has the mechanisms to make the compensation actually take place, to smooth temporary disturbances, and to plan for longer-run transitions. Some of those mechanisms have already been discussed. The standard channels of income redistribution will help. Risk-sharing arrangements with their partner banks will help exposed firms deal with temporary ups and downs. Ultimately, it is the banks that bear the capital risk for physical assets stranded by permanently changing conditions—which means these costs are socialized. The banking system's capacity to plan, finance, and facilitate the emergence of new industries can help shift worker-members from declining niches to rising ones—whether by retooling existing firms or helping people migrate to new ones. This is not fundamentally different from how the system responds to domestic changes in taste or technological developments.

But all of this assistance with adaptation at the industry, firm, and worker levels will be made easier with a macrolevel strategy to spread both the burdens and the windfalls of international change across the economy, rather than leaving them concentrated in exposed sectors. Although the network of economic connections spreads across borders, two important nodes in particular remain very national. One is the currency. Its value relative to other currencies affects all whose income and costs are primarily denominated in it. The other is the labor market and the wage structure. Firms recruit from the same pool whether or not their products are exposed to international competition. Pay and conditions cannot get too out of line between sectors without inducing people to move. And, of course, egalitarianism implies that pay and conditions should not depend on whether or not someone happens to work in a trade-exposed sector.

In our model, both of these nodes are anchored by public agencies. The central bank acts as the market maker for the domestic currency, and the labor board sets benchmark wages. The strategy we advance draws on the Nordic model of wage coordination, which has helped countries combine high and egalitarian incomes with a high degree of openness to trade. The strategy works more by managing wages than managing the exchange rate, but to see why this is so requires an understanding of what determines the value of a currency and what that value means for the economy.[24]

Foreign Exchange and the Value of the Currency

What determines the value of a currency? In the first instance, what people are willing to pay for it. A state can issue currency at will, but it can't declare what it will exchange for. An exchange rate peg—a fixed rate of exchange with some other currency—must be sustained by a public agency (usually the central bank) committing to buy or sell as much of its currency as the rest of the market wants at the set rate. It will not run out of its own currency to sell, because it can always issue more. But it can easily run out of other countries' currencies if other actors keep selling its own currency back to it. That means it can prevent appreciation indefinitely, but prevent depreciation only so long as foreign exchange reserves hold up. Where the state does not try to maintain a fixed peg in this way, the currency floats, its value left to the market—though the central bank can still have an influence by strategically buying and selling even if it does not commit to a particular rate.

So what determines what people are willing to pay for a currency? Actors decide to exchange one currency for another for a variety of reasons: to import something, to buy or sell an asset, to make contractual payments to someone abroad, or to transfer funds to family. Exchanging one currency for another, of course, always involves finding someone willing to switch currencies in the other direction. Currency dealers absorb imbalances in the very short run, quoting exchange rates, taking all comers at those rates, and letting their currency inventories fluctuate for a while. But they respond quickly and change their quoted prices in response to imbalances of supply and demand, and this is how exchange rates adjust.

Under capitalism today, currency conversion associated with capital flows dwarfs conversion associated with trade. Managers of financial portfolios move between currencies in pursuit of the highest rates of expected returns for a chosen level of risk. This means that they keep an eye on differences in interest rates between currencies and also on expected movements in exchange rates. Changes in the expectations of financial traders drive movements in exchange rates. In this environment it is not helpful to say that supply and demand determine what a currency is worth, because traders can quickly pile in or out of a currency if its value gets out of line with expectations. In other words, supply and demand rapidly adjust according to assessments of where rates should be, given relative interest rates, inflation rates, and expectations of future movements. This is why most countries today let their exchange rates float, rather than maintaining a peg. In a world of rapid capital mobility, speculators can overwhelm national foreign exchange reserves quickly if they form a collective opinion that the fundamentals are unsound.

But in the model we have described, capital movements into and out of the socialist country's currency will be much less important. Within the country, there are no financial or real assets for foreigners to invest in. There is no private asset ownership at all, beyond bank deposits and the consumer durables people have at home. The central bank has a monopoly on foreign exchange (though the other banks act as its agents) and allows currency exchange only for trade and tourism. Nonresidents have no official way of accumulating deposits within the system, and residents no official way of acquiring assets abroad. This will not entirely suppress capital movements. There will always be workarounds for the determined—for example, by disguising asset acquisition in an import payment or as spending on vacation abroad or even by varying the timing of trade settlements to take advantage of expected exchange rate movements. But there will be vastly reduced potential for large and rapid capital movements in or out of the currency, which will allow interest rates on domestic deposits to remain detached from rates of return abroad.

This makes the foreign exchange situation more like that which prevailed for many capitalist countries in the post–World War II decades of capital controls. Trade rather than capital flows will dominate the foreign exchange market. Other currency transactions—related to foreign borrowing or investment and aid transfers—will be managed publicly at a national level. International public borrowing should be done only with extreme caution, especially in the absence of trusted international financial architecture negotiated between like-minded countries.[25]

The viability of capital controls does not mean that a socialist state should adopt the other tenet of Bretton Woods and maintain a fixed exchange rate peg to another currency or basket of currencies. This would require the central bank to maintain a foreign currency reserve large enough to weather any foreseeable period of international payments deficit. Defending the peg could pull macroeconomic policy away from a focus on full employment, forcing austerity. A flexible exchange rate can absorb some of the impact of international fluctuations in prices and demand. And while exchange rate movements bring some uncertainty of their own, the banking system can help firms hedge exchange rate risk, especially if importing and exporting firms face offsetting risks. The central bank will act as market maker for its own currency, and will still need some reserves of foreign exchange to provide liquidity and smooth fluctuations.[26] In some circumstances, it may make sense to hold the exchange rate steadier for longer. But it will generally not try to hold it steady against a tide.[27]

In the absence of other international flows, those tides will mainly reflect changes in trade patterns. A stable currency (relative to the currencies of trading partners) implies that at going exchange rates, desired sales of the currency to purchase imports are being matched by desired purchases from the proceeds of exports. Essentially, exports earn the foreign currency with which imports are purchased. An imbalance between intended imports and intended exports will also manifest in an imbalance of desired purchases and sales of currency, which the central bank must sooner or later allow to move the exchange rate.

Wages, Incomes, and Trade

Given that the socialist country is mostly insulated from private capital flows, it again becomes useful to frame macroeconomic policy in the old Bretton Woods terms, as a problem of balancing "internal" and "external" constraints.[28] Internal balance is domestic full employment and price stability; external balance is exchange rate stability. With capital flows out of the picture, consistently meeting both of these targets simultaneously depends on policy control over both domestic spending and the domestic wage-cost structure.[29]

The basic reason demand management is not enough to secure macroeconomic balance is that the trade balance and demand for domestic commodities each depend on both domestic spending and domestic wage-costs relative to international tradables prices—the "cost ratio." If policy must take the cost ratio as given, then full employment and exchange rate stability might call for different levels of domestic spending. For example, the level of spending associated with full employment could also be associated with a spiral of depreciation and inflation, and policy might be pressed back toward austerity.

The trade balance depends on domestic spending because imports will vary along with spending—because some proportion of whatever people buy will be imported—while exports are unaffected, depending instead on spending abroad. It depends on the cost ratio because this determines the viability of domestically producing tradables, both exports and import-competing products.

In nontradables industries, product prices tend to move with domestic costs, which are dominated by wage-costs. All firms face the same wage structure and can respond together. In tradables industries, on the other hand, the response to domestic costs is more limited, because they compete with firms abroad who do not face the same cost structure. The boundary between "tradable" and "nontradable" is quite blurry. Some things are tradable but at relatively high transport cost or with quality differences that make imports less than perfect substitutes. Such things provide limited protection to domestic producers. Some things cross the line over time—for example, when improvements in digital communications make international provision of some services easier. In any case, more commodities will cross the boundary from nontraded to traded as gaps between domestic and foreign costs shift relative to these objective and subjective costs of trade. Around the core of tradable products whose domestic producers are already in close competition with producers abroad, there is a fringe of firms who have some room to move with respect to international prices, but who would find that space tightening as domestic costs rise.[30]

In any case, if left to run its course, and taking other factors as given, a rising ratio of domestic costs to the relevant international tradables prices will tend, over time, to squeeze the profit margins of tradable-producing firms. Well before they become completely unviable, their lower relative profitability will lead firms or their worker-members to shift investment and activity to nontradables. But residents cannot continue indefinitely consuming the same volume of tradables as before if domestic producers are producing both fewer exports and fewer things that could be imported. Exports exchange for the foreign currency that is used to pay for imports. "External balance" ultimately requires some combination of lower overall real domestic expenditure and a shift in the allocation of expenditure from tradables to nontradables.[31]

However, with exchange rate flexibility, such a situation will not run its course. The value of the currency moves much more quickly than industries transition. The tension between "internal balance" and "external balance" was felt much more acutely when countries committed to fixed exchange rates. A flexible exchange rate gives macroeconomic policy more room to move. It means policymakers do not find themselves forced into emergency macroeconomic austerity to prevent a drain of foreign currency. It helps to absorb and disperse the impact of short-term shocks and cyclical fluctuations and also helps with adjustment to longer-run international changes. This is because it is easier for exchange rates to move in both directions than for the domestic cost structure to move in terms of the domestic currency.

It is especially difficult to move nominal domestic wages and other costs downwards. Prices and especially nominal wages have long been "sticky down" in modern capitalism, and there is no reason to expect things to be different under socialism. People tend to resent and resist direct cuts to the money value of wages more than they resist—at least the modest—erosion of real wages by inflation. Prices tend to be somewhat more flexible, but downward adjustment is still difficult for firms to bear while wages and financial commitments remain fixed. Deflation is more painful than inflation—usually requiring an extended period of high unemployment and widespread firm failures to grind prices and wages down. A falling currency lowers the domestic cost structure relative to that of international trading partners with much less trouble.

It is not cost-free, however. Other things being equal, a lower value of the currency means that the prices of internationally tradable commodities are more expensive relative to domestic incomes. Or, to put it another way, real incomes are lower. If a depreciating currency prompts domestic reactions that raise nominal wages and other incomes to maintain their real value, this counteracts the stabilizing effect of the depreciation. This is a major reason why policymakers were reluctant to adjust exchange rates under Bretton Woods, even in the face of major balance-of-payments crises. In full employment conditions, wages and prices were prone to adjust to catch up with the higher tradable prices after devaluation, reopening the payments deficit and building pressure for further devaluation. Unless there was some framework for managing the distributive effects, devaluation was not an alternative to austerity but at best a supplement.

For socialist policy, domestic demand management and wage-benchmark policy must work together to dampen macroeconomic disturbances from international markets and spread around the costs and windfalls of shifting trade fortunes. To ensure this happens, policymakers must:

1. Set the overall level of benchmark wages to maintain stable *average* profit margins *over the long run* for firms in the tradables sector. This means that wages in both tradable and nontradable sectors grow according to domestic productivity growth and long-run trends in the world prices of domestically produced tradables. Prices in nontradables can find their own level, as firms in these industries all face the same domestic costs.
2. Allow the value of the currency to move. As the only foreign exchange dealer, the central bank should absorb very short-run imbalances in supply and demand, to provide liquidity and smooth fluctuations. But it should not try to hold the rate in the face of a persistent imbalance.
3. Avoid adjusting benchmark wages in the short run in response to local price movements sparked by changes in the value of currency. Let short-run fluctuations in trade fortunes be

absorbed by profit margins or the value of personal incomes, where they can be addressed by the risk-spreading mechanisms of the banking system and, if necessary, by the tax-and-transfer system. If the fluctuations come from temporary shocks on world markets, they will eventually fade and should not be locked into the wage structure. Longer-term changes of fortune will be addressed over time through the benchmark wages.

4. But do adjust other components of domestic demand in response to the effects of export fluctuations on output and especially employment. Unlike wage adjustments, aggregate demand can be moved in both directions without too much trouble.

It is, of course, not always easy to identify in advance which shifts are likely to be temporary and which more lasting—and thus forecast what is necessary to maintain average profit margins in tradables over the long run. But macroeconomic policy has always been an art rather than an exact science. The main point is to let wage benchmarks adjust slowly and exchange rates adjust more quickly, as the latter moves more easily in both directions.

Note that adjusting benchmarks to maintain average profit margins in tradables does not guarantee the viability of any firm or even industry. The tradables sector is composed of many industries, whose fortunes will vary from one another enormously. Inevitably, some will decline and others rise over time, due to changes in technology, tastes, and international development, and the consequences are something to manage through the long-run planning of the banking system.

The wage benchmarks set centrally by the labor board are an important anchor for the whole wage structure. This does not give policy complete control over wages. As explained, firms can choose to pay premiums over the benchmarks for some or all members, and it is quite likely these premiums will sometimes respond to demand and price and exchange rate movements in ways that run against policy. For example, a surge in international demand for a particular major export may leave the producing firms with fat margins. Policymakers may judge the surge temporary and so not justifying a general benchmark wage increase, which would be difficult to reverse later. The firms receiving the windfall may feel more confident, and increase worker-member wages above the benchmark.

However, the system blunts such impulses in two ways. First, in capitalism, securing a wage increase is the only way workers get a share of the windfall at all, whereas worker-members in a democratic firm already get their share through their dividends from profits. In the latter case, raising wages further above the benchmark implies confidence that the good times will continue indefinitely, which could get the firm into trouble if fortunes reverse—and this is likely to make worker-members more cautious.

Second, the wage-benchmark system implies and reinforces egalitarian norms in coordinating wage-setting across the economy. Even without hard constraints on breakaway wage drift for the fortunate, the presence of institutions for economy-wide wage-setting solves some of the fiendish collective action problems involved in solidaristic wage coordination. Today, in contrast, privileged workers asked to voluntarily restrain wage claims below what they could achieve generally expect the benefits to flow to their employers, not to lower-income workers.

Ultimately, if full employment is sustained, the real income available to distribute across the socialist community depends on domestic productivity and the terms of trade—that is, on the relative value of what the country exports compared to what it imports. There is nothing inherently more valuable or admirable about production for export than production for domestic use. Export industries generally represent production where the country has a relative advantage so that labor applied there generates more value for residents through trade than it would generate if applied directly for domestic consumption. There is no reason to promote exports beyond this point of relative advantage, but it is worth planning investment and fostering new industries where doing so builds durable advantages.

Ultimately, there is no one-size-fits-all answer to the question of how much a country should engage in trade. Larger countries can maintain higher incomes with less trade because there is room for economies of scale across a wider range of products within the domestic division of labor. Smaller countries, by contrast, need higher trade–GDP ratios for higher incomes because their productivity depends more on specialization.

Taken together, we've now laid out the architecture of our model. We began by arguing for democratic firms operating in markets as the basic unit of production, combining workplace self-government with the informational advantages of price coordination. We then explored how such firms might be embedded in a public financial system that socializes risk, directs investment, and prevents private wealth from snowballing and becoming a source of economic power. From there, we turned to the problem of system-wide coordination—how investment, employment, wages, and price level can be governed at the macroeconomic level.

We have shown how monetary and fiscal policy, exercised through public banking and public control over investment, can sustain full employment without recurring crises. We have argued that a wage benchmark system can loosen the link between employment and inflation, allowing the gains of growth and productivity to be shared without price spirals. And we have shown how openness to trade and exposure to world prices need not undermine a socialist economy, provided that capital flows are controlled and the costs and benefits of international integration are deliberately spread across society.

This is our promised blueprint for a feasible socialism. Markets are retained, but they are embedded within democratic control and egalitarian ends. Investment is coordinated but not micromanaged. Macroeconomic constraints are acknowledged but treated as social facts to be governed rather than immutable laws to be obeyed. The model rests on institutions—public banks, democratic firms, wage-setting bodies, and elected governments—that are meant to shift economic power away from wealthy individuals toward collective decision-making.

None of this will convince everyone, and it is not meant to. The architecture we have presented invites objections from multiple directions. From the Right will come familiar claims about inefficiency and unfreedom. From parts of the Left will come egalitarian worries about competition and incentives. The chapters that follow confront these challenges head-on.

9

Will Socialism Fail Again?

For many critics, the Soviet experience settled the question of socialism once and for all. Rather than seeing it as a failure of one model, they take it as proof of the folly of any attempt to transcend capitalism. Some celebrate capitalism on its merits, understanding private ownership of society's productive forces as an essential component of human freedom. Others merely accept it as something we can't rid ourselves of without making everything worse in the process. Either way, these critics see the dysfunction of the "actually existing socialist" economies and the events that led most of them to stop "actually existing" as a powerful vindication of their perspective.

Where we argue that the combination of democracy in politics and different socialist economics can produce better results, these critics—whether libertarians or social democrats—abhor the very idea of "trying again" and courting a second disaster.

One powerful way of expressing this attitude comes from the late polemicist Christopher Hitchens. He had, for most of his career, been a socialist critic of the Soviet model. The slogan of the tiny left-wing group where he'd started his political life was, "Neither Washington nor Moscow, but International Socialism." He seemed to have a residual commitment to this possibility until the last decade of his life. His initial explanation of his eventual loss of faith was simply that he could no longer imagine socialism happening. The victory of capitalism was too complete.

But in some of his final writings he hinted that this might not be such a bad thing after all, and in those moments, he drew on the same metaphor we've been using—of a failed socialist *experiment*. Do we really want, he sometimes asked, to *experiment* on the entire population?[1]

The problem is that, like it or not, by virtue of having been born into a society, we're all always subjects in a social "experiment" of one kind or another. We're all dealing with economic and political conditions not of our choosing, and the results are often unpredictable. Even when a system has existed for as long as capitalism has, its future evolution can keep everyone strapped in for that particular ride to all kinds of places they would never have chosen to go.

Instead of signing individual consent forms as you would for a literal experiment, you are enlisted to participate in a set of arrangements by being born. There is no way to *individually* opt out of the economy short of going to live in the woods. In practice, the best we can do is to exercise some *collective* control over which kind of experiment we deal with through the mechanisms of political democracy. It's surely one of the grave faults of the Communist Parties that once ruled the Soviet Union and the "People's Democracies" of Eastern Europe that they didn't allow their populations to fully exercise this right. But it's also worth noting that the same populations were denied the same right during the process of transition to capitalism. No popular referenda were held on whether to privatize state assets. Instead, these societies were plunged into a *capitalist* experiment without their consent.

The denial of this right to economic self-determination is a grave injustice regardless of the direction in which the citizens of any society are being marched. We're advocates not just of a democratic form of socialism but of a democratic road to getting there.

Even so, you might think that there's something to the intuition underlying the "no more experiments" position that our response doesn't adequately address. You might be skeptical that our model of socialism would function any better than the Soviet one did. Or you might grant that it would be a political and economic *improvement* over what existed in the Stalinist past but still think that an economic machine designed along the lines we propose would be considerably less functional than the one we already have. You might also worry that socialist democracy wouldn't coexist for long with a dysfunctional economy and conclude that our kind of socialism would end up in the same authoritarian morass as its Soviet predecessor.

Finally, you might think that even if we can adequately answer these challenges at an engineering level, powerful moral objections would remain. In other words, whether or not this new version *could* survive, you might not think socialism deserves another chance.

In what follows, we'll address a series of objections, starting with a philosophical one. Even if we could achieve a workable socialism, is this a goal worth striving for? Or does economic collectivization necessarily trample on individual rights?

Your model requires the nationalization of property in key sectors of the economy, which are currently in private hands. And though most existing businesses would find a place in your market sector, they would be reorganized against the will of existing owners and handed over to workers. Doesn't this require massive violations of the property rights of existing owners?

Historically, this has been one of the most popular objections to socialism of any kind, but it's one of the critiques we find the least compelling. The objector is essentially smuggling their normative conclusion into their premises.

To see the point, start with an example of the sort of thing that might happen during the transition to socialism. John owns a factory with a hundred workers. A socialist government has just been elected, and John is worried. The government hasn't yet acted on its most radical promises but the situation is changing every day and he doesn't want to take any chances. John plans to close the factory and move his operations to a country with a friendlier administration. The workers catch wind of this plan, and they get organized. One of them, Susan, is elected by the other ninety-nine as their representative. She lobbies the new government, pressing the workers' case and demanding that the factory be immediately nationalized and its management handed over to a workers' committee.

Suppose Susan's efforts succeed. Have John's property rights been violated?

Note that this example is carefully chosen to meet the objector on their ideological home turf—a situation in which it may feel plausible that a capitalist has a right to his means of production in much the same way that you have a right to your phone or your car or a particularly beloved leather jacket. The reality is that a traditional capitalist like John, who runs a reasonably large firm in which he combines the roles of owner, financier, manager, and entrepreneur, has already become rare. Increasingly, even in medium-sized businesses, these roles tend to be disentangled. But the intuition that he has a moral right to hold onto the business is strongest when all of that stays entangled, so that's how we've kept it here.

Also note that there are ways this story could end short of John getting *nothing*. The workers, for example, may decide that he did a good job steering the ship and decide to ask him on as a high-level manager. He'd now be accountable to his fellow workers, but he could still end up in a great situation financially—and even with some level of continuity with his previous role. Even if this didn't happen, a socialist government might well decide to offer financial compensation to expropriated owners.

The socialist ideal is a leveling of private wealth to a point where no large-scale inequalities remain. But it's possible that the political judgment of the time would be that some accumulated wealth is deserved. Over time, the tax system could be used to reabsorb much of it into the public treasury and, in any case, since money could no longer be used to purchase pieces of money-making ventures, it would be far less self-propagating. And any socialist system worth its salt would presumably include an inheritance tax of 100 percent of assets over some fairly minimal threshold. Whatever argument can be made that many business owners "earned" their wealth, surely no similar argument can be made on behalf of those owners' heirs.

That's what we think, anyway. But let's assume that John furiously disagrees. He thinks that the firm is his in exactly the way that the beloved old leather jacket is his—his to keep, sell, give away, pass on to his heirs, or set fire to—and that neither the oh-so-generous offer of staying on as a manager in a firm he'd no longer own nor the prospect of being paid a generous compensation would ever justify this brazen act of theft. If someone violates your property rights and then deposits some money in your bank account, they've still violated your property rights.

Is he right? To answer this question, we need to start by clarifying the terms of the question. What kind of "rights" are we talking about?

If the elected government does what Susan asks and passes a law nationalizing factories like John's, they haven't violated his *legal* rights at all. If you still think John's property rights have been violated, you must think that these are *moral* rights not legal ones. But what does it mean to have a moral right to some piece of property? Presumably, that you're entitled to use it and to stop other people from using it. The real question is why John is in fact morally entitled to his factory and its products in a way that Susan and her fellow workers are not.

Here, defenders of capitalist property rights might respond by appealing to intuitions about the immorality of "coercion." But that won't work. All distributions of scarce resources rest on coercion. No one really advocates a world without some system for deciding who gets to use which resources when, and it's easy to see why. If such a world—what Matt Bruenig calls a "Grab What You Can World"—somehow got going, it wouldn't last long. The question is never "coercion" versus "no coercion." It's always *which* claims are backed with force.[2]

To underline that last point, it's absolutely true that if Susan gets her way and John's factory is expropriated and placed under worker management, John is being prevented—by force!—from doing what he wants with the factory and its products. If he enters the nationalized factory at night and tries to sneak away with some of the equipment, the cops will be called on him. But it's equally true that a government that rejects Susan's demand and continues to recognize John's property rights will be preventing the workers—by force!—from doing what *they* want with that property. If the workers in this second scenario try to carry out the expropriation on their own, physically occupying the factory floor and barring the doors, John can have Susan and her fellow malcontents arrested. The two cases both involve the same kind of coercion.

A more careful critic might clarify here that they aren't advocating sweeping moral prohibitions on "force" or "coercion" but a narrower principle about the "initiation" of force. On its face, this sounds plausible. Nearly everyone agrees that, as a general rule, it's wrong to initiate conflicts with people who are just minding their business. If Smith is sitting on a park bench reading, Jones walks up to him and punches him in the face, and Smith hits him back just as hard, we all take it as a given that Jones is the one who has some explaining to do.

A popular anti-redistribution argument runs with this intuition and simply extends the idea of "force" from attacking someone's *person* to taking away their *property*. Matt Kibbe's 2014 libertarian manifesto is entitled *Don't Hurt People and Don't Take Their Stuff*. In his view, if Susan leads her fellow workers in occupying John's property and he calls the cops and has her arrested, she's the one who "initiated" force by trying to take away what belongs to John.[3]

But there are two problems here. First, the first half of Kibbe's title contradicts the second. Every time you recognize some piece of the world as one person's "stuff" that no one else is allowed to "take," you're carving out an exception to the general prohibition on hurting people. A "Private Property, No

Trespassing" sign is a threat to hurt people who aren't hurting people. Part of what's being granted by a legal recognition of property is precisely the right to issue these sorts of threats. In G. A. Cohen's words, "A property distribution is just a distribution of rights of interference." If you want a consistently enforced rule against hurting people who haven't hurt you first, you cannot recognize property rights at all. What you get instead is Grab What You Can World.[4]

Second, rhetoric about hurting people or taking "their" stuff in any argument over redistribution simply assumes the very issue in dispute. There's no dispute about what is part of John's person—which hands are his hands, which feet his feet. The dispute is about what external stuff is "John's stuff"? Again, if it's the stuff he's *legally* regarded as having, a lawful expropriation wouldn't count as taking "his" stuff because it would now be the People's Stuff. On the other hand, if "his stuff" means "the stuff he's morally entitled to have," a moral prohibition against taking "his stuff" is vacuous. It amounts to saying *it would be wrong to take whatever stuff it would be wrong to take.*

It could be that John worked hard to build up his business. He and those who take his side would probably put a lot of emphasis on this point to build public sympathy for his moral claim to the factory. Their view would be that he built it, it's his, and he shouldn't have to sell it to the government if he doesn't want to.

Many socialists would argue that the premise is entirely spurious. The employees, they'd argue, are the ones actually doing the hard work; John is just a parasite. We think this is overstated. Some forms of managerial labor, for example, are socially necessary and would be performed by *someone* in any system—whether a capitalist, a manager hired by the capitalist, or a manager hired by a workers' committee. It's common in smaller firms for capitalists to perform a good bit of this kind of labor themselves instead of delegating it all to managers. Like we said, John is one such capitalist, and he poured his blood, sweat, and tears into building up the business. If you think performing labor gives you at least some claim on the fruits of that labor, he now has at least some claim on his factory and its products.

There are at least three problems, however, with using this argument to ground a claim that nationalizing the factory violates John's rights. First, even if you accept that property claims can be justified by hard work, it's unlikely that John's individual claim would outweigh the aggregated labor-entitlement claims of his hundred workers. Second, there are a number of plausible theories about who is morally entitled to which resources that don't rest on labor entitlement at all. As we've seen, the moral philosophies of Cohen and Rawls fall into this category. Third, even if you *do* think that it's wrong to expropriate businesses still owned by individuals who did lots of work to build them up, this won't be enough to ground a more general objection to expropriation. What about businesses that are, for example, inherited or purchased by owners who had no hand in building them up and who then simply hire others to perform the management tasks?

Ultimately, if you want a world in which those who perform lots of labor for a firm are guaranteed to exert some meaningful control over how things are run and how the profits are divvied up, you should be rooting for the larger transition to socialism of which the expropriation of John's factory would be one small part.

Robert Nozick, building on a moral framework developed by John Locke, argued that someone is entitled to a piece of property when they can trace their claim on it to morally legitimate acts of "original acquisition" like homesteading unowned property. We don't find this theory plausible. We care about how much inequality and avoidable human misery a set of arrangements is generating *right now*, not whether those arrangements came about in the right way. But a more basic problem, as Nozick himself would eventually acknowledge, is that so much of the economic history of the world is so distant from these requirements that, even if we accepted Nozickian principles in the abstract, it's unclear how much they could actually be applied in practice.[5]

We suspect that the more basic intuition underlying pop-libertarianism is something like a moral version of "possession is nine tenths of the law" or a vague sense that if people accumulate wealth by "playing by the rules" as those rules are currently constituted, it's unfair to take it away from them. But these are just general prohibitions on progress. There are times in history when patterns of possession, and the rules that generate them, require revision. Now is one of those times.

Even if expropriation were morally defensible, would the social upheaval required to carry it out really be worth the risk? Why not stop at social democracy?

Attempts to leapfrog to long-term socialist goals in unfavorable conditions or without the kind of democratic majority necessary to ensure a relatively smooth transition can lead to disastrous results. This note of caution should serve as a guide for how to fight for socialist goals, not as an excuse for abandoning them.

The most advanced social democracies are the most just and livable societies humans have so far built. While there have been some rollbacks of the welfare state, even today, countries like Denmark, Norway, Sweden, and Finland have strong labor unions, large public sectors, and expansive social programs that meet the material needs of their citizens to a remarkable degree. Nevertheless, for at least three reasons, we see socialism and not just social democracy as the North Star of future civilizational progress.

The first is ideological. Even in Sweden in the 1970s, at social democracy's high-water mark, most direct participants in the economy had no real choice but to work for capitalist employers. Hence, they took orders from people with no democratic accountability to them and had no direct say in how their firms' revenues were divided. It's good that a strong labor movement gave them a degree of influence—but workers shouldn't need to threaten industrial action every time they want to exert influence on what goes on in the places where they spend half their waking lives. If a king or dictator is relatively weak and can often be influenced to adopt popular policies by a fear of unrest in the streets, that's a good thing. But democracy is better. We don't think this principle stops at the entrance to the workplace.

The second is pragmatic. Social-democratic gains made within a framework that keeps the existing ruling class in place are innately unstable. Some reforms are harder to unwind than others, but keeping the levers of production and investment in the hands of capitalists ensures that, when pressures mount, those gains will be vulnerable. Battles that seemed to have been won will have to be fought over and over. In the long run, even in an advanced social democracy, the best way to secure gains won't be to rest on the laurels of these victories but to keep going and make deeper inroads against capitalist property relations.

Finally, it's easy to conduct this discussion as if social democracy were something that's always existed—as if Norway got its social wealth funds and strong labor unions as some sort of package deal with its lutefisk and fjords—but that's not reality. The Nordic welfare states are the messy, imperfect, and incomplete fruits of a ferocious history of class struggle. And it's far from clear that they could have been achieved if many of the people who fought for them hadn't been guided by the North Star of socialism.

In your model, the state sector is larger than in highly social-democratic countries like Norway. And your "private" sector is not really private at all: Worker-controlled firms depend on public banks, and labor boards set binding wage benchmarks. With so much economic power concentrated in public institutions, shouldn't we worry about political authoritarianism?

States can be "large" and "powerful" in multiple senses. Take a state whose entire judicial system consists of a few judges who each hear hundreds of cases a day and a few executioners who wait outside the courtroom with guillotines at the ready. What we've just described is, all else being equal, considerably *smaller* than a state with the vast bureaucracy necessary to support meaningful due process and humane, rehabilitative punishment.

Or take an example from US history. The American state before the Civil War and the passage of the Thirteenth Amendment lacked the constitutional power to outlaw slavery. It was, in that sense, *less powerful* than the state that emerged from the war, but the expansion of its power went along with a historic expansion of individual freedom.

Simply put, not all forms of state-largeness and state-powerfulness are created equal. The question in every case is whether a particular form of state power enhances or diminishes the rights and freedoms of the people it governs—whether we're talking about those people's rights *against the state* or against private actors like slave owners or capitalists. We would argue that the outright nationalization of some capitalist firms and the transformation of others into partnerships between workers and the state sector would considerably enhance the overall autonomy of the vast majority of human beings whose interests are at stake.

Of course, the freedom of business owners to make their own decisions about whether to sell, give away, or hold onto their businesses would be trampled by even the gentlest transition to socialism. The same can be said of the Thirteenth Amendment and the right of slave owners to decide if or when to free their slaves. We aren't suggesting that capitalist business owners are morally equivalent to slave owners. Our point is a far more general one—that the question of whether any given expansion of the size or power of the state makes a society more or less authoritarian can't be decided only by looking at the effect on one subset of impacted parties.

Consider a less dramatic example than the abolition of slavery. Laws against mandatory overtime interfere with the ability of employers to do what they would have previously been free to do, but they create a situation in which ordinary workers have more control over their working conditions. The scope of state agency expands, the scope of capitalist agency retracts, and the scope of worker agency expands.

To see this last point more vividly, think about two examples of people trying to board planes from Chicago to Glasgow. One potential passenger is on a US government "no fly list." The other just can't afford a ticket. If either of them somehow gets past airport security and attempts to board the plane anyway, their subsequent interactions with, first, airline employees and then armed agents of the state will play out in exactly the same way. Nor is this a case of some special socialist notion of "positive freedom" being substituted for freedom from interference ("negative freedom"). In both cases, people trying to perform the same action are being *interfered with* in the same way.

Libertarians would presumably say that, while barring access to the person on the "no fly list" is a rights violation—since the list exists outside of normal due process procedures—barring access to the person who can't afford a ticket is fine. The latter comports to their preferred mechanism for distributing scarce resources, which is just letting the chips fall where they will in a free market. But if the question is whether someone's negative liberty has been restricted, libertarian approval or disapproval is beside the point. That liberty has been restricted.

This isn't to say that everyone should have a legal right to board any flight for any reason at any time. We won't run through all the obvious problems with such a proposal or its equivalents for other forms of consumption. Suffice to say that *of course* many resources are limited and *of course* there needs to be some way to ration them out. Some restrictions on negative freedom are justified. We even agree with the defenders of existing capitalist markets that letting people earn incomes in money and spend the money on any package of goods within their budget is a reasonable way of managing access to many kinds of scarce resources. It's grotesquely inappropriate for goods like health care and education, but our model assumes the continued use of money to ration out access to seats on airplanes and many other things. That's more authoritarian than simply letting everyone board every flight. But the value of having a society in which air travel continues to exist in some logistically useful fashion outweighs the disvalue of that decrease in freedom.

The fact remains that a more egalitarian distribution of money means a more egalitarian distribution of (negative!) liberty. If the reliance of firms on funding by public banks, for example, helps to stabilize postcapitalist economic structures, then (a) more of the population get more *direct* power over the part of their lives they spend at work and (b) given that there's no getting around limitations on freedom of access to limited resources, those limitations are at least spread around far more evenly than they are under capitalism. In both cases, it's hard to see how that could fail to count as a considerable net decrease in economic authoritarianism.

But maybe the worry is really about *political* authoritarianism. One version of this argument goes like this: Meaningfully exercising political freedom requires a plurality of institutions. It's important to have, say, a free press that's willing to print things the government would prefer to keep quiet. It's important to have buildings owned by people who might be happy to let dissident groups meet on their premises. It's important to have book publishers who are willing to publish books critical of the status quo. If our contemplated socialist state either owns the buildings and the publishers and the newsmagazines outright or else finances the firms that directly own these things, there's surely at least some reason to worry that none of them will be sufficiently independent of that state.

A preliminary point to make here is that any defender of capitalism who pressed this concern would be putting themselves in an odd argumentative position. After all, they would be conceding that far less political freedom is enjoyed in an inegalitarian society by those who can't afford to buy media companies and decide what's published by them or who have to worry about losing their livelihood if their boss dislikes their politics.

Of course, if meaningful political freedom were to be limited for everyone tomorrow under socialism, it would be cold comfort that it's *also* unacceptably limited for the working class today under capitalism. We want a society where ordinary people have *much more* freedom to influence the political process than they currently enjoy in capitalist democracies.

A better response starts from noticing that, in those capitalist democracies, people who rely on the public sector for their livelihood don't necessarily live in fear of angering state officials. In fact, in at least some countries, they enjoy far *more* political freedom than employees of the private sector. Even in Donald Trump's America, if you work at a public university, you can't easily be fired for the political opinions you express on social media, because the *government* punishing someone for their political opinions violates the First Amendment's protection of freedom of speech. If you work at a private college, you have no such protection. Given similar constitutional protections in a future socialist state, denying financing to a newspaper because of the political content of the editorial page would be similarly unconstitutional—just as, under the capitalist status quo, a zoning board that denied a permit to build a mosque because the board was made of Christian fundamentalists would be opening themselves up to a lawsuit.

It's true enough that, if we're imagining a socialist state without strong constitutional protections of free speech, then regulatory interference could be used as forms of indirect censorship. Then again, if we imagine a *capitalist* state without such protections, the government can simply censor or shut down newspapers that print things that displease state officials. Not to put too fine a point on it, numerous capitalist states do exactly that. Private ownership of many buildings wasn't enough to give dissidents a legally allowed place to meet in Augusto Pinochet's Chile, and private ownership of newspapers in modern Saudi Arabia isn't enough to make it possible in practice for those newspapers to print things that displease the crown. Nor, on the other side of the coin, does public support for state universities around the United States stop them from being used to host meetings by radical opponents of the status quo.

Of course, citizens of a socialist democracy will have to be just as vigilant as their capitalist equivalents in defense of freedom of speech, freedom of the press, and other crucial civil liberties—but they won't start out at any sort of disadvantage because of the socialization of the means of production. In fact, given that a socialist society would plausibly be one in which average citizens have more free time and financial security and thus more people would have the bandwidth for involvement in the political process, the socialist citizens would have a comparative advantage.

As Robert Nozick asked, what's wrong with "capitalistic acts between consenting adults"? Why doesn't your model allow traditional capitalist employment contracts for those who want them?

It's true that many things that would be troubling if they were the result of force can be justified if they're the result of the enthusiastic consent of everyone involved. We deny that the capitalistic acts performed under capitalism meet this standard. Workers submit to employment contracts ceding control over the environments in which work and how the proceeds of their work are distributed not because this happens to be their preference but because of what Marx called the "mute compulsion" of economic circumstance. But what about capitalistic acts performed under better circumstances—ones shaped by the institutions of our preferred form of market socialism? Aren't those consensual? If so, shouldn't they be allowed?

Certainly any system that depends on mass suppression of what people would choose to do is likely to be fragile. Black markets would develop for such activities, and the bigger they got, the more people's confidence in the formal system would decline. The more this happens, the stronger the case for reconsidering any particular prohibition.

It doesn't follow from this, though, that *all* prohibitions are unreasonable. As far as we know, every economic system that's ever existed has prohibited at least some possible exchanges, and ours is no exception. There are some critical restrictions at its core.

Firms must be democratic. They can't pay sub-benchmark wages. All saving and borrowing must occur within the unified public banking system, with no parallel private credit markets. In all of these examples, there may well be cases in which "consenting adults" on both sides would have reasons to sign off on prohibited employment or lending arrangements. We see these as prisoner's dilemma situations: Individuals may be better off defecting so long as most people play by the rules, but everyone loses once defection reaches a critical mass. We concur with the overwhelming body of mainstream liberal and conservative thought in holding that there's a legitimate role for regulation in solving at least some collective action problems. The interesting debates aren't about that general principle but about particular applications of it.

Small-scale exchanges of labor don't generally need to be prohibited, just as societies that restrict gambling in many ways don't take an interest in small-stakes poker games in private basements. Problems arise only when things get to a larger scale and become more organized, such that they undermine socially determined norms of wages and conditions.

Even where the regulatory state does have a role, our model already allows for a plurality of work arrangements. Self-employed professionals and tradespeople will no doubt continue to thrive under socialism. We discussed earlier the gray area likely to emerge between genuine independent contracting—the graphic designer who provides images for a number of firms' websites—and Uber-style faux-independent contracting that would really be a way of denying membership rights to dependent workers. Regulation will be necessary to ensure that everyone has a voice in the workplaces they are functionally a part of.

Would this kind of regulation, intended to protect people, instead deny them their rights to traditional employment? Under socialism, would a large minority of society, funneled into roles as worker-members of cooperative firms, harbor frustrated dreams of becoming disenfranchised wage laborers?

We say "a large minority" because no society could hope to satisfy all the preferences of every minority, no matter how small. Some libertarians insist that a free market is a "utopia of utopias" in which the dreams of even the smallest minority can be satisfied so long as they don't infringe on the dreams of others. But their argument rests on an equivocation. Whether someone's dreams are fulfilled is a different question from whether they *would* be fulfilled if that person commanded the financial resources necessary to fulfill them. Under capitalism, those who can't afford their preferred "utopia" are out of luck. Not only is that system not a true "utopia of utopias" in which there is room for everyone to live out their fondest hopes, but in the ways that matter most, it becomes *less* utopian the closer it moves to a libertarian's idea of a "truly free market," in which those who get the short end of the stick are left to their own devices. Forget founding your own utopian community. You won't even be able to stay awake long enough to watch the occasional movie if your boss can keep you at work for fourteen hours a shift by threatening to fire you if you object.

The segment of our socialist society whose dreams of wage labor the objector worries about also couldn't be a *majority*. A majority motivated by such dreams could simply use the democratic political process to reinstate capitalism. So, the real question is: How worried should we be about a large minority of socialist citizens harboring unfulfilled dreams of being a traditional worker?

In the world that now exists, it's exceedingly rare for a capitalist to simply sign over the deed to their company to someone else in exchange for being relieved of the burden of decision-making and kept on the payroll as an hourly worker. The idea that the preference for submission over responsibility just happens to be far more common at the bottom of society than at the top is more than a little reminiscent of Thomas Jefferson's potshot about aristocrats who believe that "the mass of mankind" were "born with saddles on their backs" while a "favored few" came into the world "booted and spurred."

But perhaps this is too ungenerous to the objector's point. One thing that holds back many people who would otherwise prefer being booted and spurred to being saddled from even *trying* to make the leap to starting their own businesses is a reasonable fear of the consequences of failure. No one wants to lose their house or their child's college fund by making an ill-advised attempt to leap from wage labor to economic empowerment. The decision not to try may not be an easy or pleasant one, but it's often quite rational. Even a *successful* leap can involve a level of stress that they might be wise to avoid. Moreover, the desire to maximize the time and energy a worker has for their off-the-clock pursuits is every bit as legitimate as their resentment of workplace despotism.

Does any of this add up to a reason to carve out a greater space than our vision does for worker disempowerment? We don't think so. In fact, our model is already responsive to this bundle of concerns at several distinct points.

First and most obviously, we agree that the costs of taking a leap into business ownership under capitalism are unduly onerous. In fact, one of our objections to capitalism is precisely that we don't think anyone should have to choose between the unattractive options of accepting subordination at the workplace or taking extreme economic risks. That's one of the reasons why our model finances investment through the public banking system, rather than expecting workers to finance their firms from their own savings or debt. We don't want anyone to have to stake their family home just to get a worker-controlled enterprise off the ground. It's also why we're so insistent on pairing worker empowerment with an expansive welfare state. We've established that firm failure is necessary to keep the economic wheels turning efficiently. But we don't accept that the price of failure needs to be ruination.

Similarly, if part of the motivation of the workers who we are supposed to believe would long for a return to wage labor is a desire to *just clock in and clock out and get on with the more important part of their lives*, we concur that it's good and reasonable that many socialist citizens will seek to maximize the amount of time and energy they have left over after their working day is done. We're optimistic that a producer-empowered society would react to technological progress with steep reductions in the workweek. We also don't envision a massive expansion of meetings. The election of top management, combined with everyone voting on operating agreements, doesn't necessitate that every individual worker be forced to spend time in committees themselves. As with civic participation in the political sphere or participation in labor unions in capitalist workplaces, we expect a wide range in attitudes toward these matters. Some people will spend weeks arguing with their friends about workplace matters, while some will be largely apathetic.

In the middle of this spectrum, even many worker-members who don't care about actively shaping firm strategy may care quite a bit about blocking bad ideas that threaten working conditions they want to defend. The election of bad leadership or the approval of ill-advised clauses in their firm's operating agreements could lead to loss of revenue and hence adverse consequences for their own wallets. These consequences will likely command their attention to a greater extent than, say, the consequences of elections for citizens in a capitalist democracy, which may be less tangible. For better or worse, though, even this is no guarantee of a high uniform level of participation. The point of democracy, in either politics or economics, isn't that everyone has to take an interest in any given decision. It's that people have a right to a reasonable say, should they choose to exercise the right, in the decisions that touch their lives.

Remember too that, when it comes to workers whose preferences for stability, security, and stress-avoidance are the greatest, the labor-managed firm is not the only option in our model. In addition to the ranks of the self-employed, we also include a considerably expanded public sector.

For workers in this sector, the texture of everyday life might not be dramatically different from the best version of what's available today. Public agencies are funded and directed from above, with ultimate oversight exercised by an elected national government. In our vision, public sector workers will have collective bargaining rights and influence over working conditions and service delivery. But ultimately it's a democratic state that determines any given agency's mission and scope. Unless the subordinated labor fetishists we're considering have a specific longing to be salaried employees of rich men rather than of the state, it's hard to see why the existence of a large public sector wouldn't solve the problem.

Finally, it's worth remembering that the "capitalistic acts between consenting adults" issue isn't different in any fundamental way from, say, the "subminimum wage labor among consenting adults" or the "72-hour workweeks among consenting adults" issues. There are many employment contracts some individual workers would voluntarily sign which would be prohibited by law in any normal capitalist democracy—and that's a very good thing. Firms without a floor on pay or a ceiling on working hours would have obvious competitive advantages over ones that were held down by those restrictions, so the best way to prevent these practices from becoming common is just prohibiting them.

It is well worth sacrificing a part of individual workers' freedom of contract in order to erect a collective barrier that protects the entire working class against being economically pressured into accepting repugnant forms of domination. No one but the most extreme libertarians really disagrees with this point on the level of principle. The far more interesting and controversial question is whether worker disenfranchisement in the private sector is on the list of unacceptable forms of domination. Those who believe that it's just and proper for society to be divided into a class of the saddled and a class of the booted-and-spurred should be willing to make their case on its merits, instead of taking refuge in the fact that—*like all other prohibited contracts*—this is one that some workers would have been happy to sign.

There would be far too little innovation without private finance, and providing adequate incentives for individuals who come up with innovative ideas would require inequalities incompatible with their status as coequal worker-members.

The assumption that innovation would be starved without private finance greatly underestimates the role played by the public sector under contemporary capitalism. The economist Mariana Mazzucato argues in her book *The Entrepreneurial State* and elsewhere that the United States is the home of an unusually high number of firms bringing cutting-edge innovations to the market not because the US and Europe differ culturally or because an unusually laissez faire regulatory environment provides more room for private sector geniuses to flourish but precisely because of the outsize role of the American state in promoting such innovations.[6]

She points out, for example, that just about everything that makes a glistening new smartphone "smart" is a product of innovation funded by the public sector. The internet itself was the child of the US military's Advanced Research Projects Agency Network (ARPANET). The Global Positioning System started as another military project—NAVSTAR. Touchscreen technology "was created by the company FingerWorks, which was founded by a professor at the publicly funded University of Delaware and one of his doctoral candidates, who received grants from the National Science Foundation and the CIA." Even voice-activated personal assistants like Apple's Siri have Defense Department roots.

Nor is the US state's role in fostering innovations that are sometimes misattributed to the private sector unique to the role played by the military-industrial complex. Pharmaceuticals are a particularly good case-in-point, since detailed data is available. Not only did research funded by the National Institutes of Health contribute to all 210 new drugs approved in the United States between 2010 and 2016, but many of these were genuinely revolutionary. These drugs were not incremental adjustments to drugs already on the market—or drugs with superficial changes made purely to allow a new company to slap its brand on a preexisting concept. Here too, Mazzucato reports, the public sector is doing the heavy lifting—"most of the really 'innovative' new drugs, i.e. new molecular entities with priority rating, come from publicly funded laboratories."[7]

Even so, you might be concerned that however good states can be at promoting technological innovations, they're not going to be good at turning them into new products or pioneering new business practices. What about the breakthroughs that really do happen within the private sector?

We'd make a few points here. First, those innovations happening *within* the private sector doesn't mean that they are the "natural" result of private genius being left alone to create its wonders. Even under today's corporate capitalism, business people receive plenty of government support, and such support has played a significant role in the early financing of iconic firms like Apple. Let's put those examples to one side for the moment, though, and think about companies doing new and innovative things exclusively as a result of *private* funding. In a timeline where the whole finance sector had been nationalized, is there any special reason to think loan officers at public banks would have been more likely to dismiss these entrepreneurs' applications than loan officers at private ones? If the concern is that we need a multiplicity of financing entities to maximize the chances of innovators finding one that takes them seriously, we address that with a multiplicity of public banks that each have considerable autonomy.

Second, we'd question the assumption that innovation—even innovation in business practices—primarily reflects the work of solitary geniuses. Steve Jobs branded himself very well, but many of the ideas a black-turtleneck-clad Jobs would ultimately announce to great fanfare originated in the brains of his employees.

Third, even if we *did* assume the centrality of solitary geniuses to innovation, there are straightforward ways in which our model could accommodate incentives for standout contributions. We've already discussed some of these ideas, like rewards for research and development breakthroughs, in chapter six.

There are even ways in which a socialist system could accommodate incentives for those participating in the creation of a firm. When a core group of founders come together to apply to a public bank for the initial funding, they will participate in the drafting of a legal operating agreement before they recruit other members. Founders can award themselves a generous share of profits during this initial period to compensate for their efforts. Of course, even the size of that first share will be constrained by the realistic requirements of recruiting worker-members accustomed to fairly egalitarian arrangements, but the chance to benefit from more income during this initial term will still be a real incentive for founders.

Finally, our system also has channels for encouraging and financing innovations in commodity production that are common across market economies. In the commodity-producing sector, firms pursue profit and their worker-members have every incentive to develop new products that people would want, and more cost-effective ways of producing existing ones. When someone has an idea for an innovation that might pay for itself, the public banks stand ready to provide investment funding, whether the idea comes from within existing democratic firms, within a public agency, or from people hoping to set up a new firm to develop it. Ideas can also come from within the banks themselves. Part of their role is to take the initiative in organizing the establishment of new cooperatives.

The role of the individual entrepreneur and the venture-capitalized start-up model can be overemphasized in explaining capitalist dynamism. But it has a place, and our model has room for something like it. In the capitalist version, entrepreneurs and the funders who get in early are motivated by the slim chance of enormous windfalls. Many failures are permitted, even expected; they are understood as the price of the lottery ticket. In our system, there is no pool of private capital for the wealthy to buy lottery tickets with. But the public banking system can put some portion of its resources toward high-risk, high-return bets. If the regular banks are not taking enough such risk, special investment banks can be set up with a mandate to do so.

The upside reward to the individual entrepreneur is limited by the cooperative firm model: Windfalls will be shared among the worker-members. This is not really so different from founders sharing risks and rewards with early hires by paying them partly in stock options—though it is likely these will be shared among a wider group than in an equivalent capitalist firm. Then there is the nature of the windfall itself. Capitalist start-ups and their funders aim to win by establishing a dominant competitive position in the market niche they pioneer. The dream is to gain more than the mere first mover advantage and secure monopoly rents indefinitely, whether from intellectual property or network effects. Our model aims to do away with these indefinite monopoly rents.

It seems to us that the fact that innovators would no longer be able to hit on a good idea and then rest on their laurels, raking in an unending passive income, is a virtue of our system rather than a drawback. It's a virtue because it better fits our egalitarian ideals, of course, but it's also a virtue in that *it provides a greater incentive for innovation*. Someone who has a good idea and knows that in a few years they'll be expected to pull their weight within the firm they've started will have a powerful motivation to come up with their next good idea—either to prove to their fellow workers that they're so indispensable they deserve to continue to get an oversize share of revenue under the *next* operating agreement or to repeat the cycle as the founder of a new firm.

There's also the question of the impact on other potential innovators. Under the existing regime of capitalist ownership structures and intellectual property protections, the social price of innovation is not simply a one-off bonanza for the founders; it is also the effects of ongoing barriers to competition. These effects loom large in the list of reasons why Silicon Valley is as hated as it is admired.

If some innovation comes at the price of windfalls, it is better to pay the price up front and then make sure the innovation is available to all comers. If the temporary windfalls that come with being first movers are not enough to motivate this kind of innovation, then it can be rewarded more directly with public prizes and bounties. In other words, instead of letting the first developer of a technology or platform control it for many years and squeeze whatever juice they can from it, they can simply be given their juice as soon as certain benchmarks indicating a successful product are met. Not only is this likely to be cheaper in the long run, but it also allows others to iterate on the innovation to meet user needs, rather than locking users in with the originator. This can enable innovations that are blocked under the current system.

We think it is likely that such windfalls can be much more modest than those going to those who win the tech lottery in modern capitalism and still motivate the desired level of innovation. But if the price turns out to be higher, there is nothing to stop a socialist society from deciding to pay it: Even very large one-off prize-type windfalls are preferable to wealth based on indefinite private monopolies. Prizes can potentially be targeted at smaller groups than whole firms, if that is judged necessary. A side-effect of the system is that it may draw in different kinds of people and different kinds of ideas from those drawn to winner-take-all start-up culture. Who knows what innovations we are missing because they start in the heads of people who prefer economic security or are turned off by the long hours and pressure-cooker culture of start-ups?

That said, we'll freely admit that there's a large element of speculation in this answer. The capitalism that exists now is an enormously complicated machine with countless moving parts. The hypothetical socialism we've sketched out will be one too if it ever comes to pass.

We think it's plausible—very plausible—that there would be *more* innovation under our model than there is under capitalism. But there's no way to be sure of that in advance. The real question is whether the bare possibility that retaining capitalism *might* lead to a somewhat faster rate of innovation is even close to being a sufficient reason to tolerate the poverty, large-scale economic inequality, workplace authoritarianism, and hollowing-out of political democracy that characterize extremely materially unequal societies. Our answer is a resounding no.

What about efficiency problems stemming from the expanded role of the state in the economy? Shouldn't that trigger concerns about the very "soft budget constraints" you discussed already, which bedeviled earlier versions of socialism? How do you prevent inefficient firms from lobbying the state to avoid bankruptcy or a large public sector becoming a drag on the more productive parts of the economy?

We certainly concur that one of the most important lessons of twentieth-century socialism is the danger of soft budget constraints. In the Soviet bloc economies—and even in reform experiments like Hungary's New Economic Mechanism—inefficient firms were rarely allowed to fail. Their survival was treated as a political imperative to avoid unemployment, to maintain local patronage networks, or simply because no one had strong enough incentives to pull the plug.

The result was systemic waste. Resources stayed locked up in low-productivity sectors, dragging down growth and leaving the economy vulnerable to stagnation. Avoiding this trap is crucial for any future socialist project.

Our model explicitly builds in mechanisms to keep budget constraints hard. Worker-controlled firms, financed by public banks, operate under clear rules. They must meet the financial commitments they have agreed to with the banks and also pay their worker-members precommitted wages. Those wages must at least meet benchmarks determined by the labor board. A firm that cannot meet these obligations is bankrupt.

As explained in chapter five, the financial arrangements between firms and their partner banks do make allowances for certain risks inherent in doing business. A firm's revenue is always uncertain to some degree, because the ups and downs of demand are unpredictable. Costs are also subject to unexpected change.

Under capitalism, such risks are ultimately borne by stockholders, who are not guaranteed any fixed dividend payments in advance: They are the residual claimant who takes whatever is left over. There are no outside stockholders in democratic firms. If these firms financed themselves entirely on the basis of debt with a fixed payment schedule, they would be insanely leveraged, their worker-members subject to large swings in personal income. For this reason, the financial arrangements with banks are structured differently, so that payment obligations are higher in good times and lower in bad. The specific details depend on the industry and the nature of the risks. In some cases, it works as if the bank were the owner of the fixed capital assets, with the firm paying to rent the capacity it uses. In other cases, it might be more like a hybrid debt–equity instrument, with banks insuring against short-run losses at the price of a share of profits from success.

These variable financing arrangements do not soften the budget constraint any more than equity financing, asset rental, or risk-shifting derivative contracts do under capitalism. They adjust payment obligations systematically, for good reasons, but do not relax the obligation to meet payments that come due. They are designed to appropriately socialize some of the risks and some of the profits from the use of social resources. They are not subject to ad hoc adjustment simply to protect a firm from unpleasant consequences. They do not shield democratic firms from the need to avoid waste and manage themselves efficiently or absolve them forever from adapting to changes in technology and customer tastes.

This discipline is partly because the benchmarks used to adjust firm obligations in line with market ups and downs are based on industry-level measures, not firm-specific ones. Because these benchmarks move with conditions across the sector, a firm exporting pasta sauce is protected from a temporary decline in demand caused by a recession in a key foreign market—a shock affecting the industry as a whole and beyond the control of either the firm or domestic policymakers. But it is not protected from slowing demand caused by the firm's failure to adapt to preferences for new flavors, while competing firms' revenues hold up because they have adapted. It is not protected from cost overruns arising from the inefficient running of the plant either.

Bank models of industry-level risks and trends will themselves adjust over time. The decline in the whole industry's pasta sauce exports may at first be treated as within a normal range of volatility. But if it turns out over time to be a more sustained decline due to a general shift in consumer tastes away from pasta, the banks will not bear the losses forever. They will adjust their models of the pasta sauce industry to take into account the reduced prospects, and the new models will price and allocate investment in the industry differently as firms reach their next refinancing negotiations.

Firms that fail to meet benchmarks over time would not be endlessly propped up with new injections of public money. Sometimes restructuring will be a viable option, as it often is for flailing firms under capitalism. Otherwise, the firm will close. Its assets and some worker-members may be absorbed by more successful cooperatives. Others will move on to cooperatives elsewhere in the economy or to the public sector, with the strong welfare state we envision cushioning the human costs of failure.

In the more egalitarian world this model could bring about, failure wouldn't have to be a social tragedy. It can be accepted as a necessary part of producing more wealthy, productive, and just societies.

Under our model, no individual faces poverty simply because the firm they worked for didn't succeed, which lessens political pressure to soften budget constraints. Unlike the command economies of the past, inefficient firms won't be artificially kept alive, and productive resources won't be indefinitely tied up by political inertia. Through a combination of rigorous public financing standards, real firm-level competition, and universal guarantees of social security, we aim to preserve the vital pressures that make an economy dynamic without reproducing the brutal insecurity of capitalist unemployment.

In your system, banks are very important. Wouldn't bankers just become the nomenklatura of the system, a privileged class controlling investment and using their position to empower themselves?

Public banks do indeed occupy a key role in our model. They fund investment in the market sector, collect information, and even play an entrepreneurial role, scouting for opportunities and assisting with the set-up of new cooperatives. But it is essential that they channel democratic decisions and respond to people's needs, rather than becoming autonomous powers.

Banks in our system are public utilities. They fund and partner with firms but are themselves part of the noncommodity sector, ultimately directed and overseen by a democratic state. They are not cooperative firms themselves. Any profit they make flows to the public treasury. Their decision-makers receive bonus income and have job security linked to the bank's financial performance, to motivate careful investment that responds to market signals. These payments resemble the dividends received by worker-members in democratic firms, but the metrics on which they are based are determined by policy outside the banks themselves.

The information collected and generated by the banks—partner firm operations, revenue, costs, and more—will be public, as will their own books. This transparency, combined with specialist monitoring by the central bank, is a check against self-enrichment, favoritism, or any kind of fraud, and also serves to assist investment planning across other banks and firms.

Unlike capitalist banks, banks in our model do not take deposits. The sole source of the funds they lend is the central bank. This raises the question of why the system has multiple banks at all, instead of having investment decisions made directly by the central bank. But this separation of decision-making avoids a concentration of power over investment. A plurality of banks allows for multiple views. Investment decisions are about visions of the future, which are inherently unpredictable, no matter how much data is available. With multiple banks, firms have places to go for second opinions, and no collective is too dependent on a single partner firm.

This arrangement also allows for multiple kinds of banks with different purposes. Most banks will be tasked with pursuing a high rate of return for a given degree of volatility—which is ultimately about keeping investment responsive to people's private goods preferences. Other aims are pursued directly by the noncommodity public sector, which is funded directly from the public treasury and central bank. But some banks will have mandates to fund investments for things that are considered desirable and well suited to being run by democratic firms, but which do not reach the benchmark expected returns that would see them funded by regular banks: for example, to support a depressed region or to develop an infant industry.

Within this system, there is nowhere for unchecked power to develop. The banks making investment decisions do so according to parameters set from outside, with open data, and with clear criteria for assessing their results. The central bank, where higher-level decisions are made and implemented, is separated from decisions about individual investments.

This raises the question of democratic responsiveness. In our view, democratic control of investment does not mean voting over the allocation of funds down to every last cappuccino machine and wind turbine. Democratic deliberation at too fine-grained a level of detail would lead to incoherence. The rationale for having a market sector in the first place, set out in chapter four, extends to letting market signals generally guide investment in that sector. Letting individuals direct the share of resources allocated for their personal consumption means having investment respond to their decisions. This is why the expected rate of return remains the baseline for allocating investment within the commodity sector in our model.

There are nevertheless many channels through which democratic decisions influence investment. There is the high-level decision about how much of production to devote to investment, and how much to current personal and collective consumption. There is the decision about the relative size of the market and public sectors. Even within the market sector, democratic decisions can influence the flow of finance. Funds can be allocated directly for specific purposes through investment banks. Interest rate and other subsidies or penalties change the parameters of regular bank decision-making, even while they are guided by expected return and risk within those parameters. Regulation can block particular investments entirely. And in the noncommodity sector, investment decisions are of course made directly by state agencies.

We have not fully specified how these decisions are made democratically. The general model is compatible with a number of possibilities. The system might just be democratic in the familiar sense that the public bodies involved—public sector departments, the central bank, and other banks—are ultimately under the control of an elected national government, which sets their parameters and priorities and appoints their senior directors. But there could easily be multiple sites for democracy at different levels: national, regional, local, and sectoral. Ultimately, the details can only be worked out through experimentation with what works and meets people's aspirations.

Didn't worker self-management fail in Yugoslavia?

After breaking with the Soviet Union in 1948, Yugoslavia's leaders rejected administrative planning not only for geopolitical reasons but because its limitations had already become clear. Self-management was soon introduced as a key part of their efforts to decentralize economic decision-making, weaken ministerial control over production, and empower workers.

Workers' councils exercised genuine authority over internal pay scales, employment decisions, and the use of enterprise surpluses. This went far beyond the power that workers had either in Soviet-style economies or the capitalist West.

Even so, we don't think Yugoslavia is the most instructive case for evaluating the kind of socialism we propose here. The

Yugoslav model combined enterprise self-management with a radical decentralization of banking, fiscal authority, and economic governance. By the 1970s, decentralization functioned less as an economic experiment than as a shaky political settlement aimed at holding together a multiethnic federation. This makes it much harder to tell whether later failures reflected problems with worker-managed firms themselves or with the broader institutional environment in which they operated.[8]

Yugoslavia's system as a whole was very different from the one outlined in this book. While firms were decentralized, the state lacked the tools needed to manage a modern economy. Investment flowed through a fragmented, regionally organized banking system rather than through unified public banks accountable to national priorities. This structure emerged directly from the 1974 Constitution, which granted extensive veto powers to the republics and made coherent federal economic policy politically impossible. There was no effective mechanism for countercyclical fiscal policy, no economy-wide wage coordination, and no credible commitment to maintaining full employment. When demand fell or sectors stagnated, adjustment happened through inflation, unemployment, interregional balancing, and eventually heavy reliance on foreign borrowing.

These outcomes are often blamed on supposed flaws in labor-managed firms: workers hoarding jobs, resisting restructuring, and prioritizing short-term income over long-term growth. But this gets the causality wrong. Yugoslav firms behaved defensively because they were operating in an unstable macroeconomic environment in which firm survival was the best protection against unemployment and social dislocation. In the absence of institutions capable of stabilizing demand and reallocating labor and investment systematically, soft budget constraints and political bargaining became substitutes for coherent economic policy.

Our model is designed precisely to avoid this type of failure. It treats markets not as self-regulating mechanisms but as tools that require a state capable of managing them. It recognizes the need for decisions at the workplace level to be properly coordinated as part of the division of labor across the economy and that market coordination alone is prone to dysfunction. A public banking system and other macroeconomic levers are vehicles for this conscious coordination. A robust welfare system separates worker security from firm survival, so that enterprise contraction or failure does not translate into mass unemployment.

Yugoslavia is a cautionary tale about workplace democracy being introduced without the institutions needed to sustain it. But the lesson isn't that economic democracy is impossible—it's that we need a better blueprint for it.

If welfare state guarantees are very expansive, how do you compel people to work in the competitive commodity-producing sector?

In any society with broad welfare guarantees—where no one faces destitution for being unemployed—there's always a potential worry about how to maintain enough participation in socially necessary labor. Our model recognizes and deals with this.

First, the competitive sector we envision would look very different from what exists under capitalism today. Workers would have real control over their workplaces, a genuine stake in the outcomes of their labor, and the ability to participate democratically in decision-making. Many of the most alienating and degrading features of capitalist work would be dramatically reduced. For many, work under these conditions would be far more attractive and meaningful than wage labor under capitalism.

Second, while the welfare state ensures that no one falls through the cracks, it doesn't promise a life of luxury without work. Basic income supplementation and strong public services would ensure dignity and opportunity, not lavishness. Under socialism, as today, most people would have powerful material incentives to seek employment in order to afford a wider range of goods, services, and personal comforts. There are also very real social and mental benefits to work. Even under capitalism, part of the reason many workers experience frustration during bouts of unemployment is because of the loss of those nonmaterial benefits.

Finally, our model anticipates that as productivity rises, the workweek will shorten, and the burden of labor will lighten. With guaranteed access to good education, health care, and a real floor of material security, individuals would have the freedom to pursue a mix of employment, study, family life, and creative endeavors. The goal isn't to coerce people into endless labor for its own sake—it's to make sure that participation in the economy is meaningful, fairly shared, and tied to collective flourishing. A humane balance between necessary work and personal freedom is part of what makes our vision of economic democracy superior both to capitalism and earlier experiments in state socialism.

In chapter seven, we acknowledged and discussed some tensions between income security and incentives and suggested some ways to manage them. We argued that there is a case for a modest unconditional subsistence income. At the very least, no socialist society is going to let people starve in the street under any conditions, and it is best to be honest about that. But those who cannot work due to sickness or disability, those who are retired, and those caring for young children or other family members in need deserve more than mere subsistence. There is also a case for higher support for those who are out of work not by choice but temporarily and are looking for work. This means imposing conditions on these higher-level benefits, and with conditions come difficult questions about policing them. What works and what doesn't will have to be worked out from practical experience. The level of the unconditional income relative to the more generous needs-based benefits and the nature of their conditions is subject to change through democratic politics. Ultimately, meeting people's needs depends on people's work, and if the gap between pay and unconditional income turns out to not be enough to motivate enough people to do that work, it can and will be changed. We're optimistic that, in a more egalitarian and less materially precarious society, there will be less zero-sum thinking about benefits and far less cruelty in public discourse about them.

There's no way to be certain in advance about how such large changes to the structure of investment and firm management would play out in practice. Aren't you asking people to take a big risk?

Wherever possible, and consistently adhering to core socialist goals, we've sought to build on ideas that have a good track record in the real world. Nordic social democracy can be thought of as a kind of "partial" democratic socialism. The "full" democratic socialism we propose is self-consciously continuous with it.

Where it goes further, we can generally point to promising precedents. Cooperatives already exist under capitalism, and while they may be doomed to occupy a marginal place in the economy as long as capitalists dominate the investment process, we know that they can function well once they're up and running. Our labor boards build off precedents in postwar Australia. And public banking has a long history in liberal capitalist societies. What we're proposing is a way of combining and building on these precedents to finally end the division of society into a class of owners and a subordinate working class.

We think we've given good, strong reasons to think this combination would be a workable one. It's true, though, that we don't and can't traffic in absolute certainty. Perhaps a new system would run into problems that neither we nor our critics can currently anticipate, and it would have to be abandoned in favor of another or even of returning to capitalism. The bare possibility of such a setback, though, would be a poor reason to leave the painfully clear injustices of class society in place forever without even trying to build an alternative.

We know, of course, that the objections we've covered don't exhaust the ones that could be made from a perspective to our right. Capitalism is the overwhelmingly globally dominant system. Support for it is the firmly established common sense of political and media classes the world over. It's easy to assume that the procapitalist consensus *must* be rooted in intellectually powerful considerations, even though a glance through history should be enough to remind us that *every* well-established system commands similarly widespread consensus in its epoch. Who in the twelfth century thought that political systems where subjects choose their rulers would turn out to be *more* stable in the long run than ones based on hereditary monarchy? Or that there was an economically viable alternative to feudalism in which agricultural laborers could come and go as they pleased rather than being legally bound to the estates of particular nobles? If anyone had dared make such suggestions, they would have been rejected by the greatest philosophical and theological minds not just as insults to the will of God but as laughably impractical.

Of course, it doesn't follow from the court intellectuals of that era being wrong that ours are too. These things have to be judged case by case. But no one who believes that dramatic historical progress is even sometimes justified can rest easy in the assumption that the consensus of *our* epoch must be correct just because it's the consensus.

10

Is This Even Socialism?

Let's turn now to an entirely different set of objections. In the last chapter, we addressed readers who felt our model of socialism went too far—from libertarians urging us to celebrate capitalism to social democrats who share much of our outlook but think we should ultimately make peace with it.

There are other readers, though, who harbor an entirely different bundle of concerns. They'll have nodded along, perhaps impatiently, to much of what we said in response to the objections from our right. But they'll note that the objections that move *them* have yet to be touched on.

In many cases, like the social-democratic readers who are skeptical of a horizon beyond capitalism, the readers we're addressing now might agree with us on the contemporary politics of supporting labor unions and universal health care and raising the minimum wage. But they regard our long-term vision as insufficiently visionary.

The socialist left has always had a culture of raucous and fractious political debate—sometimes maddening and sometimes invigorating. After all, socialism's core premise is that ordinary working-class people can and should remake the world in their own interests. We believe, with the Trinidadian socialist C. L. R. James, that every cook can govern. That means that everyone deserves to have a say about strategy and tactics, about principles, and about the long-term goals of our movement.

Some readers unpersuaded by our model will think that what we're talking about isn't socialism at all but only a strange sort of collectivized capitalism. Others may grant that we're talking about a version of socialism but think that, by maintaining an important role for the market as a coordinating mechanism, it's a version that could only exist for a short time before being devoured by a resurgent capitalism. Finally, some might just think that another form of socialism would be preferable to the one we propose.

This list of our responses to various objections from the left is surely incomplete. But we hope it at least advances the conversation.

The psychology of market subjects is twisted in selfish and competitive directions. In assuming that we still need markets even after the end of capitalist property relations, you seem to be assuming that we're stuck with this psychology. But why not expect—and establish the kinds of socialist economic institutions that would promote—something better?

Pessimism about human nature isn't our primary motivation for retaining market mechanisms in a model of socialism. Help yourself for the sake of argument to extremely optimistic assumptions about the *motivations* of market actors, and you're still left with the problem of coordinating a complex and ever-shifting bundle of fine-grained consumer preferences with production. Price signals get that job done and it's hard to see what else would, even if the "new socialist man" that Che Guevara dreamed of walked the earth.

Perhaps the most hopeful guesses some socialists have made on all these counts will turn out to be correct. The selfless new socialist man *will* walk the earth, information problems *are* solvable, and so on. If so, that's great news. But then our goal here can be understood as a kind of backup plan. If some or all of these hopes don't come to pass, we want to show that this wouldn't be a good enough reason to give up our hopes for a radically more democratic and egalitarian future.

This answer might not satisfy the objector, though, because their concern might run in the opposite direction—not that we won't *need* market mechanisms if the perceived "moral inadequacies" of human psychology can be overcome, but that the very persistence of those mechanisms tends to propagate the moral inadequacies.

In *Why Not Socialism?*, G. A. Cohen argues that market competition encourages us to interact with our fellow human beings on the basis of fear and greed. To see his point, imagine that Tom and Jerry work at competing worker-controlled firms. To the extent that Tom worries that Jerry's firm will thrive at the expense of Tom's firm, Tom's attitude toward Jerry is defined by fear. Jerry's success will be Tom's failure. On the other hand, to the extent that Tom hopes that his firm will outcompete Jerry's, Tom will be driven by greed to be indifferent to Jerry's misfortune. This contrasts with the value of community that Cohen hoped would be a hallmark of the marketless socialist future.[1]

People who see each other as part of a community understand themselves to be *in it together*. They try to serve each other's interests. Of course, when Tom's relations with Jerry are defined by a communitarian spirit, Tom doesn't expect to serve Jerry's interests and get nothing in return. He's not a saint who gladly suffers freeloaders. Instead, he expects that Jerry will do his part just as Tom does, each serving and being served by the other—the way friends and family members support each other.

All else being equal, to whatever extent the design of economic institutions can encourage people to relate to each other with a spirit of community, that's a point in favor of those institutions. It's undeniable that markets involve competition and it's true by definition that people who see one another as competitors, whether in a basketball game or a marketplace, will seek to advance their own interests at one another's expense. We could simply acknowledge that this is a shortcoming of our model of socialism and argue that it's made up for by the benefits of a thriving economy unhindered by the information and incentive problems bound to beset attempts at totally marketless economic coordination. Even Cohen explicitly allowed for economic efficiency as one of the competing values that had to be balanced against his socialist value of community.

As it happens, though, we think we can improve on this kind of response. While a morally tragic level of psychological deformation caused by the market *might* be a price worth paying for economic abundance, we're not convinced that the mechanisms contemplated by our model would exact this price.

To understand why not, notice that not all forms of competition involve markets. Make Tom and Jerry bright young bureaucrats with the same skill set in a totally marketless socialist economy. When a new job opens up at the state planning commission, they both apply. Both know the other is interested and both hope to outshine the other. Do we need to worry that their relations have been poisoned by community-destroying impulses of greed (for Tom's success at the expense of Jerry and vice versa) and fear (that Jerry will be successful at the expense of Tom and vice versa)?

Not really. Competition between friends might be unpleasant, but against the backdrop of a vastly more humane society where no one is worried that the price of failure will be raising their children in poverty, we think any psychologically deforming consequences will be minimal. The same point applies to the competition that would exist in a model of socialism that retains a role for markets. No one on the socialist left worries much about the psychic agonies of upper-middle-class kids who dream of writing the Great American Novel, are outshone in literary competition with their peers, and end up resigning themselves to becoming dentists. It's not clear to us why anyone should worry much more than that about the agonies of a worker-member in a basically egalitarian society who might suffer frustration when the venture she poured her energies into fails and she either becomes a member of an expanding labor-managed competitor or falls back on the cushion of a welfare state before getting a job in the public sector.

If you *do* think that's an unacceptable level of psychic agony, we'd submit that this is a problem not realistically solvable by better social design. Reminder: In the most extravagant "Fully Automated Luxury Communism" you can stretch your mind to imagine, a society where no one even *remembers* that there were once such things as markets and money, romantic competition will exist, competition for artistic prestige will exist, and so on. Failure in any of these domains can sting. This might be a good time to remember Freud's description of the goals of psychoanalysis, which can also stand as a description of the goals of the socialist project. The point, he said, was to convert "hysterical misery" into "ordinary unhappiness."[2]

Even in the absence of class inequality, the different profitability of different firms and sectors of the economy would be a significant source of material inequality.

We take this concern seriously. All else being equal, we want as much egalitarianism as possible. That's why our model includes several mechanisms to at least partially correct for interfirm disparities. It's worth briefly reviewing these before considering how we should feel about whatever inequality remains.

First, remember that there are three sources of income in our model—wages, residual dividends, and public transfers. The last of these is organized by the state, and how much anyone gets does not depend on the profitability or budget of any particular firm. In chapter seven, we sketched an outline of how income taxes and transfers can be used to redistribute personal income to meet needs and soften market inequalities. How that sketch is filled out or adjusted by any particular socialist state is a policy question, not a model question. Different governments might deal with the trade-offs in different ways. But transfers will counteract at least to some extent the impact of interfirm inequality on individual incomes, as well as support those out of the labor force entirely, like retirees. We also described how the system will moderate wage inequality with the benchmarks set by the labor boards.

Even under capitalism, the Nordic countries show that a combination of coordinated determination of wage floors and local bargaining of wages above those floors can considerably reduce labor income inequality without undermining efficiency.

One of the motivations for the firm-financing system at the core of our model is precisely to diminish intersector inequality as much as possible. Our model treats the means of production as socially owned. Firms may take the initiative in directing investment and are the custodians of the buildings and equipment they use. But investment is financed by the public banks, and firms pay for their means of production as if they were leasing them. This prevents workers in capital-intensive industries—say, oil or data infrastructure—from reaping disproportionate gains simply because their firm's assets happen to be especially lucrative. What matters most in our model isn't how profitable your sector is but how efficiently your democratic firm is run.

On top of this greater egalitarianism in the foundational economic arrangements, every tool capitalist states currently use to reduce inequality would still be available to governments in a socialist society—only they'd likely work better. Redistributive taxation is just one lever among many. Social-democratic governments have used everything from public housing and free education to antitrust law and regional development subsidies in efforts to flatten the social pyramid. If you're skeptical about how effective these measures have been under capitalism, fair enough. But much of that skepticism reflects the fact that such policies are being deployed within a system still dominated by capital. In a classless society where economic power is broadly diffused and political democracy has been deepened, those same tools would be operating on a far more favorable terrain.

If it turned out that all of this put together was insufficient to *completely* eliminate intersector inequality, we would count that as a mark against our model—though one that's compatible with it being better overall than any of the alternatives on the table. When it comes to inter*firm* inequality, though, things are a lot more complicated.

We started by saying that, *all else being equal*, we want as much egalitarianism as possible—but at the interfirm level, all else is not entirely equal. To be sure, there are all sorts of powerful motivations for egalitarianism that hold at this level. Cohen's concern about inequalities beyond our control certainly applies here—some firms might be more profitable than others because they happen to have a high concentration of unusually naturally talented people as worker-members. There are also all the usual concerns about the *effects* of inequality (regardless of whether it's generated at the intersector or intrafirm level) ranging from the way that economic inequality that's allowed to metastasize beyond a certain level might lead to inequality in political influence to much more basic concerns about human dignity. All of this militates in favor of interfirm equality. But as powerful as the value of equality is, it's not the only value that has to be considered. Economic efficiency is a real and powerful value that gives us a reason to want to allow some material advantages to accrue from success in the marketplace. All of us interact with the economy as consumers as well as workers, and we all benefit in that capacity from firms seeking competitive advantage.

Like capitalist firms, collectives of workers compete not just for customers but for labor. Unlike capitalist firms, they do this against the backdrop of an egalitarian society in which people will be far less likely to feel stuck in their positions because of the costs entailed by trying to switch jobs. Not only does our system give workers direct voice in their firms through workplace democracy, but it also gives them more genuine opportunity for exit than they have under capitalism. If they feel a given workplace is poorly managed, worker-members empowered by living in a just society can leave and take jobs elsewhere—or even start a rival firm. This socialist market mechanism complements state regulation and oversight to help put pressure on all firms to treat people fairly and respond to what workers actually want.

But for that dynamic to work, the competition has to be on a level playing field. If some firms are vastly more profitable than others due to sectoral advantages or inherited assets, workers' ability to choose which one to join starts to look less like freedom and more like economic gravity. Ensuring at least *rough* equality between firms—especially in access to capital and residual income—helps preserve the benefits of market choice without letting new hierarchies take root.

Actually, what you're describing isn't socialism at all but only a kind of collective capitalism. Real socialism requires the abolition of markets and money.

This objection can be taken in a few different ways. We'll take them one at a time, starting with what previously socialists have meant by "socialism."

Marx called the way an economy is organized a "mode of production." Any given society's mode of production is defined by the relationship between the "immediate producers" and whoever controls the productive resources. The relation between peasants and aristocrats defines the feudal mode of production. The relationship between workers and capitalists defines the capitalist mode of production. Marx's own most common expression for the mode of production he hoped would come after capitalism was that it would be a society of "associated producers."

As we've seen, he said very little about what the rule of associated producers would actually look like. To be fair to the objection we're considering, though, what little he did say gestured at a society structured very differently than our model of socialism. Unlike some later Marxists, he didn't equate capitalism with commodity production per se, but he did seem to take it for granted that capitalism and commodity production would exit the historical stage together. For example, in *Capital* he wrote that the labor-time notes that might entitle citizens of a socialist society to a certain quantity of consumer goods in exchange for work contributions would "no more [be] 'money' than a theatre ticket is."[3]

This is as good a time as any to reiterate that our goal isn't to try to demarcate the outer limits of what might be possible as socialism develops but only to convince skeptics that there's a form of socialism that would represent both a feasible and a desirable shift from the status quo. Nevertheless, there's clearly a disconnect between our model and Marx's predictions about socialism (and those of many other early socialists). Would Marx regard a society in which the subordination of workers to capitalists had been superseded by collective ownership and workers' democracy, but where markets for many goods and services persist, as a form of socialism? The only honest answer is that there's no way to know.

Moving from Marx to the socialist movements of the late nineteenth and early twentieth centuries, the emphasis of such movements was certainly on the extension of democracy into the economic sphere. This was the original, literal meaning of "social democracy" before the Russian Revolution—when the term was used by all socialists and not just the movement's moderate wing. When the logistical problems of economy-wide planning weren't yet well understood, most such socialists assumed that upon the full enactment of economic democracy the role of markets would not just be *diminished*—as it is in our model—but ended entirely. We don't know whether they would have regarded our kind of socialism as the genuine article because they took it for granted that "rational planning" would lead to better results in any case.

Later, debates about what did or didn't count as "real" socialism centered around the different reactions of different parts of the global left to "actually existing socialism." Some, of course, were starry-eyed apologists for these regimes. Others had a more realistic view of them but still regarded them as flawed instances of socialism.

Others thought they weren't socialist because they weren't workers' democracies. Even Yugoslavia, where forms of self-management were implemented, was a one-party state. Those socialists who would disqualify the USSR and the rest from the "socialism" label on *these* grounds should regard our model as a robustly socialist one.

On the other hand, some socialists thought these nations were nonsocialist because they hadn't "overcome the commodity form" in favor of pure "production for use." In other words, even though there were no capital markets in the Soviet Union, workers were still paid in money and still used it to buy consumer goods. If you regard this as incompatible with socialism, our model is similarly nonsocialist.

The claim that the Soviet Union was nonsocialist because it was nondemocratic makes some sense to us, although it's less clear that the power and privileges of bureaucrats in those societies added up to full-fledged *class* distinctions, given that those with the highest status and the most decision-making power within the system didn't *own* the means of production. However you slice these conceptual issues, though, that system was very far from our preferred form of socialism. Our linguistic preference is to avoid the claim that it "wasn't socialist" if only to avoid even the appearance of a "no true Scotsman" evasion of the lessons of the Soviet experience.

The claim that it wasn't socialist because the employees of its state-owned enterprises were paid in rubles and used these at grocery stores is less interesting to us because it's unclear whether *any* society that could come into existence in the foreseeable future would be "socialist" in the sense of achieving complete and sustained marketlessness.

Historically, "production for use rather than exchange" has defined economies where small, tightly knit groups like families or hunter-gatherer bands were consuming most of what they produced. It has also described systems where the immediate producers weren't paid in exchangeable money because they were forced to produce by slave owners or feudal lords. What's never existed has been a society in which the widespread production of goods primarily consumed by strangers was (a) undertaken voluntarily by the immediate producers and (b) organized in any way other than "for exchange."

Of course, the fact that something hasn't yet existed doesn't mean it never could. Perhaps the system we've laid out here would evolve in a direction that satisfies both (a) and (b) in the future as technology advances and more and more of the work that currently has to be done by humans is automated away. Perhaps we'll reach a point where so little still must be done that it can get done through everyone pursuing their own projects without consumption having to be tied to labor contributions at all. And perhaps, by the time that happens, we'll have figured out a satisfactory way of allocating consumption that respects everyone's privacy and autonomy (no committee looking over your shoulder at your shopping list) but also doesn't look suspiciously like a *market* for consumer goods (as so many "marketless" models that have been proposed so far do).

That long-term possibility remains deeply speculative. From where we stand today, we believe a desirable socialism purged of all market elements is out of reach. The more immediate and practical question is whether the kind of system we can build—a democratic, egalitarian economy with a role for markets but without capitalists—should count as a form of socialism. We think it should.

It's worth taking a long step back and reminding ourselves that "socialism"—like "democracy" or "feminism" or any number of other important political terms—is a word that's been defined in different, though overlapping, ways over the long history of its use. On a descriptive level, the boringly correct answer to any question like "Was the USSR socialist?" or "Is the model we propose in this book socialist?" is "It depends on what you mean."

The more interesting dimension of the question is normative rather than descriptive: In what sense of "socialism" does it *matter* whether a given society qualifies? In other words, when we ask whether a particular model or historical example is "socialist," we're really asking whether it embodies the values and goals that make socialism worth striving for in the first place. So, the more basic question lurking behind "Is such-and-such society socialist?" is "What kind of 'socialism' do we care about?"

All three of us have chosen to dedicate our lives to the struggle for socialism. It's a goal that matters to us for both principled and consequentialist reasons. On reflection, we suspect that most other socialists would find they had similar motivations for their ideological commitments. We think everyone has a basic right to have their material needs met, to have realistic prospects for pursuing a wide variety of life choices, and to have at least a roughly equal share of power over the institutions that touch their own lives and the lives of the people they care about. We think the power imbalances built into capitalist property relations are fundamentally unjust. Beyond this, we think that a great many of the ills that afflict capitalist society are downstream of its inherent disparities in property and power. In a society with no structural guarantee that everyone will be treated decently, many won't be. Many of the issues that people would be able to work out for themselves if they had the material foundation to live a good life are sources of unnecessary suffering and conflict under capitalism.

In the sense of "socialism" that matters most for these priorities, our model is absolutely a socialist one. It's a realistic blueprint for a society that would, for the first time, combine egalitarianism in distribution and democracy in production with the abundance of high-tech modernity. It would be the first society since the Neolithic Revolution not divided into a class of producers and a class of exploiters. If you're a socialist who can't get excited about that, we'd very gently suggest that you *should*.

Even if this model is a kind of socialism, it's one that would collapse back into capitalism. As long as markets exist and play a large role in the economy, equality is unstable and sooner or later class divisions will reemerge.

The possibility that a postcapitalist economy could collapse back into a capitalist one is real. Some socialists of previous generations assumed that this was impossible. Just as capitalist societies never revert to feudalism, whatever political crises they face, socialist ones would never revert to capitalism. Once the needle of history has advanced along its track, there's no going back.

Even some Trotskyists and other critics of the authoritarian state socialism of the Soviet Union assumed until quite late in the Gorbachev era that, however severe the political crisis faced by the system, capitalism couldn't be restored without a civil war. That prediction ended up being badly mistaken. A system that doesn't deliver enough prosperity and freedom to enough people can be unwound regardless of what socialists think does or doesn't count as historical progress.

Above and beyond this general point, there are specific reasons to worry about the stability of *market* socialism. We've already acknowledged a version of this concern. If it somehow came to pass that worker-owned firms predominated within markets governed by capitalist-era rules, that would be a highly unstable combination.

In the regular churn of market competition, some such firms would go out of business, while others would prosper, and still others would hang on by the skin of their teeth. Under such circumstances, you'd have a pool of unemployed workers with an incentive to look for any source of a stable income as well as firms that had strong incentives to do what the Basque cooperative Mondragon, for example, has often done when it's expanded its operations into new territories—take on new workers as wage laborers rather than as worker-members. After wage labor once again became a large element of the economy, it's all too easy to imagine that the firms that employed it would have the competitive advantages over those that did not.[4]

That's precisely why our model doesn't leave markets governed by capitalist rules. We think a new set of property relations must be stabilized and sustained by a new set of institutions. Hence the nationalized banking sector, constitutionally restricted to giving out grants to worker-managed firms; the labor boards shaping conditions within those firms; the expansive welfare state we take as the baseline of our socialism; and the strict prohibition on accumulating inherited wealth, to name just a few of the features that make our model something fundamentally different from a capitalist market that merely happens to be populated by firms with noncapitalist ownership structures.

The objection could be pressed further, though. Isn't there an analogy between our own pragmatic reason for not wanting to stop at social democracy and the nonmarket socialist's concern that market socialism would collapse back into capitalism? It's all very well to say that we're imagining a scenario in which socialist laws mandating egalitarian arrangements have been put into place and a new, more democratic political system reigns. But why couldn't all this be reversed just like the reforms of social democracy can be reversed?

On one level, the answer is that, yes, it all *could* be reversed, and indeed that this is also true of a hypothetical scenario in which some sort of nonmarket socialism has been achieved. The question in either case is how worried we should be that it *would* be reversed.

In the case of nonmarket socialism, the best reason to worry about everything being reversed is that new forms of economic planning without markets would simply fail to deliver the goods in the way Soviet planning failed to deliver them. Remember, we're specifying planning *without markets* because our position is that planning and markets aren't at odds. We think markets in sectors where markets make sense can go hand-in-hand with an expanded role for state planning elsewhere. Planning where planning makes sense can happen more easily when planners don't have to worry about how many of which kinds of toothbrushes to produce.

The best reason specific to *our* kind of socialism to be worried about all this progress being reversed is that, however well-designed our markets may be, it's in the nature of markets to have winners and losers. Even if mandated worker management in the market sector, income benchmarks set by the labor board, restrictions on inherited wealth, and the various redistributive mechanisms already outlined function to severely limit the *size* of the gap between winners and losers, they wouldn't eliminate it entirely. It's fair to worry about any inequality in the economic sphere having downstream effects on the political process that could undermine socialism.

Wouldn't more prosperous firms, which might well chafe against the restriction stopping them from reinvesting some of their profits in hiring wage laborers with whom they wouldn't have to share decision-making power or dividends, exert disproportionate political influence? If so, would this be enough to ground the concern that, parallel to our worry about a capitalist class that uses its economic power to exert political influence and reverse social-democratic gains, there would be successful political pressure from the most successful worker-controlled firms to let them disenfranchise new hires and that capitalism would thus bit by bit be reinstated?

While it's difficult to rule out any such scenario a priori, we also shouldn't be too quick to overstate its likelihood. Let's think a bit harder about the mechanics of various ways that economic success can translate to political power under capitalism so we can see how many of these worries would carry over to our form of socialism.

Under capitalism, one of the most important ways firms can exercise political power is to threaten to relocate their operations to more politically favorable climes. A capitalist can effectively tell politicians, "You like all these jobs we provide and the taxes we pay? It sure would be a shame if something happened to that."

Even under capitalism, the capacities of individual firms to do this are wildly uneven. A manufacturer may be able to move to another jurisdiction with lower wages, lower taxes, or laxer regulations, but a package delivery service or dental clinic will not. On the whole, though, the capitalist class cumulatively exercises political power on the basis of the individual power of many of its members to relocate their operations or withhold investment.

A slight variation on this source of power is the threat that a capitalist can simply liquidate one business and reinvest the money in another without shifting anything around geographically. An old firm can simply be shut down, its assets sold to the highest bidder, and the workers left out in the cold. Alternatively, it can be sold to a venture capital firm that wants to squeeze a bit more juice from the operation before doing much the same thing.

All of these are potent enough threats to strike fear into the hearts of even militant trade unionists and firebrand left-wing politicians. Capitalists don't even have to say they'll do these things for their will to be exerted on their workforce or on the political process. The commonsensical knowledge that these options exist can be enough to get the job done.

Capitalists can exercise their class power to influence political decision-making in crasser ways too, of course. They can legally bribe politicians through campaign contributions. They can influence the voting public by funding think tanks or buying up media institutions to promote their preferred political messages. They can even force workers to sit through propaganda on the job.

A few of these methods are just ways that having lots of money can translate into political influence without that money having to either derive from or be translated back into the ownership of economic enterprises. As such, in principle, they could continue to be ways that individuals with more money to throw around could exert political influence under socialism. For example, in the scenario sketched out in our previous chapter, in which some "legacy" concentrations of wealth continued to exist during the first generation of socialism, the holders of that wealth could use it to bribe political decision-makers. Doubtless, some would try. But it's hard to imagine that a push toward socialism powerful enough to overcome entrenched capitalist resistance and expropriate the means of production in the first place would be politically weak enough to be undone by a few bribes.

Recall, too, that such legacy accumulations would soon disappear and that collective ownership of the means of production would cut off the source of the most extreme inequality of individual wealth. Moreover, the vast majority of the methods of translating economic success to political power listed above rely not just on minor or even major variations of *income* but the translation of wealth into *class power*. For example, no matter how much money you managed to save up under market socialism, the rules of the market wouldn't let you use it to buy a media organization, fire journalists whose message wasn't congenial to you, and replace them with propagandists for the restoration of capitalism. In our model, any media organizations that weren't part of the state sector would be worker controlled.

So far, we've been considering the economic power of individuals, but what about firm-level economic power? A common way of expressing this concern is to say that the bad incentives of a revenue maximizing firm don't have much to do with who *owns* it and reaps the revenue. That's true to a point, though, as we'll see, only to a point.

Here's a plausible case where it *is* true: Since collective firms still have an incentive to maximize revenue-per-worker, might they try to block regulations that would force them to abandon cheap but polluting production methods or that would phase out a product that turns out to be carcinogenic?

These incentives would be weaker than those some workers might have under capitalism to defend the continued production of public bads in order to protect their jobs. Our model comes packaged with the cushion of a considerably enhanced welfare state, and it seems probable that an egalitarian society characterized by extreme worker empowerment would take retraining and a just transition far more seriously than these things are generally taken in capitalist states. Even so, some incentive to push for the undesirable policy would exist. The real question is: What kind of tools would they have at their disposal to bring it about?

Individual workers might work out some way to use their personal incomes to promote the cause of maintaining the public bads, but at this point the shape of the problem doesn't seem dramatically different from the one that would be posed by individual employees of a decommodified, state-owned company using their power as democratic citizens to advocate against the loss of their jobs.

Turning from the public bads example back to the original issue of market winners of any kind using their success to push for rewriting the legal rules in directions that point toward the piecemeal restoration of capitalism, it's striking how few of the old capitalist tools would still be at their disposal. They could hardly threaten to move their operations overseas or close shop entirely, for example, without pointing the economic gun directly at their own livelihoods. If they were to try an investment strike, the public banks would simply fund another cooperative in the industry instead. Maybe they could democratically decide to subject themselves to propaganda on the clock but it's hard to see how that would do much for their cause.

It's true that worker-members at the more successful firms would have a bit more free time to go to capitalist-restorationist rallies or a bit more spending money for plane tickets to Washington DC to lobby lawmakers than worker-members at less successful firms. Any such political inequality is certainly troubling, and minimizing it as much as possible is one of many reasons why our model includes so many mechanisms for restraining inequality. But how worried do we realistically need to be that this would be a powerful mechanism for capitalist restoration?

Remember that, first, we're talking about a dramatically more egalitarian society than any that has ever existed under global capitalism. Everyone would have a degree of financial stability and free time that would allow for greater participation in the political process. Not everyone would want to take advantage of this opportunity, of course. Lots of people are bored by politics and want to spend their free time doing other things. But this applies to a percentage of the comparatively more successful worker-members as well as to a percentage of the comparatively less successful ones.

Finally, remember that even the most successful worker-members would have a pragmatic, nonideological reason to fear a return to capitalism. Institutional safeguards against workplace disenfranchisement that a worker-member at a successful firm has a short-term incentive to undermine also protect that very worker from falling into wage labor if their own firm goes belly-up. You might be skeptical that such long-term considerations would carry much weight. But the balance of interests at play here isn't obviously different from other familiar cases.

Think of a worker tempted to cross a picket line during a long strike but choosing instead to hold strong. Or a healthy thirty-year-old who supports universal health care because she knows she might someday become sick. Or a gainfully employed person who supports unemployment insurance—even at the cost of paying slightly higher taxes because they understand they might one day need it. In each case, short-term incentives push one way, while long-term solidaristic reasoning pulls the other. There's never a *guarantee* that the solidaristic impulse will prevail. But neither social insurance schemes nor the labor movement would last very long if it never did.

In short, no significant element of society would have an unambiguous interest in restoring capitalism, and even if it did, it wouldn't have much power to do so. Too few of the means by which economic success can be turned into political power under capitalism would persist after the transition to socialism.

Nor are we convinced that what incentives would exist in this direction are much greater under market than marketless socialism. Imagine a form of top-to-bottom planning that worked much better than the Soviet system. It would still be true that some people in that system would have incentives to favor capitalist restoration. Maybe you think that under such circumstances people would be so ideologically committed that no one would act on such incentives. We're skeptical.

Certainly, if you don't help yourself to that convenient premise, it's easy to imagine a clever and energetic bureaucrat tired of making a regular workers' wage and being accountable to state institutions convincing themselves that they'd be wildly successful as a capitalist captain of industry. But would either bureaucrats in the marketless scenario who fit this description or any successful worker-members in the market scenario who would like to wrestle ownership rights from the rest of society be able to convince a majority of the population to go along with them?

You could try to prevent the issue from coming up in the first place by making deep compromises with the democratic ideals that motivate the socialist project in the first place and simply ban the expression of procapitalist political views. But as the former leaders of East Germany can tell you, doing that is no guarantee that capitalism won't be restored all the same. The real question is whether the new system improved people's lives enough that they'll want to keep it. If so, the restorationists will quickly become the equivalent of Americans who call themselves "monarchists" in 2026—a curiosity with zero power to turn back the clock.

Under capitalism, it isn't truly capitalists who reign. Rather, market forces pull everyone's strings, including the capitalists. The domination of capitalists over workers is ultimately just a symptom of this more basic domination of everyone by the abstract imperatives of economic value. The combination of workers' control of production with market coordination would leave this problem in place.

We would grant that there's a sense in which abstract market forces generate the class divisions of capitalist society. Given less restrictive markets than the ones we envisage, firms would be free to offer people contracts as disenfranchised wage laborers. Even worker-controlled firms would have an incentive to do this for new hires. And in a situation in which a socially enforced floor for allowable contracts doesn't rule this out, many people would be incentivized, prisoners' dilemma–style, to accept such offers. This would be especially true in the absence of strong social supports financed by redistributive taxation.

But all of this is equally true of many economic practices that have long since been swept into the dustbin of history. In a world where people were still legally allowed to sell themselves into indentured servitude, for example, many desperate people would end up doing so. Nevertheless, indentured servitude has long been something that citizens of liberal capitalist nations read about in history books. So we should resist the logical leap from "market forces help give rise to a phenomenon" to "there is no way to historically transcend the phenomenon without abolishing markets." History gives clear examples of societies where markets continue to exist in some domains durably eliminating practices that might thrive in the petri dish of less restricted markets.

It's true enough that many of the worst things about capitalism result from capitalists simply responding to market incentives, and in that sense it's reasonable to describe their strings as being pulled by "market forces" or "the abstract imperatives of economic value." So, for example, the working class before the passage of laws legally restricting the working day had to work longer hours than serfs did on medieval estates. Even though they were less thoroughly dominated than serfs, the capitalists dominating them (unlike feudal lords) were in market competition with each other, and this gave them an incentive to squeeze every available drop of labor. From this example, we can generalize: Separating labor from ownership and giving owners the incentives that arise from market competition is very bad for the working class.

Would it still be a problem, though, if only the "market incentives" half of this combination existed? Certainly, as we've acknowledged throughout this book, there are public bads that even labor-managed firms would be incentivized to pursue. We've argued that a socialist society would be far better equipped to mitigate these public bads than a capitalist one, and that cooperative firms with perverse incentives would have far less power than private capitalists do to obstruct that mitigation. The more basic question is whether it would be bad, not for society in general, but for the worker-members themselves, if they continued to be "dominated" by the incentives that arise from market interaction.

A sharp articulation of this worry comes from Søren Mau in his book *Mute Compulsion*. Mau says that "what is actually transmitted by the market is not *information* but rather compulsory commands communicated through the movements of things." His worry is that, even if the "vertical" domination of workers by capitalists were smashed through workers' control of production, the "horizontal" power of market forces over everyone would remain. Collectives of workers who had to respond to price signals, producing more of this and less of that, wouldn't be truly in charge of their own destiny, since they'd be in the business of obeying the market's "compulsory commands."[5]

We agree that, in an inegalitarian society in which some people have vastly more buying power than others, it's objectionable that price signals cater to the haves over the have-nots. Given a more reasonable distribution of wealth, though, we see far less of a problem than Mau does with market-transmitted "commands."

The socialist ideal was never that people would stop serving or being served by one another. It was that, instead of dividing society into classes of masters and classes of servants, we'd serve and be served by each other as free and equal citizens. A viable form of socialism needs *some* mechanism to ensure that the goods and services being produced are ones those citizens actually want. If the direction of production toward desired consumption isn't being "commanded," whether mutely by markets or in some other way, then not only are socialist citizens' interests being poorly served as consumers, but their working hours are being wasted.

After the triumph of socialism, wouldn't worker-members of socialized firms just reproduce inequality at the international level—exploiting labor in countries that remain capitalist and in particular in the Global South?

As socialists and internationalists, our concerns about inequality, oppression, and exploitation should know no borders.

World markets convert domestic differences—like gaps in wages and capital intensity—into systematic transfers of value from the Global South to North. Left to its own devices, a newly socialist economy could still source cheap inputs from poorer regions and sell higher-value goods abroad, enjoying an advantage that looks like the old unequal exchange in new clothes. Nothing about cooperative ownership automatically overturns the hierarchies baked into global trade.[6]

But we should also resist a fatalistic picture of development as a dinner party with a fixed number of seats at the table, which are occupied in perpetuity by the first arrivals. In the postwar period, late industrializers such as South Korea and Taiwan, and more recently Communist Party–led China and Vietnam, transformed themselves from poor societies into industrial powers. This evolution depended on state intervention as much as markets and often produced stark new inequalities, but it also demonstrates that development is not a zero-sum game. The banquet table can be expanded and rearranged, and a socialist society ought to be more—not less—ambitious about hastening that process.

A socialist society would have more than just moral reasons to want development to spread beyond its borders. By helping accelerate development elsewhere, a socialist society would be building not only fairer terms of exchange but also the social stability and prosperity that make international cooperation possible.

Higher wages and rising standards of living abroad also mean larger markets for socialist industry, more secure supply chains, and more opportunities to share in technological advances. A socialist society would be strongest not as a solitary island of equality but as part of a widening community pursuing egalitarian development. And even beyond these pragmatic points, we certainly think a socialist polity would have a moral duty to help export its egalitarian gains abroad.

It might be useful to think about the French Revolution here. The revolution began in a specific polity, under specific pressures. But the initial breakthrough in 1789 widened the horizon of what was possible for millions outside France. To be sure, the realities of war and power often led the revolutionaries to compromise or abandon their egalitarian commitments in their foreign policy. But there's a broader point here. A baby born in 1789 who was lucky enough to reach old age would see the liberal capitalist order spread to much of the world by the end of their life. There are complicated reasons for those global changes in economics and politics, and not all of it can be traced to the French Revolution. Even so, it was a major factor. Some of the initial effect had to do with decisions of the revolutionary leadership we *would* want to emulate, like offering refuge and resources to help radicals abroad. More importantly, though, the fall of France's ancien régime showed at a propagandistic level that the old class societies were fragile and could be overcome and electrified observers throughout the world. The Russian Revolution initially had a somewhat similar effect, though it was lessened in many parts of the world over time as the severe shortcomings of Soviet-style state socialism became clear. We're optimistic that a version of socialism that was economically viable and politically desirable in a way that model was not would produce a deeper and longer-lasting impulse toward emulation around the world.

As we discussed in chapter eight, socialism is not autarky. The point is not to withdraw from the world economy and wall oneself off. Enver Hoxha's Albania is a grim example of what such a course can produce: isolation, stagnation, and immiseration. Cutting oneself off from trade would squander the benefits of specialization and the circulation of knowledge that can accelerate development. It would also harm poorer nations that depend on access to more advanced markets.

The socialist answer is deliberately egalitarian international planning of the global division of labor, involving capital transfers to enable sustainable development and the financial architecture to accommodate it. This becomes thinkable with the emergence of a bloc of socialist countries or, in an intermediary phase, a bloc of some fully socialist countries and some still-capitalist ones governed by sympathetic social-democratic governments who are committed to egalitarianism at a world scale. An individual high-income, wealthy socialist country concerned about exploiting low-wage production in poorer countries does not help by abstaining from trade with them. Even if its citizens can be convinced to give up some or all of the material benefits they receive from cheap labor and other resources elsewhere, it is better to transfer those benefits back as part of a coordinated, international program of capital transfers—and to put diplomatic effort into building the bloc of countries among which such coordination can take place.

Whatever policy form it'll take—and we discuss a model of trade policy in chapter eight—the job of socialists is to make sure that inequality between working people around the world is only temporary and that freedom and equality can be enjoyed everywhere. As Frederick Douglass put it, "No man can put a chain about the ankle of his fellow man without at last finding the other end fastened about his own neck."

Even if market socialism could be a stable system, its dynamics will be closer to capitalism than you hope. The imperatives of competition would force worker-managers to engage in a kind of "self-exploitation."

Strictly speaking, exploitation is the forced transfer of the product of the labor of the immediate producers to a separate ruling class. That wouldn't happen under a model of economic democracy.

Nevertheless, there's something to this worry. Whether or not it would technically count as a form of exploitation, we don't want a socialist market where worker-controlled firms are locked in a race to the bottom, slashing their own wages and benefits just to remain competitive.

We take these concerns seriously enough to include multiple safeguards at the core of our model. For one, an extensive social wage affords people greater exit opportunities from stressful workplaces. Second, while capitalism has no "minimum wage" for profits flowing to owners, in our model workers have to collectively pay themselves a regular salary. These payments have to meet benchmarks set by wage boards—an element of state economic planning that hedges against the impulse to take the low road of growth through sweating one's own labor. As discussed previously, one anticipated effect of these benchmarks is that less successful cooperatives will be driven out of business if they can't meet them, with their worker-members absorbed by more successful firms.

We'd urge any readers not satisfied with this combination of safeguards to take a long step back and think about why we're putting forward a model of feasible socialism in the first place. We don't think the transformation of wildly inegalitarian capitalist markets into the far more circumscribed socialist markets we've described would completely eliminate every trace of market-driven pathology. Nor is our goal to shut down anyone's aspirations to move even further in an egalitarian direction. If, at a later phase of socialist development, ways of going beyond the point where our model leaves off without incurring unacceptable costs in efficiency or other important values opened up, we would regard that as an excellent outcome. The whole point of our project is to expand the imaginations of those who can't picture a realistic and appealing way of transcending capitalist property relations in the first place.

We want to show, accessibly but at a level of detail that can't easily be dismissed, that a better world is possible. If it turns out an *even* better one is available, well, that's better yet. Meanwhile, some tendency toward metaphorical "self-" exploitation is a lot better than the relentless and merciless *literal* exploitation of capitalism. Some inequality between sectors or between more talented and less talented workers counteracted by a large welfare state is a lot better than the staggering levels of inequality generated by existing capitalist markets.

We aren't trying to set the outer limits of progress. We're trying to show we aren't eternally stuck with *this*.

11

Civilizational Progress

For most of the 300,000 years since Homo sapiens first appeared, we lived in small, largely nonhierarchical bands of hunter-gatherers. These societies were highly egalitarian but hard to romanticize. Many aspects of life were harsher than they are now. Without writing, the cultural memory and intellectual exchange we take for granted was impossible. Without modern medicine, infant and child mortality was high, and routine injuries or infections could prove fatal. And while those who survived early dangers might live into old age, existence remained fragile and uncertain.

Nor was the absence of a ruling class in this era any sort of achievement. It wasn't the product of a successful revolt against hierarchy but of material limits. Before the Neolithic Revolution kicked off ten thousand years ago, there wasn't enough surplus to sustain a class freed from the work of hunting and gathering.

If human history were the length of this book, the last six pages would feel like an eternity. These pages represent the millennia of kings and pharaohs, feudal lords and industrial magnates. The subordination of the many to a nonworking elite hasn't lasted as long as it seems—but it's easy today to mistake it for a law of nature.

That doesn't mean that things have been static. In recent centuries, movements rooted in the idea of innate human equality have had mass purchase. It's been almost two and a half centuries since a Paris crowd stormed the Bastille and their representatives decided that they weren't representing estates of fundamentally different kinds of human beings—aristocrats, commoners, and clergy—but a whole society of citizens. In 2026, that understanding has come close to becoming a global consensus. Even the world's most cruel and capricious dictators feel the need to hold sham elections. Outside of a few anachronistic islands of monarchy or theocracy, the idea that rulers can legitimate themselves in any way other than by at least pretending to secure the consent of the governed is unimaginable.

Nor has this shift taken place only on the terrain of ideological justification. Multiparty elections, freedom of the press, and similar innovations—so recent in the long sweep of history that they would constitute just a single paragraph in our book—are now found, in varying degrees, around the world. Even within the workplace, the coercion of chattel slavery, serfdom, indentured servitude, and the like has mostly disappeared. Arrangements that were simply facts of life for many centuries are regarded by the overwhelming majority of our contemporaries as inconceivably heinous violations of our "human rights."

Even the mute compulsion of the market no longer has free rein. The degree to which that compulsion has been softened has waxed and waned with the balance of class forces, but for more than a century the power of capital was constrained by the countervailing powers exerted by labor unions, left-wing political parties, and the unevenly distributed fragments of socialism won within capitalist states. The position of the capitalist class in advanced democracies, in that sense, has resembled that of early constitutional monarchs. They were still dominant but forced to accept charters of rights and to share power, however unequally, with elected parliaments.

The real question, for some time, has been whether this halfway house is the best we can do. And we mean that "we" in the broadest possible sense. The late democratic socialist David McReynolds was in a bar in Greenwich Village when the Soviet Union launched its Sputnik satellite into space. The news was announced, and McReynolds got excited. He exclaimed, "We did it!" Another patron, confused, said, "You mean *the Russians* did it." McReynolds responded, "No, we. Us. The human race. *We* put something in space." That's the "we" we have in mind.

It would be hard to overstate the size of the chasm separating the technological level of a species that launches satellites into space from what had been achieved anywhere in the world at the time Parisians were storming the Bastille. Such rapid progress is a testament to human ingenuity, certainly, but it should also make our collective failure to move beyond class society more striking.

If something as exciting as the Sputnik launch happens tomorrow, and we pull out our phones to look up news about it, the quality of the videos on our tiny screens will be far better than the television at that bar in Greenwich Village. We live in a world where vaccines against a novel virus can be developed and deployed in under a year. Artificial intelligence may be set to make such rapid strides that many commentators throw up their hands and refuse to make predictions about what our world will look like in a few more decades.

Yet the socioeconomic fundamentals of our world feel less malleable than ever. Francis Fukuyama argued in his 1992 book *The End of History and the Last Man* that while conflict, war, and political dissension would continue, the fundamental questions about how to organize a society, once at issue in the Cold War, were no longer in dispute. However much people fought about the details, or even temporarily regressed in this or that area, the basic combination of liberal democracy and capitalist economics was the final form of our social existence. Liberalism had decisively won the contest of ideas.

We hope Fukuyama is right about the political half of the equation, and that the reversion to authoritarianism in some countries in the decades since *The End of History and the Last Man* will turn out to have only been a temporary setback in an overall trend of democratization. But is he right that the march of democratization will forever stop at the doors of the workplace? Even putting aside the strategic arguments we've made in this book about social-democratic advances being vulnerable to reversal if the structures of capitalism stay in place, the more basic question—at the level of McReynolds's "we"—is whether even a highly regulated and constrained capitalism is really the best we can do.

The average British citizen in our era would be horrified by any suggestion that King Charles should be awarded the powers enjoyed by monarchs in even the early days of parliamentary democracy. The pomp and ritual fluff of the monarchy is one thing, but the idea that someone would have a real say in waging wars, collecting taxes, or shaping policy simply because of the family he was born into would offend their sense of justice—even if that power was far from absolute. Why, then, should we accept the less than absolute but still significant power of capitalists over workers' lives—power that often extends more intimately into workers' lives than the power of monarchs ever did.

In many workplaces, especially ones where workers have to interact with customers, employers can dictate when workers are or aren't allowed to talk to one another—and even which subjects of conversation are off-limits. In many nonunion workplaces, for instance, discussing how much you're paid is forbidden. Plenty of monarchs throughout history have criminalized blasphemy or political speech—"we should have a republic," for example—but subjects of even the most despotic monarchies didn't have to maintain absolute silence during certain hours as is required in some workplaces. And we know of no despot in history who ever decreed that his subjects must smile on cue—yet that is routine in customer service jobs today.

At some firms, the boss can decide when you go to the bathroom. If you worked in the corporate panopticon of a warehouse, like the one that might have packaged this book, the exact route you took to and from the restroom might have been electronically monitored to make sure you weren't taking longer than you needed to. One of our simplest premises is that this kind of arbitrary power by some humans over others, unmediated by mechanisms for securing the consent of the governed, should be offensive to our sensibilities as free people.

Even if we thought the halfway house of social democracy was built on a stable foundation, we'd reject capitalism on these moral grounds. If the halfway house could stand for a thousand years, that would certainly diminish the urgency of the socialist cause. But it would take nothing from the justice of that cause. And sadly, we think social democracy is built on a fault line. As our late friend Michael Brooks once put it, only "taking pieces off the board" by taking away capitalists' economic power can truly secure gains workers have already won. Thus, for pragmatic reasons no less than reasons of justice, we continue to believe that the Left's North Star should be the end of class society.

The problem to which this book has addressed itself is that, for many understandable reasons, even many thinkers and activists who are deeply committed to egalitarian values have stopped seeing that star when they scan the night sky. Perhaps what once looked like a star to them was just a passing Soviet satellite that's long since crashed back to Earth.

Isn't socialism something that humanity already tried and found wanting? Why should we think there's a better version of it waiting to be achieved?

If you're a socialist who wants to shrug off these concerns without seriously engaging with them, there are a variety of rhetorical strategies available to you. You can argue that the twentieth-century experiments in collectivization weren't genuine examples of socialism because they failed to meet the most optimistic expectations of pre-1917 radicals. (Many similarities to the old society remained! They didn't figure out how to completely do without money!) While you're at it, you can insist that a priori worries about socialist calculation are just the ideological reflex of the existing society against the very idea of future transformation. You can say that the victorious proletariat will have to sort through the questions of socialist construction through a collective, democratic process of trial and error and that it's arrogant and antidemocratic for socialist intellectuals to try to anticipate the results. You can say that, just as feudal monks trying to reason about the shape of a society without lords and serfs would be unlikely to predict stock markets and limited liability corporations, it's equally futile for us to try to fathom how the socialist future will function.

All of these moves can be and have been made in eloquent ways by writers with enough Marxist rhetorical panache to make anyone already inclined to accept the evasion nod vigorously. The problem is that none of it adds up to much more than an exhortation to *have a little faith*. Listeners critical of capitalism but wary about the prospects for a successful socialism will be about as convinced by any of this as an atheist would be by a reminder that God moves in mysterious ways.

We've tried to strike a course between either taking refuge in these strategies of evasion or learning to live with a more humane capitalism. Our approach has, instead, been to take seriously the calculation and incentive problems pointed out by our ideological enemies, to learn the bitter lessons of the socialist experiments of the twentieth century, and to lay out a vision of a postcapitalist future that's fully consistent with those lessons.

So, how have we done?

One way to think through that question is to adopt the late Marxist sociologist Erik Olin Wright's framework. In his book *Envisioning Real Utopias*, Wright argues that proposals for social transformation should pass a three-stage test. First, we need to ask if the proposal is *desirable*. Second, if so, is it *feasible*? Finally, Wright argues, *after* we've decided whether the vision is desirable and whether it's logistically feasible, we should ask whether it's *achievable*.

Let's apply these tests to our model of socialism. Working backward, we do continue to think that socialism is achievable for the same reasons previous generations of socialists did. The collective action problems involved in mobilizing the working class to fight to end its exploitation are enormous, but it remains true that people who have to sell their lives to capitalists have both a collective interest in and a collective capacity to bring about socialist transformation. The bulk of this book has thus been devoted to questions of feasibility. But what about desirability?

In a chapter called "What's So Bad About Capitalism?," Wright presents eleven objections to the capitalist status quo.

1. Capitalist class relations perpetuate eliminable forms of human suffering.
2. Capitalism blocks the universalization of conditions for expansive human flourishing.
3. Capitalism perpetuates eliminable deficits in individual freedom and autonomy.
4. Capitalism violates liberal egalitarian principles of social justice.
5. Capitalism is inefficient in certain crucial respects.
6. Capitalism has a systematic bias toward consumerism.
7. Capitalism is environmentally destructive.
8. Capitalist commodification threatens important broadly held values.
9. Capitalism, in a world of nation states, fuels militarism and imperialism.
10. Capitalism corrodes community.
11. Capitalism limits democracy.

Presumably, a desirable alternative to capitalism should represent a significant improvement on at least several of these fronts. Ideally, it should tackle all eleven. Let's see how our model fares.

1. *Capitalist class relations perpetuate eliminable forms of human suffering.*

Wright offers three reasons to think capitalism produces eliminable human suffering. The first and most straightforward is that capitalism is a system of *exploitation*. Workers don't own their means of production, so a separate class of private owners decides how the fruits of workers' labor are distributed. A second way in which capitalism produces eliminable human suffering is that *technological change* leads, in the context of capitalist property relations, to workers with newly redundant skills or roles being thrown away like so much obsolete machinery. Note that the concern here doesn't depend on any controversial prediction about automation causing long-term unemployment. Even if these changes take away old jobs with one hand while creating new ones with the other, the process is going to be shot through with stress, anxiety, and periods of economic pain. And the third mechanism just generalizes from the first two. The imperatives of *profit-maximizing competition* lead firms to throw working people under the bus whenever workers' interests diverge from the interests of the firm. An obvious case would be capital moving from country to country in search of lower wages.

On all three of Wright's subpoints, our model of socialism should be a great improvement over capitalism. It completely eliminates exploitation in the Marxist sense, since all of the firms engaged in revenue-enhancing competition would be controlled by the workers themselves. Technological change isn't eliminated, of course—nor should anyone want it to be!—but workers whose interests are at stake have a voice and a vote in the decision-making about how to wield new technologies to their collective benefit. And that point generalizes.

2. *Capitalism blocks the universalization of conditions for expansive human flourishing.*

The issue here goes beyond just eliminating the cruelties involved in letting some citizens fall into poverty. It's also not *just* a matter of equality, which we'll address when we get to Wright's fourth objection to capitalism. It's a question of unleashing human potential. Socialists have always wanted everyone to be able to develop their powers in ways that let them live flourishing lives and have objected to social structures that impede this.

Of course, no model of social organization can eliminate all obstacles to the exercise of human potential. Someone might not realize their potential because they married the wrong person, or chose an unsatisfying career, or suffered a debilitating medical crisis. If we were theologians, we might worry about why a just God would allow some of these things to happen, but we recognize that doing away with all of these obstacles is beyond what can be accomplished by any economic system. The question, instead, is whether we can clear away the particular obstacles to human flourishing that result from oppressive economic structures. Here, we think our kind of socialism would represent a long step in the right direction.

First, remember that the most expansive form of social democracy (what Robert Heilbroner called "Slightly Imaginary Sweden") is the starting point on which our model builds. We assume an expansive welfare state, including not just social-democratic staples like tuition-free university education and socialized health care but direct cash payments to all adult citizens. All of this means, for example, that if you're a single mother of three children who decides a decade into holding down a job in a coffee-growing cooperative that you would be more fulfilled as a dentist, you would be able to go back to school without paying tuition, you wouldn't worry about your children's health insurance while you were outside of the labor force, and you'd be able to stay in the same house. The transition might still involve some difficulty, but far less than it would in today's United States, or even in Fully Real Sweden.

Second, workplace democracy would give workers with an aptitude for managerial tasks far more opportunity to exercise their abilities. Moreover, even workers with no such interest are far more likely to find satisfaction in what they're doing in a situation in which they have a direct stake in the firm's success and managers are accountable to them (and hence don't approach managerial tasks primarily in a spirit of whip-cracking). This point shouldn't be exaggerated. Work is still work when you own the place, and the world that exists right now is full of small business owners who spend their days fantasizing about retirement. But it's also true that a vast market in "be your own boss" self-help literature exists not *just* because the consumers of this literature hope that their bank accounts will grow if they make the leap from workers to self-employed small business owners but because they feel unfulfilled in their current jobs and they see more opportunity for fulfillment from work over which they exercise some control.

A typical citizen of the socialist society we envision would have a greater ability than workers do under capitalism to pursue interests and develop capacities unrelated to their careers. In some cases, as with Stephen Jay Gould's famous observation about potential new Einsteins who have "lived and died in cotton fields and sweat shops," the result of all of this could be scientific breakthroughs being made by amateurs, artistic masterpieces being crafted in garages, and so on. But equally we expect that there would be a flood of terrible poetry, unreadable novels, and unlistenable new bands being formed as multitudes of people were freed to explore by trial and error where their true talents lay. We would celebrate this too as a symptom of progress.

3. *Capitalism perpetuates eliminable deficits in individual freedom and autonomy.*

As Wright rightly emphasizes, the heart of the capitalist employment contract is a commitment by workers to do what they're told. All else being equal, the only sense in which they have the freedom to refuse orders is that they possess what we've already argued is the relatively feeble freedom of *exit*. But without *voice*, exiting just means entering a new relationship of domination on much the same terms. A choice of masters is better than no choice at all but it's a far cry from freedom from mastery.

It's true enough that a self-employed petty proprietor has more individual autonomy than even a worker-member in a democratic firm. But as Marx was already rightly emphasizing in the nineteenth century, advanced economies inevitably involve large groups of people working cooperatively. The real choices are whether this collective work is done under conditions of collective ownership or whether it's combined with workplace dictatorship. If a retreat to a world of small farmers and small artisans was already unrealistic in the nineteenth century, it's inconceivable in the twenty-first. Transitioning in that direction would involve a vast reduction in living standards, and no society has ever voluntarily regressed in that way. We can, however, go forward to a world of socialized ownership and workplace democracy.

4. *Capitalism violates liberal egalitarian principles of social justice.*

As we discussed in the introduction to this book, the level of inequality baked into capitalist economic structures goes far beyond what would be permitted by John Rawls's theory of distributive justice. Our model does far better in this regard. We've acknowledged that worker-owned firms trying to maximize income per member might vote for pay scales that aren't perfectly egalitarian. Higher salaries might be offered either for certain managerial roles involving lots of stress and responsibility or conversely for particularly dirty or dangerous jobs. But these are inequalities an agent deliberating from behind the veil of ignorance may well accept. They could see how they might benefit from them even if the particular combination of talents they ended up with weren't the ones that would translate into getting the long ends of these particular sticks. After all, the pay scales would have to be voted on by people who actually *knew* they were getting the short end of the stick (and decided the trade-off made sense). Nothing similar can be said in defense of capitalist structures whereby CEOs make hundreds of times more than ordinary workers and the wealthiest people don't live off of wages or salaries at all.

Of course, if you reject Rawlsianism in favor of an even more demanding egalitarian standard like Cohen's "socialist equality of opportunity" principle, our model might not measure up quite as well. Even there, though, Cohen saw his standard as a North Star toward which we should try to come as close as we can, given real-world constraints on our ability to engineer a viable system. And our system moves us very far in the direction of Cohen's North Star.

5. *Capitalism is inefficient in certain crucial respects.*
As Wright acknowledges, capitalism is far more efficient as an engine of economic prosperity than earlier systems. Our hope is that, insofar as it retains market mechanisms, our model will retain many of these sources of efficiency. However, he mentions several sources of capitalist inefficiency, including "the underproduction of public goods; the under-pricing of natural resources; negative externalities; monitoring and enforcing market contracts; pathologies of intellectual property rights; and the costs of inequality."

Of the six, our model does the least to reduce the inefficiencies involved in enforcing market contracts. We still have markets, and myriad contracts will still need to be enforced. Disputes over performance, interpretation, and breach will not vanish. Even there, though, our kind of socialism represents a step forward. It is arguable that cooperative enterprise, with more equally shared benefits and risks, would have weaker incentives to engage in predatory contracting than capitalist firms and would thereby help foster a greater degree of trust in market exchange. But when disputes do arise, a socialist state could make contract enforcement cheaper and more reliable by maintaining specialized public arbitration boards or courts, reducing reliance on private legal services. The state could also promulgate default contract templates for common transactions, cutting down on bespoke legal drafting, reducing uncertainty, and lowering the likelihood of conflict.

Two examples of inefficiency Wright gives are "the costs associated with supervising employees within the labor process, and the enormous paperwork costs of paying for medical care through a system of decentralized private insurance." The first is greatly reduced in our market sector, given the dramatically shifted incentives created by worker management, and the second is eliminated in even social-democratic systems with public health care provision.[1]

Our model also greatly reduces inequality by creating an expansive welfare state, by directly moderating labor income inequality through the wage-benchmark system, and most importantly by ending the class divisions that are inequality's most basic source under capitalism. It also addresses the chronic underpricing of natural resources by more robustly empowering the public sector to impose taxes and fees that internalize ecological costs directly into market prices. In this way, resource use would be disciplined without distorting the broader market mechanism, and the revenues generated could be reinvested in public goods. Likewise, negative externalities—from pollution to unsafe products—can be curbed through a combination of environmental taxation, clear regulatory standards, and public ownership in key sectors.

We don't claim that every source of inefficiency under capitalism would be erased by the move toward market socialism. We do, however, claim that this move would unleash tremendous progress in the right direction.

6. Capitalism has a systematic bias toward consumerism.

Of the eleven, this is the criterion that needs the most clarification. Much of what's often labeled "consumerism" could more neutrally be called "valuing having a higher quality of life in respects that require the economic cooperation of others." Any external object that satisfies a human desire that most people aren't able to make for themselves (which is a very long list in a high-tech society) is necessarily purchased in order to be consumed. There's nothing wrong with that.

When workers in capitalist workplaces go on strike and win a better contract, for example, their improved wages mean they can buy more consumer goods for themselves and their families. We think that's a good thing! Similarly, we think it would be excellent if a transition to social ownership and workplace democracy meant that future revenues in the market sector were distributed in a more egalitarian way and hence more working people were able to watch more movies, drive nicer cars, live in more spacious and pleasant residences, eat better food, and take their kids on nicer vacations.

But the specific worry about "consumerism" Wright directs our attention to is one we should take seriously. He isn't concerned here with the ecological damage caused by the production of some consumer goods (which is covered separately in the point below). Nor is he interested in scolding people for wanting too many things. Indeed, he acknowledges that one of the virtues of capitalism is that it facilitates increased productivity over time. His concern is that productivity increases can in principle be used to either increase the number of outputs being produced (even while keeping labor time constant) or keep outputs steady (even while reducing labor time), and capitalism contains a systematic bias toward the former. In other words, a predictable effect of capitalist economic structures is that, putting aside any questions about how evenly or unevenly either extra consumption or extra leisure time is distributed through the population, productivity gains are vastly more likely to generate more consumption than more leisure.

We take *this* seriously because, just as we want ordinary people who want fashionable clothing and bigger television sets to have those things, and we take pride in the successes of the Left and the workers' movement in delivering them, we similarly want everyone to be able to spend more time with their loved ones, and we agree that a desirable alternative to capitalism would secure more of that. We're optimistic that our model would secure more of both.

It's worth noting that, even under capitalism, some of the countries whose social contracts have been most powerfully shaped for the better by powerful labor unions have the least pronounced "consumerist" bias in capturing productivity gains. The Nordics, historically, had lower per capita GDPs than the United States overall but higher GDPs *per hour worked*. This is surely at least some evidence that, where workers have more power to decide whether to capture productivity gains with more goods or more leisure, they're more likely than nonworking business owners to capture at least some of the gains with reduced working hours. If so, that trend would likely be even more pronounced in our model, in which operating agreements are unilaterally decided by the workers themselves.

It's true that, at least to some extent, competitive pressures can be expected to limit this tendency *at the firm level* in our model. But the long history of the workers' movement successfully pushing for reductions in working hours makes us think that, given sufficient power, producers can and will fight for shorter workweeks and more leisure *at the state level*. At any rate, in different ways at both levels, democratic socialism puts the decision about how to balance greater leisure against greater goods precisely where it should be—in the hands of people whose lives are at stake in these decisions.

7. *Capitalism is environmentally destructive.*

For reasons laid out in our discussion of cooperatives producing environmentally damaging products, we think that worker-members even in, for example, an oil-drilling cooperative would have *fewer* bad incentives for opposing worthwhile environmental regulations compared to the owners of capitalist oil companies. More importantly, we also argued there that the levers available to them to act politically on these incentives would be dramatically diminished compared to the political levers available to capitalist CEOs. And, of course, our position is that energy production belongs in our fully public sector.

What bears emphasizing, though, is that a strong public sector in a socialist economy is uniquely positioned to set the "rules of the game" in ways that facilitate environmentally responsible outcomes. Cooperative firms may still face temptations to cut corners, but a robust state sector—with direct ownership in energy, infrastructure, and other commanding heights—has both the capacity and the legitimacy to enforce uniform environmental standards, levy ecological taxes and fees, and direct investment toward sustainable technologies. This is not an afterthought to the system but a built-in feature: The state has far greater reach and fewer conflicts of interest than any patchwork of regulatory mechanisms set on top of a fundamentally privatized economy ever would.

John Roemer argues that a capitalist society generates a powerful political constituency for many public bads, because private returns from the activities that generate them are concentrated in the hands of small groups of wealthy people who have the incentive and resources to defend them. Even if these people are themselves affected by the public bads, the income they get from the activities far more than compensates them. But in a socialist society, such private gains are more evenly distributed and so a much smaller part of any individual's income; because they are more modest, they are more likely to be outweighed by the effects of the public bads. So even if people were motivated by self-interest alone, a more egalitarian society is likely to see more support for regulation to limit environmental damage and other negative externalities.[2]

We don't claim that our model would entirely negate every ecologically bad incentive for individual actors that exists under the current system. We do claim, however, that combining the diminished bad incentives within cooperative firms with the vastly enhanced regulatory and ownership capacities of the public sector would likely result in a cleaner and more livable world than capitalism has been able to deliver.

8. *Capitalist commodification threatens important broadly held values.*

Our model is built to counteract this tendency. It enshrines certain goods as social rights and therefore outside of the market altogether, while also embedding the principle of social ownership of the means of production through both a strong state sector and a socialized cooperative sector. To whatever extent groups of workers might see opportunities in commodifying uncommodified domains, they would confront the constitutional mandates of the public banks that serve as custodians of social property.

Still, while our model assumes a state that offers a wide variety of decommodified goods as its starting point, one concern might be that the state would be unstable—that it would be susceptible to erosion by bad incentives and political machinations of some market actors. There are a few reasons, though, why we're optimistic that the gains of democratic socialism would prove sustainable.

For one thing, even under capitalism, universal social programs, once established, often require intense political struggle to reverse. Under socialism, the incentives pushing toward commodification would be far weaker. No cooperative eyeing a chance to marketize a public good would stand to gain anything remotely comparable to what wealthy shareholders or CEOs capture under capitalism.

For another, the points made in our discussion of industrial cooperatives resisting environmental regulation apply here as well. Even if some individuals were tempted by short-term gains—say, bulldozing a public park for profit or privatizing childcare—they would face the organized resistance of all the other citizens who value parks and childcare, without a clear structural advantage in the political contest. And as we noted earlier, they could not dominate public discourse through media ownership or similar means, since journalists themselves would be either public employees or worker-owners, not subordinates of private media moguls.

All this is to say, conflict and debate over the boundaries of the market will continue, and they will be resolved in the political sphere. But the social gains of decommodification, once established, should prove resilient—protected both by institutional safeguards and by the broad constituencies that benefit from them.

9. *Capitalism, in a world of nation states, fuels militarism and imperialism.*

Here, we think the case on behalf of our model is robust. It would be too much to claim in advance that it would be absolutely impossible for wars to break out between fully democratic socialist societies. That's an empirical question that remains to be tested, and we're well aware that not all causes of geopolitical conflict are straightforwardly economic. Even so, there are excellent reasons to think war between fully democratic socialist states would at the very least be extremely rare—certainly, far more rare than wars between capitalist countries.

Under capitalism, a significant share of military conflict is tied up with economic competition—over resources, markets, and strategic advantage. This has often taken the form of imperial expansion, with all its attendant human costs. If you remove a class of private owners with a direct stake in expanding investment opportunities abroad, you weaken some of the underlying pressures that have historically driven that expansion.

That doesn't mean a socialist society would be incapable of acting coercively toward weaker neighbors. It's not hard to imagine situations where it might. But the distribution of gains would look very different. Instead of flowing to a relatively small group with strong incentives to pursue and defend those gains, any benefits would be spread broadly across the population. And once those gains are diffused, they become much less politically decisive. Any "upside" of expansion would be modest for most people, while there's no obvious reason why the costs would be less severe than they are in class societies.

Second, even under capitalism, wars between internally politically democratic states are extremely rare. However one explains this phenomenon, it would be quite surprising if making democracy more meaningful made wars between democracies *more* likely. It's plausible that at least one mechanism for preventing wars between democracies is that, when people in one country get to see the debate about war play out in another, it becomes harder to dehumanize them, and we expect far more robust public debate in societies not dominated by wealthy elites.

Finally, war is the ultimate expression of inequality. The working-class majority of society always bears the brunt of the cost, at the same time that, even in formally democratic countries, they have far less say in foreign policy than other layers of the population. It's working-class people who are used as cannon fodder on the front lines (while the more privileged have far more ways out of that duty); it's working-class people who are most likely to die when cities are bombed; and it's working-class people who suffer the most from the economic deprivations experienced by nations at war. As such, manufacturing popular consent for war and imperialism is often hard work for political elites, and the general populace often sours on wars long before high-level decision-makers decide to agree to a peace treaty. There is perhaps no single social change more likely to make war rare than economically (and hence politically) empowering the great mass of the population.

10. *Capitalism corrodes community.*
In *Why Not Socialism?*, Cohen complements his "socialist equality of opportunity" principle with a socialist "principle of community." The idea here is that we want a society in which human interactions are shaped, as much as possible, by a nonmarket reciprocity according to which we help and expect help from others because we care about them and they care about us. Most of us intensely value our families and our friendships, for example, in part because families and friendships are islands of this kind of interaction in a society in which we often otherwise scramble over each other for economic opportunities.

To the extent that our model retains a significant role for markets, we might stand accused of falling short in the degree to which we're giving space to the value of community. We argued in the introduction, though, that insofar as our model dramatically reduces inequality and precarity, we've thereby taken very long steps in the direction anyone who values community in Cohen's sense should want.

To make that point more vivid, imagine that you had a brother with a bad gambling habit who lost everything in high-stakes poker games. Assume that this isn't a compulsion outside of his control. He's simply making unwise decisions of his own free will. If so, his losing everything doesn't violate the socialist equality-of-opportunity principle. Even so, if you saw him sleeping on a park bench, you wouldn't just keep walking on the grounds that it's his own damn fault. The reason you wouldn't do this is because he's connected to you by bonds of mutual caring as part of the smallest-scale and most intense form of community (a family).

Of course, it's not psychologically realistic for us to all be exactly as emotionally invested in the fate of any random stranger as we would be in our own siblings, but that doesn't mean we have to have a society where we're all socialized not to make eye contact with the homeless. In the far more egalitarian society we envision, it's plausible that seeing someone sleeping in the streets, too dejected to seek help from the state, would be so shockingly rare that socialist citizens would react to it the way you or I would react even now to seeing a stranger having a heart attack. They would perceive it as an emergency requiring immediate attention. Even with markets continuing to play an economic role, the move toward a far more egalitarian future could dramatically increase the extent to which we all see our fellow citizens as within the sphere of people we care about—as being, in other words, part of our larger community.

11. *Capitalism limits democracy.*

This is the single test on which the merits of our model are the most obvious. We would completely end the subordination of workers to profit-seeking capitalists. Just about every direct producer in the economy (who wasn't self-employed) would either be an employee of the public sector or a worker-member in a cooperative. With greatly enhanced economic equality and hence greatly enhanced political democracy, the public sphere would be far more meaningfully the property of the public as a whole. And worker-members, as we've emphasized, would be citizens of economic republics rather than subjects of economic kings and queens. Our form of socialism would extend democratization well beyond anything that's been achieved anywhere in human history.

Showing that this would be more democratic isn't the problem. The challenge is to show readers that such a world of greatly enhanced democracy is *possible*.

It's always useful to remember that everything that's now in the past was once in the future. Forms of progress we take for granted once seemed impossibly fanciful. No one in France in, say, 1500, thought their descendants would be living in a republic. Few of the revolutionaries who would go on to proclaim that republic at the end of the eighteenth century could have imagined extending full democratic rights to women. Even fewer in the early American republic thought the descendants of slaves would one day achieve every legal right enjoyed by whites or be elected to high public office.

In those capitalist countries that have traveled furthest in a democratic socialist direction, things like free public health care and free public higher education, powerful unions that bargain to set wage levels for entire industries, social wealth funds that play a powerful role in the economy, and huge portions of the public living in high-quality public housing have simply become *the way things are*. Many Swedes and Danes and Finns and Norwegians would deny that there's anything especially "socialist" about these historic achievements of their countries' socialist movements. That's how progress works. What was once unimaginable becomes unremarkable.

Our hope is that the socialization of the foundations of the economy will one day be like that. It will just seem *obvious* that this is how things are. The same way we've traveled so far technologically from the launching of Sputnik that we take the existence of satellite-guided navigation for granted every time we get into our cars, we look forward to the day when we've traveled so far socially that the very thought of having to submit yourself to the will of a capitalist to make a living will seem bizarre. Being told that the cutting-edge progressive position taken by many social-democratic politicians was once *co*determination, whereby only *part* of the boards that ran companies were elected by the workers, will be like being reminded that advocacy of minor limits to the power of kings was once considered dangerously subversive.

Of course, this hope may not come to pass. The future isn't written and there's no guarantee that the political struggles that are yet to come will go our way. What we do know is that there's little chance of achieving a new kind of society if even the renegades of the twenty-first century who are dissatisfied with capitalism have no confidence in the possibility of a realistic, viable alternative. Without a conviction that something better can come after capitalism, the inequities of the current system appear like bad weather or the inevitability of aging and death—unfortunate facts to be endured, not injustices that can be ended.

Books about economic models of the future can't dislodge economic systems. Only a powerful workers' movement can do that. But the participants in such a movement must believe that something better is possible, and it's here that we hope to have made a contribution.

Acknowledgments

Many people helped make this book possible. We are grateful to Seth Ackerman, Nicole Aschoff, Vivek Chibber, Asher Dupuy-Spencer, Melissa Flashman, Mark Martin, and John Roemer, among others, for their support, feedback, and assistance at various stages of the project. Thanks also to Artemis Brod for careful and thoughtful copyediting.

Bhaskar would also like to thank his wife, Emily Morrow. Ben would like to thank the analytical Marxism reading group in Los Angeles for their engagement and encouragement. He also wants to take this opportunity to remember Michael Brooks, a dear friend to both him and Bhaskar, whose voice was sorely missed as we worked on this project. Mike would like to thank his wife, Raych, and daughter, Frankie, for their love and tremendous support and to acknowledge the students in his Political Economy of Socialism seminar—Philippe Alais, Sam Gardiner, Alex Glase, Lucas Kao, Patrik Kertesz, Matt McKelvie, Tilly Shim, Jack Stubley, Haonan Song, and Vivek Waller—for discussions that sharpened his thinking throughout the writing process.

Notes

1. The Return of Politics

1 Karl Marx, *Capital*, trans. Ben Fowkes and David Fernbach, vol. 1 (Harmondsworth: Penguin Books, 1976 [1867]), 98.
2 Ludwig von Mises, "Economic Calculation in the Socialist Commonwealth," trans. S. Adler, in *Collectivist Economic Planning*, ed. F. A. Hayek (London: Routledge & Kegan Paul, 1935 [1920]).
3 Karl Marx and Friedrich Engels, *The German Ideology* (Moscow: Progress Publishers, 1964 [1846]), 45.
4 G. A. Cohen, *If You're an Egalitarian, How Come You're So Rich?* (Cambridge, MA: Harvard University Press, 2000), 58–78.
5 Peter Hudis, *Marx's Concept of the Alternative to Capitalism* (Chicago: Haymarket Books, 2013), 3.
6 John Rawls, *A Theory of Justice* (Cambridge, MA: The Belknap Press, 1971), 136–42.
7 G. A. Cohen, *Why Not Socialism?* (Princeton: Princeton University Press, 2009), 14–18.
8 Nick Romeo, "How Mondragon Became the World's Largest Coop," *The New Yorker*, August 27, 2022; *AFL-CIO, Executive Paywatch 2024: CEO Pay and the S&P 500* (Washington, DC: AFL-CIO, 2024), which reports that in 2023 the average CEO-to-median worker pay ratio across S&P 500 companies was 268:1; "Un ejecutivo del IBEX cobra 73,5 veces más que sus trabajadores," *Cadena SER*, April 14, 2025, which notes that executives at IBEX-35 companies earn on average 73.5 times more than their employees.

9 Oskar Lange, "On the Economic Theory of Socialism," parts I and II, *Review of Economic Studies* 4, nos 1–2 (1936–7): 53–71, 123–42.

10 F. A. Hayek, "The Nature and History of the Problem," in *Collectivist Economic Planning*, 1–40. We discuss the debate in chapter four. For a succinct overview of the key contributions from a market socialist perspective, see John Roemer, *A Future for Socialism* (Cambridge, MA: Harvard University Press, 1994), 28–36.

11 Gregory Dow, *The Labor-Managed Firm: Theoretical Foundations* (Cambridge: Cambridge University Press), 116–27.

12 Mark Fisher, *Capitalist Realism: Is There No Alternative?* (Winchester: Zero Books, 2009).

2. The Plans That Failed

1 Nikita Khrushchev, *Khrushchev Remembers*, trans. and ed. Strobe Talbott with an introduction, commentary, and notes by Edward Crankshaw (Boston: Little, Brown, 1970), 266.

2 In other accounts, Khrushchev merely banged the table with his fist while his shoe was visible on his desk.

3 "Nikita S. Khrushchev Sees Consumer Gains; Soviet to Outproduce US, He Tells Parliament," *New York Times*, April 11, 1958.

4 Robert Gillette, "Remaking the Revolution: New Soviet System; Perestroika; Bold Shift in Economy," *Los Angeles Times*, October 27, 1987.

5 Marx and Engels, *The German Ideology*.

6 Karl Marx, *Critique of the Gotha Programme* (New York: International Publishers, 1938 [1875]). Marx distinguishes between a "first phase of communist society" and a "higher phase of communist society." He does not call the first phase "socialism." It was Lenin, in *State and Revolution*, who systematically codified Marx's "lower phase of communism" as socialism and reserved communism proper for the higher phase.

7 Marx and Engels, *Manifesto of the Communist Party* (London: George Allen & Unwin, 1888 [1848]); Friedrich Engels, "Outlines of a Critique of Political Economy," in *Karl Marx and Friedrich Engels: Collected Works*, vol. 3 (New York: International Publishers, 1975 [1844]).

8 Karl Kautsky, *The Labour Revolution* (London: National Labour Press, 1924), 149.

9 Tony Cliff, *Lenin: Building the Party (1893–1914)* (London: Pluto Press, 1975), 77.

10 Vladimir Lenin, *The State and Revolution: The Marxist Theory of the State and the Tasks of the Proletariat in the Revolution* (Moscow: Progress Publishers, 1970 [1917]), 17–20, 111–12.

11 Vladimir Lenin, "The Impending Catastrophe and How to Combat It" (September 1917), in *Collected Works*, vol. 25 (Moscow: Progress Publishers, 1977), 354–7, quoted in Alec Nove, *An Economic History of the USSR* (London: Penguin Books, 1989), 34–5.

12 Leon Trotsky, *Terrorism and Communism: A Reply to Karl Kautsky* (Ann Arbor: University of Michigan Press, 1961 [1920]), 102.

13 S. A. Smith, *Russia in Revolution: An Empire in Crisis, 1890 to 1928* (Oxford: Oxford University Press, 2017), 282.

14 Vladimir Lenin, "The Tax in Kind (The Significance of the New Policy and Its Conditions)," April 21, 1921, in *Collected Works*, vol. 32 (Moscow: Progress Publishers, 1965), 332.

15 John Marot, "The New Economic Policy Was the Alternative to Stalinism," *Jacobin*, December 18, 2019.

16 Robert Himmer, "The Transition from War Communism to the New Economic Policy: An Analysis of Stalin's Views," *The Russian Review* 53, no. 4 (1994).

17 Nove, *An Economic History of the USSR*, 95.

18 Moshe Lewin, *The Making of the Soviet System: Essays in the Social History of Interwar Russia* (New York: Pantheon Books, 1985), 94.

19 Robert C. Allen, *Farm to Factory: A Reinterpretation of the Soviet Industrial Revolution* (Princeton: Princeton University Press, 2003).

20 We'll often use "command economy" as it's a more familiar term for readers. But the system is more accurately described as an "administered economy," as many of its features were shaped not by direct command but by more complex bureaucratic mediation.

21 Paul R. Gregory, "The Stalinist Command Economy," *The ANNALS of the American Academy of Political and Social Science* 507, no. 1 (1990): 18–25.

22 It's been noted that, as the Soviet model evolved, planning became "less 'physical' than the stereotype; planners set targets

for the value of industry outputs using plan prices that were supposedly fixed but in fact the factories themselves exerted considerable influence over prices, and could push them up under certain conditions to make the plan easier to fulfil." Mark Harrison, "Five-Year Plan," *The Encyclopedia of Modern Europe: Europe Since 1914; The Age of War and Reconstruction*, ed. John Merriman and Jay Winter (New York: Scribner, 2006).

23 Paul G. Hare, *Central Planning* (London: Routledge, 1991), as cited in Seth Ackerman, "The Red and the Black," *Jacobin*, Winter 2013.

24 Joseph S. Berliner, *Factory and Manager in the USSR* (Cambridge, MA: Harvard University Press, 1957), 13–14.

25 Ibid., 15.

26 Ibid., 18.

27 Eugène Zaleski, *Planning for Economic Growth in the Soviet Union, 1918–1932* (Chapel Hill: University of North Carolina Press, 2011).

28 Michael Ellman, *Socialist Planning* (New York: Cambridge University Press, 2014), 13.

29 Miklós Haraszti, *A Worker in a Worker's State: Piece-Rates in Hungary* (Harmondsworth: Penguin Books, 1977).

30 Ibid., 45, 132. Though workers like Miklós Haraszti didn't yet feel it individually, at the enterprise level many of these classic features of administered economies were being combatted in his native Hungary.

31 Ellman, *Socialist Planning*, 260–2.

32 Milan Vodopivec, "The Labor Market and the Transition of Socialist Economies," *Comparative Economic Studies* 33, no. 2 (1991): 123–58.

33 Daniel S. Hamermesh and Richard D. Portes, "The Labour Market Under Central Planning: The Case of Hungary," *Oxford Economic Papers* 24, no. 2 (1972): 243, 246. In China, like in the Stalin-era USSR, however, a high percentage of labor was allocated administratively from 1958 until the mid-1980s.

34 Joseph Stalin, "The Tasks of Business Executives," February 4, 1931, in *Works*, vol. 13 (Moscow: Foreign Languages Publishing House, 1954), 38. "Socialist sixth of the world" was a term used by supporters of the Soviet Union like English priest Hewlett Johnson to describe the USSR's land mass.

35 Giacomo Corneo, *Is Capitalism Obsolete?: A Journey Through Alternative Economic Systems* (Cambridge, MA: Harvard University Press, 2017), 124.

36 Khrushchev would also seek extensive growth through his "Virgin Lands" campaign, which from 1954 aimed to bring millions of hectares of land in Kazakhstan, Siberia, and other regions under cultivation. Khrushchev, quoted by Valery Vasiliev, "Failings of the *Sovnarkhoz* Reform: The Ukrainian Experience," in *Khrushchev in the Kremlin*, ed. Jeremy Smith and Melanie Ilic (London: Routledge, 1991), 112–32.

37 Leigh Phillips and Michal Rozworski, *The People's Republic of Walmart: How the World's Biggest Corporations Are Laying the Foundation for Socialism* (London: Verso, 2019).

38 Roemer, *A Future for Socialism*, 43–4.

39 Michael Ellman, "Lessons of the Soviet Economic Reform," *Socialist Register* 5 (1968): 29.

40 Leonid Kantorovich, "Mathematical Methods of Production Organization and Planning," trans. Robert W. Campbell and W. H. Marlow, *Management Science* 6, no. 4 (1960 [1939]): 366–422.

41 Ibid., 376.

42 Michael Ellman, "Leonid Kantorovich," in *Russian and Western Economic Thought: Mutual Influences and Transfer of Ideas*, ed. Vladimir Avtonomov and Harald Hagemann (Cham, Switzerland: Springer, 2022), 433.

43 Ivan Boldyrev and Till Düppe, "Programming the USSR: Leonid V. Kantorovich in Context," *British Journal for the History of Science* 53, no. 2 (June 2020): 10.

44 Joseph S. Berliner, "Soviet Management from Stalin to Gorbachev: A Comparison of the Harvard Project and SIP Interviews," working paper, Soviet Interview Project, University of Illinois at Urbana-Champaign, 1988.

45 Cosma Shalizi, "In Soviet Union, Optimization Problem Solves You," *Crooked Timber*, May 30, 2012.

46 János Kornai, "A General Descriptive Model of Planning Processes," *Economics of Planning* 10, nos. 1–2 (1970): 12–13.

47 Ellman, "Leonid Kantorovich," 437.

48 Seth Ackerman, "Socialism Can Work. Cybersocialism Can't," *Jacobin* (forthcoming).

49 "Evsei Liberman on Socialist Economic Planning," WNYC Radio, November 19, 1962.

50 Paul R. Gregory and Robert C. Stuart, *Soviet and Post-Soviet Economic Structure and Performance*, 6th ed. (New York: HarperCollins College Publishers, 1994), 295–6.

51 Jan Adams, *Economic Reforms in the Soviet Union and Eastern*

Europe Since the 1960s (Basingstoke: Palgrave Macmillan, 1989), 40.

52 Yakov Feygin, *Building a Ruin: The Cold War Politics of Soviet Economic Reform* (Cambridge, MA: Harvard University Press, 2024), 9.

53 Mark Harrison, "Economic Growth and Slowdown," in *Brezhnev Reconsidered*, ed. Edwin Bacon and Mark Sandle (Basingstoke: Palgrave, 2002), 59.

54 Robert Pear, "Evolution in Europe; Soviet Experts Say Their Economy Is Worse Than US Has Estimated," *The New York Times*, April 24, 1990.

55 János Kornai, *The Socialist System: The Political Economy of Communism* (Princeton: Princeton University Press, 1992), 391.

56 Béla Balassa, "Collectivization in Hungarian Agriculture," *Journal of Farm Economics* 42, no. 1 (1960); Z. Edward O'Relley, "The Changing Status of Collectivized and Private Agriculture under Central Planning: To Increase Output, State Socialist Hungary Combines Private with State Enterprises," *The American Journal of Economics and Sociology* 45, no. 1 (1986).

57 Kornai, *The Socialist System*, 481.

58 Béla Balassa, *The Hungarian Economic Reform, 1968–1981* (Oxford: Pergamon Press, 1981).

59 Ellman, *Socialist Planning*, 64.

60 Adams, *Economic Reforms in the Soviet Union and Eastern Europe Since the 1960s*, 86.

61 Kornai, *The Socialist System*, 481.

62 Ibid., 403.

63 Béla Balassa, "Reforming the New Economic Mechanism in Hungary," *Journal of Comparative Economics* 7, no. 3 (1983): 253–76.

64 Ibid.

65 Ellman, *Socialist Planning*, 66.

66 Chinese leaders in the 1980s studied Hungary while planning their own reform attempts, visiting government departments, scientific institutions, industrial enterprises, and rural cooperatives. But they ultimately resolved the contradictions of market socialism through the restoration of capitalism under the watchful eye of a powerful state. While we think the example of Hungary is more instructive, Yugoslavia's self-managed model offers another market socialism case study, which we discuss in chapter nine.

67 Kornai focused particularly on enterprises in socialist countries

undergoing market reforms like Hungary, Poland, and Yugoslavia, but his insights extend to other state socialist models, as well as to capitalist systems. János Kornai, Eric Maskin, and Gérard Roland, "Understanding the Soft Budget Constraint," *Journal of Economic Literature* 41, no. 4 (2003): 1095–136.

68 Lenin, *State and Revolution*, 70–5. Gosplan, to an impressive degree, actually got the accounting part down; it just struggled with the control.

69 Paul R. Gregory, "Soviet Bureaucratic Behaviour: Khozyaistvenniki and Apparatchiki," *Soviet Studies* 41, no. 4 (October 1989): 511–25. Alec Nove, *The Soviet Economic System* (London: George Allen & Unwin, 1977), 33.

70 Alec Nove, *The Economics of Feasible Socialism Revisited* (London: HarperCollins Academic, 1991), 75.

71 Ibid., 68–82; Ellman, *Socialist Planning*, 35.

3. Solving the Economic Problem

1 Diane Elson, "Market Socialism or Socialization of the Market?" *New Left Review* 1, no. 172 (1988): 3–44.

2 Lange, "On the Economic Theory of Socialism," 54.

3 Lionel Robbins, *An Essay on the Nature and Significance of Economic Science*, 2nd ed. (London: Macmillan and Co., 1935), 16.

4 From the perspective of Pareto optimality, the problem is not that the monopolist gains at the expense of others: Fixing this would make the others better off only at the expense of the monopolist, and so would not be a Pareto improvement. The improvement left on the table could be realized if the monopolist were able to discriminate on price between different customers, selling some units more cheaply to those who will not pay the higher price.

5 Charlie Giattino, Esteban Ortiz-Ospina, and Max Roser, "Time Use," *Our World in Data*. Global Change Data Lab, 2020. The housework category includes time spent shopping.

6 For visions of life beyond productivism, see Juliet Schor, *Plenitude: The New Economics of True Wealth* (Melbourne: Scribe Publications, 2010); and Kate Soper, *Post-Growth Living: For an Alternative Hedonism* (London: Verso, 2020).

7 Lange, "On the Economic Theory of Socialism," 60.

4. What Do Markets Do?

1 David McNally, *Against the Market: Political Economy, Market Socialism and the Marxist Critique* (London: Verso, 1993), 170.
2 Marx, *Capital*, vol. 1, 168–9.
3 Marx, *Capital*, vol. 1, 171–2. It can be confusing that in the very same chapter Marx appears to find the "substance" of value in "socially necessary" labor time, which sounds like something that might be measured directly from technical aspects of production. But how much labor time is "socially necessary" for producing something is a variable that depends on the scale and technique of production, and these technical choices depend on relative prices, wages, and interest rates. In other words, socially necessary labor time is not an immovable point from which all these other variables can be determined. On the dependence of socially necessary labor time on the scale of demand, see I. I. Rubin, *Essays in Marx's Theory of Value*, trans. Miloš Samardźija and Fredy Perlman (Detroit: Black & Red, 1972 [1928]), 185–221.
4 Marx, *Capital*, vol. 1, 171.
5 Mises, "Economic Calculation in the Socialist Commonwealth."
6 The fact that something is a public good or subject to externalities does not necessarily mean it is best delivered through noncommodity production. It may instead be dealt with by regulation or through public subsidies or purchases. Conversely, the allocation of even some unambiguously private goods may be improved with some collective decisions. For example, economies of scale in producing something may be lost when it is produced in smaller runs with minor variations. On related issues, see Charles Kindleberger, "Standards, as Public, Collective and Private Goods," *Kyklos* 36, no. 3 (1983): 377–96.
7 Lange, "On the Economic Theory of Socialism," 62; Paul W. Cockshott and Allin Cottrell, *Towards a New Socialism* (Nottingham: Spokesman, 1993), 103–10.
8 Ernest Mandel, "In Defence of Socialist Planning," *New Left Review* 1, no. 159 (1986): 17.
9 As clothing prices have fallen over the decades, Americans have taken the opportunity to spend relatively less on clothes and more on other things—from 10 percent of their consumer budgets in 1950, clothing made up closer to 3 percent by 2010. Robert J. Gordon, *The Rise and Fall of American Growth: The US Standard of Living since the Civil War* (Princeton: Princeton

University Press, 2016), 348. When the price of something falls, there is an *income effect* in expanding real purchasing power, with different people allocating the savings to very different things that are not at all close substitutes. This effect is hard to describe without using the language of prices and budgets, but a system that tried to do without prices and budgets would need to find a way.

10 It is possible to have a system with prices and budgets without buying and selling as such. Lange writes that we can use the term "price" in the wider sense of "terms on which alternatives are offered," or the narrower sense of "exchange ratios on a market." Lange, "On the Economic Theory of Socialism," 55. Prices in the former sense can be used for administrative purposes in accounting without any kind of exchange taking place. Hahnel's proposal is of this type.

11 Robin Hahnel, *Democratic Economic Planning* (Milton Park: Routledge, 2021), 90.

12 Ibid., 94.

13 As Diane Elson asks in response to Mandel's proposal, "Once their basic items have been ordered for the plan period, what happens if the size and composition of households change unexpectedly (for instance through births and deaths) or needs change because of sickness or change of work or change of location?" Elson, "Market Socialism or Socialization," 24.

14 Hahnel, *Democratic Economic Planning*, 125.

15 Alec Nove, *The Economics of Feasible Socialism Revisited* (New York: HarperCollins Academic, 1991), 69–71.

16 Schor, *Plenitude*; Guy Rundle, *A Revolution in the Making: 3D Printing, Robots and the Future* (South Melbourne: Affirm Press, 2014).

17 This does not mean monetary incomes will be equal. There are good egalitarian reasons for different incomes (such as different choices about how much to work in producing for others and different needs due to disability or life stage) and also reasons why income distribution will fall short of the egalitarian ideal, though much less than under capitalism.

18 Lionel Robbins, *The Great Depression* (London: Macmillan, 1934), 151.

19 Lange argued that each person's social dividend share should be proportional to their earnings from paid labor, so as not to interfere with choices about work. Lange, "On the Economic Theory of Socialism," 64–5.

20 Lange seems to presume that individual workplaces eventually face decreasing returns to scale, so that average cost rises with quantity, at least past a point. If returns to scale are constant, average cost will be too, and a manager would be prepared to produce any amount so long as the price of the product were at least as high. Lange's planning board would need to supplement prices with quantitative directives, based on how much customers want to buy at that price. Since it appears that there is nothing preventing workplaces from achieving constant returns by simply duplicating their existing technical set-up (getting identical outputs from an identical combination of inputs), Lange must believe there are organizational inefficiencies involved in larger workplaces.

21 If marginal cost of some product is higher than the average cost per unit, the workplace will be generating a profit, because the price at which the output is sold exceeds the average cost of producing it. But in Lange's system, this is taken as a signal to set up new workplaces producing that product. This additional supply will only be bought by customers at lower prices, and each individual workplace will adjust its output accordingly. This process reaches equilibrium when each workplace is producing the amount according to which the price of a unit of output equals the average cost. Note that this all follows from Lange presuming decreasing returns to scale. If returns to scale are constant once a point of efficient scale is reached, which is probably the case in most industries, things are simpler. A price can be set at the average cost, and the total output of that product determined by how much people want to buy at that price. This output can be divided between an arbitrary number of workplaces, so long as they are all large enough to reach the point at which returns to scale level off.

22 Lange, "On the Economic Theory of Socialism," 62.

23 This is not to say that price adjustment would be the only, or even the main, tool of intervention. The state can still ban, cap, or otherwise regulate "bads" and directly organize the public production of "goods." We discuss these issues with respect to our own system in chapter six. Lange, "On the Economic Theory of Socialism," 62.

24 F. A. Hayek, "The Use of Knowledge in Society," *American Economic Review* 35, no. 4 (1945): 524.

25 In fact, the possibility of cutting corners on quality raises a

problem for nonmarket algorithmic socialism, which we discuss in the next section.

26 Francis Spufford, *Red Plenty* (Minneapolis: Graywolf Press, 2012), 101.

27 Roemer, *A Future for Socialism*, 37–45.

28 Nove, *The Economics of Feasible Socialism Revisited*, 75.

29 In a number of works, Sam Bowles and Herb Gintis have conceptualized this as a "contested exchange," and we return to this in more detail in the next chapter.

30 This is not always the case. Sometimes labor practices can be improved from workers' perspectives while also boosting their productivity. In the next chapter we argue that workplace democracy, in the context of cooperative commodity production, is a good way of finding these unambiguous efficiency gains.

31 Though the term "soft budget constraint" suggests local units operate with monetary budgets, the concept is more broad. It applies to any loosening of expectations that local managers follow the efficiency rules, whatever they may be, even in a hypothetical system without monetary budgets. Kornai, Maskin, and Roland, "The Soft Budget Constraint": 25.

32 Roemer, *A Future for Socialism*, 39.

33 This applies also to the choices producers make about inputs provided by other producers.

34 Note that the points here apply not only to consumer products but also to produced intermediate goods used in production.

35 Mandel, "In Defence of Socialist Planning," 28.

36 The price adjustment would likely be small and temporary, since it is relatively easy to switch recipes without changing equipment or workforce. The production adjustment would in theory restore a price equilibrium in which both kinds of pasta sauce are sold at their cost of production. Though Lange originally presented his system as operating through price adjustments, it is possible to imagine a similar system that would operate by changing quantities ordered from workplaces, rather than price adjustments in the short term—just as in capitalism firms in many industries tend to adjust prices infrequently and respond to changes in demand directly with changes in output.

37 Nove, *The Economics of Feasible Socialism Revisited*, 72.

38 Lange, "On the Economic Theory of Socialism," 53.

39 McNally, *Against the Market*, 173–4.

5. Workplace Democracy and Finance

1 Roemer, *A Future for Socialism*, 122–3.

2 Giacomo Corneo, *Is Capitalism Obsolete?: A Journey Through Alternative Economic Systems* (Cambridge, MA: Harvard University Press, 2017), 128–51.

3 Samuel Bowles and Herbert Gintis, "The Distribution of Wealth and the Viability of the Democratic Firm," in *Democracy and Efficiency in the Economic Enterprise*, ed. Ugo Pagano and Bob Rowthorn (New York: Routledge, 1994), 82. Residual income is what is left over from revenue after deducting all production, interest, and other costs. Costs here include wages, as discussed below.

4 Caring responsibilities can have a big impact on the amount of paid hours people can and want to take on in a workplace. Compensation for this is better done universally from public funds rather than left to the policies of individual firms. We discuss such transfers in chapter seven.

5 For a classic source on the economics of technological change, labor, and wages, written at the height of centralized wage-bargaining in Australia, see W. E. G. Salter, *Productivity and Technical Change* (Cambridge: Cambridge University Press, 1960).

6 Jan Tinbergen, *Economic Policy: Principles and Design* (Amsterdam: North-Holland, 1956). On how these tensions played out in Australia, see Michael Beggs, *Inflation and the Making of Australian Macroeconomic Policy, 1945–85* (London: Palgrave Macmillan, 2015) and Michael Beggs, "Labour in the Technocratic Frame: Macroeconomic Policy and Wages in 1950s Australia," *Labour History* 121 (November 2021): 129–54. On Nordic systems of collective bargaining and the interaction of national floors with firm-level wage-setting, see Magne Mogstad, Kjell G. Salvanes, and Gaute Torsvik, "Income Equality in the Nordic Countries: Myths, Facts, and Lessons," *Journal of Economic Literature* 63, no. 3 (2025): 791–839.

7 Armen A. Alchian and Harold Demsetz, "Production, Information Costs, and Economic Organization," *American Economic Review* 62, no. 5 (1972): 777–8.

8 Lange, "On the Economic Theory of Socialism," 64–5.

9 "Competence" is defined here in terms of usefulness to the employer's goals—profit, in the case of a firm, and other targets in the case of a public agency. Needless to say, workers may have other ideas about counts as competence.

10 "Contested exchange" is a concept developed by Samuel Bowles and Herbert Gintis; see especially "A Political and Economic Case for the Democratic Enterprise," *Economics and Philosophy* 9, no. 1 (1993): 75–100. See also Carl Shapiro and Joseph E. Stiglitz, "Equilibrium Unemployment as a Worker Discipline Device," *American Economic Review* 74, no. 3 (1984): 433–44.

11 Amartya Sen, *Development as Freedom* (Oxford: Oxford University Press, 1999), 112–16; Lange, "On the Economic Theory of Socialism," 62.

12 On "exit" and "voice," see Albert O. Hirschman, *Exit, Voice, and Loyalty: Responses to Decline in Firms, Organizations, and States* (Cambridge, MA: Harvard University Press, 1970).

13 Bowles and Gintis, "A Political and Economic Case for the Democratic Enterprise."

14 Robert A. Dahl, *A Preface to Economic Democracy* (Berkeley: University of California Press, 1985), 115.

15 Dow, *The Labor-Managed Firm*, 94–104, 111.

16 Bowles and Gintis, "A Political and Economic Case for the Democratic Enterprise," 92–104.

17 Variations on this point have been made by a number of writers. Alec Nove argues that capitalism tends to suppress producer preferences: *The Economics of Feasible Socialism Revisited*, 191. Jacques Drèze treats workplace conditions as public goods for a firm's workers, which capitalist firms will inefficiently underproduce: Jacques H. Drèze, "Some Theory of Labor Management and Participation," *Econometrica* 44, no. 6 (1976): 1125–39. Gregory Dow argues that workplace democracy may "yield efficiency improvements relative to capital-managed firms by aligning firm policies more closely with worker preferences": Dow, *The Labor-Managed Firm*, 121.

18 John Roemer, "Market Socialism Renewed," *Catalyst* 4, no. 1 (2020): 26–7.

19 The classic papers are Benjamin Ward, "The Firm in Illyria: Market Syndicalism," *American Economic Review* 48, no. 4 (1958): 566–89; and Evsey D. Domar, "The Soviet Collective Farm as a Producer Cooperative," *American Economic Review* 56, no. 4 (1966): 734–57. The idea is presented particularly clearly by James E. Meade, "The Theory of Labour-Managed Firms and of Profit Sharing," *Economic Journal* 82, no. 325 (1972): 402–28.

20 It is one of the key reasons Corneo gives for rejecting worker management. *Is Capitalism Obsolete?*, 142–5. Dow tries to

explain the persistence of this argument: *The Labor-Managed Firm*, 78–81.

21 Jaroslav Vanek, *The General Theory of Labor-Managed Market Economies* (Ithaca: Cornell University Press, 1970), 56–7. For a review of the empirical research, see Dow, *The Labor-Managed Firm*, 93–4.

22 Eirik G. Furubotn and Svetozar Pejovich, "Property Rights and Economic Theory: A Survey of Recent Literature," *Journal of Economic Literature* 10, no. 4 (1972): 1156.

23 Michael C. Jensen and William H. Meckling, "Rights and Production Functions: An Application to Labor-Managed Firms and Codetermination," *Journal of Business* 52, no. 4 (1979): 469–506.

24 Jensen and Meckling, "Rights and Production Functions."

25 Dow, *The Labor-Managed Firm*, 152–4.

26 Ibid., 63.

27 Jaroslav Vanek, *The Labor-Managed Economy: Essays* (Ithaca: Cornell University Press, 1977), 171–85.

28 Ashley Fang et al., "Trends in Australian Corporate Financing," *Reserve Bank of Australia Bulletin* (December 2015): 37.

29 More technically, a firm should invest in a project when the net present value of expected cash flows is positive, when discounted by the going market rate of return on other assets of the same beta. Expected cash flows are the average of possible cash flows, with each possibility weighted by its probability. Though idiosyncratic risks do not matter when calculating the beta, they do affect expected cash flows. A business model of buying bulk lottery tickets has a negative expected return despite its risk being completely uncorrelated with the market.

30 Since debts are a liability of a firm and not individual members, people may simply leave the firm in this event. This is one of the reasons why a viable system requires firms to meet minimum wage rates for their member-workers and to go out of business if they are unable to meet these.

31 Marc Fleurbaey, "Economic Democracy and Equality," in *Market Socialism: The Current Debate*, ed. Pranab K. Bardhan and John E. Roemer (Oxford: Oxford University Press, 1993). Vanek devised a system of dual property rights dividing ownership between a financing "basic owner" and the "usufruct owner" that uses the asset in production and pays a variable rent to the basic owner but has secure tenure. See Jaroslav Vanek, "Some Fundamental Considerations on Financing and the Form

of Ownership under Labor Management," in *The Labor-Managed Economy: Essays* (Ithaca: Cornell University Press, 1977).

32 That is, the beta. Note that this does not mean the bank can ignore risks specific to the firm. Unnoticed risks mean an inaccurate assessment of expected returns. For example, a speculative investment in a new technology with a small chance of success will have a low expected return even though its risk may be uncorrelated with anything else.

33 Kornai, Maskin, and Roland, "The Soft Budget Constraint," 26–7.

34 Firms might also of course find themselves persistently underperforming, but this is self-limiting. If not compensated by some attractive feature of the work, members would drift off to better prospects. If performance is so poor that the firm cannot meet its obligations to partner banks, it will sooner or later be liquidated.

35 We have mentioned some of this literature in this chapter: Alchian and Demsetz, "Production, Information Costs, and Economic Organization"; Furubotn and Pejovich, "Property Rights and Economic Theory"; Jensen and Meckling, "Rights and Production Functions."

36 See essays collected in Pranab K. Bardhan and John E. Roemer, eds., *Market Socialism: The Current Debate* (Oxford: Oxford University Press, 1993); Samuel Bowles et al., eds., *Markets and Democracy: Participation, Accountability and Efficiency* (Cambridge: Cambridge University Press, 1993); and Ugo Pagano and Bob Rowthorn, eds., *Democracy and Efficiency in the Economic Enterprise* (London: Routledge, 2002).

37 An important exception is David Schweickart, who proposed a combination of markets and workplace democracy. Schweickart's vision has been a key inspiration for this aspect of our model. See David Schweickart, *Against Capitalism* (Cambridge: Cambridge University Press, 1993); and *After Capitalism* (Lanham: Rowman & Littlefield, 2011). Gregory K. Dow, "The Labor-Managed Firm, Jaroslav Vanek and Me," *Journal of Participation and Employee Ownership* 3, nos. 2/3 (2020): 123–34.

6. What Does the State Do?

1 Ralph Miliband, *The State in Capitalist Society: The Analysis of the Western System of Power* (London: Weidenfeld and Nicolson, 1969).
2 The responsibility categories are taken from Richard A. Musgrave and Peggy B. Musgrave, *Public Finance in Theory and Practice*, 5th ed. (New York: McGraw-Hill, 1989).
3 Lange, "On the Economic Theory of Socialism," 61–2, 125–6.
4 Musgrave's argument is specifically about the provision of public goods, but his points apply also to limits on negative externalities. Richard A. Musgrave, "Provision for Social Goods in the Market System," *Public Finance = Finances Publiques* 26, no. 2 (1971): 304, 313.
5 As Paul Samuelson put it in a seminal paper for this paradigm: "The failure of market catallactics in no way denies the following truth: given sufficient knowledge the optimal decisions can always be found by scanning over all the attainable states of the world and selecting the one which according to the postulated ethical welfare function is best. The solution 'exists'; the problem is how to 'find' it": Paul A. Samuelson, "The Pure Theory of Public Expenditure," *Review of Economics and Statistics* 36, no. 4 (1954): 389.
6 And, for similar reasons, to more comprehensively regulate public bads, though this is outside the scope of Musgrave's argument.
7 Musgrave, "Provision for Social Goods in the Market System," 319–20.
8 It is of course possible to have different tax and expenditure mixes in different parts of the country through state and local government taxing power.
9 Joan Robinson, "Consumer's Sovereignty in a Planned Economy," in *On Political Economy and Econometrics: Essays in Honour of Oskar Lange* (Oxford: Pergamon Press, 1965), 520.
10 John Kenneth Galbraith, *The Affluent Society* (London: H. Hamilton, 1959).
11 Musgrave, "Provision for Social Goods in the Market System," 320.
12 Dean Baker has developed a number of plausible alternative models for publicly funding research and creative work without a restrictive intellectual property regime. For an overview, see Dean Baker, Arjun Jayadev and Joseph Stiglitz, "Innovation, Intellectual

Property, and Development: A Better Set of Approaches for the 21st Century," AccessIBSA.org, July 2017.

13 George A. Akerlof, "The Market for 'Lemons': Quality Uncertainty and the Market Mechanism," *The Quarterly Journal of Economics* 84, no. 3 (August 1970): 488–500.

14 In "family" and "household" here and elsewhere, we include all kinds of tight personal relations. The "household sector" simply refers to work done informally, not for a wage or other forms of exchange.

15 Nancy Folbre, "Reforming Care," *Politics and Society* 36, no. 3 (September 2008): 376.

16 Nancy Folbre, *The Rise and Decline of Patriarchal Systems* (London: Verso, 2021), 209.

17 Janet C. Gornick and Marcia K. Meyers, "Institutions that Support Gender Equality in Parenthood and Employment," in *Gender Equality: Transforming Family Divisions of Labor* (London: Verso, 2009).

18 Nicholas Barr, *The Welfare State as Piggy Bank: Information, Risk, Uncertainty* (Oxford: Oxford University Press, 2001).

19 Gornick and Meyers, "Institutions that Support Gender Equality," 19.

20 Diane Elson, "Market Socialism or Socialization of the Market?," *New Left Review* 1, no. 172 (December 1988): 29; and Johanna Brenner, "Democratizing Care," in *Gender Equality: Transforming Family Divisions of Labor*, ed. Janet C. Gornick and Marcia K. Meyers (London: Verso, 2009), 184.

21 Fully institutional care is more often necessary with the elderly, who are more likely to lack nearby family and, in cases of disability, require around-the-clock professional care.

22 Robinson, "Consumer's Sovereignty," 514.

23 Elson, "Market Socialism or Socialization," 8. Robinson, "Consumer's Sovereignty," 71, 80.

24 Waves of privatization have seen many such industries returned to private hands, with convoluted regulatory systems intended to force or simulate competition, in practice often guaranteeing captive income streams to investors.

25 For an excellent account of rents from a number of forms of monopoly, see Brett Christophers, *Rentier Capitalism: Who Owns the Economy, and Who Pays for It?* (London: Verso, 2020).

26 Cory Doctorow, *Enshittification: Why Everything Suddenly Got Worse and What to Do About It* (New York: MCD, 2025).

27 Elson, "Market Socialism or Socialization," 7.
28 Robinson, "Consumer's Sovereignty," 521.
29 Though Robinson writes of wholesalers, the same logic applies to supermarket chains and other large retailers. Robinson, "Consumer's Sovereignty," 521.
30 Elson, "Market Socialism or Socialization," 32–42.
31 Elson also proposes a wage commission, the functions of which are already provided for in our labor commission.
32 Elson, "Market Socialism or Socialization," 32.
33 The worker-membership system can accommodate part-time and even seasonal work. Dividends can be distributed on a pro rata basis according to hours worked over the relevant period.
34 Nove, *The Economics of Feasible Socialism Revisited*, 194.
35 We do not necessarily agree, though, that a large multisite firm is incompatible with meaningful democracy. Participatory democracy may be impossible at such a scale, but we see no reason why the representative democracy we envision as the norm, in which workers elect the board, would be less meaningful in a large firm.
36 Nove, *The Economics of Feasible Socialism Revisited*, 194.

7. Income, Equality, and Housing

1 Ronald Dworkin, "What Is Equality? Part 2: Equality of Resources," *Philosophy and Public Affairs* 10, no. 4 (1981): 284.
2 Amartya Sen, "Equality of What?" in *The Tanner Lectures on Human Values*, vol. 7 (Cambridge: Cambridge University Press, 1987), 203–4; G. A. Cohen, "Equality of What? On Welfare, Goods and Capabilities," *Louvain Economic Review* 56, nos. 3–4 (1990): 366.
3 Duncan K. Foley, "Resource Allocation and the Public Sector" (PhD, Yale University, 1966), 50. Foley's "envy test" appeared in his doctoral thesis; on its remarkable influence among economists, see Hal R. Varian, "Dworkin on Equality of Resources," *Economics and Philosophy* 1, no. 1 (1985): 110–25. It seems to have come to the philosopher Dworkin's attention through this economic literature. Dworkin, "What is Equality? Part 2," 285.
4 This framework avoids the "expensive tastes" problem of utility egalitarianism because it takes "expensive" into account. It

recognizes that the resources devoted to catering to these tastes might instead have produced more for others or allowed them more leisure.

5 Sen presented this as a type of egalitarianism in "Equality of What?" Sen, Martha Nussbaum, and many others have developed the approach since.

6 Barr, *The Welfare State as Piggy Bank*.

7 This is not to say that market pay rates necessarily compensate these things fairly—a problem we pick up in the next section.

8 John Rawls, *Political Liberalism* (New York: Columbia University Press, 1993), 182. Philippe Van Parijs, "Why Surfers Should Be Fed: The Liberal Case for an Unconditional Basic Income," in *Distributive Justice*, ed. Julian Lamont (New York: Routledge, 2012).

9 As Diane Elson puts it, the desire for "steak and wine sometimes" is enough incentive for most people to take on a share of the work, even if they are guaranteed the income for "lentils and water." Elson, "Market Socialism or Socialization," 29.

10 Lange, "On the Economic Theory of Socialism," 64–5.

11 There is a theoretical approach to reconciling endowment equality and efficiency. It essentially involves taxing talent—the endowment—rather than income resulting from the use of the talent. The talented then start from behind, income-wise, and need to apply their talent in paid work to catch up. Rawls once commented that this seems a way of implementing Marx's "from each according to their ability" without depending on the transcendence of scarcity or self-interest. "Reply to Alexander and Musgrave," *Quarterly Journal of Economics* 88, no. 4 (1974): 654. But it has almost always been put as a thought experiment rather than a practical proposal. It would depend on the accurate assessment and valuation of talent, while disincentivizing people from revealing it. Even if the assessment could somehow be done, it would push people to use their talents only in commodity production or in other paid work. It penalizes those who would rather use their talents in uncommodified ways—as Musgrave put it, the "recluses, saints, and (nonconsulting) scholars." "Maximin, Uncertainty, and the Leisure Trade-Off," *Quarterly Journal of Economics* 88, no. 4 (1974): 632.

12 The seminal paper in this literature claims its relevance even to centralized nonmarket socialist economies: "Even in a highly socialist economy, where all who work are employed by the

state, the shadow price of highly skilled labor should surely be considerably greater than the disposable income actually available to the labourer." J. A. Mirrlees, "An Exploration in the Theory of Optimum Income Taxation," *Review of Economic Studies* 38, no. 2 (1971): 175. See reviews by Joel Slemrod and Jon Bakija (*Taxing Ourselves: A Citizen's Guide to the Debate over Taxes*, 4th ed. [Cambridge, MA: MIT Press, 2008], 121–7); and A. B. Atkinson and Joseph Stiglitz, *Lectures on Public Economics* [Princeton: Princeton University Press, 2015], 40–4). And for a useful guide written for a general audience by economists at the forefront of this research, see Emmanuel Saez and Gabriel Zucman, *The Triumph of Injustice: How the Rich Dodge Taxes and How to Make Them Pay* (New York: W. W. Norton, 2019).

13 We have discussed some of these reasons in the previous chapter, in the context of Bowles's and Gintis's theory of employment as a "contested exchange." Other models emphasize the costs to both sides of an employment relationship of finding new jobs/employees in conditions of imperfect information about one another and considerable uncertainty about alternatives. Alternatively, high marginal tax rates may discourage high earners from bargaining for more in the first place, in which case gains go to the rest of the population through lower prices to customers or higher incomes to others in their firms. Piketty, Saez, and Statcheva discuss the importance of bargaining power to optimal taxation, and model a situation in which higher marginal rates reduce returns to the bargaining and rent-extraction efforts of high earners. Thomas Piketty et al., "Optimal Taxation of Top Labor Incomes: A Tale of Three Elasticities," *American Economic Journal* 6, no. 1 (2014): 230–71.

14 Peter Diamond and Emmanuel Saez, "The Case for a Progressive Tax: From Basic Research to Policy Recommendations," *Journal of Economic Perspectives* 25, no. 4 (2011): 165–90.

15 On Nordic systems today, see Mogstad, Salvanes, and Torsvik, "Income Equality in the Nordic Countries," 791–839.

16 As of 2022, across the OECD about 70 percent of households live in dwellings they own, with or without a mortgage. OECD, OECD Affordable Housing Database: HM1.3 Housing Tenures. Paris: Organisation for Economic Co-operation and Development, 2024.

8. Macroeconomic Policy

1 The course of this project in Australia is traced in Beggs, *Inflation and the Making of Australian Macroeconomic Policy*.

2 It is also possible to set a quantitative lending target over a period and allow the interest rate to adjust to bring demand for funds in line with this fixed supply. But it is simpler to conduct day-to-day policy by setting the rate and allowing supply to adjust to demand in the short run. The authorities will set the rate according to their estimate of how much investment will take place and adjust it accordingly if investment runs faster or slower than desired. Even though the target is quantitative—the flow of investment financed over the year—it is usually operationally easier to manage it by price. In some circumstances, there might be reason to also set a quantitative limit directly and ration credit at the going rate.

3 The central bank can also use risk-sharing contracts with banks if policymakers want to affect the pricing of risk.

4 Such a scheme was advocated by Keynes in his 1940 pamphlet *How to Pay for the War*, and variations on the theme have sometimes been implemented under capitalism. Not only were these schemes directly influenced by Keynes's specific plan—such as the measures implemented in the UK's Finance Act 1941—but the basic principle has resonated in other policies. For example, the Australian compulsory superannuation system partly originated as a way of negotiating pay deferral to dampen demand amid the inflation of the 1980s.

5 Individual savings decisions do not combine to determine investment under capitalism either. As Keynes argued, it is truer to say that investment creates the savings.

6 Deposits in their accounts are mostly ephemeral, on their way to funding firm investment or on their way back to repaying the central bank, with profits distributed to the public purse. Banks will operate with some working capital, into which repayments from its partner firms flow, and from which its repayments to the central bank come. This may well be managed as an overdraft with the central bank rather than a positive account. In any case, since the banks are public institutions, any worries about spare liquidity feeding into more finance than authorities intend can be dealt with by simply canceling excess deposits or lowering overdraft limits.

7 People are free to choose to save from income during working

years in order to have more to spend in retirement than they would get from the pension. This raises the question of whether the pension entitlement should be the same for everyone or whether more should go to those who earned more over their working years, through whatever combination of more hours and higher pay rates. The first seems more egalitarian on the face of it, but if higher earners respond by privately saving over their working years, actual consumption in retirement will be unequal anyway. Since providing for the retired is a question of real resources at the time of provision and not about the value of financial claims accumulated, there is a case for managing this publicly where demographic and workforce trends can be planned for appropriately, rather than leaving it to individual private savings accounts. The distributional aspects can be managed through the progressive taxation system—essentially collectively deciding a higher level of saving for those with higher earnings. A managed system can also take into account gendered imbalances in paid work and earnings, to the extent that the system does not fix these elsewhere.

8 Exceptions can be made where people are immigrating or emigrating, with "abroad" here including all investments outside the formal system and not only those in other countries. Digital currencies make it harder than ever to locate transactions geographically. The point is the border between the socialist financial system and outside transactions, which may not in fact be a geographical border.

9 Meade, "The Theory of Labour-Managed Firms and of Profit Sharing," 413–14.

10 Meade's argument is this: When a cooperative firm expands membership, it divides its fixed costs over more members, increasing income per member. But, assuming diminishing returns to labor, each additional member brings less income than the last, decreasing income per member. In equilibrium, the firm will have expanded to the point that these counterposed forces balance out. When an upward shift in demand then increases the price of the product, the balancing point of maximum income per member will fall. Downsizing would increase the income per member for the majority of members left after the downsizing. A democratic firm will therefore respond to an increase in demand by reducing its output and membership—and vice versa for a fall in demand.

11 There is a lot of variation between capitalist countries in how

easy it is for firms to quickly hire and fire workers, and unsurprisingly, labor productivity is less procyclical where employment is more "flexible" from the employer's point of view. The United States—with an unusually flexible labor regime—is also unusual in having had modestly countercyclical labor productivity in recent decades. See Maarten Dossche, Andrea Giovanni Gazzani, and Vivien Lewis, "Labor Adjustment and Productivity in the OECD," *Review of Economic Dynamics* 47 (January 2023): 111–30.

12 Nove, *The Economics of Feasible Socialism Revisited*, 70.

13 This is because each new member gets a share of profit as well as a wage, unlike a new worker in a capitalist firm, who gets only the wage. Collective firms have an incentive to expand while there are increasing returns to scale, because each new worker-member added will increase income per worker, and thus more than pay for everyone. But once a workplace is big enough that returns to scale flatten out, individual incumbent members of a collective firm no longer see their own incomes rise with further expansion. The *owners* of capitalist firms keep increasing their income with expansion so long as marginal output continues to exceed the marginal combined cost of labor and capital, because new workers do not get a share of profits.

14 As discussed above, specialist investment banks may have a mission to assemble new firms in depressed areas or infant industries, charging a lower baseline interest rate on investment.

15 Michał Kalecki, "Political Aspects of Full Employment," *Political Quarterly* 14, no. 4 (1943): 322–31; Milton Friedman, "The Role of Monetary Policy," *American Economic Review* 58, no. 1 (1968): 1–17; Joan Robinson, *Essays in the Theory of Employment* (London: Macmillan, 1937), 3–29. See Robert Pollin, "The 'Reserve Army of Labour' and the 'Natural Rate of Unemployment': Can Marx, Kalecki, Friedman, and Wall Street All Be Wrong?" *Review of Radical Political Economics* 30, no. 1 (1998): 1–23; and Engelbert Stockhammer, "Is the NAIRU Theory a Monetarist, New Keynesian, Post-Keynesian or a Marxist Theory?" *Metroeconomica* 59, no. 4 (2008): 479–510. Marx's analysis of the reserve army of labor was developed under gold and silver standards that constrained chronic inflation, leading him to assume that wage growth outpacing labor productivity would cut directly into profits.

16 For an analysis of Reserve Bank of Australia thinking and policy along these lines, see Michael Beggs, "Monetary Policy and

Unemployment," in *Wrong Way: How Privatisation and Economic Reform Backfired*, ed. Damien Cahill and Phillip Toner (Melbourne: La Trobe University Press, 2018); and "Monetary Policy," *Journal of Australian Political Economy*, no. 92 (2024): 166–88.

17 For a classic statement of this ideology at its height, see the OECD's 1994 *Jobs Study*.

18 Olivier Blanchard and Justin Wolfers, "The Role of Shocks and Institutions in the Rise of European Unemployment: The Aggregate Evidence," *Economic Journal* 110, no. 462 (2000): 2, 17–18.

19 James Forder, *Macroeconomics and the Phillips Curve Myth* (Oxford: Oxford University Press, 2014).

20 Tinbergen, *Economic Policy*, 84.

21 For an account on the workings and tensions of wage arbitration in Australia, see Beggs, "Labour in the Technocratic Frame," 129–54; and *Inflation and the Making of Australian Macroeconomic Policy*. For overviews of Nordic wages policy, see Lars Calmfors, "Pattern Bargaining as a Means to Coordinate Wages in the Nordic Countries," Working Paper no. 1517 (IFN Working Paper, 2025); and Mogstad, Salvanes, and Torsvik, "Income Equality in the Nordic Countries," 791–839.

22 Richard Jackman, "European Unemployment: Why Is It So High and What Should Be Done About It?," in *Unemployment and the Australian Labour Market*, ed. Guy Debelle and Jeff Borland (Sydney: Reserve Bank of Australia, 1998), 47.

23 In any case, market power will generally be associated with a fatter margin of revenue over nonlabor costs, rather than a continually increasing one. Market power may, however, make it easier for firms to pass on other cost increases as price increases, helping to sustain an inflationary process already underway. See Isabella M. Weber and Evan Wasner, "Sellers' Inflation, Profits and Conflict: Why Can Large Firms Hike Prices in an Emergency?," *Review of Keynesian Economics* 11, no. 2 (2023): 183–213.

24 Calmfors (2025) provides a clear overview of the model and its specific forms in Denmark, Finland, Norway, and Sweden. Most of these countries have moved to coordinated bargaining rather than fully centralized wage determination.

25 Shared reserve pools and credits along the lines of Keynes's original vision for the International Monetary Fund could help stabilize the international division of labor and facilitate development within a socialist bloc.

26 The lack of capital flows into and out of the currency isolates it from destabilizing speculation, but also from stabilizing speculation in which private dealers dampen temporary imbalances because they expect them to come right.

27 In certain circumstances, an exchange rate peg could make sense—for example, if the country does much of its trade with a larger country or currency bloc. But this should require broader monetary and macroeconomic cooperation among allies.

28 The classic analysis is in James E. Meade, *The Theory of International Economic Policy, I: The Balance of Payments* (Oxford: Oxford University Press, 1951). Meade received the economics Nobel Prize for this work in 1977. In what follows we assume that domestic producers of tradable commodities are a relatively small part of their global markets, so that domestic cost structures and demand do not affect international prices. This keeps the analysis simpler, and is realistic for most countries. This is based on the dependent economy approach to trade theory, mainly developed by Australian economists (with some contributions from a visiting Meade) and popularized around the world especially by Rudiger Dornbusch. For an overview, see Phillip Edmund Metaxas and Ernst Juerg Weber, "An Australian Contribution to International Trade Theory: The Dependent Economy Model," *Economic Record* 92, no. 298 (2016): 464–97.

29 This is what Jan Tinbergen was referring to in the remark quoted above, that "wage rates have to be a deliberate instrument of economic policy if employment targets and monetary equilibrium are to be pursued at the same time": Tinbergen, *Economic Policy*, 84. Note that Tinbergen, like Meade, went on to win a Nobel Prize in economics—these were not marginal figures.

30 Statistical classifications of products and industries as "tradable" or "nontradable" often use data on the proportion actually traded. For example, the Australian Bureau of Statistics counts as "tradable" any product for which final exports or imports makes up more than 10 percent of domestic supply.

31 In poorer countries, not only are incomes lower overall, but internationally tradable commodities tend to be more expensive relative to locally produced nontradables. For example, the average local wage goes further on local food and services than it does on consumer electronics, compared to the average wage in a richer country.

9. Will Socialism Fail Again?

1 Ben Burgis, *Christopher Hitchens: What He Got Right, How He Went Wrong, and Why He Still Matters* (Winchester: Zero Books, 2021), 114–32.
2 Matt Bruenig, "How a Reductio ad Absurdum Works," MattBruenig.com, January 29, 2014.
3 Matt Kibbe, *Don't Hurt People and Don't Take Their Stuff: A Libertarian Manifesto* (New York: William Morrow, 2014).
4 G. A. Cohen, *On the Currency of Egalitarian Justice, and Other Essays in Political Philosophy* (Princeton: Princeton University Press, 2011), 176.
5 Robert Nozick, *Anarchy, State and Utopia* (New York: Basic Books, 1974).
6 Mariana Mazzucato, *The Entrepreneurial State: Debunking Public vs. Private Sector Myths*, rev. ed. (London: Penguin Books, 2018).
7 Ekaterina G. Cleary, Jennifer M. Beierlein, Navleen Surjit Khanuja, Laura M. McNamee, and Fred D. Ledley, "Contribution of NIH Funding to New Drug Approvals 2010–2016," *Proceedings of the National Academy of Sciences* 115, no. 10 (2018): 2329–34.
8 For an analysis of Yugoslavia's political economy, see Susan L. Woodward, *Socialist Unemployment: The Political Economy of Yugoslavia, 1945–1990* (Princeton: Princeton University Press, 1995).

10. Is This Even Socialism?

1 Cohen, *Why Not Socialism?*, 11.
2 Corey Robin, "Socialism: Converting Hysterical Misery into Ordinary Unhappiness," *Jacobin*, December 10, 2013.
3 Marx, *Capital,* vol. 1, 188.
4 For a critical survey of Mondragon, see Sharryn Kasmir, *The Myth of Mondragon: Cooperatives, Politics, and Working-Class Life in a Basque Town* (Albany: State University of New York Press, 1996).
5 Søren Mau, *Mute Compulsion: A Marxist Theory of the Economic Power of Capital* (London: Verso, 2023).
6 David Schweickart, "The Politics and Morality of Unequal

Exchange: Emmanuel and Roemer, Analysis and Synthesis," *Economics and Philosophy* 7, no. 1 (1991): 13–36.

11. Civilizational Progress

1 Erik Olin Wright, *Envisioning Real Utopias* (London: Verso, 2020), 56–60.
2 Roemer, *A Future for Socialism*, 55–9.

Index

Ackerman, Seth, 52
administered economy. *See* command economy
Advanced Research Projects Agency Network (ARPANET), 313
aggregable utility, 79–80
aggregated supply and demand
  Gosplan, 39
  macroeconomic fluctuations, 266–7, 289
Albanian isolation, 352
Alchian, Armen, 146–8, 152–3
algorithmic planning and algorithmic (price) socialism, 18, 86, 97, 109, 114–35, 207
  central planning board, 115–16, 118, 131
  choices about production as choices about people, 125–9, 391n29
  competitive general equilibrium, 114, 116–17
  cutting corners on quality, 121, 391n24
  equipment and built environment, 118–19
  following instructions, 123, 125
  individuals, 115–16, 390nn18–20, 391n22
  information required, 115
  internalizing externalities, 118
  limits of, 122–34
  outputs for people, 129–34, 391nn32–33, 391n35
  workplace managers, 116, 120–1
alienation, 73, 84, 86, 98, 155, 325
Allen, Robert C., 38
Allende, Salvador, 52
Andropov, Yuri, 56–7
ARPANET (Advanced Research Projects Agency Network), 313
Australian wage determination, 145, 240, 327, 401n4
autarky, 279, 352

banking system. *See* public banking system
bankruptcy, 62, 64–5, 318
Barr, Nicholas, 204, 229
Berliner, Joseph S., 41–2, 64
Blanchard, Olivier, 272–3
blueprint (proposed model). *See also* socialism
  challenges to, 7–8, 292

democratic firms, 19–20, 88, 137–82
engineering issues, 7–10
housing, 89–90, 240–3
income distribution, 224–40
macroeconomic policy, 90–1, 245–92
market sector, 88, 92–136
national labor board, 89, 91, 142–5
need for, 4, 6
overview of, 86–91
public banking system, 88–90, 209–12, 249–62
public sector and noncommodity production, 88, 183–223
tax and transfer system, 89, 236–9, 253–6
trade, 90–1, 278–92
values and goals, 10–11, 15
Bolsheviks, 32–6
Bowles, Sam, 153–5, 181, 391n28, 400n13
Brenner, Johanna, 204
Bretton Woods system, 274, 284–5
Brezhnev, Leonid, 56
British National Health Service, 69
Brooks, Michael, 360
Bruenig, Matt, 297
Bukharin, Nikolai, 36

capabilities approach, 228, 230
Capital (Marx), 93, 336
capitalism
abstract market forces, 348–9
banking system and investment, 249–50
collective capitalism, 336–40
competition, 207–8
concerns socialism would collapse back into capitalism, 340–8
consensual capitalistic acts, 307, 312
versus democratic firms, 15–16, 158–66, 180–2
economic problem, 77–83
ending capitalist realism, 23–6
equity finance, 171
as experiment, 294
freedom and property rights, 85
fundamentals of, 72–3
housing, 240–1, 243
inefficiency in crucial respects, 367–8
meritocratic principles, 12–13
objections to, 2–5, 73–4, 362–76
blockage of conditions for human flourishing, 363–5
class relations perpetuate human suffering, 362–3
commodification threatening important values, 371–2
corrosion of commodity, 374–5
environmental destructiveness, 370–1
inefficiency in crucial respects, 367–8
limitation of democracy, 375–6
perpetuation of deficits in freedom and autonomy, 365–6
promotion of militarism and imperialism, 372–4
systematic bias towards consumerism, 368–70
violation of principles of social justice, 366
versus previous systems, 2
public versus private goods, 190–1
the state, 183, 185, 187
unemployment, 150, 263–8
“utopia of utopias,” 309

victory of, 1, 293
wages and marginal disutility of work, 148
care work, 194, 200–6, 392n4
decision to have children, 204
divergence of preferences, 201–2
gender relations of care, 201–2
at household level, 201, 397n13
job accommodation for, 204–5, 397n20
quality and availability, 204
socialized costs, 202–3
support for care and for providers, 202
central banks, 90, 321–3, 401n3, 402n6
competition between banks, 251–3
deposits and consumer spending, 256–9
financial controls, 259–61
foreign exchange, 282–5, 288
integrating monetary and fiscal policy, 253–6
lender-of-last-resort action, 64
macroeconomic policy, 248–53
Central Intelligence Agency (CIA), 56, 313
central planning. *See* command economy
Charles III, king of the United Kingdom, 359
childcare, 72, 144, 203–5, 372
China, 351, 384n33, 386n66
CIA (Central Intelligence Agency), 56, 313
civilizational progress, 356–77
objections to the capitalist status quo, 362–76
socialism as North Star of, 301–2
Cockshott, Paul, 100–1
coercion, 3–4, 73, 297–8, 373
Cohen, G. A.
inequalities beyond our control, 335
obstetric metaphor, 11
principle of community, 331–2, 374
property distribution, 299–300
socialist equality of opportunity principle, 14–15, 25, 366
collective bargaining. *See* labor unions and collective bargaining
command (administered) economy, 38–69, 384n30
agency problems, 63–5
algorithmic socialism, 115–16, 118, 120, 123–4, 131, 135, 138
analysis of failure of, 68–9
authoritarianism, 5
concealment of production figures, 43–4, 63–4
cybersocialism and optimal planning, 48–52
example 1940s-era factory, 41–3
factory conditions, 43
Gorbachev's reforms, 57
hoarding of labor and material, 43, 63–4, 68
Hungarian market socialism, 58–63
income distribution and wages, 44–5
Khrushchev's reforms, 44, 46
Liberman's proposals, 53–4
material-balance planning, 40, 383n22
Mises's challenge to, 96, 109
number living under, 57
as organizing principle, 69
public-planner agency problem, 65–7
quasi–labor market, 44
simple model of, 40
Soviet Union, 53
stagnation, 56

Stalinist period, 45–6
technological lag and stagnation, 47
tendency towards shortage, 68
terminology, 383n20
commanding heights, 24, 34, 370
commodity-producing market sector. *See* market sector
common property problem, 162–4, 166–8, 178, 180
communism. *See also* Soviet Union
experimentation on entire population, 294
global rivalry, 1
Hungary, 58–63
socialist and communist phases, 29, 382n6
competitive general equilibrium, 18, 97, 112–13, 116–17, 135, 189–90, 207
consumer choice, 96, 98–109
care decisions, 201
cigar and cigarette exchange example, 99
necessity of, 133
personal and collective consumption, 106–8
price and quantity signals, 108
pricing, 100–3, 389n9
products not well suited to, 100, 388n6
shops, 103–6
socialist argument for, 98–100
consumerism, capitalism's systematic bias towards, 368–70
contested exchange, 150–3, 181, 391n28, 393n10, 400n13
contract law, 77–9, 111
cooperatives (co-ops), 20–3. *See also* democratic firms
Bolsheviks, 37
environmental issues, 370–1
example of working for, 71–2
expansion, 21–3
finance issues, 21–2, 321
firm failure, 21, 320
innovation and individual entrepreneurs, 316
macroeconomic policy, 243–4, 268–9
versus regular firms, 15–16
versus worker-controlled firms, 20
Corneo, Giacomo, 394n20
Cottrell, Allin, 100–1
coverture, 20–1
Critique of the Gotha Program (Marx), 95
cultural property, 194–7
currency value, 261, 282–5, 287–8, 405nn26–27
cybersocialism, 48–52, 114
Cybersyn, 52

Dahl, Robert, 154
decentralization, 7
algorithmic planning, 97, 115, 119, 131
Hungary, 65
private insurance, 367
Soviet Union, 46, 62
wage bargaining, 276
Yugoslavia, 323–4
decommodification, 24, 29, 346, 371–2
deflation, 263, 287
democratic firms, 7–10, 19–21, 137–82, 308–12
asset buffers, 176
capital controls, 261–2
versus capitalist firms, 141
case for, 146–58
changing output without changing membership, 264–5
commodity production, 24
conflicts of interest, 220
constitution of, 140
contested exchange, 150–3
versus co-ops, 20

culture of solidarity, 233
defined, 140
development of concept, 180–2
efficiency, 154–6
equipment and built environment, 169
expansion, 24
finance issues, 24, 140–1, 167–79, 209
investment partnership, 169–75, 394–5nn29–32
options for, 176–9, 395n34
intangibles, 177–8
interest, 169–70
labor markets versus grocery stores, 146–7, 152
less flexibility and greater security, 265
long-run equilibrium of, 264
membership markets, 164–7
monitoring and surveillance, 151
need for, 152–8
possibility of firm failure, 25
problems of, 158–67
membership markets, 164–7
perverse responses to market signals, 159–63
public sector, 218–23
purpose of, 219
representation of interests, 138–9
response to market conditions, 159–63
risk management and reduction, 169–74
safeguards, 139
shifting the boundaries of, 215–18, 398n32, 398n34
skepticism of, 138
socialist models without, 138
structural asymmetries, 158–9
unemployment, 263–4
wages, 141–9
benchmark system, 139, 142–5, 210
fixed, 141–2
marginal disutility of work, 148–9
wage differences, 142–3, 389n16
wage-setting and labor board, 142–5
worker preferences versus consumer preferences, 156–7
Demsetz, Harold, 146–8, 152–3
Diamond, Peter, 239
distributive inequalities, 14–17, 366
Don't Hurt People and Don't Take Their Stuff (Kibbe), 298
Douglass, Frederick, 353
Dow, Gregory, 155, 158, 164–5, 181, 393n17
Dulles, Allen, 47
Dworkin, Ronald, 225

"Economic Calculation in the Socialist Commonwealth" (Mises), 8
economic problem, 75–87, 387n4
capitalist solutions to, 77–83
identifying, 75–7
rational allocation of resources, 75–7, 79
socialist solutions to, 83–91, 98
education, 194, 197–200
liberal response to inequality, 235–6
periodic work, 179
popularity of public services, 197–8
positive spillovers, 189
relationship between training and competence, 148, 393n9
Soviet Union, 35
support for unemployed, 24
uncertainties, 198–9

workplace democracy in the public sector, 221–2
efficiency/inefficiency, 83–6
algorithmic planning, 122–30
capitalism's inefficiency in crucial respects, 367–8
choices and efficiency in trade, 280
concerns over expanded role of the state, 318–20
democratic firms, 154–6
financial discipline, 20
Pareto efficiency and optimum, 49, 80–1, 86, 112, 189–90, 195, 387n4
private insurance, 200
reconciling personal freedom with, 95–6
as socialist virtue, 10
soft budget constraints, 128, 175
Ellman, Michael, 67–8
Elson, Diane
childcare, 204
command economy, 207–8
household composition changes, 389n13
incentives, 399n9
public commissions and network coordinators, 214–15, 218
socialized markets, 75, 195, 208, 212
wage commission, 398n30
The End of History and the Last Man (Fukuyama), 358
Engels, Friedrich, 29
The Entrepreneurial State (Mazzucato), 313
environmental issues, 18, 65, 84, 370–1
Envisioning Real Utopias (Wright), 361
equality/inequality, 224–44
capabilities approach, 228, 230
concerns about material inequality, 333–6
concerns over international-level inequality, 351–3
conditional income transfers, 232
differences in skills and talents, 234–6
disability compensation, 232
distinction between those who cannot work and those who can, 230–2
effect on incentives, 229–33, 399n7
endowments, 225
fundamental problem with capitalism, 73
guaranteed minimum income, 231
housing, 240–3
inability to socialize labor, 225–6, 230
of income, 225–6, 234–40
inter-firm level, 334–5
lottery of birth, 224
markets and unequal outcomes, 225
private insurance, 200
Rawls' theories, 11–17
satisfaction with what one gets, 227–8
as socialist virtue, 10
taxation, 237–9
trade-off between income redistribution and efficiency, 236–7
unemployment benefits, 232
of utility, 227, 399n4
equality of opportunity principle, 13–14, 25, 366, 374–5
exchange rates, 91, 99, 274, 282–4, 287–9, 405n27
exit, possibility/power of, 129, 147–8, 150–4, 220–1, 354
capitalism, 3–4
costliness of, 151, 154

partial owners of capitalist firms, 161
right to a voice, 153, 213, 335, 365
skills tailored to labor sector, 221
supply and demand for labor, 150
exploitation
concern that class relations perpetuate human suffering, 362–3
Lenin's views, 31
self-exploitation, 139, 143, 353–5
expropriation, 31–2, 296–301, 344

Factory and Manager in the USSR (Berliner), 41
Finance Act, 401n4
FingerWorks, 313
fiscal policy, 248, 253–6
Fisher, Mark, 26
Folbre, Nancy, 201
Foley, Duncan, 227–8, 398n3
foreign exchange, 62, 282–5, 288
French Revolution, 352, 356–8, 376
Friedman, Milton, 271
Fukuyama, Francis, 358
A Future for Socialism (Roemer), 138

Gagarin, Yuri, 47
Galbraith, John Kenneth, 193
The General Theory of Labor-Managed Market Economies (Vanek), 180
Gintis, Herbert, 153–5, 181, 391n28, 400n13
glasnost, 57
Global South, 351
Glushkov, Victor, 50
golden rule (Kantian) optimization, 157
Gorbachev, Mikhail, 56–7, 341
Gornick, Janet C., 202–3, 205
Gosplan
alternate USSR, 6–7
cybersocialism, 49
example 1940s-era factory, 42
founding of, 38
functions of, 38–40
Hungarian market socialism, 60
immense responsibilities of, 66–7, 387n68
goulash communism, 63
Gould, Stephen Jay, 365
"Grab What You Can World," 297, 299
grain-procurement crisis, 36–7
guaranteed minimum income, 231, 233, 239, 244, 255
Guevara, Che, 330

Hahnel, Robin, 103–5
Haraszti, Miklós, 43–4, 64, 384n30
Hayek, F. A., 8, 66, 109, 180
market competition, 86, 135
planning problem, 18, 48–50, 114, 124
use of knowledge, 119
health care, 194, 197–200
popularity of public services, 197–8
private insurance, 200, 367
uncertainties, 198–9
Heilbroner, Robert, 364
Hitchens, Christopher, 293–4
horizon problem, 161–2, 164, 166–8, 177–8, 180
housing, 89–90, 240–3, 376, 401n16
capitalist system, 240–1, 243
equality/inequality, 240–3
maintenance and renovations, 242–3, 253–4
public ownership and secure tenure, 242

rent, 242
Soviet Union, 62, 68
unusual nature of, 240–1
How to Pay for the War (Keynes), 401n4
Hoxha, Enver, 352
Hungarian market socialism, 58–63, 386n66
agriculture, 58–9
Kádár's background, 58
New Economic Mechanism, 59–63, 318
recollectivization, 58
revolution, 58
turning inwards, 61

ideological externalities, 191
immediate producers, 2–3, 196, 336, 338, 353
imperative planning, 60
imperialism, 372–4
incentives
algorithmic planning, 97, 128
effect of equality on, 229–33
as euphemism for discipline, 98
information and incentive problems, 95, 97–8
innovation, 313–18
Lange versus Hayek, 18
reconciling personal freedom with efficiency, 95
warped, 65
income effects, 264, 266, 389n9
indicative planning, 39, 60
inefficiency. *See* efficiency/inefficiency
inequality. *See* equality/inequality
inflation, 246–7, 263, 269–78
Australian wage determination, 401n4
bailouts, 175
capitalist acceptance of, 249, 287
centralized bargaining, 274–6
cost ratio, 286
Hungarian market socialism, 60, 62
market power, 277, 405n23
NAIRU, 269–72
responsibility of stabilization, 187, 244
wage-benchmark system, 291
information problems, 7, 48, 62, 95, 97–8, 101–3, 122, 330
innovation
concerns about, 17, 313–18
democratic firms, 156
incentives and financing for, 196, 313–18
Soviet Union, 46–7
workplace tyranny, 3
intellectual property, 177–8, 194–7, 209, 316, 367
intergenerational wealth transfer, 226, 259, 297, 300, 342
interpersonal utility comparisons, 79–80

Jacobin (magazine), 52
Jefferson, Thomas, 309
Jobs, Steve, 314
Johnson, Hewlett, 384n34
journalism and news media, 189, 195–7, 345, 372
Justice as Fairness (Rawls), 15

Kádár, János, 58–9
Kalecki, Michał, 207, 271
Kantian (golden rule) optimization, 157
Kantorovich, Leonid, 48–52, 121–2
Kautsky, Karl, 30
Keynes, John Maynard, 281, 401n4, 405n25
Khrushchev, Nikita
embracing Kantorovich and his co-thinkers, 50
Khrushchev's thaw, 46
program to catch up with the US, 27–8

reforms, 44, 46, 53
shoe incident, 27, 382n2
Virgin Lands campaign, 385n36
Kibbe, Matt, 298
Kornai, János, 51, 64, 128, 175, 387n67
Kosygin, Alexei, 54, 60

Labor-Managed Firm, The (Dow), 164, 181
labor unions and collective bargaining, 88, 153
Nordic social democracy, 301–2, 369
public sector, 220–1, 312
unemployment, 273–5
workplace tyranny, 3
Lange, Oskar
algorithmic planning, 17–18, 96–7, 109, 114–24, 135, 207, 390nn18–20
competitive general equilibrium, 97, 112–13, 116–17, 135, 207
dual meaning of price, 389n10
freedom of choice of occupation/consumption, 85, 152
labor market, 234–5
market of consumers' goods, 100
price structure and public costs, 189–90
price system and rational prices, 86–7
rational allocation of resources, 76, 79, 81
regular employment relations, 148–9
shadow prices, 188–9
Law on State Enterprises, 57
Lenin, Vladimir
accounting and control, 65
civil war, 34
commitment to revolution, 30–1
death of, 35
economic complexity, 31
inspiration from German war economy, 31–2
nonexistent preconditions, 32
repressive state apparatus, 68
requisitioning, 34
socialist and communist phases, 382n6
Lewin, Moshe, 37
Liberman, Evsei, 53–4
limited liability, 64–5, 361
linear programming, 48–50, 52
Locke, John, 300

macroeconomic policy, 245–92
bailouts, 175
banking system and investment, 90, 249–62
cash economy, 262
central banks, 250–3, 256–7, 259, 261, 321–3
compared to capitalist system, 249–51
competition between banks, 251–3, 401n2
consumer credit, 259–60
deposits and consumer spending, 256–62, 402nn6–8
financial controls, 259–62
handling consumption demand, 255
housing, 243, 254–5
integrating monetary and fiscal policy, 253–6, 401n5
payments system, 250
personal saving, 258–9
private financial relations, 260–1
separating investment lending from deposit-taking, 250–1
specialized development banks, 252

compared to capitalist system, 249–51, 259–60
conditions of deliberate public intervention, 248
downturns, 245–6
fiscal policy, 248, 253–6
inflation, 246–7, 263, 269–78
monetary policy, 248, 253–6
responsibility of stabilization, 186
trade, 90–1, 278–92, 405nn25–7
changes in the international situation, 280
choices and efficiency, 280
converting resources into products, 279
currency value, 288
exchange rate flexibility, 283–5, 287
foreign exchange and value of currency, 282–5
tradable commodities, 278, 286, 288, 406n30
wage benchmarks, 288–90
wages and incomes, 285–92, 406n31
unemployment, 246–7, 263–78, 405n23
assumptions regarding, 263–4
changing output without changing membership, 264–5
compared to capitalist system, 263–8
income effects of fluctuations in demand, 266
inflation, 269–78
risk-sharing arrangements, 266
slack, 267–8
wage benchmarks, 145
Malenkov, Georgy, 49
Mandel, Ernest, 100–1, 131
market irrationalities, 73–4, 83
marketless planning, 8, 23, 96, 122–3, 127, 130–1, 332. *See also* algorithmic planning and algorithmic socialism
markets. *See* market sector
market sector, 78–9, 92–136, 207–18
algorithmic planning, 114–35
central planning board, 115–16, 118, 131
choices about production as choices about people, 125–9, 391n29
competitive general equilibrium, 114, 116–17
cutting corners on quality, 121, 391n24
equipment and built environment, 118–19
following instructions, 123, 125
individuals, 115–16
information required, 115
internalizing externalities, 118
limits of, 122–34
outputs for people, 129–34, 391nn32–33, 391n35
workplace managers, 116, 120–1
antisocialist challenge to planning, 109–12
aspects of production not suited to, 100, 185, 188–9, 194, 388n6
cement-production planning example, 110–11
challenge of coordinating division of labor, 92
competitive general equilibrium, 112–13
concerns over psychology of market subjects, 330–3
information and incentive problems, 95, 97–8
innovation, 315

marketless planning, 96
markets as Janus-faced institutions, 92–3
not private sector, 185
overview of, 88
personal consumer choice, 96, 98–109
price system, 93–4
public banks, 209–12
public wholesalers as intermediaries, 212–15, 398n28
role in production organization, 96–7, 109–22
roles of, compared to public sector, 184–6
shifting the boundaries of firms, 215–18, 398n32, 398n34
socialist skepticism about markets, 93
socially rational use of resources, 111
market socialism, 69–70, 75, 109, 207, 341–2, 345
concern about self-exploitation, 353–5
Hungarian market socialism, 58–63
Nove's model, 86, 217
Roemer's model, 86, 163, 181
Marx, Karl
applying labor power in full self-awareness, 95, 97, 388n3
commodity fetishism, 93–4
compared to authors' model, 336–7
competition, 207
cooperative workers in advanced economies, 365
to-each-according-to-their-basic-needs ideal, 228, 230, 399n11
immediate producers, 4
mute compulsion, 307
price system, 93–4
reserve army of labor, 270, 404n15
socialist and communist phases, 29, 382n6
socially necessary labor time, 388n3
studying capitalism, 29
vision of consumption decoupled from work, 9
writing recipes, 4
material-balance planning, 40, 383n22
Mau, Søren, 350
maximin (maximizing the minimum), 17
Mazzucato, Mariana, 313–14
McNally, David, 135
McReynolds, David, 357–9
Meade, James, 263–4, 268, 403n10, 405n28
membership markets, 164–7
Meyers, Marcia K., 202–3, 205
militarism, 372–4
Mises, Ludwig von, 66, 81
antisocialist challenge to planning, 8, 96, 109–12, 135
cigar and cigarette exchange example, 99
information problem, 48
price system, 17
Mondragon Corporation, 15–16, 341
monetary policy
central banks, 248
integrating, 253–6
interbank money market, 250
interest rates, 209, 258
NAIRU model, 272
moneyless systems, 7–9
Musgrave, Richard, 190–2, 396n4, 399n11
Mussolini, Benito, 49
mute compulsion, 307, 357
Mute Compulsion (Mau), 350

Nagy, Imre, 58
NAIRU (nonaccelerating inflation rate of unemployment), 269–72
National Institutes of Health, 313
national labor board, 89, 91, 142–5
National Science Foundation, 313
natural monopolies, 195, 208
NAVSTAR, 313
negative income tax, 231, 233, 239
negative liberty, 304–5
Nemchinov, Vasily, 50
network coordinators, 214–15, 218
Neurath, Otto, 11
New Economic Mechanism (NEM), 59–63, 318
New Economic Policy (NEP), 34–9
New York Times (newspaper), 47
NHS. *See* British National Health Service
nonaccelerating inflation rate of unemployment (NAIRU), 269–72
noncommodity production. *See* public sector and noncommodity production
Nordic social democracies
  civilizational progress, 301–2, 376
  decentralized pattern bargaining, 276
  GDPs, 369
  partial democratic socialism, 327
  wage coordination, 145, 240, 282, 333–4, 405n24
Nove, Alec, 86, 106, 134, 217, 220, 267, 393n17
November Revolution, 30
Nozick, Robert, 300, 307
Nyers, Rezso, 59

obstetric metaphor, 11
optimal planning, 50–2
optimal taxation, 89, 237–9, 400n13

paid family leave, 205
Pareto, Vilfredo, 49, 80
Pareto efficiency and optimum, 49, 80–1, 86, 112, 189–90, 195, 387n4
participatory planning, 7, 103, 215
perestroika, 57
perfect competition, 18, 81, 159, 190, 209, 263–4
Pigou, Arthur Cecil, 79
Pinochet, Augusto, 306
"Plan, Profit, and Bonus" (Liberman), 53–4
Prague Spring, 56
Pravda (newspaper), 53
price signals, 62, 108, 118–19, 161, 330, 350
price socialism. *See* algorithmic planning and algorithmic socialism
price system/structure
  central administration of, 275
  consumer choice, 100–3, 207–8, 389n9
  dual meaning of price, 389n10
  fixed wages, 142
  Hungarian market socialism, 61
  Lange's views, 17, 86, 190
  Marx's views, 93–4
  price signals, 108, 111–13, 330
  socialist skepticism and capitalist response, 93–4
  wage compression, 240
prisoner-of-love dynamics, 201
product differentiation, 129–31, 213

property rights, 77–80, 85, 180, 295–301, 395n31
public banking system, 168–75, 209–12, 249–62
  barriers to competition, 211–12
  bonuses, 251–2
  cash economy, 262
  central banks, 250–3, 256–7, 259, 261, 321–3
  compared to capitalist system, 249–51
  competition between banks, 251–3, 401n2
  concerns over bankers as privileged class, 321–3
  consumer credit, 259–60
  data analysis and collection, 214
  demand fluctuations, 267
  democratic responsiveness, 322–3
  deposits and consumer spending, 256–9, 402nn6–8
  financial controls, 259–62
  formation of new entrants, 210
  handling consumption demand, 255
  housing, 254–5
  innovation, 314–15
  integrating monetary and fiscal policy, 253–6, 401n5
  interest, 169–70, 209
  investment finance, 188, 192, 308, 310
  investment partnership, 169–75, 394–5nn29–32
  payments system, 250
  personal saving, 258–9
  plurality of banks, 210–11
  private financial relations, 260–1
  risk management and reduction, 169–74
  risk sharing, 139
  risk-sharing arrangements, 266
  separating investment lending from deposit-taking, 250–1
  specialized development banks, 252, 403n14
  state's control of, 186
  unemployment, 263
public sector and noncommodity production, 81, 183–223
  allocation of funding, 221–2
  aspects of production better suited to, 100, 185, 188–9, 194–206, 388n6
  balancing public and private goods, 190–5, 396nn4–6, 396n8
  budget constraints, 186
  care work, 194, 200–6
  concerns of political authoritarianism, 302–7
  double task of contesting and transforming the state, 184
  education, 194, 197–200
  goal, 184
  health care, 194, 197–200
  innovation, 313–14
  intellectual and cultural property, 194–7
  main responsibilities of, 187
  more complete accounting, 189–95
  nonexcludable and nonrival goods, 195
  roles of, compared to market sector, 184–6
  shaped by market environment, 185–6
  state-largeness and state-powerfulness, 302–3
  sustaining the benefits and minimizing their problems of markets, 207–8
  tools for action, 187
  worker representation, 221–2
  workplace democracy, 218–23

quality signals, 132–3
quantity signals, 108, 113

Rákosi, Mátyás, 58
Rawls, John, 11–17, 142, 231, 300, 366, 399n11
Rehn-Meidner framework, 275
research and development (R&D), 177, 196, 314. *See also* innovation
residual income, 19, 140–1, 167–8, 336, 392n3
Road to Serfdom (Lange), 135
Robbins, Lionel, 76, 79, 114
Robinson, Joan, 207–8, 212–15, 218, 271
Roemer, John, 86, 123, 129, 138, 157, 163, 181, 371

Saez, Emmanuel, 239
Samuelson, Paul, 396n5
Schumpeter, Joseph, 207
Schweickart, David, 395n37
scissor crisis, 36
Sen, Amartya, 152, 228
shadow prices, 48, 103, 188–9, 400n12
Shalizi, Cosma, 51
Smith, Adam, 93
Smith, Steve, 33
social choice theory, 191
socialism
  critique of capitalism not enough, 2
  double task of contesting and transforming the state, 184
  early manifestations of, 29–30
  engineering issues, 7–10
  example of life under, 71–2
  as experiment, 293–4
  idea that details will sort themselves out, 4–5
  need for vision of something better, 2
  objections to, 74, 294–355
    bankers as privileged class, 321–3
    capitalist employment contracts, 307–12
    collapsing back into capitalism, 340–8
    collective capitalism, 336–40
    competition and self-exploitation, 353–4
    domination, 348–50
    efficiency problems, 318–20
    failure of worker self-management, 323–5
    innovation without private finance, 313–18
    international-level inequality, 351–3
    material inequality, 333–6
    political authoritarianism, 302–7
    property rights, 295–301
    psychology of market subjects, 330–3
    risk, 327–8
    stop at social democracy, 301–2
    welfare state guarantees, 325–7
  personal freedom, 83–5
  productive efficiency, 83–5
  right to economic self-determination, 294
  shaking association with totalitarianism and long lines, 68
  socialist and communist phases, 29
  three-stage desirable-feasible-achievable test, 361–2
  values and goals, 10–11, 15
socialist calculation debate, 17, 74–5, 84, 96, 109, 135, 180, 360
socialist equality of opportunity principle, 13–14, 25, 366, 374–5

socialized markets, 75, 207–18, 397n23
 public banking system, 209–12
 public wholesalers as intermediaries, 212–15, 398n28
 shifting boundaries of firms, 215–18, 398n32, 398n34
soft budget constraints, 64–5, 128, 175, 318–20, 324, 391n30
solidarity and communitarian spirit, 157, 233, 275–6, 290, 331–2, 347, 374–5
Soviet Union, 32–47
 after capitalism's victory, 4
 austerity measures, 36
 Bolsheviks, 32–6
 civil war, 33–5
 command (administered) economy, 38–47, 383n22
 division of labor, 121–2
 economic chaos, 32–3
 end of, 4, 57
 Gorbachev's reforms, 57
 industrial policy, 33
 New Economic Policy, 34–9
 nonsocialist claim, 337–8
 passport system, 44–5
 production of unwanted goods, 28
 program to catch up with the US, 27–8
 requisitioning, 33–4
 restoration of market exchange, 34
 scissor crisis of grain procurement, 36–7
 Stalinist terror, 37–8
 steel industry, 67
 thought experiment of democratic USSR, 5–7
 war communism, 32–4
Spufford, Francis, 121
Sputnik, 28, 47, 357–8, 376
Stalin, Joseph
 administered economy, 45–6
 criticism of NEP, 36
 foremen, 42
 grain-procurement crisis, 36
 taking on real and imagined enemies, 37–8
Stasi, 68–9
State and Revolution, The (Lenin), 30–1, 65

tax and transfer system, 89, 186–7, 243, 289, 296–7, 333–4
 allocating between commodity and noncommodity production, 193
 capitalism, 82, 343
 environmental taxation, 349, 368
 fiscal policy, 253–6
 inheritance tax, 297
 labor income inequality, 236–9
 negative income tax, 231, 233, 239
 optimal taxation, 89, 237–9, 400n13
 price structure adjustment, 190
A Theory of Justice (Rawls), 15
Time (magazine), 53
Tinbergen, Jan, 145, 274, 405n29
Tonnenideologie, 62, 67
trade, 278–92, 405nn25–7
 benchmark wages, 288–90
 changes in the international situation, 280
 choices and efficiency, 280
 converting resources into products, 279
 currency value, 288
 exchange rate flexibility, 283–5, 287
 foreign exchange and currency value, 282–5
 tradable commodities, 278, 286, 288, 406n30

wages and incomes, 285–92, 406n31
Trotsky, Leon, 32, 35–6
Trump, Donald, 306

unemployment, 128–9, 231–3, 246–7, 263–78, 403nn10–11, 403n13, 405n23
assumptions regarding, 263–4
capitalism, 150–1, 154, 156, 206
changing output without changing membership, 264–5
compared to capitalist system, 263–8
income effects of fluctuations in demand, 266
inflation, 269–78
risk-sharing arrangements, 266
slack, 145, 267–8
unfreedom, 3–4, 73, 83, 292
unions. *See* labor unions and collective bargaining
United Nations, 27
unpaid work, 82, 201
US General Accounting Office, 56
USSR. *See* Soviet Union

Vallander, Sergei, 49
Vanek, Jaroslav, 160, 167–82, 263, 268, 395n31
Van Parijs, Philippe, 231
veil of ignorance, 12–16, 366

wage benchmark system
contractor firms, 217
democratic firms, 89, 139, 143–5, 210
discretion to pay margins above, 142, 239–40
international markets, 288–91
macroeconomic policy, 249, 276–8
public sector, 220
responding to concerns, 302, 308, 317–18, 333, 342, 354
trade, 288–90
wage compression, 240
war communism, 32–4
Weimar Republic, 30
welfare state, 25, 198, 310, 332, 345
expense of, 231
maintaining labor participation, 325–7
new welfare economics, 79
Nordic social democracies, 301–2
objections to capitalist status quo, 364, 367–8
as piggy bank, 203, 229
pressure to compete for jobs, 273
Why Not Socialism? (Cohen), 330, 374
"Why Surfers Should Be Fed" (Van Parijs), 231
Wolfers, Justin, 272–3
worker pay ratios, 381n8
workplace democracy. *See* democratic firms
World War I, 30
Wright, Erik Olin, 361

Yugoslavian worker self-management, 323–5, 337, 386n66

Zaleski, Eugène, 43, 67